947.C

0          0

This book is to be returr
the last date stamped below.

RUSSIA IN

This book is !

# RUSSIA IN THE ERA OF NEP

Explorations in Soviet Society and Culture

EDITED BY

## SHEILA FITZPATRICK,

## ALEXANDER RABINOWITCH,

AND

## RICHARD STITES

INDIANA UNIVERSITY PRESS

*Bloomington and Indianapolis*

This book was brought to publication with the assistance of a grant from the Joint Committee on Soviet Studies of the American Council of Learned Societies and the Social Science Research Council
© 1991 by Indiana University Press

The paper used in this publication meets the minimum requirements of American National Standard for Information Sciences—Permanence of Paper for Printed Library Materials, ANSI Z39.48-1984.

MANUFACTURED IN THE UNITED STATES OF AMERICA

Library of Congress Cataloging-in-Publication Data

Russia in the era of NEP : explorations in Soviet society and culture
/ edited by Sheila Fitzpatrick, Alexander Rabinowitch, and Richard Stites.
    p.   cm. — (Indiana-Michigan series in Russian and East European studies)
   Includes bibliographical references (p.   ) and index.
   ISBN 0-253-32224-3 (cloth). — ISBN 0-253-20657-X (paper)
   1. Soviet Union—Politics and government—1917–1936.  2. Soviet Union—Intellectual life—1917–1970.  3. Soviet Union—Economic policy—1917–1928.  I. Fitzpatrick, Sheila.  II. Rabinowitch, Alexander.   III. Stites, Richard.  IV. Series.
DK266.R82   1991
947.084—dc20                                90-25044

2  3  4  5   95

# CONTENTS

# PREFACE

One of the most exciting and influential collective intellectual enterprises in which scholars of Russian history and politics were engaged in recent years was the Seminar in Twentieth-Century Russian and Soviet Social History. From its first meeting in Philadelphia in 1980, the seminar, conceived initially by Moshe Lewin and Alfred Rieber of the University of Pennsylvania, brought together historians from the United States, Great Britain, and Western Europe to consider broad analytical problems that cut across the traditional 1917 dividing line. In contrast to the conference mode of traditional scholarly gatherings, the seminar was structured to encourage innovative approaches and new research; to bring the knowledge and insights of scholars working on disparate but related problems to bear on broader central themes and issues; and to identify important questions and fruitful avenues for future investigation. Most important, the seminar brought together younger and more senior scholars in a small setting that allowed them to think creatively about major problems of twentieth-century Russian and Soviet social history. The success of the seminar is evidenced by its durability, by its popularity as a forum for scholarly discussion, and by the many publications that have been enriched by their authors' participation in it.

Previous meetings focused on the Russian and Soviet peasantry (1982), the Imperial and Soviet bureaucracy (1983), and the social history of Soviet Russia during the Civil War (1984). Work presented in preliminary form at the Civil War seminar was developed and subsequently published as *Party, State, and Society in the Russian Civil War: Explorations in Social History*, edited by Diane P. Koenker, William G. Rosenberg, and Ronald Grigor Suny (Bloomington, 1989). A seminar on industrialization and change in Soviet society during the 1930s was held in 1988.

The present volume, on the transformation of urban and rural society and culture in Russia during the era of the New Economic Policy of the 1920s, grew out of work presented at the fifth seminar in the series, held at Indiana University in 1986. The main themes of the book and the historical context in which they are considered are elaborated by William G. Rosenberg in the introduction that follows. We should like simply to mention here that when we began planning the NEP seminar, perestroika and the rethinking of Soviet history had barely begun. It is our hope that this book will shed useful new light on one of the key historical moments in this discussion.

The essays included in this volume convey only in part the rich and rewarding contributions and discussions that animated the seminar. The editors wish to express deepest appreciation to all our colleagues who attended and whose comments and criticisms helped shape the present book: Susanne Ament, Dorothy Atkinson, Kendall Bailes, Henryk Baran, William Burgess, John Bushnell, William Chase, Ben Eklof, Barbara Engel, Laura Engelstein, Loren Graham, Peter Kenez, Christel Lane, Mary McAuley, Roberta Manning, Daniel Orlovsky, David Ransel, Blair Ruble, Ronald Grigor Suny, Lynn Viola, James Von Geldern, Allan Wildman, Richard Wortman, and Reginald Zelnik.

The NEP seminar and the preparation of this volume were made possible by generous support from the Joint Committee on Soviet Studies of the American Council of Learned Societies and the Social Science Research Council and by assistance from the Indiana University Office of International Programs and Russian and East European Institute.

# I

# INTRODUCTION

## NEP RUSSIA AS A "TRANSITIONAL" SOCIETY

*William G. Rosenberg*

As students of Soviet history know quite well, the period between the end of the Civil War and the onslaught of collectivization and rapid industrialization in late 1929 is known as NEP because of a series of new economic policies introduced by the Bolsheviks in the spring of 1921. These had to do first and foremost with ending food requisitions from the countryside and eliminating tight restrictions on private trade and production. With victory in the Civil War assured, the confiscation of grain and the effort to maintain rigid controls on the pricing and distribution of goods no longer made political or economic sense. Wholesale peasant resistance had culminated in massive uprisings in Tambov province late in 1920, just as the anti-Bolshevik "Whites" and their European allies were being defeated. Workers in Petrograd and elsewhere appeared on the verge of revolt over scarcities and harsh working conditions. Opposition had broken out openly within the party itself. Early in March 1921 sailors at Kronstadt seized the island fortress to demand "land and bread" and a Soviet government without the Bolsheviks. Bolshevik leaders everywhere were quickly persuaded that the party had to retreat, at least for a time, that the policies of "War Communism" had to give way to a more relaxed period of recovery and transition.

The first task was to reduce tensions in the countryside. The introduction of NEP consequently involved the end of grain requisitioning and the imposition instead of a fixed tax in kind. It was anticipated that these two measures would increase food production, since peasants could expect to retain whatever was left after taxes and consume or market it to their own advantage. Surpluses were also to be distributed through private as well as state trading networks, and at prices largely determined by supply and demand. It was hoped this would lead to a more efficient (even if less equitable) system of distribution and free the party itself from much of the responsibility for assuring that citizens were adequately provided.

Major changes were also promised in industry. In many sectors, a much freer market was to replace the highly centralized system for allocating scarce industrial resources and setting prices. Strict labor regulations were to be relaxed, especially those associated with Trotsky's policies of labor "militarization" in 1920. In some enterprises, "bourgeois" managers and other administrative persons would be invited to resume their old positions. Many of those who had emigrated would also be welcome to return, especially if they had essential skills and qualifications. Limited private enterprise was authorized, particularly in consumer goods and services. The party's immediate goal was the recovery of agriculture and industry from seven devastating years of war and revolution.

Lenin and his comrades also hoped for party unity. This involved accepting in large measure the sharp criticisms expressed by "Democratic Centralists," the "Workers' Opposition," and other factional groups, particularly as they pertained to arbitrariness and excessive political centralization.[1] The autonomy of regional and local organizations would consequently increase. The frightening and often arbitrary use of force would give way to a period of orderly politics, involving "active participation of all members in the life of the party, in deciding questions, and in building the party organization."[2] Concessions were made in the direction of free discussion and criticism, although factions were specifically proscribed.

These changes have persuaded many historians that had Lenin not been severely incapacitated by strokes in 1922 and 1923, the entire course of Soviet history would have been different. His illness in December 1921 seriously weakened the leadership role of the Politburo, leaving Stalin and others relatively free to carry out policies on their own. In May 1922 Lenin suffered partial paralysis and temporarily lost the ability to speak. In mid-December he suffered two additional strokes. By March 1923 his political activity was effectively at an end, almost an entire year before his death in January 1924. The principal political question of the time, consequently, was who would succeed him as head of the party and chairman of the Council of Ministers.

The logical choice appeared to be Trotsky, founder of the Red Army, commissar of war, and arguably the country's most charismatic figure. Few understood Stalin's ambitions in this regard, or appreciated his shrewd ability to use the power he was developing as party secretary to such great advantage. Partly for this reason, partly because Stalin's subsequent dictatorship was itself so important for Soviet and world history, the ensuing "struggle for power" has captured historians' attention. The 1920s are traditionally seen as years of political transition. The important benchmarks are the 23rd, 24th, and 25th party congresses, held from 1924 to 1927, where Stalin's patronage gave him the power to strip Trotsky, Zinoviev, Kamenev, and others from their posts and expel them from the party; the most frequently cited documents of the period include Lenin's famous "Testament" (in which he castigates Stalin and calls for his removal); Trotsky's attacks on Stalin and his bureaucracy in "The New Course"; and the articles and speeches of Preobrazhenskii, Bukharin, Zinoviev, and others about the nature of Soviet Russia's economic course—the appropriate path to industrialization.

Most historians have consequently regarded the important issues of the 1920s to be those relating to a society "in transition" between Leninism and Stalinism. The questions that have most often been asked have to do with the struggle for power itself, the degree to which Stalin's success stemmed logically from Leninist institutions and outlooks, the relative importance of ideology and political organization, and whether Stalin's subsequent rule reflected the logical end of NEP or a fundamental corruption of Bolshevik values and institutions. NEP has thus taken on special importance as a "breathing space" between the revolutionary upheavals of 1917–21 and the "great change" of the 1930s. For some, it also seems an attractive alternative model, in its relative freedom and openness, of communist politics and society "in the making."

The problem with these "traditional" perspectives is not that they are wrong. Each of these questions is obviously important. One can readily understand why they have drawn the attention of able historians, and why they continue to be of vital interest in and outside the Soviet Union today.

Yet the task of understanding NEP requires a much broader conceptualization of the processes of "transition." What happened in Soviet Russia during the 1920s was not simply a retreat from the harsh politics of War Communism to liberalism, back to harsh authoritarianism under Stalin. Rather, NEP was a period in which those in power were forced somehow to come to terms with complex social and cultural residues of prerevolutionary Russia, implicitly at odds with ongoing goals of building a socialist or communist order. Insofar as NEP proved to be a "breathing space," it was because a complex and variegated society needed to move more slowly toward these goals in order to cope with the profound consequences of revolutionary upheaval. From the party leadership's viewpoint, this meant moving forward cautiously so as to minimize resistance, a position some regarded as "retreat." From the point of view of most ordinary Russians, however, NEP meant conserving recent gains and protecting comfortable traditions, while also experiencing continuing and contradictory pressures for further change.

In the most general terms, the result was a continued period of social tension. Traditional social relations and attitudes reappeared both inside

the party and in society at large, despite the years of revolutionary struggle.
So did a wide range of other outlooks, customs, and social relations described in this volume. At best these reflected resilient prerevolutionary
social and cultural forms which could, with difficulty, be incorporated into
the tasks at hand. At worst, they were inimical to the party's basic goals for
Russia's development and future. Despite sharply different viewpoints
about the tempo of change and how these goals might be realized, no one
in the party saw Soviet Russia's future as anything but an industrialized,
modern society, standing alone or with others as a powerful socialist
alternative to the developed capitalist nations of the West. To achieve this,
the legacies of the past had to be overcome: through attrition, absorption,
or repression.

Thus the processes of transition which NEP reflects did not turn simply
on Bolshevik politics but on the broad social and cultural axes connecting
what tsarist Russia had been to what Soviet Russia was about to become;
and the transitional elements of NEP did not have to do only with Soviet
Russia's transformation from an essentially preindustrial order to a powerful, autonomous state, but also with creating in the course of that change
the fundamental elements of a new Soviet social order, culture, and national identity, and selecting the most appropriate methods to do so. NEP, in
other words, reflected a Soviet society, a Soviet nation, "in the making," to
paraphrase Moshe Lewin, creating its own culture, social order, and state
system. The crucial questions historians still have to ask of this period have
less to do with struggles for power than with the complex and consequential interactions between social and cultural components of resistance and change.

By way of background to the issues at hand, let us briefly look at some of
the principal social legacies of the revolution and Civil War. One of the
most dramatic had to do with fundamental demographic changes wrought
by the fighting itself, as well as by hunger and disease. In December 1926,
the Soviet regime conducted the first comprehensive census in Russia since
1897. According to best estimates, the total population would have been
approximately 175,000,000 had growth continued between 1914 and 1926
without unnatural interference. The actual population was 147,028,000,
indicating a deficit of approximately 28,000,000 persons.[3] Since the annual
prewar growth rate of approximately 1.7 percent was undoubtedly somewhat less during this period and the rates of infant mortality were ex-
ceptionally high, some substantial proportion of this deficit must be attributed to those unborn or unable to survive infancy. But at least 2,000,000
men died in the war between 1914 and 1917; and reasonable estimates
indicate that almost 3,500,000 died from disease after the Bolsheviks came
to power, some 834,000 from typhus alone in 1920.[4] The horrifying

famine of 1921–22 claimed additional tens of thousands, especially among children; 31 percent of the 1926 deficit, in fact, is attributed to those whose birth years were 1917–21.[5]

The deficit revealed by the 1926 census thus reflects an extraordinary national trauma. Few families survived without grievous personal losses, regardless of their politics. Whole communities were decimated or uprooted. Difficulties were especially severe for women. By the end of the Civil War, the loss of able-bodied men had left tens of thousands of households in dire straits; as late as the 1926 census, when new births had begun to redress the imbalance somewhat, there were still only 83 males in Soviet Russia to every 100 females among those twenty-five to twenty-nine years of age, and 88 to every 100 for those thirty years old or older.[6] Despite high infant mortality, moreover, just over half the population in the countryside in 1926 was under twenty years of age, reflecting both the period's staggering toll on adults and the very high rate of new births between 1922 and 1926 (some 19.2 million). This increased the burdens women had to bear for family maintenance and reflected the enormous problems of child care and support with which Soviet society was now forced to contend.

Whether these difficulties were greater in urban or rural Russia is hard to determine. An extraordinary migration took place from cities and towns to the countryside between 1917 and 1923, particularly in the northern industrial area around Petrograd, before being reversed rather dramatically, as Douglas Weiner shows in his essay below. Despite a rapid increase in urban growth during 1924–25, the 1926 census indicated that the Soviet Union remained overwhelmingly rural, with as much as 82 percent of the total population living outside cities and towns.[7] It was not until the census year itself that the urban population exceeded prewar figures. This was largely a result, of course, of the general collapse of Russian industry and the expectations, often false, that food would be easier to obtain outside the city. But Soviet supply organs were invariably more concerned with the well-being of urban than of rural areas, and certainly it was the peasants who suffered most in the famine, insofar as such judgments can properly be made.

There was no question, however, that the virtual collapse of Russian industry and commerce wreaked havoc almost everywhere. Gross national income may have fallen by more than 60 percent between 1913 and 1921.[8] Most of this decline was caused by the collapse of industrial production, equally divided in rough terms between producers' and consumers' goods.[9] The output of coal, for example, which stood at slightly more than 29 million tons in 1913, was less than 9 million tons by 1920, and only 12.7 million tons by the beginning of 1923. Iron ore extraction had fallen from 9.2 million tons in 1913 to 129,000 by 1921, increasing only to 505,000 by

1923. The declines in other sectors were comparable. One remarkable consequence of this can be seen in production levels for motor vehicles and agricultural equipment, especially tractors. In all of Soviet Russia only 100 cars and trucks were produced for 1924, and only 11 tractors! No significant production of other heavy agricultural equipment (grain combine harvesters, for example) was recorded until 1930.[10]

These critical deficiencies in production, moreover, were both cause and consequence of broader social patterns. For one, the revolutionary upheaval as a whole had been particularly hard on industrial managers, engineers, technicians, and other members of Russia's small but vital "technological intelligentsia," as it has been called. Efforts to restore the role of "experts" in the factories were frequently resisted; even many of those who were willing to accept the new regime felt themselves forced into emigration. Statistics here as elsewhere are estimates at best, but as many as 2 million people may have fled abroad between 1917 and 1921, overwhelmingly from the educated and propertied social groups. Some analysts suggest the figure might be higher.[11] Many were landed gentry whose estates had been seized by the peasantry, and whose lands had contributed a disproportionate share of surplus production in the countryside. Others carried away technological knowledge essential to rapid industrial recovery. The same was true for those involved in commerce, transportation, and other services. The very centrality of social conflict to the 1917 revolution made the decimation of these social groups far greater than many Bolsheviks themselves desired, although the party's own deliberate efforts at encouraging class warfare hardly improved matters, at least from an economic point of view.

Similarly, the decimation of professional groups such as doctors and teachers had serious consequences for education and basic medical care. The 1926 census again reveals some interesting figures in this regard. For all of Russia's rural population, for example, approximately 50 percent of which indicated some basic ability to read and write, there were only 170,900 professional schoolteachers, or 1 for every 705 rural inhabitants. The situation with health care was far worse. Fewer than 7,000 trained doctors served a population of more than 120 million in the countryside— one for every 17,000; and their geographical distribution, like that of the teachers, was hardly uniform.[12] The results were huge pockets of illiteracy, ignorance, and poor health, often many miles from towns or other administrative centers where rudimentary services might be available.

Finally, in industrial areas themselves, the collapse of production clearly threatened basic elements of Bolshevik support. Soviet currency was unstable, and so were real wages. Unemployment had become a common phenomenon, reaching as high as 1.3 million in 1924 and 1925 even as industrial production steadily increased. Worker unrest over wage and other issues was not uncommon. Again, NEP allowed the market to "solve" some of these difficulties; and migration to and from the countryside was a common way to cope with erratic conditions of employment. But this hardly eased conditions in the villages or brought Soviet Russia as a whole the promise of social betterment.

The manner and degree to which all of this challenged the hopes and goals of the October Revolution should become clearer in the essays that follow. There is little question, however, about the ways in which seven years of war and devastation had "ruralized" Soviet Russia, to borrow another term from Moshe Lewin, and left the fledgling socialist state relatively "primitive" in comparison with the relatively urbanized and industrialized West. This constituted both a theoretical and a practical danger. Theoretically, socialism simply could not develop on an agrarian base, at least according to the Bolsheviks, and neither could the communist order which would ultimately follow. Industry was the foundation of material well-being. Since socialism and communism were both "higher stages" of historical development than capitalism, it was "necessarily" the case that Soviet citizens would eventually enjoy a higher standard of living than countries in the West. In practical terms, the extraordinary hostility with which many in the West continued to regard the "Soviet menace" raised the specter of further military conflict, in which an essentially agrarian society would clearly be at a serious and perhaps fatal disadvantage.

To restore and develop Russia's industrial base, however, Lenin's government needed huge amounts of capital. Initially, party leaders had expected that this would come from Western Europe, once the Bolshevik Revolution had spread abroad. As it became increasingly clear that few states were likely to follow Russia's lead, however, the problem of accumulating adequate investment resources from within became correspondingly acute.

Raising capital through high levels of taxation meant "squeezing" the peasants in ways that were likely to rekindle the conflicts of War Communism during 1918–20. Hiding taxes by imposing them as sales levies on consumer staples was problematic in terms of the market, the administrative machinery necessary for efficient tax collection, and comparable dangers of popular resistance. Most important, there was a real question whether this method would prove adequate for the amount of capital that needed to be raised. Peasant demand was relatively inelastic, and peasants constituted the overwhelming mass of Russian consumers. The most hopeful possibility was exporting grain and other raw materials, as tsarist Russia had done, and using the income both to purchase industrial machinery from the West and to build new plants. This, however, depended on a substantial increase in the levels of agricultural productivity and output, weak precisely because of the relatively "primitive" conditions of the Soviet countryside.

The centrality of this problem soon led to major debates over the proper course of Soviet economic development, and it was largely on this basis that the political factions associated with Stalin's "struggle for power" were formed. On the "right," Nikolai Bukharin and others insisted the party turn its "face to the village." Peasants had to be encouraged to produce as much as they could, to "enrich themselves," since increased rural prosperity would fuel the engine of commerce and trade and provide the party with the agrarian surpluses it so desperately needed. Strongly and at times bitterly opposed were those such as Evgenii Preobrazhenskii, who sharply criticized the party's growing dependence on the peasantry and the market, and who, with Trotsky and others, urged that the struggle against these capitalist residues be renewed. As Moshe Lewin has shown so well, strong political undercurrents swirled beneath the surface of these debates. Each viewpoint held different implications for the role of the party and the future character of the state.[13] At the same time, the turbulence itself gave Stalin an extraordinary opportunity to build alliances seemingly based on principle. His imaginative argument that socialism could be built "in one country" without exploiting either peasants or workers was a politically astute "middle" ground, more than making up in its appealing optimism for all that it lacked in substantive content. Concentrating his own efforts on building the party machine (and invoking Lenin's image at every opportunity), the future dictator left others to struggle with such complex questions as the capitalization of industry, urban-rural terms of trade, and the degree to which a socialist society could indeed be constructed in a hostile world if the difficult problems inherent in Soviet Russia's social and cultural inheritance were not rapidly overcome.

All this has been well documented in the literature. What has not been carefully investigated, and what our seminar on NEP was designed to take up, is the nature of NEP society and culture, and particularly the social and cultural interactions which developed under NEP between urban Russia and the countryside.

These matters are central to our understanding from several perspectives. First, they are intrinsically important. The status of the family, of working-class women, and of the relations between men and women more generally are determining elements of urban and rural culture generally, and must be understood if the complexities of Soviet social and cultural development are to be unraveled. An analysis of the artel and social relations in Soviet industry cannot help but provide important insights into the actual state of affairs inside the factory, just as a careful analysis of private trade, labor conflict, or the question of class and consciousness each relates to central issues in the history of Soviet workers. The same is true for studies of village conflicts, the rural police, or the Red Army's role in "socializing" the peasants. Each of these deals with fundamental aspects of rural life in the 1920s and touches issues basic to understanding the Russian countryside. Along with explorations of more specific aspects of urban and rural culture—literature, songs, the character of the urban intelligentsia, and the complex question of festivals and rituals—each deserves close attention as an important point of entry into the very nature of urban and rural existence.

At the same time, careful analyses of urban and rural society and culture are central to the question of whether NEP might have represented an alternative basis for Soviet socialism had the Stalinist revolution not intervened. As Stephen F. Cohen has suggested, history written without an exploration of lost or defeated alternatives always reinforces the notion that what actually happened was historically logical, if not inevitable.[14] Whether NEP constituted the foundation for a viable socialist order depends, of course, on one's definition of "socialism." An answer also requires a good deal of speculation about international as well as domestic politics. But the question is a vital one to any society seeking to construct a socialist or communist order without the heavy burdens of Stalinist central controls, much less the brutal authoritarianism of the 1930s and the accompanying horrors of forced draft collectivization and industrialization. Its exploration requires a comprehensive understanding of how conducive the social and cultural conditions of early Soviet Russia actually were to these objectives.

Finally, however, and perhaps most important, the nature of Soviet society and culture under NEP was itself a crucial determinant, along with Stalinist politics, the nature of the party apparatus, and other, more familiar elements of Soviet history in the 1920s and 1930s, of the very processes of transition which actually did occur, structuring the possibilities for change. The very character of state building during NEP, for example, was necessarily affected by the degree of compatibility or conflict between the fundamental objectives set by the party and those of society at large. Insofar as the creation of a modern industrial order required the emergence in Russia (as it had elsewhere in the contemporary world) of an autonomous, centralized state apparatus, liberated from and dominant over corporate social structures such as the church, the village commune, or even the industrial artel, the state and its agents had to penetrate insulated areas of social life and extend the state's political and cultural hegemony. This necessarily involved conflict and resistance, but the extent of each, and the degree to which each might have altered the character of the state itself in this period of transition, depended on how far removed urban and rural society and culture actually were from the state's declared objectives. In any state system, the degree of coercion is related, at least in part, to the pervasiveness of consensual values and commitments. Hence the brutal authoritarianism which accompanied Stalin's "revolution from above" after 1929 was undoubtedly connected to the party's failure under NEP to develop broad support, institutionally as well as culturally, for the "modernizing" tasks at hand.

A similarly broad task was the creation of a socialist society itself, one whose institutions, social relations, and culture roughly corresponded to the revolutionary goals of October. The very meaning of such central elements to Soviet Russia's future as "legality" or "social equality" depended as much on the social and cultural residues of the past as on Bolshevik ideology; and whatever the party's ultimate position on such things as the status of women or the superordinate role of law, the degree to which they ultimately found reflection in Soviet life was at least to some extent the result of interactions between towns and villages, between leaders and led, and between those "above" in all areas of social life and those "below," inside the party and out.

If we are to continue to think of NEP as a period of transition, in other words, we must understand far better than we do the ways in which the society and culture of the 1920s may have structured what followed. This requires, first of all, a much better understanding of NEP culture and society itself—the task of the essays that follow.

## NOTES

1. Each of these groups had emerged during the Civil War to oppose ways in which they felt the party apparatus was violating fundamental revolutionary principles. See the discussion in Robert V. Daniels, *The Conscience of the Revolution* (Cambridge, Mass., 1965), chaps. 3–6.

2. *Desiatyi s"ezd RKP/b. Mart 1921 goda. Stenograficheskii otchet* (Moscow, 1963), p. 563.

3. Tsentral'noe Statisticheskoe Upravlenie, *Vsesoiuznaia perepis' naseleniia 1926 g.*, 56 vols. (Moscow, 1928–33), vol. 17, table 1, p. 2.

4. E. Z. Volkov, *Dinamika naseleniia SSSR za vosem'desiat let* (Moscow, 1930), p. 190.

5. F. Lorimer, *The Population of the Soviet Union: History and Prospects* (Geneva, 1946), p. 39. See also Volkov, *Dinamika*, chap. 5.

6. Lorimer, *Population*, p. 42.

7. TsSU, *Vsesoiuznaia perepis'*, vol. 17, p. 6.

8. *Bol'shaia Sovetskaia Entsiklopediia*, 2nd ed., vol. 29, p. 302.

9. R. A. Clarke and D. J. I. Matko, *Soviet Economic Facts, 1917–81*, 2nd ed. (London, 1983), pp. 10–12.

10. Ibid., pp. 83–98, 105–109.

11. H. von Rimscha, *Der russische Bürgerkrieg und die russische Emigration 1917–1921* (Jena, 1924), pp. 50–51. See also Lorimer, *Population,* p. 39.

12. TsSU, *Vsesoiuznaia perepis',* vol. 34, pp. 160–61.

13. M. Lewin, *Political Undercurrents in Soviet Economic Debates: From Bukharin to the Modern Reformers* (Princeton, 1974).

14. Stephen F. Cohen, "Bukharin, NEP, and the Idea of an Alternative to Stalinism," in *Rethinking the Soviet Experience* (New York, 1985), pp. 71–92.

# II

# THE PROBLEM OF CLASS IDENTITY IN NEP SOCIETY

*Sheila Fitzpatrick*

> *Class relations* are considered very important by Communist leaders, in accordance with their program. The *class principle* is applied in many contexts. It is also often necessary to speak of *declassing* and of *declassed* groups: "the *declassed* petty-bourgeois intelligentsia" . . . "the mass of *declassed* persons, the unemployed, the mass that has lost its sharply defined class profile, the mass of social fragments." . . .
>
> —A. M. Selishchev, *Iazyk revoliutsionnoi epokhi* (Moscow, 1928), p. 105.

NEP was the great age of detailed Marxist analysis of Soviet society. The statisticians collected data on the class composition of every conceivable social institution and organization, including the Communist Party. The peasantry was diligently analyzed to identify the breakdown into class categories of "poor peasant," "middle peasant," and "kulak." The social origins of state officials and university students were repeatedly investigated and tabulated. The statistical department of the party's Central Committee issued guidelines on occupations and class classification: gravediggers and chauffeurs, it turned out, were "proletarian," but domestic servants, porters, and shop assistants belonged to the class of "junior service personnel" *(mladshii obsluzhivaiushchii personal).*[1]

It was not just intellectual curiosity that led the Bolsheviks to collect these sociological data on such a large scale. They needed the information in order to carry out their own class-discriminatory legislation, which affected people's everyday lives as well as social status in the new society. Class membership and social origin were criteria in deciding many practical

12

questions such as university admissions, allocation of rations (at the beginning and end of the 1920s), and housing priority.[2] Members of "alien" social classes, including private traders, rentiers, and kulaks, were not even allowed to vote, according to the 1918 Constitution of the Russian Republic, and local authorities could exercise discretion in adding persons with suspect social and political backgrounds to the ranks of the disfranchised (*lishentsy*).[3]

The Bolsheviks considered that detailed knowledge of the class breakdown of Russian society was essential for political reasons. Without information about the balance of class forces, the revolutionary regime could not assess its strength or distinguish friends from enemies. Since the regime was defined as a dictatorship of the proletariat, its natural source of support in the society was the proletariat and the poor peasantry (*bednota*). Its natural enemies were the bourgeoisie, the remnants of the old nobility, and, in the countryside, the kulaks.

This Marxist approach to politics had served the Bolsheviks well in 1917, when urban society was visibly polarized between bourgeois "haves" and proletarian "have-nots," and peasants were seizing land and driving the old landowning nobility from the countryside. By 1921, however, it was a different story. The *memory* of class polarization remained strong, and the passions of revolutionary class war volatile. But the class structure itself had collapsed, the old possessing classes had disintegrated, and even the proletariat had almost vanished from the scene. The great polarization of proletariat and bourgeoisie had become a polarization of shadows and surrogates.

War, revolution, civil war, and famine in the years 1914–23 were the main causes of this debacle. The landowning nobility and capitalist bourgeoisie had been annihilated as classes by revolutionary expropriation and emigration. The old bureaucratic elite had suffered a similar eclipse as a result of the fall of the tsarist regime. In the countryside, the emerging class differentiation of the peasantry that Stolypin's agrarian reforms had sought to stimulate had been wiped out, at least temporarily, by the spontaneous "Black Repartition" of 1917–18 and the revival of the peasant commune.

Worst of all, from the Bolshevik point of view, the industrial working class, battered by hunger in the towns and the closure of industrial plants and mines, had fragmented and dispersed during the Civil War. A million or more workers had left the towns for the villages and were now, to all appearances, peasant cultivators of the land.[4] In addition, hundreds of thousands of workers had gone into the Red Army or left the factory to take up managerial and administrative positions in the new governing institutions of Soviet power; other factory workers had become artisans and small traders on the black market. The proletarian coach that had brought Cinderella to the revolution had turned into a pumpkin.

The phenomenon of "declassing" was not restricted to industrial workers. In the tumult of the revolution, millions of citizens of the former Russian Empire were in the process of moving—from one occupation to another, from one place to another, from one social status to another, from an old life to (perhaps) a new one. Men conscripted into the Imperial Army returned home, and then in many cases departed again to serve as volunteers or conscripts in the Red Army or the White Army (some served sequentially on both sides). Inhabitants of northern cities fled to the south and east but often returned as the White armies retreated. Former nobles became bookkeepers and black-marketeers. Volga residents fled west from famine or dispatched their children from the stricken areas. With the demobilization of the Red Army at the end of the Civil War, almost five million young men were released to go home to their villages or former urban residences and jobs—or, perhaps, to go somewhere else. The railway stations were full of soldiers, homeless children (besprizornye), and citizens in transit to destinations that often proved illusory.

As the demographic and social turmoil began to settle in 1923–24, Bolshevik officials, sociologists, and statisticians tried to assess the new situation, paying particular attention to the society's class structure and the class position of individuals. But the task proved extremely difficult. In Perm, for example, an attempt in 1924 to identify the class position of university students produced extraordinarily complex and ambiguous findings that left the investigating officials baffled:

> "What did your parents do before [the revolution]?"
> "My father is a worker, here is the document."
> In the document, which is twenty years old, it says: "Metalworker in depot of the Singer Company."
> "And what did he do in 1918?"
> "He worked here as a baker, he was in a baker's artel. . . ."
> "Hm, a metalworker and a baker," says the registrar in bewilderment. "And then, in 1919 and 1920, where did he work?" . . .
> ". . . The ARA [American Relief Association] offered Papa a place as an inspector. . . . He worked as an ARA inspector until 1923. . . . And then he was unemployed for a year."
> "What does he do now?"
> "Now he has a job. Here is the document from the Labor Exchange."
> It reads: "Sent at the request of a private entrepreneur to 'manage the office.' . . ."[5]

If this degree of occupational and social mobility was baffling to the Bolsheviks, it was also bewildering and frightening for the individuals concerned. Was that Perm student's father, in his own eyes, a temporarily declassed proletarian or a new recruit to the ranks of the white-collar petty bourgeoisie? Was his social self-identification shared by his daughter, who needed to qualify as a proletarian in order to stay in college? If she satisfied the examining registrar, would she feel herself to be proletarian? If she failed, would she accept a petty-bourgeois identity?


## The Bolsheviks and Proletarian Identity

The most desirable class identity in NEP Russia—proletarian—was, for that reason, the most problematical. The Bolshevik Party defined itself as the party of the proletariat and the events of October as the proletarian revolution. The industrial working class had, for the most part, supported the Bolsheviks in October. The Bolsheviks assumed that this class would also provide the necessary social support for the new revolutionary regime, the "dictatorship of the proletariat."

But what if this turned out not to be so?

In 1920 and 1921, the Bolsheviks confronted a double disaster. In the first place, the industrial working class had largely disintegrated. In the second place, many of the remaining workers had become alienated from the Bolshevik Party, as was evident in the strikes in Petrograd in early 1921 and the Kronstadt revolt. Within the party, the Workers' Opposition had mounted a significant, although ultimately unsuccessful, challenge to the Bolshevik leadership.

All this produced a brief crisis of faith in which leading party members (including Lenin) hovered on the brink of disillusionment with the Russian working class.[6] But it proved impossible for the party to abandon the proletarian connection. A majority of all party members in 1921 had been workers before the revolution and defined themselves as proletarian. The party's intellectuals, who often saw themselves as having adopted a "proletarian" identity when they became revolutionaries, were also emotionally committed. The intellectuals, moreover, felt caught on the horns of a Marxist dilemma. If the proletariat was no longer the base of support, on what class did the party and the new Soviet government depend? To that question, there was no acceptable answer.[7]

The party remained proletarian by self-definition; and at the beginning of 1924, with the announcement of the mass recruitment of workers known as the Lenin levy, the party leaders did their best to turn this premise into reality. For the Bolsheviks, however, the word *proletarian* was not simply a synonym for *working-class*. Real proletarians had to have proletarian consciousness, which from the Bolshevik standpoint implied commitment to the revolution and the Bolshevik Party. There were many actual workers at the beginning of the 1920s who failed this test and were therefore shown to be "accidental elements" in the working class, people whose mentalité was essentially peasant or petty-bourgeois.

There were also increasing numbers of "proletarians," often but not invariably members of the Bolshevik Party, who had once been workers by occupation and social position but were now, in the aftermath of the revolution, Red Army commissars and commanders or cadres in the new soviet and party bureaucracies. It was necessary for the Bolsheviks to distinguish them from "workers at the bench,"[8] while at the same time emphasizing their continuing proletarian identity.

By the early 1920s, therefore, analyses of the class composition of institutions, including the Bolshevik Party itself, used two categories for class identification—"before" and "after" the revolution. The first category, social position, was based on social origin and occupation in 1917, or in some cases occupation at the moment of joining the Bolshevik Party. The second category was current occupation. Thus, a working-class party cadre would be listed as working-class by social position and white-collar (sluzhash-chii) by current occupation. A Bolshevik worker who had been a peasant at the time of joining the party would be listed as peasant by social position and worker by current occupation.[9]

For Bolshevik purposes, the "before" category was the crucial one. What really mattered about class, from the Bolshevik standpoint, was its implication for political attitudes. If someone had been a member of the exploiting classes on the eve of the revolution, he or she was likely to regret the passing of the old regime and to dislike the Bolsheviks. But someone who had belonged to the exploited masses was probably on the side of the Bolsheviks and the revolution.

There remained a residual problem about the "before" category, namely, that social origin (proiskhozhdenie) and prerevolutionary occupation did not always coincide. For example, it was common for a worker to have been born and to have spent his early years in the village. For purposes of party entry and the like, his social position was defined as proletarian. But what was the right category for a former worker, village-born, and now a cadre? The answer was still proletarian, even though the individual in question might have spent less than ten of his thirty years actually working in a factory.

Since there were many such cases, the Bolsheviks instinctively moved toward a concept of formative proletarian experience as a determinant of class position. There were no formal guidelines, but as a rule of thumb, seven or more years' experience as a worker in a factory before the revolution (or before joining the prerevolutionary Bolshevik Party and becoming a professional revolutionary) was assumed to make a man proletarian.

In addition, it became widely accepted that Red Army service as a volunteer during the Civil War also constituted formative proletarian experience, at least for persons of lower-class urban or peasant backgrounds. Thus, a young man of provincial, probably peasant, origin could legitimately claim that he qualified for the rabfak (the workers' preparatory school that was a steppingstone to higher education in the 1920s): "Why don't they take me? I served in the Red Army as a volunteer, I am worthy, I have earned the rabfak."[10]

### Proletarian and Working-class Identities

When workers of the older (prerevolutionary) generation described themselves as "proletarian," this was a sign that their consciousness had been raised by contact with the Bolsheviks or other revolutionary intellectuals. The word would not otherwise have been a part of their vocabulary. *Proletarian* was sometimes used interchangeably with *worker (rabochii)*. But it was most often used to denote a particular type of worker—one who had participated in labor organizations and protests, had identified with the workers' factory (or shop) collective, and was aware of capitalists as the class enemy and the tsarist state as the capitalists' ally.

When the Bolsheviks spoke of the proletariat in the 1920s, they still thought above all of the type of worker "tempered in the revolutionary struggle." But the revolutionary struggle was over, and this kind of proletarian consciousness probably could not be reproduced in future generations.[11] As the Bolsheviks gradually redefined the concept of proletarian consciousness into a notion of revolutionary and ultimately civic responsibility, the distance between the ideal proletarian and the actual worker grew larger.

With the revival of industry and re-formation of the working class in the 1920s, new working-class mentalités emerged and old ones revived in new forms. Among the recognizable working-class (but not completely "proletarian") identities of NEP was that of the skilled worker with ties to the land. Although Marxist sociologists of the 1920s often tried to minimize or explain away these ties, they seem to have been strengthened in the Civil War years, when many workers (including skilled workers) went back to the villages. Perhaps the most interesting feature of workers' "ties to the land" during NEP is that they were in many cases ties to the improving farmer—sometimes the worker-peasant himself,[12] sometimes a close family member. In some industries, such as textiles in the Ivanovo region, whole communities of workers were involved in profitable farming.[13] The scale of this phenomenon was recognized only at the end of the 1920s (and then only semipublicly), when many skilled workers and their families were threatened with dekulakization.[14]

Another emerging working-class mentalité might be described, with apologies to Lenin, as "trade-union consciousness." The trade unions of NEP, whose tone seems to have been set by male, middle-aged, firmly urban workers who had been in the factories before the revolution, were committed to working within the system, but also to defending labor's (or the unions') interests against Soviet management. Since unemployment was high, the unions did their best to enforce closed-shop rules and limit the influx of nonunionized peasants. Their bias was not only antipeasant but to some degree antiwoman and antiadolescent as well, because it was assumed by most trade unionists that adult, urban males needed the jobs most.

Young workers of the postrevolutionary cohort often had prickly relations with their elders in the factory. They were said to be disrespectful, overconfident, and not amenable to collective discipline.

> The lads do not always want to obey the administration or the foreman or anyone else. If, for the good of production, they get transferred to worse work in another shop, they make objections and threaten to give both the foreman and the administration a thrashing. Boys still wet behind the ears beat their chests and declaim: "What did we fight for!"[15]

Youth unemployment was high, and it was hard for young people to get a factory job. Those who did were an educated and ambitious group, little different in sociocultural profile[16] and political culture[17] from their white-collar and student peers, whose sights were often set (consciously or unconsciously) beyond the factory. Young proletarians were an elect group in NEP society. They were the *smena,* the coming generation, the future builders of socialism. The Komsomol and party wanted them as members, and every educational institution in the country wanted them as students to meet its proletarian quotas. To be a young, skilled male worker in the 1920s was to have a new kind of proletarian consciousness—that of a potentially upwardly mobile proletarian *vydvizhenets.*

### The Bourgeois "Other"

> In the revolutionary years . . . many words changed their meaning in connection with the circumstances of the time and with the moods and sufferings of social groups. . . . *Bourgeois* and *petty-bourgeois* [now] have a pejorative meaning.[18]

The bourgeoisie was, of course, the antithesis of the proletariat in Marxist analysis. Its old elite social role was one the Bolsheviks particularly disliked, yet in some respects it could be seen as inheriting. In Soviet usage of the 1920s, the term *bourgeois* was applied to the class enemy in general, as well as to three distinct social groups in NEP society: *"byvshie"*[19] (members of the old privileged classes, including the landowning and bureaucratic nobility), Nepmen, and the noncommunist intelligentsia.

Although Russia had lost a large part of its prerevolutionary elites during the years of war, revolution, and civil war, as a result of expropriation and emigration, the old "bourgeoisie" was still seen as a threat by the Bolsheviks. This was because of the possibility of a capitalist revanche staged from abroad. As Lenin explained:

> They [the Russian bourgeoisie] have retained their class organization abroad, as an emigration which probably numbers one and a half to two million persons and possesses more than fifty daily newspapers of all the bourgeois and "socialist" (that is, petty-bourgeois) parties, the remnants of an army, and many links with the international bourgeoisie. This emigration devotes all its strength and resources to the destruction of Soviet power and the restoration of capitalism in Russia.[20]

The *byvshie*—those of the former privileged classes who had remained in Russia—were assumed to be potential allies of the Russian and foreign capitalists abroad. Bolsheviks feared their influence in Soviet society, even when (as was generally the case) they occupied humble positions, steered clear of politics, and tried to conceal their past. Their children, also seen as a possible source of corruption, were barred from the Pioneers,[21] the Komsomol, and, as far as possible, higher educational institutions.

Nepmen—the "new bourgeoisie" of private entrepreneurs engendered by NEP—were also regarded with great distrust and suspicion. While Nepmen, like *byvshie*, showed few signs of political activism or aspiration, the Bolsheviks still thought of them as potential challengers and future leaders of a return to capitalism, and they regarded their reticence as a sign of cunning. Although their activities were no longer illegal, as they had been when they operated on the black market under War Communism, this did not convey any marked increase in social tolerance on the Bolshevik side. Nepmen were caricature figures, depicted as bloated and rapacious exploiters, "stroll[ing] along the alleys with self-important expressions in the company of their overfed, incredibly well-groomed wives, dressed to kill."[22]

The majority of Nepmen seem to have been parvenus, not descendants of the old merchant and capitalist business classes.[23] Nevertheless, the possibility of links' being forged between Nepmen and members of the old elites was anxiously monitored, and one observer (a contemporary criminal investigator) claimed that "Leningrad Nepmen eagerly married brides with princely and ducal titles and in their lifestyle and manners imitated the old Petersburg 'high society' in every way."[24] Still more alarming, and more plausible, was the danger of rapprochement between Nepmen and the new Soviet elite. Under NEP conditions, the most profitable entrepreneurial activities were across the boundary of the public and private sector, and the Nepman's function as a *tolkach*[25] made him a valuable contact for Bolshevik managers and industrial officials.

In Soviet discourse of the 1920s, educated professionals (members of the intelligentsia) were also "bourgeois," unless they had proved otherwise by joining the Bolshevik Party before the revolution. The term Bolsheviks used for the intelligentsia was *bourgeois specialists*. This had an ironic ring, since historically the Russian intelligentsia had supported radical causes, prided itself on being above class, and despised the commercial bourgeoisie as philistine. Nevertheless, the intelligentsia had been one of the elites of prerevolutionary society; and, unlike other prerevolutionary elites, it had emerged from the upheaval of revolution and civil war more or less intact, unsympathetic to Bolshevism, and strongly conscious of its identity as a group. The Bolsheviks had some reason to fear the intelligentsia as a viable competing elite with pretensions to moral if not political leadership.

"Bourgeois specialists" remained a relatively privileged group in the 1920s, because the Bolshevik leaders concluded that their skills were irreplaceable. But this policy was not popular with the rank and file of the party or its urban lower-class sympathizers. "Whatever privileges you give them, it's like the proverb—'No matter how much you feed the wolf, he still looks to the forest' . . .," one soviet deputy from the provinces complained.[26]

"The word '*intelligent*' is becoming a term of abuse,"[27] an Old Bolshevik intellectual commented with alarm in the mid-twenties. *Intelligentshchina,* an unambiguous pejorative, was widely used during NEP, especially in Komsomol circles, to describe attitudes that were liberal, vacillating, weak, and lacking the necessary Bolshevik quality of *tverdost'* (tough-mindedness). The disgust with which many lower-class Bolsheviks viewed the intelligentsia is well conveyed in a report by a Workers' Control official on the Stanislavsky Theater in Moscow. The theater people mocked the Bolsheviks' slogans and sneered that their red banners were "aesthetically displeasing," and the general manager was

> a repellent manifestation of a class that has had its day, a sycophant. . . . Today he shakes our party member's hand and tries to bow low to him, but in fact he hates that Communist to the depths of his soul, hates everything Communist, every value that the working class and the party inculcates.[28]

### Bourgeois and Petty-Bourgeois Tendencies

Bolsheviks often used a "genealogical" approach to class in the 1920s, although this upset the party's intellectuals.[29] Once a bourgeois, always a bourgeois was what this meant in practice. But that did not mean that members of other classes were safe from the siren song of the bourgeoisie. The Bolsheviks believed that their revolution had interfered with the society's natural progression to capitalism, and they were constantly on guard against a spontaneous reversion. "Bourgeois" and "petty-bourgeois" influences were everywhere. Persons of any social class were liable to succumb to them.

Discussion of "bourgeois" and "petty-bourgeois" tendencies could sometimes be taken more or less literally. For example, a worker whose wife was in trade might be said to be under petty-bourgeois entrepreneurial influence, and a worker-peasant who clung to his plot of land in the village might be thought to show petty-bourgeois proprietorial instincts. In other cases, however, the accusations had a more tenuous connection to social reality. For example, Bolshevik Oppositionists and persons who had once belonged to other political parties were identifiable ipso facto as bourgeois or petty-bourgeois.

There were serious reasons for the party to fear embourgeoisement of its cadres. In taking power from the old ruling classes, the Bolsheviks risked inheriting materialist bourgeois values and style of life as well. This was described in the 1920s as the danger of "degeneration," that is, loss of the party's revolutionary dedication. Such degeneration might occur, Bolsheviks feared, if party cadres were corrupted by *byvshie,* Nepmen, and bourgeois intellectuals, or by contact with the foreign capitalist world.[30]

Nepmen might corrupt the Soviet officials with whom they did business by arousing "aspirations toward the 'easy life' " and using "bribery and all kinds of small services, entertainments, and 'gifts.' "[31] As noted above, this was not an idle fear. In Moscow, at least, Nepmen, members of the old intelligentsia, and party leaders mingled in the café society of NEP, and it is reasonable to suppose that in this milieu "bourgeois" values were more likely to influence Communists than vice versa.

Bolsheviks also feared degeneration of cadres through contact with the bourgeois specialists with whom they worked. It was assumed that the cadres would feel themselves at a social and cultural disadvantage, since the *spetsy* were likely to know more about the business at hand than their Communist superiors; and they might react by imitating and assimilating the values of the *spetsy.*

There were dangers on the domestic front, too, if cadres of lower-class origin married wives who came from the old privileged and educated classes. Such marriages were not uncommon and often had a visible effect on the Communist husband's lifestyle: a growing taste for luxury, christening of children, and social interaction with "alien class elements," including the wives' relatives, were noted as consequences of such misalliances. The party's Central Control Commission received many complaints from rank-and-file Communists about cadres who had married out of their class. For example:

> Is it permissible for an old party man to indulge in a personal life that is often philistine and petty-bourgeois (with an aristocratic wife and so on)?

> How does the Central Control Commission react when our party members, especially those holding responsible positions, throw over their peasant or working-class wives and families and go off with priests' daughters and the former wives of White officers?[32]

Solts, chairman of the Central Control Commission, sympathized with the concerns expressed in these notes. He told young Communists:

> We are the governing class, and that's how we ought to think of ourselves. Rapprochement with a person of the camp hostile to us ought to provoke such public criticism that a person would think thirty times before making such a decision. . . . People ought to think many times before deciding to marry a wife from an alien class.[33]

In addition to the fears about bourgeois influences in Communists' private lives, young Communists and Komsomol members, in particular, were concerned about petty-bourgeois influences, namely, the danger of succumbing to *meshchanstvo*, petty-bourgeois philistinism and vulgarity. The term *meshchanstvo*, derived from the prerevolutionary urban *soslovie* (social estate) *meshchane*, was always used pejoratively. This usage had its roots in the discourse of the prerevolutionary Russian intelligentsia, for whom the values associated with *meshchanstvo* constituted the antithesis of the values of the intelligentsia.

For Communist youth, *meshchanstvo* was the antithesis of proletarian, revolutionary values. But this had a special meaning. In the young Communist milieu of NEP, *meshchanstvo* meant oppressive, patriarchal, narrowly conventional views about sex, marriage, and the family. The implication (rejected by many older party members, including Lenin) was that proletarians and Communists should liberate themselves from any such conventional restraints on their personal lives:

> Don't think that your family—husband, child, and so on—should constitute an obstacle to you or me if our feelings for each other are deep and sincere [wrote the young "proletarian" writer Aleksandr Fadeev in 1924]. We live in the Land of Soviets, and it would be shameful for us to behave like petty-bourgeois philistines [*pokhodit' na meshchan*].[34]

## Rural Identities

> Nobody is trying to work his way into the prosperous peasantry [*lezt' v zazhitochnykh*] now. Everyone is trying to work his way into the poor peasantry, because that has become more advantageous in the village.[35]

The Bolsheviks and other Russian Marxists believed that the peasantry was divided (or at least in process of dividing) into classes, with "kulaks" exploiting the "poor peasant" class, while "middle peasants," as yet undifferentiated, occupied the social terrain between the two extremes. This view of the peasantry and its development was disputed in the 1920s by neo-Populists such as A. V. Chaianov and has since been contested by many historians and sociologists.[36] It was certainly problematical in its application to the Russian peasantry of the NEP period, if only because of the equalizing effect of the redistribution of land in 1917–18.

Nevertheless, forms of economic and sociocultural differentiation did exist in the Russian peasantry in the 1920s. Some peasants were wholly dependent upon cultivation of their allotments for survival. Others had important secondary occupations (trades, crafts, seasonal departure [*otkhod*] to wage-earning jobs in mines, factories, and commercial agriculture), many of which brought them in contact with the town. *Otkhodniki*, in particular, had long been associated with the introduction of urban artifacts and mores into village society.[37]

The Bolsheviks were inclined to interpret all conflict within the peasantry as class conflict between exploited poor peasants and exploiting kulaks. While the existence of a class basis might be disputed, conflict of various kinds existed. During the Civil War, when *otkhodniki* and worker-peasants were forced to return to the villages and make a living on the land, often without the animals and equipment to render this feasible,[38] many conflicts arose between the new arrivals and the old inhabitants. Probably the new arrivals, with their urban experience, skills, and literacy, were disinclined to defer to the elders of the commune. When *otkhod* and opportunity for outside earnings diminished in Saratov province in the mid-1920s, the former *otkhodniki*, "poor peasants" in terms of their capacity to support themselves by agriculture alone, "were forced to stay in the village, and entered into sharp conflict with the kulak bosses [*verkhushka*].[39]

Conflict also arose on the basis of generational differences, often in connection with *otkhod*, which was particularly common among younger male peasants, or the return of young men from military service. In Tver, for example, where out-migration and *otkhod* had long been a basic fact of peasant life, there were major generational conflicts over culture.[40] The fashion of the 1920s for the young male peasants of Tver was "Civil War" dress (Red Army uniforms or homemade imitations, worn with wide leather belts and *budennovki*). Young peasant women in the region were similarly attracted to styles of modern urban dress which their elders deplored.[41]

It is reasonable to assume that peasants who were young and had had contact with modern urban mores through wagework in the towns or military service were more likely than other peasants to sympathize with Soviet power.[42] The Komsomol, whose constituency was youth, proved one of the most effective purveyors of Soviet values in the countryside. Young peasants who had served in the Red Army probably played a similarly important role.[43] In 1927, more than half the chairmen of Russian rural soviets were Red Army veterans.[44]

If the Bolsheviks' description of their rural sympathizers as poor peasants and their opponents as kulaks was simplistic, this is not to say that the class categories they applied to the peasantry were meaningless. The terms *poor peasant* and *kulak* had long had meaning in the village. Moreover, they acquired additional meaning in the 1920s, because the Bolsheviks gave them practical significance. A new "poor peasant" role was created after the revolution as a result of the fact that the Bolsheviks rewarded people identified as poor peasants. Similarly, a new "kulak" role came into existence because the Bolsheviks punished people identified as kulaks.

The basis of "poor peasant" identity was the possession of an allotment too small for its cultivation to support the peasant family. Poor peasants were therefore peasants who were in danger of being forced off the land and often had to seek outside income as *otkhodniki*. The basis of "kulak" identity was officially the exploitation of poorer peasants, as manifest, for example, in the hiring of nonfamily labor. In practice, however, *kulak* was often almost synonymous with *prosperous peasant*. In many areas, kulaks often had nonagricultural earnings (from trade, milling, and so on) as well as a comparatively large area under cultivation. Both poor peasants (with below-average sown area) and prosperous peasants (with above-average sown area) tended to be more literate than other ("middle") peasants.[45]

During NEP, peasants often denied the existence of any special group of poor peasants in the village ("We have no poor peasants; we are all poor peasants").[46] This should be taken with a large grain of salt, since it was surely aimed primarily at the tax collector. Later, during the collectivization and dekulakization campaign at the beginning of the 1930s, peasants also often denied the existence of kulaks. But such denials were not characteristic of the NEP period, when the term seems to have been used fairly freely by peasants as well as Soviet officials.

The main benefit available for "poor peasants" in the 1920s was release from the agricultural tax. Poor peasants also had preference in educational, Komsomol, and party admissions, at least in principle, and were supposed to have first rights to jobs in industry and clerical and administrative jobs in the rural soviets. "Kulaks" were penalized by being deprived of the right to vote, and they had last priority of access in all situations where poor peasants had first priority. The existence of such penalties and rewards presumably meant that the original premise—that poor peasants were Soviet sympathizers, and kulaks were hostile—became, at least to some degree, a self-fulfilling prophecy.

In some contexts, notably taxation, poor peasants were recognizable by their marginal status as cultivators. But in other contexts (education, Komsomol membership, jobs) it was probably their literacy and status as past or present *otkhodniki* that enabled officials to identify them as candidates for advancement *(vydvizhenie)*. Potential kulaks were well aware of their position during NEP, and they often took care to avoid behavior likely to earn the label. In Siberia, a survey of peasant reading habits disclosed that kulaks bought "mainly juridical books" and knew more about the Soviet Land Code and the Criminal Code than most local lawyers.[47]

Since it was advantageous for a peasant to "work his way into the poor peasantry," this group undoubtedly contained many persons who were essentially impostors in the category—particularly prosperous peasants and rural priests and their children, who were officially disadvantaged but tended, like the poor peasants, to have above-average literacy. The disadvantages of kulak status had the reverse effect. Prosperous peasants in danger of being labeled kulaks often took evasive action: for example, hiring out their own labor (and horse) to a horseless peasant in order to create the image of a "poor peasant."

### Masking and Unmasking of Class Identity

> Tear off each and every mask from reality.
>
> —RAPP slogan of the 1920s[48]

The NEP structure of rewards and penalties based on class created the temptation for anyone with an "alien" class identity to conceal it or invent a new one. This sometimes involved outright falsification. However, given the fluidity of Russian society in the 1920s, it was often a question not so much of falsification as of making selective use of different elements of one's personal and family history. The former noble, now working as a *spets*

or an accountant in some government institution, might reasonably describe himself simply as a white-collar worker. The child of a village priest
whose peasant wife cultivated the family allotment might well feel that
"peasant" identity was appropriate as well as advantageous.

Class identity was generally determined on the basis of an individual's
statements about himself, although the authorities might ask for
documentation from local soviets and employers, and a claim that was not
congruous with the individual's appearance and manner might be immediately challenged. Since persons from "alien" classes did not have the
right to vote, local soviets were supposed to identify them and exclude
them from the electoral register. However, rigorous investigation of an
individual's class position usually occurred only when he sought admission
to the Komsomol, the party, secondary school, or university, or in the
course of one of the periodic purges of party and Komsomol membership,
the student body in universities and secondary schools, and white-collar
employees in the bureaucracies.

The conscious creation of desirable class identities took various forms.
One way of creating a new identity was to change occupation or choose a
different occupation from that of one's parents. It was common, for example, for the child of an urban white-collar or professional family to try to
establish proletarian identity by working in a factory for a few years before
college. This was usually done for practical reasons—sometimes for urgent
reasons of self-preservation[49]—but was not usually done entirely cynically.
For many adolescents of the NEP period, there was romantic appeal to the
idea of the factory and proletarian toil.

For young people with "alien" class backgrounds, another way of creating a new class identity was adoption by a friend or relative with better
social credentials than the parents. For example, a priest arranged for his
son to be adopted by an uncle who was a village teacher in order that the
child should not be barred from further education on grounds of his social
position.[50] The son of another priest tried to persuade a relative who was a
Soviet official to adopt him, partly for career reasons, but partly because he
had rejected his parents' values after going away to school and wanted a
"Soviet" identity.[51]

Such cases were invariably complex, since they brought into play all the
tensions inherent in the relationship between parents and their growing
children. The daughter of a priest left home and "broke all ties" with her
parents, first living with her brother, an agronomist, and then working as a
nurse in order to realize her dream of going to medical school.[52] A
merchant's son, also a university student, argued before a purge commission that he had broken all "political ties" with his father, constantly
quarreled with him about politics, and thus should not be considered to
share his class identity.[53]

Young people often made unsuccessful efforts to get their parents to change their class position.

> No matter what we say or how we curse the old man [and tell him] to give up being a priest [*bros' svoe popovstvo*], it's just deception of the public, he doesn't want to listen. He's taken his stand; he says: "You make your own decisions, and so will I. What will I do at my age if I give up being a priest?" You just can't budge him.[54]

Some children of social aliens "broke ties" with their parents, or even resorted to public announcement of the fact ("I, the son of a former priest, break all ties with the clerical caste. [Signed] Iurii Mikhailovskii, teacher").[55] In one case, a man whose prospects in the party were blighted by his alien social origins took even more desperate action:

> Veit [a party member since 1923] concealed the fact that he was the son of a noble, a former assistant district police officer. When Veit's social position was disclosed, and he was expelled from the party for hiding it and for inactivity, his relations with his father worsened acutely, and in the end, Veit killed him.[56]

Although it was relatively easy to misrepresent or invent class identity, it was also common for identities to be challenged, as happened in Veit's case, with damaging consequences to the individual. "Unmasking" of concealed or fraudulently claimed class identity was a great preoccupation of Communists in the 1920s and, as a result, a constant anxiety for some segments of the population. Apart from Nepmen, kulaks, priests, and members of the former noble and merchant estates, who were directly at risk, the issue of class identity was most troubling for white-collar wage and salary earners *(sluzhashchie)*, who were particularly likely to have ambiguous class identities and to have made selective and creative use of the disparate data at their disposal.

The proletarian writers' slogan "Tear off the masks!" ostensibly referred to a literary technique by which the real person was revealed behind the social persona. In reality, however, the young Communists of RAPP tore off the masks in order to reveal class enemies. It was this instinct that brought them success in the Communist milieu of NEP and lent credibility to their dubious claims to be proletarian. Fear of hidden enemies and habitual suspicion that people might not be what they seemed were already basic components of Soviet political culture in the NEP period.

> Once, passing through Tula, I happened to stop in at the GPU. I looked, and there sat the son of our former lord [*barin*]. I was horrified. And then the train came in, and I had to go. I asked him: "What's your last name?" But he saw that the train had already come in, . . . so he wouldn't say.[57]

Such encounters, real or imagined, were frightening to Communists, especially those who were uneducated and from the lower classes. One source of anxiety was fear that the more cultured class enemy might hoodwink and manipulate them. A semiliterate peasant chairwoman of a rural soviet described her alarm when, just after taking office, she saw what she thought was a familiar name in a document and asked someone to decipher it for her. It turned out to be the name of the daughter of the old *barin,* wanting an official signature for (the chairwoman presumed) some sinister purpose. "If I had signed the piece of paper and put the [soviet] stamp on it, who knows what she might have done with that piece of paper!"[58]

For many Communists, the public unmasking of hidden class enemies seems to have been both exhilarating and reassuring. When Zemliachka, a member of the Central Control Commission, reported to a party congress on a recent purge of the Cooperatives, the *engagement* of her audience was palpable:

> [Those purged included] 109 former merchants (not people from merchant families but the actual former merchants themselves), former nobles, hereditary Honored Citizens, and persons of the clerical estate. Among those purged were 11 former ministers from various governments *(Excitement in the hall)* and . . . 49 scions of former tsarist *chinovniki,* tsarist aristocrats, big landowners, manufacturers, and merchants. Fifty-seven of those purged had criminal convictions under Soviet power, 22 had engaged in trade in the Soviet period, and 82 were former officers *(Excitement in the hall. Voices: "Aha!").*[59]

This essay has focused on a central paradox of NEP society: the fragility of individuals' class identity, on the one hand, and the social and political significance of class identity, on the other. The paradox is important for historians of the NEP period because most of the contemporary sources reflect the Bolsheviks' Marxist, class-based approach to social analysis. If we take those sources at face value, we may overlook the fact that the class roles played by Soviet citizens during NEP were often precarious and unstable. If, however, we conclude that class is an artificial category in the Soviet context, we are in danger of missing an important and unusual dimension of NEP society, namely, that presentation of a *class* self in everyday life was part of the common social experience.

Having disintegrated in the period of revolution and civil war, Russian society was in the process of re-formation and recovery during NEP. By 1928, the society was undoubtedly more structured and coherent than it had been in 1921. The industrial working class was a social reality, not just a shadowy political symbol, by the end of the decade. It was sufficiently coherent to be capable of collective action within the new trade union framework. Nepmen constituted a recognizable social type, if not a coherent group capable of political action. The "bourgeois" intelligentsia had recovered confidence and privileges during NEP, and by 1927–28 showed some tentative ambition to play a political role, or at least the role of equal partner in the Bolsheviks' modernization program. In the countryside, there were signs of internal differentiation within the peasantry based not so much on class exploitation as on intergenerational conflict and the tensions associated with the spread of modern, urban mores and Soviet influence.

In the late 1920s, in a mood of militancy and alarm that swept the party after the 1927 war scare and in anticipation of the coming First Five-Year Plan, Bolsheviks claimed that the "bourgeois" forces in society were rallying and preparing an assault on Soviet power. The question quickly became moot, because the regime launched preemptive strikes against kulaks, Nepmen, and, to a lesser degree, the bourgeois specialists, liquidating the first two groups "as classes."

The upheavals of the First Five-Year Plan period are significant in a number of ways for social historians of NEP. In the first place, the upheavals ended NEP abruptly and shattered the NEP social structure. That means that our discussion of social development during NEP applies to a chronological period of only seven to eight years. There are questions about trends that—as in the comparable case of social change in the village stimulated by Stolypin's reforms in the years 1907–15—can never be answered definitively.

In the second place, the Bolshevik allegations about "bourgeois counterattack" in the late 1920s should give social historians food for thought. Western historians have rightly been skeptical about these allegations as a description of any immediate political reality. But what about the *social* reality? What actual developments and phenomena in the society were the Bolsheviks observing that led them to make the allegations of counterattack? Did they, for example, see the Nepmen gaining coherence as a class (for which evidence is slight), or were they more concerned about the increasingly visible interaction between "bourgeois" (commercial and professional) and Soviet elites? In the countryside, did they really see a poor-peasant class emerging in the village as a result of kulak exploitation? Or did they simply conclude that the balance of forces between "modern," young, urban- and Soviet-influenced peasants and the "traditional" village leadership, still firmly in command of the commune, had shifted in favor of the former?

The impact of the Bolsheviks' preoccupation with class on social relations and consciousness is a topic that deserves serious attention. On the one hand, the Bolsheviks were offering and to some degree imposing a social framework predicated on the idea of basic class antagonism between the bourgeoisie and the proletariat. On the other hand, members of Russian society, buffeted and uprooted by the revolutionary storms, had their own need to reorient themselves and define their new positions and identities. Since it was necessary to have class identities for contacts with Soviet authorities, it would be surprising if these were not to some degree internalized during NEP. This would not preclude dual identities, or a skeptical approach to Soviet class categories. A peasant might regard himself simultaneously as a *bedniak* (if this was his Soviet persona) and as an ordinary peasant (for purposes of everyday interaction with other peasants in the village). A self-defined *intelligent* who pronounced the term *bourgeois specialist* in tones of mockery might still come to see himself as, in some essential way, bourgeois.

Finally, we come to the complex question of the *afterlife* of NEP class categories. Whether or not a kulak class existed during NEP, Soviet society of the 1930s certainly contained a real group of *raskulachennye* (those who had experienced dekulakization). It also recognized the presence of "former *bedniaki*" (prominent in the new kolkhoz administrations), "former workers" (particularly conspicuous in industrial management),[60] and a social entity "previously called the bourgeois intelligentsia." Like its NEP predecessor, the society of the 1930s often defined social identity in "before" and "after" categories. From the perspective of the mid-1930s, however, it was not the October Revolution that constituted the social watershed (as had been the case during NEP) but rather the period of collectivization and the First Five-Year Plan.

## NOTES

1. *Slovar' zaniatii lits naemnogo truda. Posobie dlia rabotnikov iacheek i komitetov VKP(b) pri opredelenii roda zaniatii kommunistov i prinimaevykh v partiiu* (Moscow, 1928), passim.

2. For a detailed discussion of this question, see Elise Kimerling, "Civil Rights and Social Policy in Soviet Russia, 1918–1936," *Russian Review*, vol. 41, no. 1 (January 1982), pp. 24–46.

3. *Sobranie uzakonenii i rasporiazhenii rabochego i krest'ianskogo pravitel'stva RSFSR*, 1924, no. 71, art. 695.

4. This was an intellectual as well as political blow to the Bolsheviks, since they had acted on the premise that, despite the presence of many recent arrivals from the village and peasant *otkhodniki* in the industrial labor force, Russia had a "mature" working class, essentially separate from the peasantry.

5. V. Sh-rin, "Chistiat (s natury i po ofitsial'nym dokumentam)," *Krasnaia molodezh'*, 1924, no. 2, p. 126.

6. See discussion in Sheila Fitzpatrick, "The Bolsheviks' Dilemma: Class, Culture and Politics in the Early Soviet Years," *Slavic Review*, vol. 47, no. 4 (December 1988).

7. "An awful situation has been created," said Iurii Milonov at the 10th Party Congress. "We find ourselves above an abyss, between the working class, which is infected with petty-bourgeois prejudices, and the peasantry, which is petty-bourgeois in essence. It is impossible to depend solely on the soviet and party bureaucracy." *Desiatyi s"ezd RKP(b). Mart 1921 g. Stenograficheskii otchet* (Moscow, 1963), p. 74.

8. According to Selishchev, the terms *rabochii ot stanka* and *krest'ianin ot sokha* were new coinages in Russian, introduced by the Bolsheviks on the semantic pattern of the German *Arbeiter von Erde*. A. M. Selishchev, *Iazyk revoliutsionnoi epokhi. Iz nabliudenii nad russkim iazykom poslednikh let (1917–1926)*, 2nd ed. (Moscow, 1928), pp. 36–37.

9. See *Sotsial'nyi i natsional'nyi sostav VKP(b). Itogi vsesoiuznoi partiinoi perepisi 1927 g.* (Moscow, 1928).

10. Rostovskii, "Khozhdenie po mukam odnogo rabfakovtsa," *Molodaia gvardiia*, 1924, no. 5, p. 212. But note that when the young Communists who headed RAPP (the militant proletarian writers' organization of the 1920s) made similar claims, these were often regarded skeptically, despite their credentials of Civil War experience, because they came from upper-class, intelligentsia families.

11. See Diane P. Koenker, "Class and Consciousness in a Socialist Society: Workers in the Printing Trades during NEP," below.

12. See, for example, the interesting biography of I. E. Kniazev, a worker whose participation in the revolutionary movement from 1905 led him to return periodically to his village in Moscow gubernia to escape the police. In 1917, impressed by the agricultural techniques of German colonists, he returned permanently to the countryside to put them into practice, becoming a prosperous peasant farmer and Soviet official by the mid-1920s. S. Leningradskii, *Ot zemli na zavod i s zavoda na zemliu* (Moscow-Leningrad, 1927).

13. See N. Semenov, *Litso fabrichnykh rabochikh prozhivaiushchikh v derevniakh i politprosvetrabota sredi nikh* (Moscow-Leningrad, 1929).

14. See, for example, the anxious discussion of this problem in *Ianvarskii ob"edinennyi plenum M[oskovskogo] K[omiteta VKP(b)] i M[oskovskoi] K[ontrol'noi] K[omissii]. 6–10 ianvaria 1930 g.* (Moscow, 1930), p. 34, and *Sessiia TsIK Soiuza SSSR 6 sozyva. Stenograficheskii otchet i postanovleniia. 22–28 dekabria 1931 g.* (Moscow, 1931), Bulletin 10, p. 13.

15. A. Bordadyn, "Rabochaia molodezh' kak ona est'," *Molodaia gvardiia*, 1926, no. 3, p. 102. For an interesting discussion of the attitudes of working-class youth, see N. B. Lebina, *Rabochaia molodezh' Leningrada. Trud i sotsial'nyi oblik 1921–1925 gody* (Leningrad, 1982).

16. For a description of a young Moscow worker's recreational and cultural habits, see S. A. Antonov, *Svet ne v okne* (Moscow, 1977), pp. 19–24, 69–70.

17. On the new political culture of young workers, see Selishchev, *Iazyk revoliutsionnoi epokhi*, pp. 198–200.

18. Ibid., pp. 192–93.

19. Literally, "former people."

20. V. I. Lenin, *Polnoe sobranie sochinenii*, vol. 44 (Moscow, 1964), p. 5.

21. See, for example, the case of young Lidiia Tolstaia, refused entry to the Pioneers on the grounds that her grandmother, widow of an admiral in the Imperial Fleet, spoke French and was "from the *byvshie*," and that her parents knew

the poets Khlebnikov and Viacheslav Ivanov: Lidiia Libedinskaia, *Zelenaia lampa. Vospominaniia* (Moscow, 1966), pp. 48–60.
22. Lev Sheinin, *Zapiski sledovatelia* (Moscow, 1965), pp. 32–33.
23. *Izmeneniia sotsial'noi struktury sovetskogo obshchestva 1921–seredina 30-kh godov* (Moscow, 1979), pp. 116–17; I. Ia. Trifonov, *Klassy i klassovaia bor'ba v SSSR v nachale NEPa (1921–1925 gg.)* (Leningrad, 1969), part 2, pp. 70–71.
24. Trifonov, *Klassy*, pp. 268–69.
25. Fixer, procurer of goods, expediter of deliveries.
26. *Tret'ia sessiia Tsentral'nogo Ispolnitel'nogo Komiteta Soiuza SSSR 5-go sozyva. Stenograficheskii otchet* (Moscow, 1931), Bulletin 10, p. 13.
27. Skrypnik, in *Biulleten' VIII-i vseukrainskoi konferentsii Kommunisticheskoi partii (bol'shevikov) Ukrainy. (Stenogramma). 12–16 maia 1924 g.* (Kharkov, 1924), pp. 64–65.
28. Karaseva (Moscow Control Commission), speaking at *III-ia moskovskaia oblastnaia i II-ia gorodskaia konferentsiia VKP(b)* (Moscow, January 1932), Bulletin 10, p. 11.
29. Iaroslavskii complained that the Bolsheviks were doing (in reverse) "almost what the White Guards do when they take a prisoner: they look to see if there are calluses on his hands, and if there are, that means he's a real criminal, a Bolshevik." *XI s"ezd RKP(b). Mart-aprel' 1922 g. Stenograficheskii otchet* (Moscow, 1961), p. 105.
30. In the early Soviet years, the masking of "proletarian" identity involved in international diplomacy caused Bolsheviks great anxiety. One memoirist, for example, recalls that in 1922, ordinary party members could not refrain from making uneasy jokes about the fact that Soviet diplomats at the Lausanne Conference had to wear tails, the formal garb of "the bourgeoisie." A. G. Zverev, *Zapiski ministra* (Moscow, 1973), p. 43.
31. Ibid.
32. *Biulleten' TsKK i RKI SSSR i RSFSR*, 1927, no. 2–3, p. 55.
33. In I. Razin, comp., *Komsomol'skii byt. Sbornik* (Moscow-Leningrad, 1927), p. 66.
34. Letter to A. A. Il'ina, 4 October 1924, in *Aleksandr Fadeev. Materialy i issledovaniia* (Moscow, 1984), vol. 2, p. 121.
35. Delegate from Western oblast, speaking at *Tret'ia sessiia Tsentral'nogo Ispolnitel'nogo Komiteta*, Bulletin 10, p. 13.
36. For example, Moshe Lewin, *Russian Peasants and Soviet Power* (London, 1968), and Teodor Shanin, *The Awkward Class: Political Sociology of Peasantry in a Developing Society, Russia, 1910–1925* (Oxford, 1972).
37. See, for example, the data on Viriatino (Tambov gubernia) at the turn of the century cited in Sula Benet, ed. and trans., *The Village of Viriatino* (New York, 1970).
38. See, for example, A. Gagarin, *Khoziaistvo, zhizn' i nastroeniia derevni* (Moscow-Leningrad, 1925).
39. V. A. Kozlov, *Kul'turnaia revoliutsiia i krest'ianstvo 1921–1927* (Moscow, 1983), p. 105.
40. This should be remembered when reading the account of traditional peasant culture in Tver province in Helmut Altrichter's essay, below.
41. L. A. Anokhina and M. N. Shmeleva, *Kul'tura i byt kolkhoznikov Kalininskoi oblasti* (Moscow, 1964), p. 145.
42. This is not to suggest an absolute correlation between "modern" attitudes in the peasantry and Soviet values. One of the main Soviet values offered to the peasantry was skepticism about religion, and in many villages a sharp decline in Orthodox religious observance was reported in the NEP period. Part of this decline, however, may be attributed to the rise of Christian sectarian influence in the countryside: the sects claimed an almost four-fold increase in membership in the

decade from 1917 (A. Angarov, *Klassovaia bor'ba v sovetskoi derevne* [Moscow, 1929], p. 32). Their appeal was at least partly to the same "modern" constituency in the peasantry, and indeed they often mimicked Soviet forms: for example, in Saratov the Baptists organized a "Day of Classless Solidarity with Brothers-in-Christ" on May 1, 1929, and in the North Caucasus they ran a "campaign against biblical illiteracy" (imitating the contemporary Soviet anti-illiteracy campaign) and even issued a Soviet-style challenge to Siberian Baptists to compete with them. *Kommunis-ticheskii put'* (Saratov), 1929, no. 19, p. 41; V. A. Kumanev, *Sotsializm i vsenarodnaia gramotnost'* (Moscow, 1967), pp. 226–27.

43. See Mark von Hagen's essay, below.

44. Kozlov, *Kul'turnaia revoliutsiia*, p. 154.

45. See table in ibid., p. 94.

46. Ibid., p. 147.

47. *Plenum Sibirskogo Kraevogo Komiteta VKP(b) 3–7 marta 1928 goda. Stenogra-ficheskii otchet* (Novosibirsk, 1928), vyp. 1, p. 21.

48. S. Sheshukov, *Neistovye revniteli. Iz istorii literaturnoi bor'by 20-kh godov* (Moscow, 1970), pp. 153, 276–77. The RAPP leader, Leopold Averbakh, took the slogan from Lenin's comment that the "realism of [Lev] Tolstoy was the tearing off of each and every mask [*sryvanie vsekh i vsiacheskikh masok*]."

49. For example, the son of a Ukrainian bourgeois family, son of a former tsarist officer who served in Petliura's National Ukrainian Army in the Civil War, created a new identity as a worker at the Kharkov Tractor Plant after his father's arrest. W. I. Hryshko, "An Interloper in the Komsomol," in Institut zur Erforschung der UdSSR, *Soviet Youth: Twelve Komsomol Histories* (Munich, 1959), series 1, no. 51, p. 96.

50. *Sudebnaia praktika*, 1929, no. 8, p. 15.

51. N. Khvalynsky, "Life in the Countryside," in *Soviet Youth*, pp. 111–14.

52. She got into medical school in Moscow a few years after leaving home in 1924 but was expelled four months before graduation (and sentenced to a term of imprisonment by a court) on grounds of concealment of social origin. It took several years of litigation to get both the university's and the court's decision reversed. *Sudebnaia praktika*, 1931, no. 16, p. 13.

53. The investigator was skeptical about this because the student still lived at home. *Krasnaia molodezh'*, 1924, no. 1, p. 126.

54. From a Perm University student's interview with the 1924 purge commission. *Krasnaia molodezh'*, 1924, no. 2, p. 127. For a similar case, see Khvalynsky, "Life in the Countryside," p. 113.

55. *Izvestiia*, 24 February 1930, p. 5.

56. *Biulleten' TsKK VKP(b)—NK RKI SSSR i RSFSR*, 1927, no. 6–7, pp. 12–13.

57. *Tret'ia sessiia Tsentral'nogo Ispolnitel'nogo Komiteta*, Bulletin 12, pp. 13.

58. Ibid.

59. *XVI s"ezd Vsesoiuznoi Kommunisticheskoi Partii (bol'shevikov), 26 iiunia–13 iiulia 1930 g. Stenograficheskii otchet* (Moscow, 1935), vol. 1, pp. 621–22.

60. See *Sostav rukovodiashchikh rabotnikov i spetsialistov Soiuza SSSR* (Moscow, 1936), where the breakdowns of industrial management distinguish not only form-er workers but those within the category who were workers at the bench in 1928.

# III

# CLASS AND CONSCIOUSNESS IN A SOCIALIST SOCIETY

## WORKERS IN THE PRINTING TRADES DURING NEP

### Diane P. Koenker

The fate of the workers in Soviet Russia in the 1920s has constituted an enduring theme of historiographical discussion, both in the Soviet Union and in the West. Underlying the famous debates about industrialization policy, whether to follow Bukharin or Preobrazhenskii, was the question of who would sacrifice the most in the name of industrial progress: the workers, whose support had made the socialist revolution possible, or the peasants, whose resistance to change and to economic modernization threatened to undermine the socialist experiment before it had fairly begun? The critical questions of social support for political alternatives also require an understanding of the Soviet working class: did they support Trotsky or did they support Stalin? If workers remain central to such inquiries, however, the conclusions are far from clear. The meaning of Soviet power for Russian workers remains ambiguous. On the one hand, workers who were vaulted into positions of power and authority can surely be considered to be victors of the revolution.[1] On the other hand, workers who stayed at their benches in the 1920s and 1930s found themselves often facing unemployment, and always facing competition from peasant migrants, from women, from new generations of Soviet workers. Either way, the role of workers remains critical. This is true whether we seek to resolve the "big questions" of Soviet history in the early period—the nature of Stalin's rise to power and the reasons for the Great Turn at the end of the 1920s—or whether we choose to explore questions less central to the prevailing historiography but no less important for our overall understanding of the process of historical change. These questions include how society organized itself under socialism, the relative influence of cultural traditions and political will on molding that society, and the relationship between ideology and practice in everyday terms.

The study of working-class history and the development of the field's paradigms and agenda have largely been based on the study of workers and the working class in capitalist societies. Working-class identity is defined in terms of a relationship with the ruling bourgeoisie: the fundamental experience of workers derives from selling their labor power on the capitalist market. From these realities of life in capitalist societies have come working-class culture and class consciousness, as well as movements for change and occasionally for the wholesale eradication of the system which fosters class distinctions. Our sense of labor-management relations, of politics, of culture as a way to distinguish workers from their class opponents is that they are all products of a system which assumes some element of class antagonism and therefore class identification.

What becomes of the "working class," its culture, its consciousness, when the bourgeois state has been replaced with a proletarian state, a proletarian society? In a workers' state, the workers are both employer and employed. Exploitation by definition disappears, since the surplus produced by the workers will belong (collectively) to the producers themselves. This naturally alters the old adversarial system of industrial relations. Politics in a proletarian society can be seen as a mobilization problem: there is no need to resolve competing claims for resources and power. Conflict, by definition, disappears from socialist society. And without conflict, can there be class? Without a working class, what becomes of its culture? These are the questions that underlie my inquiry into the social, economic, and political experience of workers in Soviet Russia in the 1920s.

The formation of a new revolutionary culture and pattern of everyday life was, of course, of primary importance to many Russian revolutionary theorists, including Trotsky, Lunacharskii, and Kollontai. Much attention has been paid to the efforts of the Soviet state to create, some say to dictate, a new proletarian revolutionary culture.[2] These questions of class and cultural transformation are broad and important ones, and it is my task to begin to explore some of them here.

With the revolution, class structure itself underwent fundamental changes, both theoretically and in reality. The working class moved from being underdogs to top dogs. The aristocracy was decisively eliminated as a privileged entity. But the role of countless intermediate groups—as large as the peasantry, as small as salaried employees—remained open to definition under the new regime. Physically, the working class also underwent a transformation: workers left the workbench for the countryside or for posts in Soviet administration; new workers, from the country and from urban families, entered the labor force in waves throughout the 1920s and after, as is well known.[3] The postrevolutionary working class was undergoing a continual process of "class formation."

But can we talk about class formation in a postcapitalist society? Without plunging headlong into theory, I wish to consider some of the attributes of the new and old working class as a way to approach the problem of class itself. I will start with those groups who were part of the traditional working class and who therefore brought with them to socialism a historical experience of class identity, a shared class culture, and, ultimately, a consciousness about who they were and where they belonged in society. An understanding of how this historical sense of class and class consciousness evolved in the first decade of socialism in Russia will help us construct a picture of the new social structure and the role of workers within it. Such an approach can illuminate our understanding of the contradictions and social tensions that plagued the Soviet Union in the first fifteen years of its existence.

Exploring these issues, the present essay focuses on a particular group, workers in the printing trades. Printers were by no means "typical" Russian workers, either before or after 1917, but they constituted a cohesive, self-conscious, articulate group of workers who generated a great deal of published material about their activities, their culture, their world view. For these reasons, as well as their history of political activism and their distinctive Menshevik political history between 1917 and 1923, a study of printers offers a rich perspective on the role of labor in the formative years of Soviet socialism.

Memoirs, histories of individual printing plants and local unions, studies of industrial health and safety, and an array of trade union journals and other publications shed important light on issues of class identity and class consciousness among printers. The primary source for this essay is the journal of the Moscow branch of the All-Russian Union of Workers in Polygraphic Production, *Moskovskii pechatnik*, for the year 1924. *Moskovskii pechatnik* appeared monthly from 1921 to 1926. Addressed to union activists and to rank-and-file workers in the Moscow printing industry, the journal served as a vehicle of mobilization, of information, and also of entertainment. It opened its pages to "worker-correspondents" who described factory events and who also registered, in the spirit of *glasnost'* that prevailed during NEP, complaints about management abuses, union indifference, and workers' lack of culture. The journal also appealed to special-interest constituencies among the union membership, with regular columns devoted to technical education, youth groups, women workers, physical culture enthusiasts, and recreational clubs. Although other unions published regular serials for their members, none appeared in the 1920s to have been as rich and varied as this and other journals published by different levels of the printers' union organizations.

Certain problems, however, are presented by the nature of these printed journals. We have been reminded recently of the fact that the Soviet press did not honor the principle of consumer sovereignty, but rather served as an instrument to mobilize the masses, to popularize official policy.[4] The trade union press, and even factory wall newspapers (which in the typographic industry were printed), did not escape this control. Certainly much of the content of *Moskovskii pechatnik* was determined by national political, economic, and trade union policy (about which more below), and selection of shop-floor contributions was also based on the leaders' and editors' sense of political priorities. Nonetheless, in order to have its message read, the leadership had to put its journal in the hands of its readers (subscriptions were voluntary, and the price was not part of a worker's basic union membership in 1924), and this required putting out a product that appealed to the rank and file.

The journal had at least three levels of readers (and contributors). The activist elite—union professionals—by and large generated its basic content. In doing so, they responded to party and trade union directives and consciously tried to fulfill national policy. Their primary readership and source of contributors were what could be labeled the *aktiv*, or rank-and-file activists: party members, factory committee members, shop delegates, women's delegates, members of commissions created in shops to study and implement union policy and services. It is possible that the union intended to reach no farther than this group. But in its attempt to mobilize ordinary printing workers, to bring them into the *aktiv*, the journal also tried to address the mass of workers, a body which was in any case far from homogeneous, even within the printing industry; it included workers of different levels of skill, family background, sex, age, and education. The final product of *Moskovskii pechatnik* and other journals reflected a dialogue among these different levels (just as the capitalist press represents a compromise among the interests of advertisers, publishers, and consumers).

Although NEP is usually dated from 1921, 1924 was an important transitional year in the history of the Soviet working class.[5] Urban workers began to share in the recovery of the economy from seven years of wartime devastation. For Moscow printers, the year 1924 marked the victory of Soviet power in their union. The All-Russian Union of Workers in Polygraphic Production (Vserossiiskii soiuz rabochikh poligraficheskogo proizvodstva), which had formed in 1919 as a parallel rival "Red union" to the Menshevik-dominated Union of Workers in the Printing Trades (Soiuz rabochikh pechatnogo dela), had been one of the last unions to face serious opposition from noncommunist Marxists. Although the union apparatus had been taken over by Communist printers in 1920, individual Menshevik printers still played a role in the Moscow union as late as 1923. But by 1924, the fierce partisan struggle that had characterized politics among printers since 1917 had abated. This political struggle reinforced a parallel battle by workers against economic pressures, resulting in a considerable wave of

strikes in 1923, but these too had ebbed in 1924 as the party sought to
become more responsive to the economic needs of the working rank and
file.[6] Consequently, the pages of *Moskovskii pechatnik* belonged to the victors
and loyally reflected the major concerns of party and state.[7] Most pressing,
in this fourth year of the New Economic Policy, was the economic position
of the printing industry. Finally recovering from the depression of the Civil
War years and the dislocations of the transition to NEP, with their atten-
dant unemployment, the industry had been told to become self-
supporting. The state would not subsidize the printed word as it had since
1917; if printers wanted jobs, they had to sell books. If they wanted to sell
books, they had to make them affordable to the mass peasant market.
Making them affordable required drastic cost cutting, and this translated
by the second half of 1924 into an all-out battle to raise labor productivity.
This was to be largely accomplished by increasing labor intensity by means
of the universal introduction of piece rates instead of hourly pay. This was
the economic reality within which printers continued to attempt to define
their position in the new society.

### Printers in Tsarist and Soviet Russia

Printers in the 1920s brought with them the accumulated traditions of
many years of self-conscious craft status, of political and professional
organization, of their importance to literate society. Naturally, not all
printers were equally imbued with this sense of tradition, but the prerevolutionary cultural heritage of printers provided this group with a unique
frame of reference around which to shape their new culture, on the basis of
which workers new to production could be assimilated.

Printing was by and large a relatively small-scale, labor-intensive craft in
Russia. Most printing workers were highly skilled, having learned their
trade through years of apprenticeship and practical experience. Like many
artisanal trades, printing was relatively exclusive: women rarely appeared
on the shop floor, and a sharply defined status hierarchy prevailed inside
the typographies. On the other hand, printworkers could expect to advance through the ranks from apprentice to skilled, to foreman and composing room chief (*metranpazh*, from the French *mettre en page*), sometimes
even to proprietor. Not all printers could hope to rise so high, but almost
all of the higher managerial personnel had begun their careers as workers
on the shop floor.

One important characteristic of the printers' exclusivity was their use of
language. Printers practiced many different specialized skills, but all
shared in the professionally specific language. They were not workers but
"toilers" (*truzhenniki*), "smiths of literature," "commanders of the leaden

army." Their printshops were "tipo's" or "nail shops" (*gvozdil'ki*); they formed not artels but corporations, companies, collegia. Especially pernicious supervisors were known as "spiders."[8]

Such inventive vocabularies were most closely associated with typesetters, the largest group of skilled workers in the industry, who worked in direct contact with writers and journalists. Typesetting was a dirty, hazardous job. Tuberculosis was a major killer of these workers, half of whom died before they were thirty-nine years old.[9] Unlike presswork, it was not noisy, and the composing room was known for its lively camaraderie, joke telling, and trick playing. Among typesetters, hierarchies prevailed based on pay level and regularity of work. Newspaper compositors received the highest compensation; some of them came to work in starched white shirts and graciously allowed themselves to be called "*barin*," "my lord." At the other end of the spectrum were teams of down-and-out casual typesetters, called "Italians," who contracted to work around the clock on rush jobs. They worked only when they ran out of money and drink, then drank away their pay again when they had finished their job.[10]

Generally considered beneath the level of typesetters in status were pressmen, who also learned their skills through apprenticeship and worked up through grades of skill and responsibility. Following them were a third skilled category, bookbinders. Supporting these skilled workers were folders, loaders, and helpers, and unskilled workers performing a series of more menial jobs. All workers in a shop were linked by their special language and by the rituals of their trade. The promotion of an apprentice called for certain ceremonies. The late arrival of a colleague (often with a hangover) summoned a ritual "typographic march"—the rhythmic clanging of metal rulers and composing sticks on type cases, sung with the words:

> They set type up, they put it away,
> They get their pay, they drink it away.[11]

The nature of work was often episodic, particularly in newspaper printshops, and printers would fill in the idle hours playing cards or dominoes and consuming the "green snake," alcohol.[12] Printing had the reputation of being one of the more alcoholic professions, and many stories are told of smuggling apprentices in and out of ventilator windows in order to purchase one more bottle of beer or Madeira. Perhaps this endemic alcoholism and general devil-may-care attitude of printworkers was linked to their short life expectancy.

The political consciousness of printers emerged from this base of craft tradition and solidarity. Their craft associations had begun with mutual aid funds of the printing elite back in the nineteenth century; these evolved into trade unions (sometimes with the help of the Zubatov organization) at

the beginning of the twentieth century, and along the way they expanded
to include more than just the highly paid top stratum of printers. In 1903,
strikes spread from printers in Baku, Tiflis, Odessa, and Kiev to Moscow,
where a general strike in September marked the first major episode of
labor unrest in that capital. Despite arrests, printers won concessions on
hours and wages from printshop owners.[13] Petersburg printers came a
little later to organization; their rise in activism coincided with the economic upturn and political thaw in 1904. Now more provocative material
could be printed, but typesetters also became aware of what was not
printed: they set type for articles and books before the censor passed on
publication, and they learned from this what had been banned. So their
very work experience helped to raise their political consciousness.[14] Even
before the 1905 Revolution, printers formed trade unions, often along
industrial rather than craft lines, and they published a series of periodicals
during their years of harried union activism between 1905 and 1917.[15] In
sum, printers brought to the revolution a rich associational tradition based
on their work experience.

### Working-class Identity during NEP

Printers were toilers, workers. If some of them considered themselves to
be "labor aristocrats," they were still laborers and worked in production.
There was no doubt about their proletarian pedigree, in contrast to many
other groups whose position in the new society was not so secure (*kustar'*
artisans, professionals, middle peasants, white-collar workers, to name a
few). But what did it mean to be a proletarian in a proletarian society? Did
printworkers lose their sense of superiority, of distinctiveness, of aloofness
from the common mass of toilers? Did they link their identity with the
party of the proletariat, the Communist Party?

Typically, a social group defines itself with reference to other groups.
"We are workers, we are not ___." So one way to explore this question of
identity is to investigate the attitudes of these printers toward other social
groups. Whom did they exclude from their midst, whom did they include?
What patterns of self-identity might correspond to a broader definition of
class, and how did such patterns evolve over time? If classes "are never
made, in the sense of being finished and having acquired their definitive
shape," as Eric Hobsbawm reminds us[16] (or is this true only under capitalism?), then the attributes of class, the limits of the definition, must also
change with time.

Let me start with the strata which were traditionally alien to the workers
of Russia: the aristocracy and the bourgeoisie. The aristocracy so com-

pletely disappeared after 1917 that there is no reference to it in working-class discourse by 1924.[17] Even in 1917, the aristocracy and bourgeoisie were already pretty well combined in one large "privileged" stratum. It was the bourgeoisie that was the traditional class enemy of the worker. In 1924, middle-class entrepreneurs were down but not out, surviving as owners of small printshops, as speculators, as "Nepmen," and, of course, still in full regalia in the capitalist West. In Moscow, there seemed to be relatively little overt hostility toward private owners of printshops. These shops tended to be small, poorly outfitted, and marginally profitable. Workers and "capitalists" together faced competition from the state-owned sector of the industry. At one private shop, when the owner was arrested for mistreating his apprentices, some of his workers circulated a petition asking for clemency.[18] Yet even before 1917, one account suggests that workers and printshop owners lived in relative harmony, that workers' class hostility was, on the one hand, generalized to the entire capitalist class and, on the other, directed at middle-level managerial people—spiders—rather than the big bosses.[19]

The more abstract "Nepmen" attracted a greater share of abuse from printers. A Comrades' Court at the Sixth Transpechat' printshop held 350 workers spellbound for four hours with scandalous testimony about relations between a worker and a man from this bourgeois milieu: a respected active young Komsomol woman had allegedly entered into a secret marriage (in a church!) with a "trader-Nepman." For some days before the tribunal, the sections of the printshop had heatedly debated her crime. Some demanded her expulsion from the Komsomol, others defended her by blaming an environment which could not be changed overnight. On hearing the case for and against the *komsomol'ka*, the court decided to expel her, a decision that brought loud applause from the audience. Only then did the factory activists reveal that the whole episode had been a "dramatization" in order to provoke discussion and "cure apathy." Friends of the errant woman were much relieved that she had not sold out to the Nepman after all.[20] More frequently, hostility toward this Soviet bourgeoisie took the form of complaints about speculative prices. The first summer of the union's rustic rest home was a great success, wrote a participant, but next year, the union cooperative should open a kiosk to sell cigarettes and matches; this would deprive local suppliers of the triple profits wrested from vacationing working-class consumers.[21]

Nepmen were easy targets, officially sanctioned class enemies. More interesting in understanding how workers defined themselves were relations within the printshops, among supervisors, specialists, and workers. One might expect that with the installation of socialist management and new opportunities for bench workers to advance to positions of authority, that old lines between "blue collar" and "white collar" would tend to disappear. Nonetheless, evidence of separatism and antagonism runs through the pages of *Moskovskii pechatnik*. The factory committee of the 39th Mospoligraf trust printshop had lodged a complaint with the trust's medical clinic about the rude and inattentive manner of one Dr. Tsatkin toward his patients. But "Working Woman N." wrote to the journal in defense of the good doctor. The initial complaint had come from the "wife of a cashier," seven months pregnant, who was miffed when the doctor routinely pronounced her healthy during a regular checkup. According to N., the "wife of the cashier" just wanted to chat and have someone pay some attention to her; the implication was that she had nothing better to do with her time. The doctor's other patients—hard-working proletarians—all thought he was an excellent physician.[22]

The gulf between the two groups within the printshop also produced a comic sketch from a vacationer at one of the union's summer rest homes. The factory "aristocrats"—office workers and similar employees—sat together at dinner, where their table conversation was exceedingly refined and polite, punctuated with "merci," "pardon," and the use of patronymics. At the proletarian end of the table, however, conversation was jesting and informal.[23] In another article, the prevalence of hostility toward supervisory personnel is admitted in a defense of the position of these employees. Workers always blame the specialists and bosses when things go wrong, it said, but workers, too, were guilty of inefficiency and waste.[24]

A sense of pride in being workers, in producing a product, also pervades the columns of *Moskovskii pechatnik*. This might be considered to be part of the official ideology, but it corresponds too closely to prerevolutionary attitudes to be entirely artificial. The campaign to raise productivity, which put great pressure on workers to reduce waste and work more intensely at the direct peril of big wage reductions,[25] generated spirited resistance. The real problem, wrote several typesetters, was authors who insisted on making round after round of corrections. The height of irony was a circular on "reducing waste in book printing," whose author insisted on time-consuming correction after correction. Obviously, said the correspondent, he had not read his own circular.[26] Such attacks on authors who made printers work harder echo the anti-intellectualism that characterized many politically conscious workers before the revolution.

Hostility and tension between white and blue collar, educated managers and proletarians, might be seen to be a temporary transitional problem: once enough managers and officials were raised up from the ranks of the proletariat, such differences of world view and of interest would disappear. This was the promise of *vydvizhenstvo*, promotion from the shop floor to the ranks of administrators. But scattered evidence from 1924 suggests that workers did not pass easily from one milieu to another, that the process of *vydvizhenstvo* did not necessarily erase the differences between the interests of workers and of managers. At the same time, the experience of some of these *vydvizhentsy* underscores the persistence of class identity and class pride. Not all promotees stopped thinking of themselves as workers; presumably some attempted to defend workers' interests and aspirations.

Three examples will illustrate. First is the classically successful *vydvizhenets*. Good Communist printers were hard to find in the early 1920s, but Ivan Dmitrievich Makushkin was an exemplar. Born in 1883 to a poor peasant family in Moscow province, he began work as a brochurist—a relatively low-skill job—at I. D. Sytin's printing plant at the age of twelve. He taught himself to read and write and was active in revolutionary and union politics from 1905. After 1917, he was a deputy of the Moscow soviet and remained active in his factory committee. He also visited his family's village to conduct meetings and inspect schools, and in 1921 he was named director of the printers' union consumer cooperative, an extremely difficult job. Makushkin was soon coopted to the board of directors of the central Moscow cooperative and represented this group to the Moscow soviet's economic department. When he died suddenly in 1924 of a cerebral hemorrhage, Makushkin was only forty-one; he died, said his colleagues, of overwork. In their tributes to Makushkin, coworkers stressed his proletarian roots, the simple worker language he used when addressing meetings, his commitment to the revolution, the respect he gained even from Mensheviks and SRs.[27] Such a man could bridge the gap between workers and leaders.

Not so the next *vydvizhenets*, a classic failure. According to the account furnished by his subordinates, F. A. Miakin had been a worker, but in 1922 he was made director of one of Moscow's biggest printing plants. At first, all went smoothly, because the shop ran itself—the workers were experienced, knew their craft, loved their printshop, "which they tenaciously held on to in the days of hunger and economic collapse." But power and money began to lead Miakin astray. On Saturdays, he would stroll into the printshop drunk; he left his middle-aged wife for a young woman who demanded to be supplied with clothing and jewelry. Apparently, Miakin dipped into the factory till to support his "grand style," and in early 1924 he and the typography's bookkeeper were arrested.[28]

Finally, there was the case of a reluctant *vydvizhenets*, who would best illustrate the tenacious worker pride of the Russian printer were it not for the story being fiction. Nonetheless, the publication of the story in the printers' journal suggests it had some resonance with real life. Typesetter Popov reluctantly left his position in his "native printshop," where he had worked twenty years, because of ill health. The story opens on Popov's empty type case, as he says goodbye to his colleagues. We next see him as a militiaman, dashing out of a beer bar, "where I used to drink like you," he tells those present, in order to respond to a call for help. When he petitions the party district committee to return him to his old job because the open air of the militiaman's life has partially cured him, he is assigned instead to an office job at a flour mill. Popov protests he is unsuited for office work and begs to return to the printshop, but party discipline is invoked and he is sent to the mill. He performs superbly there, and when the party transfers him again, a general meeting of millworkers pleads with him to stay. "I would leave you voluntarily only for the printshop," he tells them, but the party has ordered him to work in the upper echelons of a trust. A true success story! Later, Popov presides over a late-night party cell meeting at the trust. Economy measures require reductions in the trust's personnel, and Popov volunteers to be the first to leave. "I worked until now in these institutions because there was no one else to work in them, but now qualified people exist. Furthermore, I left the printshop only because of ill health, and now I am a bit better. Why should I work in an office when I can return to the printshop, yes, my 'native printshop' where I have worked twenty years." His request is granted. Popov returns home, wakes his family to tell them the good news, and then pulls out from under his bed his carefully stored case of special typographic tools, which he places in his pocket so as not to forget them in the morning. At the close of the story, Popov is warmly greeted by his colleagues on his return to his type case.[29] What message is conveyed here? In part, it is that the promise of the revolution is not that workers can stop being workers and start being bosses but that work itself becomes honorable, satisfying, and respected.[30]

## Worker Culture

One critical question for understanding workers in NEP society is how and whether these patterns of worker self-identification translated into a specific class culture, one that would help to preserve the values carried over from before revolution and that could be used as a basis for assimilating newcomers into the ranks of laborers in a socialist society. I use *culture* here in the broad anthropological sense, as a complete way of life, the sum of daily transactions in multiple arenas of workers' activity: home, society, work.[31] How did workers construct the fabric of their lives after the revolution? Did they attempt to develop a culture that was distinctively proletarian, and if so, distinctive from what? From peasant culture? Bourgeois culture? "High" culture? What were the characteristics of workers' culture? As I shall attempt to demonstrate, there were various and sometimes conflicting elements: a strong Puritan streak of hard work and sobriety (quite alien to many undisciplined printers but an important attribute of certain strata of prerevolutionary class-conscious workers), the upwardly mobile culture of night schools and promotion, shop-floor routine and tradition, family and community patterns of living. Finally, given the tremendous intellectual and agitational energy devoted to the creation of a "proletarian culture," with special rituals and institutions, with "Club Month" and public discussions of values appropriate to the proletarian society, the question must be confronted: was this "culture" that can be observed among printers dictated from above, or was it an autonomous reflection of indigenous working-class values? This is a false dichotomy in many ways: many revolutionaries had been workers, and therefore their goals frequently coincided with the aspirations of broader worker society. Therefore it is not appropriate to speak of a culture "imposed" from outside. The outside—the cultural leaders of the Soviet working class—grew up in and reflected the values of the prerevolutionary working class; the culture that emerged in postrevolutionary society therefore syncretized different aspects of what workers and activists thought was appropriate or necessary to the way they would live under socialism.

A common theme in the pages of the printers' union press, as elsewhere, was the struggle to replace the "old way of life" with the new. Just what the parameters were of the old life are not clear: presumably some of the prerevolutionary working-class culture was worth preserving. (Or had workers been so completely exploited and alienated that no aspect of the culture they created was to be bothered with?) The new culture was quite clearly a normative one: workers "ought" to be sober, collectivist, and absolutely devoted to increasing the wealth of the socialist society.[32] The real culture, which helped to define the working class after the revolution, was inevitably a blend of new and old, approved and disapproved. Nor was working-class culture homogeneous, even among printers. But from the evidence offered by the union journals, from memoirs and other sources, a preliminary sense of the general lines of working-class life can be discerned.

The workshop naturally remained central to printers' identity and to the way they lived. Printers spent eight to eleven hours a day at work (including dinner, meetings, and occasional overtime). Their political obligations were organized by shop, and their union activities and social life also revolved around the printshop.[33] Shop-floor culture among printers prior to the revolution had been exclusively male, always easygoing and often alcoholic. Rituals abounded: the name days of owners, promotion of apprentices, teasing hung-over workers, all helped to cement a sense of comradeship and belonging.

The biggest change to this culture brought about by the October Revolution was the widespread introduction of women into the printshop.

Women had been making unwelcome inroads into the printshop since the world war. In 1912 they constituted 5 percent of the workers employed in printing. In 1918 their share had risen to 16 percent (and 10 percent of the skilled typesetters). In hungry 1920, women made up one-third of the labor force in the Moscow printing industry (although only 15 percent of typesetters).[34] With the return of male printers to production over the next few years, however, and the New Economic Policy's contraction in employment opportunities, women began to be forced out of the ranks of the leaden army. In the provinces, in fact, returning army veterans began to displace women immediately after the demobilization of the tsarist army; the pressure to dismiss women beginning in 1918 was also probably due to the self-evacuation of printers seeking employment in areas better supplied with food than Petrograd and Moscow. Women were summarily dismissed from their jobs and sometimes even denied unemployment benefits.[35] By 1923 in Moscow, the share of women in the industry had fallen to 24 percent, and they constituted 10 percent of typesetters.[36]

Aside from offering more competition to male workers and thus driving down wages, what was wrong with women on the shop floor? The predominant negative image of women was that they were not serious workers; they preferred to stand about all day gossiping. A cartoon lampooning the religious observance of Maslenitsa in a 1925 issue of *Pechatnik* (the all-Russian union organ) depicts male typesetters falling all over their type cases, hanging onto bottles and glasses of spirit, while women gather in the background arguing about something.[37] Another story linked gossiping women with a generally unproletarian printshop. While linotypists stood around smoking and discussing the haymowing in their villages, the women all crowded into their washroom, some exchanging gossip and teasing a woman who had just been promoted up a skill category; older women gossiped about the new priest at the local church and his marital problems. The women here had to be chased to work by their Women's Section organizer.[38]

Such stories surely came from the old life, but male attitudes based on the old life clearly persisted. Reports of trials of male printers for what would today be called sexual harassment regularly appeared in the pages of *Moskovskii pechatnik*, clearly for their didactic as well as journalistic value. Swearing at women, or using offensive language in front of them, was a legacy of the old ways. Women in one shop feared even to ask a question about their work lest they be answered with abuse. Soviet power, wrote one of them, had made it possible for them to enter "with full rights as members of the worker family, but here at the printshop it was the reverse": women had no rights.[39] Elsewhere, an assistant instructor threatened to transfer a young woman to heavy labor unless she agreed to sleep with him. This Dubov, forty years old and married, had more than once so propositioned older women as well as young ones. The latter feared to report him, but when he was finally brought before the printshop collective, a Comrades' Court expelled him from the union for six months and recommended his firing from the plant.[40] We can deduce from such stories that the shop floor had become a less comfortable, less friendly place for the printers of old.

A second, and often stormier, source of divisiveness on the shop floor was young workers, apprentices, the so-called factory rabbits.[41] They were often portrayed as disruptive, rowdy, disrespectful. Noting the first anniversary of the Komsomol cell at the shop Notopechatnia, a worker-correspondent wrote, "To the worker family of *notopechatniki* was born their first offspring, named the 'Komsomol Cell.' " The family was not especially thrilled with their first-born, who turned out to be a bawler and who "disturbed the peace of the whole family."[42] Young workers especially resented the limited openings in printing, the difficulty of learning skills, the lingering system of personal servitude to the foremen. At the Krasnaia nov' printing works, apprentices were expected to buy the foreman a bottle of liquor every payday and to run errands for one of the factory committee members. If they refused, they would receive no favors from their superiors, testified the apprentices. When the offending factory committee member was asked by investigators if he really asked the boys to do work other than training, he replied, "You really expect that I myself should go to the store?"[43]

Conflicts between old and young workers predated Soviet power, of course, and most likely the offending foreman in 1924 had endured the very same treatment as an apprentice. Why should it cause such a fuss now? Evidently, here the revolution had created a major discontinuity in the transmission of shop-floor culture. Young people in the factories had been raised in a revolutionary epoch, and they expected more equality and opportunity than the prevailing culture was accustomed to granting. This evidence from the printing trades on the roles of women and youth suggests that shop-floor culture remained inhospitable to new claimants for membership in the "working family." In response, young workers particularly turned to other arenas of working-class life to forge their own new sense of community, as I shall discuss below.

One of the more difficult aspects of shop-floor culture to ascertain from this limited sampling of evidence is the existence of an implicit work contract. Prerevolutionary skilled workers, whether through overt or more subtle pressures, had often managed to regulate their workload and workday according to customary norms. Even where remuneration was paid by the piece in order to stimulate high production, skilled workers managed to resist "maximal" output in favor of what they considered to be "optimal"—a fair day's work for a fair day's pay.[44] It was usually the new worker, unsocialized into the shop-floor culture, who sought to utilize the piece system to maximize his own earnings. Older workers tried to teach the newcomers that there was in any case a ceiling on the wage bill, and if they worked too hard, norms would inevitably be raised for everyone. If the newcomer failed to learn this lesson, he would be taught more forceful-ly: other workers would spoil his raw materials or pour talc on the transmis-sion belt to his machine, slowing it down.[45]

One would expect that this sense of a fair day's work would continue to play a role in printshop culture into the Soviet period, even if the employer was the worker himself, through the Soviet state. Therefore, one might expect resistance from skilled workers to the universal introduction of piece rates and higher norms in the industry during the course of 1924. Evidence of overt protest would not appear in the kinds of sources I have examined so far, but there have been several instances of older, skilled workers' responding to the new piece rates in the same way the new recruits had before the revolution: by working harder, in search of more money. One union organizer lamented the disappearance of experienced workers who could take part in organizational work. They either had already moved into administrative positions or, "with the introduction of piece rates, are lured by 'big rubles.' "[46] Other workers were criticized for moonlighting—taking their four-week vacation pay (double the vacation norm because of the hazards of the industry) and spending the time filling in at other shops instead of soaking up the sun at one of the union rest homes.[47] This, too, constitutes evidence of a breakdown in the collectivism of the shop floor, an end to the implicit agreement to regulate collectively the workload.

Working-class life outside the factory is of course just as important in shaping a common culture, a sense of identity, a way of life. It is useful here to think of life outside the factory as divided into three overlapping spheres: official public life (party and trade union, the *obshchestvennyi* sphere), unofficial social life, and, most privately, family life. Activities in all spheres as well as in the workplace itself contributed to the formation of class culture. The official sphere was perhaps the most self-conscious about promoting a particular type of "culture," and most of the evidence about working-class extramural activity is filtered through the prism of union and party ideology. Nevertheless, in the pages that remain, I wish to focus on more private representations of working class-culture, in leisure activi-ties and in the family sphere.[48] The leisure time of workers was one of the most important targets of Soviet cultural policy makers, and one where lines between old and new could be clearly seen. The "old" leisure was segregated by sex: women had no leisure, only "clothing, cooking pots, and diapers." What little extra time they had was devoted to religion, definitely an "old" practice that was shared by many of the menfolk, too. At the First Obraztsovaia typography, the morning after Easter found few workers at their stations, and even by midday, the absentee rate was between 20 and 30 percent in the skilled departments, up to 50 percent among less skilled parts of the shop.[49]

And of course there was alcohol. It not only lubricated many shop-floor customs but dominated life after work as well. A typical Saturday saw workers go home to clean up and then make the rounds of the beer bars, starting with the third-rate bars and then moving up. When all the regular drinking places had closed, the diehards would continue drinking in all-night basement tea rooms. Wives often waited outside the printshop on payday, vainly hoping to intercept their husbands' pay packets before they were all spent on drink.[50]

What should replace this cultural pattern? According to official pronouncements, to begin with, the new life would be sober and secular. Workers would replace the pernicious old pastimes with participation in public life, through party, unions, cooperatives, voluntary organizations such as Friends of the Air Fleet and Friends of Children, through goodwill missions to adopted villages and military units. Workers would celebrate the open air, take excursions to scenic and historic spots, swim, engage in athletics. In this way, printers could counter the especially hazardous effects of their trade. All of these activities received extensive coverage in the trade union press, and a few overworked union organizers labored diligently to provide leisure opportunities for workers, particularly in clubs and rest homes.

Workers' clubs were the focus of much energy, controversy, and political conflict. In greeting "Moscow Club Month," the printers' union journal proclaimed that the purpose of clubs was to satisfy workers' cultural needs, develop through clubs "class-conscious fighters for communism," and give workers and their families a place of intelligent entertainment and relaxation.[51] In fact, as John Hatch has demonstrated, Proletcult, party, and unions disagreed on how clubs should accomplish these goals, but all were faced as well with the reality of club life, which was not always what they wished to see.[52] On the one hand, clubs provided the setting for new rituals of Soviet life: Komsomol Christmases and Easters, the public celebration of revolutionary holidays such as International Women's Day, May Day, November 7. Six babies were welcomed into the worker community during 1924 in a ceremony that early in the year was called a "Red Christening" but later was more consistently named an "Oktiabrina." (Two Vladimirs, two Rosas, a Margarita, and an Oktiabr' were made honorary members of the local Young Pioneers and given gifts of blankets and little red outfits by the factory committees involved.) But generally, cultural organizers lamented the lack of attention and energy that local worker collectives devoted to clubs. Moreover, the overwhelming clientele of the worker clubs were young male workers. At one district club, 65 percent of the members were young people, men outnumbering the women by two to one.[53] At other clubs, interest groups (circles) consisted mostly of workers' children, not workers themselves.[54] Such evidence suggests that older workers may have resisted the imposition of a new culture and clung instead to their traditional habits of alcoholic male camaraderie.

Among club participants, "artistic" circles, again to the consternation of organizers, and physical culture groups proved to be the most popular activities. Workers formed choirs, orchestras, and brass bands that played (sometimes for pay—another disputed practice)[55] at ceremonial occasions, but the most important cultural activity of printers, as among other worker youth, was theater. Hardly a club lacked a dramatic circle, which along with the physical culture group was usually the largest in the club. One club had two theater groups, a drama "circle" and a drama "studio"; the former followed the precepts of the Stanislavsky method, which the smaller studio group denounced.[56] Almost every public function of the clubs was treated to performances by the drama or music circles: celebrations of alternative holidays and revolutionary holidays included revolutionary plays, "living newspapers," dramatic readings, as well as traditional fare such as "The Night before Christmas." And of course there was "living theater," such as the faked trial of the Komsomol girl led astray.

Judging by the attempts of cultural organizers to suppress these activities as frivolous, it would seem that drama and music were strongly rooted indigenous elements of Russian working-class culture. Theatrical performance had become an important cultural outlet for Russian workers. It provided a way, especially for young people, to escape from the social relations at work that placed them in subordinate positions; its content provided an outlet for and expression of revolutionary strivings. It combined ego with collectivism: individual roles added up to produce a whole which often had a collectivist message. Is it too much to say that theater served for Russian working youth the function performed in early modern Europe by the charivari and carnival? What is surprising is why the *kul'turniki* so heartily disapproved of these activities.

Workers' behavior that organizers deemed to be uncultured (alcoholism, woman baiting) was labeled "old" culture (never peasant culture, but that was the implication). Cultural activities that organizers considered inappropriate for the Soviet proletariat were labeled "bourgeois," "*meshchanskie*," "*Nepovskie*." All of these were vague enough terms for a society which had never had a well-defined bourgeois culture, and the range of behaviors so labeled did not form a clear pattern. For example, a union club activist warned,

> The club, as a center of proletarian public life [*obshchestvennost'*], uniting around itself the working masses, ought to consider the natural need of workers to rest after the working day, and also the cultural needs of workers, remembering that this need, if it does not find satisfaction in the club, inevitably pushes the worker toward embracing the increasingly expanding petty bourgeois (Nep) ideology, pushes him to the beer halls, boulevard theaters, cinemas, etc., that flourish everywhere.[57]

Young printers at the union rest home who distressed the more sedentary workers with their partying and their disregard for rules and discipline ("We are the bosses here—and tough!") were also tagged as bourgeois. "When you look at all this, you are surprised; where did the factory kids learn such bourgeois bragging, lying, and hooliganism?"[58] A Komsomol veteran recalled favorite activities in his club: a living newspaper, with dramatized "articles" on religion, production discipline, and criticisms of idlers, followed by songs, games, and folk dancing. "To dance the waltz or the polka, and even more the foxtrot or tango, was then considered petty-bourgeois [*meshchanstvom*]!"[59] It is almost as if anything that activists considered too pleasurable for its own sake could not be proletarian culture, but we must remember that some of the *kul'turniki* were the radical Puritans of the labor movement. Most workers may not have felt that the revolution was endangered if they danced the foxtrot, but evidence for this is hard to find.

A final important sphere for the development of worker culture is of course the family. Shop-floor culture seems to have been an adult male preserve, and club life belonged to the young. Family life was the province of women. Wives cared for children and fed the family, some while holding down jobs in printing or other industries, others as housewives. Women workers complained of being cut off from access to culture because of their domestic duties; their chief concerns at meetings and conferences of women workers were to raise their skill levels to better their pay, and to rearrange family life to free them from some of the drudgery of domestic chores. Communal homes housed some hundreds of printer families, and every time the residents managed to construct a children's playground, the event was marked with music and speeches about the promise of Soviet power and the achievements of self-help.[60] Woman activists tried to organize canteens at their factories, to free themselves and their nonworking sisters to be able to have more time to participate in club and union activities. Such activists faced passive resistance from both women and men. Even open-minded men who approved of women's becoming publicly active did not appear to favor this activism at the cost of their own taking on more domestic duties, leading one woman correspondent to comment ironically, as some male printers slipped away from a workshop meeting, "Obviously they were going home to prepare supper for their wives."[61]

Most women in printing did not keep up the struggle to combine motherhood and membership in the factory collective; a survey of Moscow printers done in late 1923 revealed that women usually left the workforce by the time they were thirty years old. By then they had too many family responsibilities, and their health was so weakened by the double shift of work and family, and by the particular hazards of the typographical industry, that they could not expect to earn much in any case.[62] E. O. Kabo's classic study of Moscow workers in 1924 describes four families of printers. The wives were all employed, but none of them in the printing industry; in three cases, extra help in housekeeping and child care was provided by a young relative or grandmother.[63] Given the amount of time women had to devote to their domestic duties, it is difficult to see where they would find the time to respond to change and to create for themselves a new culture.

The clash of old and new attitudes within the family is described in a poignant vignette reminiscent of the modern classic short story, Natalia Baranskaia's "A Week like Any Other," or the contemporary Dasha in Gladkov's *Cement.* In this story, "The Meaning of Life—A Story from Nature," Aniuta is a Soviet superwoman, a typesetter, woman's delegate, treasurer of her communal home, a tireless organizer. The story begins at daybreak, as she rises to prepare her family for the day. Her husband, also a typesetter, has never stopped complaining in the three years since she was elected a delegate, and she thinks she would leave him if it were not for their three children. (The oldest is in a kindergarten, taken there by his father each day; the middle child is in a nursery; and the youngest, for whom there is no room in a state-run facility, is taken each morning with a supply of food and diapers to a neighbor. Aniuta must run there each noon to nurse her child.) But she cannot go back to the old life, "not being interested in anything, thinking about nothing other than children, husband, clothes, pots, and diapers." She is up especially early to make soup for the evening's supper, since she has another meeting that night. Her husband complains that she is always at meetings, that the children go hungry each night. Her coworkers, however, have her to thank for their new printshop canteen which feeds them at noon. Aniuta first organized a cooperative soup kitchen, preparing meals herself during the dinner break. When the factory committee saw her success, they stepped in and sponsored a real canteen. The costs are high for Aniuta, however: her fellow workers notice how she coughs more each day, and her marriage is painful. "This is how the woman worker under difficult conditions opens the way to a new life, to communism."[64]

### Conclusion: Class Consciousness in a Socialist Society

Let me stress that these are preliminary conclusions, but based on the evidence I have sifted so far, it appears that printers by 1924 were fumbling for an identity, that the appeal of "class" as a source of solidarity and self-consciousness had weakened since the days of 1917 and before. Printers had retained much of their old culture, but now elements of that culture (alcohol, exploitation of apprentices and women) were rejected as inappropriate and outdated. Some vestiges of the old craft pride remained,[65] but the dominant motif in the union press is not the glorification of work and the printers' craft but scolding, chastising, moralizing.

The evidence so far also suggests elements of serious schisms within the printing trade. The old class culture had been homogeneously adult and male, and new candidates for membership—young workers and women—appear in the 1920s to have been rejected and consigned to secondary spheres of cultural importance. Perhaps this was the inevitable result of a technologically progressing society; the division of labor was not a phenomenon restricted to capitalism. E. J. Hobsbawm writes of working-class wives as "the most permanent victims of proletarian culture."[66] Gareth Stedman Jones relates how public education for girls and higher wages for skilled men in England meant that the wife no longer had captive child-minders to allow her to work outside the home, and also that she no longer had to work to make up the family wage. This "liberation" from wagework led to a stricter division of roles between husband and wife.[67] In Soviet Russia, a similar role separation would make it difficult for women to reenter the culture of work on equal terms with men.

Perhaps printers also grasped for an identity in NEP Russia because the workers' revolution had made class consciousness unnecessary. Historically, class consciousness had developed as a product of a common struggle against a common outside force. Victorious, the working class had no common enemy, even though many attributes of the old class solidarity remained: craft pride, cooperativism, collectivism. How could the struggle against a dilapidated economic plant, against technological limits, against alcoholism, against the foxtrot, create a common bond stronger than the everyday forces that separated Russia's workers in the 1920s? As a hypothesis for further testing, I would argue that Russia's workers were "declassed" in the 1920s, as Lenin and Bukharin had claimed in 1919 and 1920. But they were declassed not in spite of the revolution but because of it.

Indeed, to replace the old image of class, a new idiom was finding its way into the discourse of workers in the printing trades. Whether or not this was a conscious rhetorical device, the metaphor of the "worker family" can be found throughout the pages of *Moskovskii pechatnik*, in contributions both by union activists and from worker-correspondents. I noted above the reference to the Komsomol cell as the troublesome first-born. Another worker complained that printers in government printshops were treated like "stepsons" in comparison to the "sons" employed by the big Mospoligraf trust.[68] A printer urged the construction of suburban worker settlements, where printers could keep some chickens and a garden, and be close to one another instead of sitting isolated in rooms scattered throughout the city. Such a settlement could be just like a family, he argued.[69] Perhaps the family metaphor was helpful in accommodating generational and gender divisions; perhaps it was useful in assimilating peasant workers into the urban culture. But I wonder if it could be as powerful a symbol as class had been under capitalism in binding together all working people in the new socialist society.

NOTES

Research for this paper was made possible by support from the National Endowment for the Humanities and the University of Illinois at Urbana-Champaign. I am grateful to Jim Barrett, Bill Sewell, and Allan Wildman for their helpful comments.
    1. This is the argument in Sheila Fitzpatrick, *Education and Social Mobility in the Soviet Union, 1921–1934* (Cambridge, 1979).
    2. See, most recently, Abbott Gleason, Peter Kenez, and Richard Stites, eds., *Bolshevik Culture* (Bloomington, Ind., 1985), and Peter Kenez, *The Birth of the Propaganda State: Soviet Methods of Mass Mobilization, 1917–1929* (Cambridge, 1985); also Sheila Fitzpatrick, ed., *Cultural Revolution in Russia 1928–1931* (Bloomington, Ind., 1978), and William G. Rosenberg, ed., *Bolshevik Visions: First Phase of the Cultural Revolution in Soviet Russia* (Ann Arbor, Mich., 1984).
    3. See, for example, Moshe Lewin, *The Making of the Soviet System* (New York, 1984); William Chase, *Workers, Society and the Soviet State: Labor and Life in Moscow, 1918–1929* (Urbana and Chicago, 1987); Hiroaki Kuromiya, "The Crisis of Proletarian Identity in the Soviet Factory, 1928–1929," *Slavic Review*, 44, no. 2 (Summer 1985), pp. 280–97; Paddy Dale, "The Instability of the Infant Vanguard: Worker Party Members, 1928–1932," *Soviet Studies*, 35, no. 4 (October 1983), pp. 504–24.
    4. Jeffrey Brooks, "The Breakdown in Production and Distribution of Printed Material, 1917–1927," in Gleason et al., eds., *Bolshevik Culture*, pp. 151–74; Peter Kenez, *Birth of the Propaganda State*, chap. 10.
    5. See Chase, *Workers, Society and the Soviet State;* and John Hatch, "Labor and Politics in NEP Russia: Workers, Trade Unions, and the Communist Party in Moscow, 1921–1926," Ph.D. dissertation, University of California, Irvine, 1986.
    6. Hatch, "Labor and Politics in NEP Russia," chap. 4.
    7. I am unable for the time being to pay attention to the intraparty struggle, except to note that Trotsky's and Zinoviev's names appear in the journal much more often in 1924 than Stalin's or Bukharin's.
    8. *Istoriia Leningradskogo soiuza rabochikh poligraficheskogo proizvodstva*, vol. 1: 1905–1907 (Leningrad, 1925), pp. 16, 29.
    9. Ibid., p. 54.
    10. Ibid., pp. 15–16.
    11. Ibid., p. 37.
    12. E. A. Vechtomova, *Zdes' pechatalas' 'Pravda'* (Leningrad, 1969), p. 161.
    13. V. V. Sher, *Istoriia professional'nogo dvizheniia rabochikh pechatnogo dela v Moskve* (Moscow, 1911), p. 125.

14. *Istoriia Leningradskogo soiuza*, pp. 99–100.
15. See Victoria E. Bonnell, *Roots of Rebellion: Workers' Politics and Organizations in St. Petersburg and Moscow, 1900–1914* (Berkeley, Calif., 1983).
16. E. J. Hobsbawm, "The Making of the Working Class, 1870–1914," in *Workers* (New York, 1984), p. 194.
17. Except in the expression *labor aristocrat*, which tended to be a term of abuse. Kuromiya offers a stimulating discussion of the concept in "Crisis of Proletarian Identity," and I intend to pursue the idea further in connection with my larger study of printers.
18. *Moskovskii pechatnik*, no. 19 (May 27, 1924), p. 12.
19. *Istoriia Leningradskogo soiuza*, pp. 34–35. In 1917, while relations between printers and owners suffered the same general breakdown as elsewhere in society, printers struck less frequently than most other industrial workers. Diane Koenker and William G. Rosenberg, "Skilled Workers and the Strike Movement in Revolutionary Russia," *Journal of Social History*, 19, no. 4 (Summer 1986), pp. 605–29.
20. *Moskovskii pechatnik*, no. 21 (April 1924), p. 19.
21. Ibid., no. 29–30 (September 1924), p. 17.
22. Ibid., no. 23 (June 1, 1924), p. 15.
23. Ibid., no. 29–30 (September 1924), p. 17.
24. Ibid., p. 4.
25. "Mama, can you visit my nursery today?" "No, dear one, today I have to fulfill my higher norm. If I don't meet my quota you will not have buns and apples." Ibid., no. 34 (December 1924), p. 5.
26. Ibid., p. 15.
27. Ibid., no. 23 (June 1, 1924), pp. 2–5.
28. Ibid., no. 19 (March 27, 1924), p. 9.
29. Ibid., no. 32 (October 15, 1924), pp. 5–7. The story, "Otryv," is by V. Konovalikhin.
30. There are many other facets of worker identity that require further exploration in the union journals and other sources. Attitudes toward peasants were complex: "good" peasants were adopted by factories, whose workers brought books and Soviet culture (Red weddings, Komsomol Easters) to the adopted villages; "bad" peasants sold vacationers matches and sour cream at speculators' prices. Craft loyalties and factory patriotism were other important elements of printers' identity.
31. This is the usage employed by E. P. Thompson, *The Making of the English Working Class* (New York, 1963); Hobsbawm, "The Making of the Working Class, 1870–1914," pp. 194–213; and Gareth Stedman Jones, "Working-class Culture and Working-class Politics in London, 1870–1900: Notes on the Remaking of a Working Class," in *Languages of Class: Studies in English Working-class History, 1832–1982* (Cambridge, 1983), pp. 179–238.
32. Leon Trotsky, "Not by Politics Alone," in *Problems of Everyday Life* (New York, 1973), p. 20.
33. Printers were unique in this respect; in the U.S., their odd hours tended to isolate them from other workers, causing them to socialize more completely with each other. See S. M. Lipset, M. Trow, and J. Coleman, *Union Democracy* (Glencoe, Ill., 1956).
34. *Statisticheskii ezhegodnik goroda Moskvy i Moskovskoi gubernii*, vyp. 2 (Moscow, 1927), pp. 70–71, 46.
35. For example, in Maikop, in Ufa, where women "rarely left production of their own free will," and Stavropol', where a general union meeting voted on February 3, 1918, to "remove from work the girls [*devitsy*] hired during wartime." *Iz istorii Maikopskogo soiuza pechatnikov 1906–1927* (Maikop, 1927), p. 9; *Materialy po*

*istorii profdvizheniia rabochikh poligraficheskogo proizvodstva Bashkirii* (Ufa, 1927), p. 12; *Istoriia Stavropol'skogo soiuza rabochikh pechatnogo dela (poligraficheskogo proizvodstva) 1917–1920* (Stavropol', 1927), p. 9.

36. *Statisticheskii ezhegodnik g. Moskvy*, p. 46.

37. *Pechatnik*, no. 7 (April 1925).

38. *Moskovskii pechatnik*, no. 32 (October 15, 1924), p. 12. The story is by V. Insarov.

39. Ibid., no. 23 (June 1, 1924), p. 13.

40. Ibid., no. 20 (April, 1924), p. 15. Nonpayment of union dues also could result in six-month suspensions. Other cases of harassment are reported in no. 15 (January 7, 1924), p. 16; no. 28 (August 15, 1924), p. 15.

41. *Fabzaichiki*, from the term *fabzavuch (fabrichno-zavodskoe uchenichestvo)*, or factory apprenticeship. A. M. Selishchev, *Iazyk revoliutsionnoi epokhi* (Letchworth, England, 1971 [reprint of 1928 edition]), p. 185.

42. *Moskovskii pechatnik*, no. 20 (April 1924), p. 13.

43. Ibid., no. 15 (January 7, 1924), p. 16.

44. See E. J. Hobsbawm, "Custom, Wages, and Work Load," in *Laboring Men* (New York, 1964).

45. This example is from the chemical industry rather than printing, but the principle is the same. Eduard Dune, "Zapiski krasnogvardeitsa," unpublished manuscript, Nicolaevsky Collection, Hoover Institution.

46. *Moskovskii pechatnik*, no. 28 (August 15, 1924), p. 3.

47. Ibid., no. 25 (July 1, 1924), p. 7. The two offenders were brought before a Comrades' Court for violation of professional ethics. Another similar case was reported in no. 26 (July 1924), p. 20.

48. The conflicts over culture within the official sphere, among unions, party, and Proletcult, are discussed in John Hatch, "The Politics of Mass Culture: Workers, Communists, and Proletcult in the Development of Workers' Clubs, 1921–1925," *Russian History*, vol. 13, no. 2–3 (Summer-Fall 1986), pp. 119–48.

49. *Moskovskii pechatnik*, no. 22 (May 15, 1924), p. 15. Or was this "Saint Monday" rather than "Easter Monday"? I have found little mention of the practice, common in Britain and elsewhere, of the self-proclaimed Monday holiday. See D. A. Reid, "The Decline of Saint Monday, 1776–1876," *Past and Present*, no. 71 (1976).

50. *Pervaia obraztsovaia tipografiia imeni A. A. Zhdanova za 40 let sovetskoi vlasti* (Moscow, 1957), p. 82.

51. *Moskovskii pechatnik*, no. 18 (February 27, 1924), p. 1.

52. Hatch, "Politics of Mass Culture."

53. *Moskovskii pechatnik*, no. 18 (February 27, 1924), p. 27.

54. Ibid., p. 28.

55. Ibid., no. 27 (August 1, 1924), p. 7.

56. Ibid., no. 15 (January 7, 1924), p. 21.

57. Ibid., no. 29–30 (September, 1924), p. 25.

58. Ibid., no. 27 (August 1, 1924), p. 16.

59. *Leninskii zakaz. Sto let tipografii 'Krasnyi proletarii'* (Moscow, 1969), p. 146.

60. For example, in *Moskovskii pechatnik*, no. 28 (August 15, 1924), p. 14.

61. Ibid., no. 32 (October 15, 1924), p. 18.

62. B. B. Koiranskii, *Trud i zdorov'e rabochikh tipografii* (Moscow, 1925), pp. 36–37.

63. E. O. Kabo, *Ocherki rabochego byta* (Moscow, 1927). In the fourth family, a hired nursemaid failed to work out, and the couple's infant daughter—their third child—appeared to have died from inadequate care (p. 90).

64. *Moskovskii pechatnik*, no. 34 (December 1924), pp. 4–5. The author of the sketch is M. Frid'eva.

65. Curiously, the evidence for this so far is all from Leningrad and not Moscow. Even after 1921, remembered a veteran printer, "Polygraphists were proud of the peculiarities of their trade and patiently endured its complications and inconveniences: caustic lead dust, night work" (Vechtomova, *Zdes' pechatalas' 'Pravda'*, pp. 132–33). I had expected to find more evidence of this kind of attitude, and I shall be interested to see if the Leningrad union journals differ in this respect from Moscow's.

66. E. J. Hobsbawm, "The Formation of British Working Class Culture," in *Workers*, p. 188.

67. See Stedman Jones, "Working-class Culture and Working-class Politics," pp. 218–19.

68. *Moskovskii pechatnik*, no. 18 (February 27, 1924), p. 35.

69. Ibid., no. 28 (August 15, 1924), p. 15.

# IV

# LABOR CONFLICT IN MOSCOW, 1921–1925

## John B. Hatch

Russia's industrial proletariat played a crucial role in the revolutions of 1917.[1] In Moscow and Petrograd, workers quickly availed themselves of the new opportunities created by the collapse of the autocracy, organizing trade unions and factory committees, asserting their interests in production, and participating in a rapidly growing socialist movement.[2] Radicalized after February 1917 by the continuation of the war, the polarization of Russian society, and the politicization of labor-management relations, workers formed an increasingly receptive audience for the appeals of the Bolshevik Party, which, by the time of its seizure of power in October 1917, was able to secure majority backing in Russia's main urban soviets.

By 1921, after three years of civil war, this class bore little resemblance to its 1917 predecessor.[3] In Moscow, the industrial wage-labor force declined by over 50 percent as thousands of workers left the shop floor for duties in the Red Army, the party, the unions, and the state administration, and as many more returned to the villages to escape the collapse of the urban economy.[4] In conjunction with a worsening economic situation, this process of "disintegration" had a profound and negative impact on relations between the Communist Party and the industrial working class. In February 1921 a spontaneous strike movement, sparked by a cut in bread rations and accompanied by the rise in political fortunes of the social democratic opposition, engulfed Russia's main industrial centers. The immediate crisis was quelled through repression and emergency concessions, but not before workers had registered their reappearance as an active force in industry.[5]

The New Economic Policy (NEP), officially promulgated shortly after these events in March 1921 at the 10th Party Congress, signaled a new era in the history of the Soviet working class.[6] As an experiment in market socialism, the NEP economic system consisted of the coexistence between state ownership of the commanding heights of the economy, including foreign trade, finance, and large-scale industry, and private and communal forms of small-scale production and distribution in agriculture, retail trade, and petty manufactures. The forced grain-requisitioning policies of War Communism gave way to a fixed tax in kind and a revival of the market. It was hoped that commercial agricultural production would be stimulated at rates high enough to finance industrial reconstruction and the expansion of the "socialist" sector of the economy, a developmental strategy that gave the peasantry considerable influence over the tempo and patterns of industrialization.

For workers, the NEP entailed constant upward pressures on labor productivity (which had fallen sharply since 1914) so that manufactured goods could be produced cheaply enough and in sufficient quantities to attract peasants to the marketplace. When in the fall of 1923 during the so-called scissors crisis, a severe price imbalance between manufactured and agricultural goods prevented this from happening, the consequences for workers, in the form of layoffs and work speed-ups, were dramatic. In short, industry's exposure to market forces and cost accounting *(khozraschet)*, and the empowering of management, through the principle of one-man management *(edinonachalie)*, to take those actions deemed necessary to restore profitability, made it clear that for the duration of NEP workers could expect to take a back seat in the delicate calculations by which the party felt industrialization could be financed through the market. Needless to say, this set-up ran counter to prevailing sentiments in the working class; it thus provided a stimulus for the reemergence of a spontaneous workers' movement reminiscent in many ways of the economic struggles carried out by industrial workers in other settings. What follows is an examination of labor conflict and the workers' movement in the Moscow region during the first half of the 1920s, with special attention given to the textile and metal industries.

Broadly speaking, working-class formation under conditions of the political economy of NEP—"state capitalism"—was subject to the powerful outside determinants of market economic forces, state economic and social policies, and communist political and cultural activism. "Capitalism," in this case the use of the market for purposes of accumulation, impinged daily on the world of labor, especially through unemployment and wage and productivity pressures. Balancing the influence of economic factors were "state" interventions in labor relations and, perhaps more important, the peculiarly "proletarian" character of the political organization (the Communist Party) in charge of that state and the actions it took to influence working-class formation. At the same time, class formation was a "living" process experienced and advanced by individuals and collectivities through shared experiences and outlooks; it was their response to outside pressures that is important for understanding the process of class formation. These three factors—"state," "capitalism," and worker "spontaneity" (used here in the broad sense of the term covering both spontaneous worker collective action [*stikhiinost'*] caused by historically and locally specific economic grievances, and the existence of autonomous histories and cultures that informed the outlook of workers and their reactions to the outside world)—had profound impacts on the evolution of labor activism during NEP.

With the beginnings of industrial recovery in 1923 and the influx of thousands of demobilized Red Army soldiers and returnees and newcomers from the villages, the number of employed wage laborers in Moscow's industry grew rapidly, and by 1926 exceeded pre–World War I levels.[7] Workers employed in the metal and machine-building industries constituted the largest sector of the wage-labor force within Moscow itself, but their numbers were diluted by the presence of workers laboring in a number of other industries. When Moscow province as a whole is taken into account, textile workers were by far the largest single group.[8]

The wide variations between industries (and even between factories and workshops within the same industry) in the social composition of this labor force had to do with differential degrees of mechanization, rationalization, and concentration. The most highly mechanized and/or concentrated industries, especially textiles, demanded higher proportions of unskilled and semiskilled labor, and it was in these industries that female labor predominated. In other branches, such as the printing and metal industries, skilled labor continued to play an important role in production.

The workers who filled the expanding employment opportunities during this period came mainly from two sources: children of working-class parentage and a much larger group of peasant migrants, whose preindustrial outlooks and work habits were viewed by the authorities as obstacles to the creation of a socialist work culture, and which also seriously complicated the formation of proletarian class sensibilities in broad strata of the labor force. As we have seen from studies of working-class formation elsewhere, the chasm between the urbanized, hereditary core of skilled cadre workers and the much larger mass of "new" workers was one of the key forces undermining this process during the NEP.[9]

Throughout the 1920s, peasant migrants streamed into the cities, straining the inadequate supply of housing and social services and competing with their urban counterparts for jobs. The latter circumstance was the occasion for complaints by workers and trade unions about the ineffectiveness of labor exchanges in securing preferential hiring for unemployed union members. This situation was made possible by the fact that after 1922, the NEP labor market was a buyer's market: demobilization, rural overpopulation, and the processes of concentration and rationalization ensured the existence of a substantial reserve army of the unemployed. In its efforts to achieve savings, management readily used this army as a way to hold down wage costs and, in conjunction with the rationalization of labor, to degrade skill; it also employed the threat of unemployment to intimidate potential strikers.[10] Thus, while the dequalification of skill engendered disaffection, unemployment (in tandem with state repression) often inhibited labor activism by lessening skilled workers' prospects of defending their position.

The NEP labor market strengthened management's hand in labor intensification and encouraged the emergence of divisions within the labor force between the so-called proletarian workers—a cohort of socially active, younger, educated, and (usually) male "urban" workers—and other workers, by enlisting the former's cooperation in labor intensification. These workers, many of whom were graduates of trade union vocational training courses and thus more adaptable than their older workmates to the introduction of new machinery and work techniques, were said to have "exhibited great labor heroism" and were repeatedly hailed as the most "advanced" in their attitudes toward work.[11]

The prerevolutionary cadre of older skilled workers was dedicated more to defending its relatively privileged position in production against the pressures of dequalification and intensification than it was to participating in regime-initiated efforts to improve productivity.[12] The corporate consciousness of skilled workers, often referred to at the time as "shop cliquishness" *(tsekhovizm),* was perhaps most clearly manifested in the de facto institutionalization of the prerogatives of skill in trade union wage and piece rate policies and in skilled worker participation in factory committees, conflict commissions, and technical norm-setting boards.[13]

The processes of industrial reconstruction and working-class reaggregation promoted by the NEP were characterized by sustained worker activism. Industrial disputes reflected a series of difficulties associated with Soviet labor during the 1920s, including the long-term effects of the collapse of the urban economy during the Civil War and the consequent steep drop in workers' standard of living, as well as the conditions of labor peculiar to NEP.

The numerous points of contact between the authorities and workers represented a fundamental divergence from labor relations in the imperial period. In theory, workers could expect a variety of institutions to defend their interests, including industrial party organizations, trade unions, and factory committees. But because they answered to higher authorities anxious to raise labor productivity, these institutions more often than not failed to provide this service.[14] For the resolution of labor conflicts, a vast labor arbitration apparatus was created that handled thousands of disputes over wages, dismissals, and other issues involving tens of thousands of workers.[15] Workers were successful in a substantial portion of those cases that involved management infringement of collective-agreement wage provisions. They were less successful in appealing other job actions, particularly those regarding management's right to lay off workers.[16] Despite pro-managerial biases in the functioning of some arbitration boards and the ability of management to ignore adverse decisions,[17] it should be recognized that workers utilized these grievance procedures, and often did so to good effect.

The issues that provoked workers into taking job actions varied from case to case and factory to factory, but they can be subsumed under two broad categories that in practice often overlapped: purely economic questions involving wage levels, work norms, layoffs, and labor intensification, and labor-management disputes over the limits of managerial authority. The latter spanned a whole range of conflicts, including the late or nonpayment of wages (a widespread phenomenon officially denounced by the party as a "bureaucratic distortion"), hiring and firing infractions, violations of collective-agreement provisions, and skill dequalification.[18] Although some of these problems—such as low wages or the withholding of wage payments—were across-the-board phenomena characteristic of all branches of industry, others were specific to certain industries and groups of workers. Thus, opposition to wage egalitarianism and the defense of skill were characteristic of the behavior of skilled workers, while support for wage egalitarianism was characteristic of lesser-skilled workers.

Between 1921 and 1923, Soviet industry was faced with the task of reconstruction. Workers hoped to improve on the basic subsistence levels to which their wages had declined during the preceding years and to protect jobs from threatened closures of unprofitable enterprises. Between 1921 and 1926, all branches of industry and transport in Moscow and Moscow gubernia experienced wildcat strikes or other spontaneous labor disturbances. Strike waves peaked in the winter of 1920–21, in response to threats against basic subsistence, and in the summer and fall of 1922 and 1923, when wage issues and factory closures came to the fore; during July–December 1922, for example, 65 strikes and 209 other major industrial disturbances were recorded in Moscow's state enterprises.[19] Norm revisions resulted in a series of disturbances, especially in the metal and printing industries.[20] In addition, an increasing number of disputes in the consumer-oriented textile and garment industries were tied to factory shutdowns and mass layoffs necessitated by the scissors phenomenon.[21]

Metalworkers were arguably the most active sector of the working class at this time, a circumstance traceable to the precipitous decline in wages for skilled metalworkers prior to 1921, as well as to the dwindling wage differentials between skilled and unskilled workers caused by War Communism's egalitarian wage policies. According to *Pravda*, the political fallout of this discontent was expressed in the fact that "in the [April 1921] elections to the Moscow Soviet, the active metalworker played almost no positive role. He frequently applauded Mensheviks, he frequently voted nonparty."[22] During the first eight months of 1921, a series of strikes involving a monthly average of one thousand workers and employees and lasting between two to five days hit the Bromlei metal factory, and between October 1921 and November 1922, the Rogozhko-Simonovskii district party committee discussed eight strikes and thirty industrial "disturbances," many of which undoubtedly occurred in the district's important metal factories. One of these took place at AMO over late wage payments.[23] Strikes over wages were reported at a number of other metal factories, and a series of disputes were caused by increases in work norms and the introduction of piece rates in 1923 and after.[24] According to the Moscow trade union chief, G. N. Mel'nichanskii, "disturbances over low wages that do not take the form of strikes take place in a whole series of shops and enterprises of the metal industry."[25]

Wage and norm disputes were exacerbated by labor-management tensions. At the Dinamo metal factory, archival sources reveal a series of disputes over "mistaken" wage calculations, "abnormal" wage payments, and "exploitative" wage levels throughout 1922–23.[26] Disputes were often precipitated by management's failure to fulfill collective-agreement provisions.[27] Conflicts between workers and shop foremen were not uncommon. In one case, a delegate to the 1925 congress of the Moscow Metalworkers' Union criticized management's habit of promoting shop foremen, who "turn out to be . . . the whippers-along [*pogonial'shchiki*] of the workers," and called for worker control over the naming of foremen. Skilled workers also protested the common managerial practice of filling job openings with underskilled workers and of paying workers doing similar kinds of labor different wages.[28] Distrust of management was also evidenced in attempts by metalworkers to establish managerial accountability. In the MOGES factory, a shop representative complained that "workers must know where funds are going, must control production. Layoffs were initiated in connection with the monetary reform. And what do we see? In the first instance, they lay off workers and employees. And in the trusts, everything remains as of old."[29]

In the textile industry, the strike movement correlates closely with the intense economic pressures placed on that industry as a result of the scissors crisis. These measures, which included factory shutdowns, layoffs, and labor intensification, were resisted on a mass scale by textile workers. Low wages galvanized textilists in 1922–23 in a number of large strikes, including a strike in 1922 at the Nikol'skaia textile factory in Orekhovo-Zuevskii *uezd* over unspecified "economic questions," a one-day work stoppage over wages at the Serpukhovskaia *manufaktura,* and a walkout by three thousand workers at Moscow's Trekhgornaia combine in September 1923. Earlier that summer, Zamoskvoretskii district's Tsindel' textile factory was also hit by a strike over wages.[30] In the summer of 1923, much of the labor conflict in the textile industry was tied to staff reductions.[31] Worker resentment was fueled by the perception that management exempted white-collar employees from layoffs. As in the metal industry, this resentment was increasingly directed against management and technical specialists *(spetsy).*[32]

The cost-cutting and labor-intensification measures instituted in 1924 in response to the scissors crisis sparked a series of strikes when management (backed by the trade unions) sought to increase the number of machines for which workers were responsible from one or two to three or four. One of these occurred at the Bronitskii *uezd* Krasno-Znamenskii factory after the factory committee there agreed to reduce the number of workers working on spinning mules. Worker demands for a change in this policy went unanswered, prompting a three-day strike. In this case, at least, the workers forced the order to be rescinded. This incident prompted a leading member of the Moscow Party Bureau, K. Ia. Bauman, to comment that the prerevolutionary owners of the factory had attempted to implement a similar intensification with much the same results; he criticized the local party authorities for failing to take this into account in planning the change.[33]

Labor intensification was also the occasion of a split within the textile workforce between "proletarian" workers who "enthusiastically" and "voluntarily" adopted higher norms and "backward" workers who opposed this process. At the #1 state textile factory, workers in the Mashveev dye shop voluntarily increased their workload against the opposition of shop administrators.[34] Higher production norms often were applied first to "leading" workers and only later to the labor force as a whole. When factory management at Trekhgornaia *manufaktura* placed three "conscious" female workers on multistation work, "the majority of the factory's female workers gave way to the persuasion of one irresponsible female spinner [and] demanded that these three workers cease their work on three stations."[35] William Chase argues that worker-Communists, *komsomol'tsy,* and young workers volunteered for multistation work and higher rates, taking advantage of the skills they learned in technical courses to improve their job security.[36] These tensions would spread throughout Soviet industry during NEP's final years under the pressures of rationalization and the introduction of new techniques of production.

Because of their essentially economic character and the existence of political sanctions against autonomous cross-factory organization, strikes and other job actions remained localized, centered in specific factories and shops. According to a nationwide survey conducted in 1925, the vast majority of these strikes occurred without union sanction.[37] Evidence suggests that the leadership of this spontaneous movement consisted in part of workers who, as members or supporters of the Menshevik and SR parties, had been active in the strike movement prior to 1918.[38] In the textile industry, strikes were sometimes coordinated by spontaneously organized strike committees or "parallel" factory committees,[39] and in at least some instances, strikers successfully forced participation upon workers who opposed the strike.[40] But as noted above, worker solidarity was undermined by managerial efforts to pit groups of workers against each other in competition for scarce jobs, and by tensions between "urban" and "new" workers and "skilled" and "unskilled" workers.

It is also worth noting that, on the whole, propensity toward spontaneous labor activism did not correlate with skill or sexual classifications; in fact, lower-skilled female textile workers were also the most strike-prone in the Moscow region during these years. What seems to be an important variable in determining strike propensities, especially after 1923, was not only material considerations (e.g., job pressures, wages) but also, and perhaps more important, the degree of contact between workers and soviet institutions and the acculturation of workers to urban values. Thus, "new" workers fresh from the countryside—especially textilists employed in large-scale provincial factories—were largely outside the influence of urban organizations, and their labor activism retained its uncontrolled character throughout much of the 1920s.

Work stoppages often were spontaneous and defiant reactions to adverse workplace developments. For example, garment workers in one of the shops of the Balakireva buttonmaking factory demanded an increase in piece rates when a change to inferior fuel sources resulted in lower labor productivity and, consequently, lower wages. Not content to wait for a decision through the proper channels, these workers stopped work for two hours and were joined, in the name of solidarity, by the workers from another of the factory's shops.[41] In another case, in 1925, workers in the weaving shop of the Red Banner textile factory spontaneously organized "a meeting during work for the sake of resolving the issue of rates without the permission of the factory committee and the agreement of factory management to the cessation of machine operations [*na ostanovku stankov*]."[42]

Authorities responded to this activity with a combination of strategies, including temporary or partial acquiescence to workers' economic demands, efforts to convince workers of the wrongfulness of their actions, the removal of responsible factory officials, and repression or the threat thereof. For example, in response to the Red Banner work stoppage, the factory committee "categorically recognized the impermissibility of . . . [the violation of] the correct tempo of factory labor . . . [and] trade union discipline," and it denounced the role of "suspicious characters" in these events. "Everyone knows," the factory committee's proclamation continued, and every worker . . . knows, that wages have yet to achieve adequate distribution, but every worker must ask himself the question: are we able to raise wages now? There is only one answer, as yet we cannot . . . because of . . . the urgent demands of . . . the peasant population . . . [for] cheap manufactures. . . . The rise in prices of our products, by means of wage increases, lessens the purchasing capacity of the peasantry, [and] can lead to stagnation of commercial exchange and force us to reduce industry. . . . Do not believe those who summon [you] to walk a different path, because for workers there is no other path. We say to workers that in response to any efforts to undermine our industry, to violate the peaceful life and work of our enterprises, you will immediately cease to be a member of our ranks . . . [and] in the case of any new attempt to violate . . . factory order . . . decisive measures will be adopted.[43]

Labor activism, whatever its source, had important consequences. First, as a form of mass pressure, the workers' movement gave the party, if it hoped to maintain production, little option but to acquiesce to the upward renegotiation of wages, generally outstripping increases in labor productivity.[44] This wage offensive worked throughout the 1920s at cross purposes with the party's aim to increase labor productivity. The major victim of the clash between workers' consumptionist interests and the party's productivist policies was the official trade union movement. When local union officials proved inattentive to workers' demands, the influence of their organizations in the workplace abruptly fell amid spontaneous job actions. But when the unions moved cautiously in support of workers' interests, as they increasingly did after 1924, they earned the ire of party officials anxious to promote industrialization at whatever the short-term economic cost for workers.[45] Industrial strife also contributed to a general worsening of worker-management relations and exacerbated social antagonisms between workers and technical personnel, and, at times, gave way to incipient politicization.

In this, it reflected the historic tendency for labor movements to develop political arms, the nature and extent of which are determined by the broader political system, the overall balances between social and administrative forces within that system, and the presence or absence of allies among the political elites and nonworker strata of the population. Although the successful suppression, by 1922, of the social democratic Menshevik Party and the radical Workers' Opposition marked the illegalization of independent labor politics both within and without the Communist Party, incipient politicization continued to take place on a factory level. The most dramatic expression of this occurred during the strike wave of 1923 with the appearance of the illegal, factory-based Workers' Group and Workers' Truth party factions.[46] Even after the suppression of these groups, politicization continued to characterize many labor struggles. In 1925, a prominent Moscow party official admitted to "the formation . . . of several so-called workers' groups" in certain factories "that took on the goal of a . . . broad struggle . . . against the influence of the Communist Party."[47] Another official admitted that during factory committee elections in 1925, "the most heterogeneous elements—former Mensheviks, former Communists, and nonparty [workers]—were able to openly [*nachisto*] kick out Communists." At one factory, "the most varied conglomerate of former Communists, anarcho-syndicalists, etc., gathered, and . . . it was necessary to adopt measures through our state apparatus." In this case, the entire factory committee was arrested.[48]

By late 1923, it was clear that spontaneous labor activism hindered not only the party's economic program but also the political and social stabilization of the factories. Beginning in 1924, then, the Communist Party encouraged new forms of worker activism to cope with these stresses, including the mass enrollment of workers into the party, the formation of factory-level production conferences for the assertion of worker interests in production, the periodic holding of factory committee elections to oust insensitive trade union bureaucrats, and the promotion (*vydvizhenie*) of workers into the administrative, economic, and supervisory apparatuses.[49] Mass recruitments, first carried out in 1924 and repeated in 1925 and 1927, brought tens of thousands of younger, skilled, "urban" workers into the party. While some of these workers used their newfound party affiliation to legitimize their actions (including strike behavior) in defense of workers' interests,[50] the "bolshevization" of the urban cohort had the effect of blunting the spontaneous workers' movement in those areas of industry and the labor force most accessible to Communist influence. Increasingly, nonsanctioned labor disturbances were restricted to "new" workers who remained largely impervious to political mobilization.[51]

Russian workers were energetically struggling for their economic interests long before 1918. After a brief hiatus during War Communism, the workers' movement resurfaced in 1920–21, reflecting the strength of strike traditions in the factory workforce and the urgency of economic conditions. In both periods, worker activism was primarily neither "anarchic" nor "disorganized" in nature but was well organized and logically reflected the economic concerns of the workers involved. Wage and productivity pressures mobilized workers into the collective defense of their economic interests and promoted the development of working-class sensibilities based upon the shared experience of resistance to production pressures. In doing so, the NEP industrial system undermined the formation of a "socialist" corporate consciousness in which workers might see themselves as "owners" of the means of production, with interests identical to those of management. At the same time, however, rural-urban migration, gener-

ational and gender differences, industrial differentiation, and sectionalism
continued to influence and fragment workers' conceptions of class.

Beginning in 1924, through worker mobilization, the party sought to
counter the impact of the market and other autonomous forces on class
formation by asserting the primacy of politics and party consciousness.
Mobilization enabled the party to shape working-class formation in important ways, but primarily through the "bolshevization" of young, skilled,
male urban workers. By displacing spontaneously generated economic
activism as the primary source of collective action and identity with politicized forms, the party encouraged worker-Communists to renounce economic struggle in favor of social advancement and political influence in a
system of structured opportunities. The effects this had on the workers'
movement are difficult to ascertain precisely, but during the latter part of
the NEP, in conjunction with economic improvements that affected many
workers, strike actions rapidly declined.[52]

While this policy may have derailed the development of a full-blown,
independent workers' movement of the sort found in Western democracies, it did so only incompletely, and only by significantly rearranging
relations between the NEP "state" and the industrial proletariat. For a
reproletarianized Communist Party could unreservedly back managerial
power only by seriously weakening its shop-floor credibility; nor did it have
the option enjoyed by capitalist states of standing above the impersonal
workings of the market. Thus, after 1924 the Communist Party found itself
increasingly involved in the politics of the shop floor as it attempted to
maintain its newly reaffirmed "proletarian identity" while continuing to
defend managerial authority and the NEP system as a whole.

## NOTES

1. Funding for the research and writing of this essay was provided by the
International Research and Exchanges Board, the Social Science Research Council,
the University of Michigan Center for Russian and East European Studies, and the
Graduate Division of the University of California, Irvine. The views expressed in
this essay are solely those of the author.

2. Diane Koenker, *Moscow Workers and the 1917 Revolution* (Princeton, 1981);
Steve Smith, *Red Petrograd* (Cambridge, 1983); and David Mandel, *The Petrograd
Workers and the Fall of the Old Regime* (London, 1983) and *The Petrograd Workers and
the Soviet Seizure of Power* (London, 1983).

3. On the Moscow workers' movement prior to 1918, see Victoria Bonnell, *Roots
of Rebellion: Workers' Politics and Organizations in St. Petersburg and Moscow, 1900–
1914* (Berkeley, 1983); Laura Engelstein, *Moscow, 1905: Working-class Organizations
and Political Conflict* (Stanford, 1982); and Koenker, *Moscow Workers*.

4. A. A. Tverdokhleb, "Chislennost' i sostav rabochego klassa Moskvy v 1917–
1937 gg.," *Vestnik Moskovskogo Universiteta*, 1 (1970), p. 22.

5. Leonard Schapiro, *Origin of the Communist Autocracy*, 2nd ed. (Cambridge, Mass., 1977), pp. 296–97; Paul Avrich, *Kronstadt 1921* (Princeton, 1970), pp. 35–36; William Chase, *Workers, Society, and the Soviet State: Labor and Life in Moscow, 1918–1929* (Urbana, Ill., 1987), pp. 48–52; and A. A. Matiugin, *Moskva v period vosstanovleniia narodnogo khoziaistva 1921–1925* (Moscow, 1947), p. 17.

6. Recent contributions to NEP labor history include Chase, *Workers;* and William Rosenberg, "Smolensk in the 1920s: Party-worker Relations and the 'Vanguard Problem,' " *Russian Review*, 2 (1977) pp. 125–50.

7. In 1925 there were 155,661 industrial workers employed in Moscow, compared to 148,212 in 1913. *Istoriia rabochikh Moskvy* (Moscow, 1983), p. 138.

8. In 1926, 200,000 textile workers labored in factories located in the provincial region outside Moscow. See L. I. Bas'kina, *Rabochii klass SSSR nakanune sotsialisticheskoi industrializatsii* (Moscow, 1981), p. 133.

9. See Chase's discussion in *Workers*, pp. 120–21, 246–47, and 295–96. On the cultural dispositions of new workers, see *Pravda*, Jan. 31, 1926.

10. On the protests of skilled workers over the common managerial practice of filling job openings with underskilled workers and of paying workers doing similar kinds of labor different wages, see *Metallist*, Feb. 16, 1923; *Rabota V-go Moskovskogo gubernskogo s"ezda VSRM 31 oktiabria–5 noiabria 1925 g.* (Moscow, 1925), p. 84; and Central State Archive of the October Revolution (TsGAOR), f. 100, op. 7, d. 94, l. 28 (Apr. 28, 1923). Similar tactics were used by railroad administrators in 1923. See TsGAOR, f. 5451, op. 7, d. 127, l. 16. On management's use of unemployment to defeat a strike at #1 state instrumentation factory "Geofizika" (formerly Shtabe), see *Sotsialisticheskii vestnik*, Jan. 1, 1923.

11. *Pravda*, Jan. 31, 1926. In the words of the management journal *Predpriiatie*, advanced workers held "new attitudes" toward work; that is, they were careful with factory property, politically developed, and less discriminatory and abusive toward female workmates. *Predpriiatie*, 2 (Sept. 1923), p. 23.

12. According to *Predpriiatie*, "few workers" took initiative to "improve" production, and *Pravda* admitted in 1921 that the "mass of workers" was relatively indifferent or even hostile to "the interests of the economy." Instead, they demanded personal monetary incentives in return for more work. *Pravda*, July 17, 1921; *Predpriiatie*, 2 (Sept. 1923), p. 23. On the preservation of cadre workers during the Civil War, see Diane Koenker, "Urbanization and Deurbanization in the Russian Revolution and Civil War," *Journal of Modern History*, 57 (Sept. 1985), pp. 424–50.

13. On the attitudes of skilled metalworkers, see *Pravda*, May 27 and 31, 1921; and on their reaction to piece rates, TsGAOR, f. 100, op. 7, d. 80, l. 2. On printers, see *Moskovskii pechatnik*, July 12 and Sept. 22, 1923; *Otchet pravleniia Moskovskogo gubotdela VSRPP ot 1 sentiabria 1922 g. po 1 sentiabr' 1923 g.* (Moscow, 1923), pp. 6, 27, and 30; *Otchet Moskovskogo gubernskogo otdela Professional'nogo Soiuza Rabochikh Poligraficheskogo Proizvodstva s maia 1921 g. po fevral' 1922 g.* (Moscow, 1922), p. 3; *Tretii gubernskii s"ezd Moskovskogo gubernskogo soiuza rabochikh poligraficheskogo proizvodstva 16–20 fevralia 1922 g.* (Moscow, 1922), pp. 9–10.

14. On trade union– and party-worker relations, see TsGAOR, f. 5451, op. 6, d. 45, ll. 147 and 184 (1922); and *Rezoliutsii i postanovleniia III-go s"ezda professional'nykh soiuzov Moskvy i Moskovskoi gubernii (10–14 maia 1921 goda)* (Moscow, 1921), p. 1; Chase, *Workers*, pp. 214–56; and John Hatch, "Labor and Politics in NEP Russia: Workers, Trade Unions, and the Communist Party in Moscow, 1921–1926," Ph.D. dissertation, University of California, Irvine, 1985.

15. On labor arbitration during NEP, see Mary McAuley, *Labor Disputes in Soviet Russia* (Oxford, 1969), pp. 11–35.

16. *Trud v Moskovskoi gubernii v 1923–1925 gg.* (Moscow, 1926), p. 426; *Otchet pravleniia Moskovskogo gubotdela VSRPP . . . 1922 po . . . 1923*, p. 29; and *Biulleten' Moskovskogo raionnogo komiteta Vserossiiskogo Soiuza Rabochikh Metallistov*, 1 (Jan. 1923), p. 44.

17. For criticisms of RKK enforcement of labor contract provisions, see G. N. Mel'nichanskii, *Moskovskie profsoiuzy v obstanovke NEPa* (Moscow, 1923), pp. 29–30; and *Trud*, Feb. 16, 1923.

18. Over one-half of the sixty-five reported strikes occurring in Moscow in the last half of 1922 were due to wage disputes of one kind or another. Mel'nichanskii, *Moskovskie profsoiuzy*, pp. 29–30.

19. Ibid., pp. 29–30.

20. *Izvestiia MK*, 3 (Dec. 12, 1922), pp. 60–61; *Pravda*, Aug. 22, 1922; *Otchet Krasno-Presnenskogo raikoma RKP(b) za period s 1-go ianvaria po 1-e iiunia 1923 g.* (Moscow, 1923), p. 3; TsGAOR, f. 425, op. 2, d. 34, l. 5 (Sept. 14, 1923); *Otchet. mart-dekabr' 1923 goda* (Moscow, 1923), p. 3; and *Sotsialisticheskii vestnik*, Oct. 18, 1923.

21. *Pravda*, July 4, 1923; *Biulleten'. Moskovskii gubotdel* (Soiuz Tekstil'shchikov SSSR), no. 1 (1923), p. 24; *Otchet Krasno-Presnenskogo raikoma . . . 1923*, p. 4.

22. *Pravda*, May 25 and 27, 1921. A subsequent article extended this argument to all skilled workers and pointed to the difficulties being experienced by the printers. See *Pravda*, May 31, 1921.

23. *Sotsialisticheskii vestnik*, May 2, 1922; *Otchet Rogozhko-Simonovskogo raikoma s 3-go maia po 15-e noiabr' 1922 g.* (Moscow, 1922), pp. 4 and 16; *Pravda*, Dec. 30, 1921; and Chase, *Workers*, p. 175.

24. *Sotsialisticheskii vestnik*, Apr. 16, 1923, and *Otchet. Sokol'nicheskaia raionnaia konferentsiia (30–31 maia 1923)* (Moscow, 1923), p. 54; *Otchet Krasno-Presnenskogo raikoma . . . 1923*, p. 4; and *Rabota Moskovskogo gubernskogo soveta professional'nykh soiuzov za oktiabr' 1924 g.–ianvar' 1926 g.* (Moscow, 1926), pp. 105–106; *Rabota Rogozhko-Simonovskogo raionnogo komiteta RKP(b) s ianvaria po oktiabr' 1925 g.* (Moscow, 1925), p. 24; *Biulleten' Moskovskogo raionnogo komiteta V. S. R. M.*, 2 (Jan.–Mar. 1924), p. 8; Chase, *Workers*, p. 230.

25. *XII-aia Moskovskaia gubernskaia konferentsiia RKP(b) 14–21 maia 1924 g. stenograficheskii otchet* (Moscow, 1924), p. 149.

26. TsGAOR, f. 100, op. 7, d. 80, l. 2 (July 11, 1922); d. 94, l. 5. (Sept. 28, 1923); d. 95, l. 7 (Sept. 24, 1923); and d. 98, l. 2 (May 31, 1923).

27. *Metallist*, Jan. 30, 1923.

28. See *Metallist*, Feb. 16, 1923, and July 15, 1924; *Rabota V-go Moskovskogo gubernskogo s"ezda VSRM*, pp. 79–80 and 84; and TsGAOR, f. 100, op. 7, d. 94, l. 28 (Apr. 28, 1923); TsGAOR, f. 100, op. 7, d. 98, l. 2 (May 31, 1923).

29. *Metallist*, Apr. 30, 1924. In November 1921, Dinamo workers criticized management for failing to present a detailed report on factory output. TsGAOR, f. 100, op. 7, d. 75, l. 1.

30. See *Izvestiia MK*, 3 (Dec. 12, 1922), pp. 60–61; *Pravda*, Aug. 22, 1922; *Otchet Krasno-Presnenskogo raikoma . . . 1923*, p. 3; TsGAOR, f. 425, op. 2, d. 34, l. 5 (Sept. 14, 1923); *Otchet. Mart–dekabr' 1923 goda* (Zamoskvoretskii raikom), p. 3; and *Sotsialisticheskii vestnik*, Oct. 18, 1923.

31. *Pravda*, July 4, 1923; *Biulleten'. Moskovskii gubotdel* (Soiuz Tekstil'shchikov SSSR), 1 (1923), p. 24; N. V. Poliakova, "Rabochie-tekstil'shchiki Moskvy i Moskovskoi gubernii v bor'ba za vosstanovlenie promyshlennosti v period perekhoda na mirnuiu rabotu (1921–1925 gg.)," Ph.D. dissertation, Moscow, 1953, p. 132. Worker unrest was sparked at the Gracheva ribbon factory when its closure due to a lack of orders and insufficient fuel was announced. See *Otchet Krasno-Presnenskogo raikoma . . . 1923*, p. 4.

32. Poliakova, "Bor'ba rabochikh-tekstil'shchikov za povyshenie proizvo-ditel'nosti truda v 1921–1925 gg.," *Voprosy istorii*, 6 (June 1959), p. 28.

33. *Biulleten' 4-i (Zamoskvoretskoi) raipartkonferentsii (po stenograficheskom zapisy)* (Moscow, 1925), p. 97. For other reports, see *Sotsialisticheskii vestnik*, June 20, 1925; *Rabota Rogozhko-Simonovskogo raionnogo komiteta . . . ianvaria po oktiabr' 1925*, p. 24; *Materialy piatogo plenuma Moskovskogo komiteta VKP(b) 5 iiunia 1925 goda* (Moscow, 1925), pp. 11–13 and 21; TsGAOR, f. 627, op. 2, d. 1623, l. 5 (8.I.25); f. 627, op. 2, d. 1623, l. 17; f. 627, op. 2, l. 1623, l. 9; f. 627, op. 2, d. 1613, l. 30. Factory committees responsible for supervising the transition often proceeded arbitrarily, causing widespread discontent among workers. Poliakova, "*Rabochie-tekstil'shchiki*," pp. 193–95; and *Rezoliutsii Moskovskogo gubotdela Soiuza Tekstil'shchikov za period oktiabr' 1924 g.–fevral' 1925 g.* (Moscow, 1925), p. 64.

34. Poliakova, "Bor'ba," p. 332; Matiugin, *Moskva*, pp. 66–67.

35. Poliakova, "Rabochie-tekstil'shchiki," p. 192.

36. Chase, *Workers*, pp. 40–41.

37. *Bolshevik* reported that in 1925, 96.5 percent of all strikes within the Soviet Union occurred without trade union sanction. "Nekotorye nedochety raboty prof-organizatsii," *Bolshevik* (July 30, 1925), pp. 76–77.

38. *14-aia Moskovskaia gubernskaia konferentsiia RKP(b). Biulleten'* (Moscow, 1925), p. 15.

39. *Biulleten' 4-i (Zamoskvoretskoi) raipartkonferentsii*, pp. 97–99.

40. These dynamics were observed in the Serpukhovskaia and Nikol'skaia strikes cited above.

41. *Rabota Baumanskogo raionnogo komiteta R.K.P.(b) i raionnoi kontrol'noi komissii ianvar'–oktiabr' 1925 g.* (Moscow, 1925), pp. 24–25.

42. TsGAOR, f. 627, op. 2, d. 1613, l. 47.

43. Ibid.

44. Although the workers' wage offensive was not successful everywhere, wage increases generally outstripped productivity gains in NEP's early years. See Chase, *Workers*, pp. 218–19; Hatch, "Labor and Politics," pp. 40–44; and E. H. Carr, *The Interregnum, 1923–1924* (London, 1954), p. 71.

45. *Istoriia rabochikh Moskvy* (Moscow, 1983), p. 128; TsGAOR, f. 5451, op. 7, d. 127, ll. 88, 107, and 123. In 1925, a Moscow party committee official observed that recent efforts to increase wages by 30–40 percent had been rejected and held to 10–15 percent by the Moscow party committee. *Biulleten' 4-i (Zamoskvoretskoi) raipartkonferentsii*, pp. 88–89.

46. On the Moscow Mensheviks, see John Hatch, "Working-class Politics in Moscow during the Early NEP: Mensheviks and Workers' Organizations, 1921–1922," *Soviet Studies*, 4 (Oct. 1987), pp. 556–74. On the Workers' Group episode, see Hatch, "Labor and Politics," pp. 217–21.

47. *Materialy piatogo plenuma*, p. 22.

48. Ibid., pp. 11–13.

49. On worker mobilization, see Chase, *Workers*, pp. 256–86.

50. See the discussion in Hatch, "Labor and Politics," pp. 472–75; and also *Otchet Sokol'nicheskogo raionnogo komiteta RKP(b) (mai–noiabr' 1924 g.)* (Moscow, 1924), pp. 24 and 26; *Otchet o rabote Baumanskogo raionnogo komiteta RKP(b) za period raboty mai–noiabr' 1924 g. i materialy k IV-i raipartkonferentsii* (Moscow, 1924), pp. 20 and 26–27; *Rabota Moskovskogo komiteta RKP(b) aprel'–dekabr' 1924 g.* (Moscow, 1925), pp. 63–64; and *Sotsialisticheskii vestnik*, Aug. 16 and Dec. 1, 1924, and Oct. 29, 1925.

51. Early examples of instances in which "new" workers were much more prone than "urban" workers to strike can be found in *Pravda*, Aug. 22, 1922, and *Izvestiia MK*, Dec. 12, 1922.

52. Chase, *Workers*, p. 251, n. 54.

# V

# WORKERS' ARTELS AND SOVIET PRODUCTION RELATIONS

*Hiroaki Kuromiya*

In the realm of labor, as in others, the introduction of NEP left many important social issues unresolved. The revival of old social hierarchies among workers, for instance, sharply contradicted the socialist goal of egalitarian and collective labor. True, Soviet industry lacked corporate (guild) traditions,[1] traditions that in the West had provided a historical basis for the survival of old craft hierarchies well into the age of the machine. Moreover, craft solidarity and consciousness became politically suspect under Soviet power, because they were deemed harmful to class solidarity and consciousness: craft unions gave way to industrial unions. Yet, behind the façade of monolithic industrial unionism, complex craft hierarchies and sectarianisms seem to have persisted throughout NEP.[2] How the Bolsheviks sought to solve this contradiction still remains to be closely investigated.

The present essay attempts to examine this issue by a case study of little-known folk institutions called workers' *artels,* or voluntary labor collectives, composed on the average of twelve to fifteen members.[3] The artel makes an interesting case study, because it embodied production relations that were both preindustrial and, to a degree, egalitarian and collectivist. With a paternalistic elder (*starshina, starshii,* or *artel'shchik*) as its head, it was an organization for mutual aid and collective security, a sort of transplanted village commune. As a long-established work organization, the artel was deemed expedient in the quick recovery of an economy ruined by the First World War, the revolution, and the Civil War. Much praised by the Populists in the nineteenth century, it embodied a collectivist principle of social organization that was congenial to the Bolsheviks as well. The artel, however, appeared to the Bolsheviks to be a fortress of tenacious traditions that had to be superseded by modern principles: its paternalistic elder was deemed politically unacceptable; and its collective labor and egalitarianism were believed, under the influence of Taylorism, to be unconducive to modern industrial efficiency.

This essay first analyzes some of the characteristics of the artel in the NEP period and then traces its fate in the period of Stalin's rapid industrialization. The collectivist, egalitarian characteristics of the artel did not deter the Bolshevik modernizers from violently attacking it. The attack in fact began well before 1928, the year usually associated with the onset of Stalin's revolution from above. The attack on the artel was part of the general attack on the traditional production relations inherited from the prerevolutionary years. It was an essential element of the Soviet attempt to leap from tradition to modernity. The essay suggests that despite the attack the artel died hard, influencing the way Soviet workers sought to protect their interests on the shop floor; that the attack led to much confusion concerning socialist labor; and that through this confusion an alternative concept of labor emerged in the 1930s.

## I. Workers' Artels.

One prerevolutionary observer noted that "the artel is, as a matter of fact, not an institution but rather an everyday [*bytovoi*] communal phenomenon which is peculiar to the characters and customs of the Russian people."[4] Ubiquitous as it was, another observer noted, "we cannot provide statistics about the artel. These organizations are so fluid and mobile that it is impossible to collect the data."[5] The word *artel* was applied to such a wide variety of cooperative and quasi-cooperative organizations as to defy clear definition.[6] This essay focuses on artels that furnished labor for the nationalized sector of industry and the construction sector. These artels were the most primitive and simplest and were subjected particularly harshly to rapid industrial modernization in the 1920s and 1930s.

These artels survived the revolutionary upheaval of 1917–20 almost intact,[7] and in the 1920s they existed widely among mainly marginal worker groups—construction workers, miners, lumber workers, and other seasonal industrial workers,[8] whose labor was almost entirely manual and bore little semblance to modern industrial labor. In the 1920s artel labor declined as mechanization progressed. In the late 1920s, however, it was still predominant in the construction and lumber industries; in 1928, 47.5 percent of the Donbass underground miners were organized into artels.[9]

In the mid-1920s the artels were divided into two legal categories: labor artels (*trudovye arteli*) and "ordinary" artels ("*obychnye*" *arteli [gruppy]*, or *bytovye arteli*). Labor artels existed predominantly in the construction and lumber industries, and ordinary artels were more widespread. Because many artels provided horses and other equipment for work, they were legally differentiated from those which merely sold labor. The law of 15 December 1924 defined the labor artel as "an association of persons for the joint organization and hiring out of their physical and intellectual labor to carry out work, as a general rule, from the employer's materials." The minimum number of members was set at seven, and those "who exploit hired labor for the purpose of making profits" were not allowed to join.[10] A juridical entity, the labor artel possessed formal written statutes or rules and had to be registered with the People's Commissariat of Labor. The artel was allowed to conclude contracts for work, operate limited working capital, and hire temporary workers (up to 10 percent of its standing members) under certain conditions. The members of labor artels (some of which referred to themselves as "labor communes") were deprived of trade union membership on the grounds that their purpose as associations was not to satisfy the demands of the national economy as a whole but to serve "their own particular interests"; they were often said merely to provide a screen for those who sought to preserve their own equipment.[11] Moreover, because the Labor Code and other measures for labor protection were not fully applied to the labor artels, the contractors and elders were accused of "intense exploitation of labor" under the guise of cooperative ideals.[12]

If the labor artel possessed equipment, the ordinary artel possessed none and merely sold labor. Its legal status was defined only as a group which had the right to conclude a labor agreement *(trudovoi dogovor)* with management independently (but not exclusively) of collective agreements between the trade unions and management.[13] It had no right to own working capital or to undertake formal contracts because it, unlike the labor artel, was not a juridical entity. It had no formal written statutes or rules and regulated its inner life "in a way established since olden times by the older generations."[14] Like other workers, the members of the artel had the right to join trade unions. In reality, many ordinary artels worked according to contracts or quasi-contracts. The Labor Code of 1922, which "merely takes into account the existence of [ordinary] artels as a fact," authorized them to allocate jobs among the members and to replace some members with others, thereby effectively limiting managerial power and allowing artels to act as subcontractors.[15]

These two types of artel differed little in practice and will be treated in this essay interchangeably unless otherwise noted. They survived largely outside the control and influence of industrial management and trade unions.[16] In the 1920s they preserved relations inherited from the prerevolutionary era and remained little affected by modern bureaucratic management.

In some respects, the Russian artel resembled the butty system and the *Kameradschaft* in the premechanized British and German coal-mining industry. However, the butty system seems to have lacked a mechanism of collective security, and the *Kameradschaft* was integrated into the managerial hierarchy through its leader *Ortsältester*, who was "appointed by management and not elected by his comrades."[17] Yet it was these features that characterized the Russian artel.

## II. Autonomy and Collective Security

The artel retained a certain measure of autonomy from the hierarchy of industrial management. The elder, in particular, held sway over the inner life of the artel, "a practice of many decades." This practice appeared to contemporary observers as a "vestige of the prerevolutionary era that runs counter to the existing social system of our time": "The least shrewd elder in the majority of cases becomes a virtual contractor and consequently exploits the members of his artel with impunity by shortchanging them in every way in his own interests."[18] In a word, the artel was said to be "antisocial" because of the elder's exploitation.[19]

In the Donbass coal mines, it was reported that the elders were "most often" entrusted by the party and trade union organizations to manage their artels,[20] a reflection both of the conciliatory spirit of NEP and of the lack of control of the party and trade union organizations. The elders set the output norms of their artels through negotiations with the management, allocated jobs to members, kept the records of work performed, determined the skill ranks and wage rates of the members, and selected new members "not on the basis of proper skills but on the basis of various personal considerations."[21] The elders, as before the revolution, "continued to receive 'from their office' both open and secret 'percentages.' "[22] The artel members often shared room and board, and elders were alleged to have forbidden members from eating at factory (or mine) canteens and going to meetings and clubs.[23] When artel members depended economically on the elder (who possessed equipment, horses, and carts), his influence proved "stronger than appeals to [proletarian] consciousness."[24]

From the mid-1920s, attempts were made to replace the elder with a "Soviet" leader, appointed by the management.[25] In 1927 the Central Committee of the Construction Workers' Union ordered a special investigation of artels to find out "to what extent modern technical, economic, and political conditions have affected the internal nature of the artel; how far 'the traditions of the past' have survived or been eliminated in the artel; the role of the elder at the present time; and how all this affects the work of the trade union."[26] After the investigation, the elders came under sharp attack. In October 1927 a law was enacted prohibiting, with some exceptions, elders from distributing wages to workers.[27] In 1928 the elder was stripped of his power to determine the skill ranks of the members.[28] Those elders of "ordinary" artels who "work on contract or semicontract principles (manage the internal order of the artel, make arrangements on behalf of the artel, and appropriate from the artel a certain amount of money or a percentage from the total sum of wages as a supplementary remuneration)" were expelled from the trade unions.[29] In the late 1920s attempts were also made to replace the elders of construction workers' artels with brigadiers, selected and appointed from among "party members, union activists, and poor peasants." In 1927–28 some elders, like Nepmen, were removed as "hostile anti-Soviet elements."[30] They organized "all kinds of sabotage," according to one typical report, but the efforts to replace them were optimistically said to have had a "great economic, and particularly political, effect."[31]

Similarly, in the 1920s, the elders in the Donbass coal mines came to be attacked as "kulak" exploiters. However, many were reported to hide skillfully under the cloak of *desiatniki* (the equivalent of assistant foremen in the factories) or as rank-and-file miners. They now earned only 100 to 120 rubles instead of the 300 or even 400–500 rubles they had earned before, and they were reported to entertain "malice and hatred toward all innovative undertakings."[32]

Unlike the appointed supervisors, the elders had no formal authority. Their authority came from within the artel, deriving from a group coherence and power based on *zemliachestvo:* members came largely from the same family, clan, village, district, or region, and elders were more often than not elected representatives. The artel thus replicated the old village traditions. While *zemliachestvo* may have been a legacy of the past (in the nineteenth century many artels were created from above to secure seigneurial power away from the village),[33] after the revolution construction workers' artels, for example, were organized by committees of peasant mutual aid.[34] The Bolsheviks regarded *zemliachestvo* with suspicion because it was not a class principle. From the point of view of production, however, *zemliachestvo* appeared to some to have positive effects, because, according to one commentator, it provided a group coherence.[35] Reflecting this ambivalence, Aleksei Gastev, an eminent Soviet Taylorist, contended in 1927 that the *zemliachestvo* of artels must be "either smashed or utilized cleverly."[36]

The organizational coherence of artels was based not only on *zemliachestvo* but also on a degree of egalitarianism. In the nineteenth century the members of all artels in the Donbass "without exception" rotated their jobs and divided the wages evenly except for the minors—horse drivers—who were hired separately by the artel.[37] The same "nomadic" labor of artels survived well into the 1920s. In the Donbass, according to one report, artel members "regarded it as their duty" to move from one job to another, making it impossible to determine each member's output and, consequently, his wages. Thus, the wages had to be divided equally among members.[38]

There were at least three reasons for this egalitarian practice. First, job rotation familiarized the less skilled members with skilled labor and thus performed the important function of transmitting craft skills to the younger generations. Second, collective labor was a guarantee against the interruption of work due to high absenteeism, which even in the mid-1920s stood at about 30 percent in the Donbass.[39] Third, the egalitarian division of wages protected the artel members against wage fluctuations: if the artel as a whole failed to fulfill its output norms, the burden of consequent decreases in wage bills was shouldered equally by each member.[40] Egalitarianism served as collective security, which in turn provided the artel with group coherence.

The degree of coherence certainly varied from one artel to another. The contemporary studies of artels were made mainly by those distrustful of artel labor, and therefore they tended to overstate the degree of group cohesion. Actually, many artels had to struggle hard to maintain group cohesion. In order to prevent internal conflict, some artels paid the skilled workers (hewers, in particular, who were ranked highest in the miners' craft hierarchy) separately, with other members dividing the remainder evenly.[41] In others, egalitarianism led to conflicts between the industrious and the lazy and between the skilled and the unskilled.[42] The presence of the less skilled workers in the artel pushed down its overall wages, and this became a source of conflict.[43] In construction workers' artels, the elders received the wages for all the members and allegedly divided them according to the length of each member's beard! The younger members were naturally discontented.[44]

Generally, however, the artel "strictly controlled the number of young [and less skilled] workers" to prevent its wages from declining and to avoid internal conflicts.[45] According to one observer, artel workers coordinated their labor, and their "will and conduct were aimed at observing an 'order' to ensure the maximum productivity of the artel and the possibility of making considerable extra money."[46] The coherence of the artel depended on the degree to which it safeguarded the particular interests of its members in collective fashion acceptable to most, if not all, members. Some artels perhaps embodied a grassroots mechanism of reconciling the conflicting demands for equity and work motivation.

The collective security and equity of the artel, however, appeared to proponents of scientific management (who in the 1920s enjoyed a strong influence in the political leadership)[47] to hinder the achievement of maximum labor efficiency, a hindrance deemed worse than individual craftsmen's control over their work processes. In 1911 Frederick W. Taylor noted: "A careful analysis had demonstrated the fact that when workmen are herded together in gangs, each man in the gang becomes far less efficient than when his personal ambition is stimulated; that when men work in gangs, their individual efficiency falls almost invariably down to or below the level of the worst man in the gang; and that they are all pulled down instead of being elevated by being herded together."[48] Under the influence of Taylorism, the Soviet industrial authority set about disbanding artels as soon as it managed to achieve a degree of economic recovery. The dissolution of artels was also supported by plans for the rapid mechanization of mining and construction, which would have made the traditional crafts obsolete. As early as 1924, attempts were made to divide miners' artels.[49] There followed reports of time-motion studies claiming that the dissolution of artels and the division (individualization) of labor and wages led to dramatic increases in labor productivity.[50] In 1926 the miners' union ordered the abolishment of artels.[51] In 1928 the Donbass Coal trust instructed that the artels be divided up in all mines.[52]

The construction workers' artels likewise came under attack by the late 1920s. The Central Institute of Labor (TsIT), led by Gastev, promoted the Taylorist functional organization of labor—division and specialization—in place of artel labor. This innovation met "the most formidable resistance on the part of the old construction workers organized in the so-called artels."[53] In March 1929 a national conference on construction ordered a "division of large artels into small groups" in order to introduce individual piece work, to raise labor productivity, and to abolish the institution of the "plenipotentiary" (i.e., the elder system).[54]

The attack on the artels subjected them to curious vicissitudes. The individualization of wages evoked resistance on the part of the less skilled.[55] In 1928, just at the time when serious attempts were being made to disband the artels in the Donbass, the Donbass Coal Trust declared with despair that "in a significant number of places we have failed to dissolve the artels."[56] In other places, however, the artels were forcefully disbanded. The dissolution brought workers into "senseless collisions" by depriving them of solidarity. As a result, labor discipline deteriorated, labor turnover and accidents increased, the edifying influence of the senior on the junior miners decreased, and the "technical and organizational order itself was disappearing."[57] Thrown into panic by the disappearance of the old order, mine managers and engineers came out in defense of the artels.[58] In 1929–30 the Donbass mines thus resorted to the old method of labor, which the political leadership attacked as a revival of "petty-bourgeois utilitarianism (a reversion to the old contract-type artels)."[59]

### III. Artels and Confusion over Socialist Labor

The assault on the artel was an attempt to create modern production relations. Characteristically, the onslaught preceded a clear conceptualization of production relations that were not only modern but also "socialist." Certainly in the 1920s there was a vague consensus among the Bolsheviks that they would have to be collective and more equitable and productive than capitalist relations. Even when the collective labor of artels, deemed preindustrial, was being individualized, strictly individualized labor received neither an emotional nor a technological endorsement among the Bolsheviks: it was widely believed in the 1920s that modern technological developments represented by the conveyor and the Ford system would ultimately lead to and were actually leading (in some industries) to "dequalification" of labor; and that therefore individual piece work would be unnecessary. Reflecting this belief, the 8th Trade Union Congress in 1928 advocated a transition from individual piece work to "collective bonuses."[60] In introducing the Taylorist "functional organization of labor" into the textile industry, Gastev proposed that collective wages be introduced accordingly.[61] Moreover, from 1928 to 1931, the political leadership considered grassroots egalitarianism and collectivism politically useful for preventing the economic differentiation of workers from developing into political groupings.[62]

The attack on the artel therefore caused considerable confusion concerning "socialist" collective labor. This confusion can be illustrated by the case of shock brigades. These brigades, which mushroomed in 1929 in all industries, were triumphantly proclaimed as a new, socialist form of collective labor, based not on a grassroots collective security but on a (supremely Bolshevik) "conscious" attitude toward production. "Consciousness" and self-discipline were heroically assumed to have taken the place of administrative order and supervision.[63] This assumption led shock workers and others to adopt what was referred to in the contemporary press as "unconditionally abnormal production autonomy": they constituted a "state within a state," an "autonomous, self-management production unit."[64] The majority of shock brigades, like artels, elected their brigadiers (elders) or even a collective leadership ("soviet") in explicit challenge to one-man management. In 1930, 61 percent of Leningrad shock brigades, for instance, elected their "managerial organs."[65]

Moreover, shock brigades also came to assume an egalitarian characteristic. Socialist labor implied (at least to idealistic young workers) not narrow specialization but polytechnic, despecialized labor (workers at the Stalingrad Tractor Plant justified their despecialization of conveyor labor as "a socialist revision of the Ford System"),[66] and socialist "consciousness" implied comradely egalitarianism. Thus the sixth Komsomol conference in June 1929 explicitly advocated "facilitating by all means the transition of the shock brigades to an even division of wages."[67] From a mundane point of view, the "collectivization of wages," as in the artel, relieved management of costly supervision and provided the workers with a certain security against wage fluctuations.[68]

Much confusion was apparent: the "autonomy" and egalitarianism of shock brigades thus scarcely distinguished themselves from the old artel. In the 1920s the Bolsheviks deemed traditional production relations embodied in the artels neither politically acceptable nor technically productive. Nor did they deem the more advanced, "capitalist" relations of managerial supervision and differentiated incentive payment emotionally acceptable or durable from a technological point of view. They began to attack the artels before the onset of Stalin's "revolution from above," and during the revolution they challenged "capitalist" relations. The traditional social hierarchies thus partially fell apart on the shop floor. As a result, not only artels but also older, skilled workers found it convenient to declare themselves shock brigades or communes in order to protect their autonomy and privileges.[69] In turn, some shock brigades and communes, perhaps rather naively, referred to themselves as shock artels.[70]

This confusion and the Bolshevik collectivist ethos (which received a technological endorsement) helped workers' artels to survive. When, in 1931, collective wages in general came under political attack,[71] construction workers sought to "maintain the artel system" by contending that "in the village you [the Bolsheviks] are driving peasants into collective farms, whereas here you divide us up into individuals"; "We don't want to work individually. Many died in the Solovki because they wanted to work individually in the village"; "We are for collectives."[72] Thus many construction workers' artels managed to survive intact or under the guise of a modern name, brigade, at least until the mid-1930s.[73]

Some artels survived in a "decapitated" form, as it were, because their elders were removed. Characteristically, their removal preceded the training of Soviet managerial-technical cadres. In some cases, the elders were replaced by brigadiers, supposedly appointed by management but actually elected by workers.[74] The shortage of those who would have to replace the elders was said to make the dissolution of artels difficult.[75] Individual labor needed much closer supervision and more sophisticated accounting and bookkeeping, which, however, was burdensome to lower managerial personnel. In 1930 in the Siberian coal mines, the shortage of qualified supervisors created a "tendency for individual labor and small artels to transfer to large artels" to simplify accounting and bookkeeping.[76] Construction workers' artels also owed their survival to the limited degree of mechanization of labor: in 1929 only 5 to 6 percent of construction work was mechanized, and by 1932 still only 20 percent.[77]

By contrast, in the 1930s the rapid progress of mechanization in the coal-mining industry either radically transformed or dissolved miners' artels. In 1929 the mechanized extraction of coal accounted for 24.4

percent of the total output; in 1933, 67.6 percent.[78] Inflated though these official data may be, it was still a remarkable leap. The press continued to attack the brigades as disguised artels until the summer and autumn of 1932, at which time it suddenly began to contend that the brigades had been shattered and fragmented, that individual miners were left to themselves, and that it was necessary to reconstitute and enlarge the brigades.[79] The new unskilled miners (who swamped the mines) received no technical help or guidance from elders (who had disappeared) or fellow miners (who worked individually) and regarded a resort to sheer muscular power as the best method of work.[80] The old underground authority structure had crumbled. In 1933, in an effort to restore underground order, the government sought to strengthen one-man management in the pit and to re-create brigades on the basis of collective piece work and job rotation.[81] In practice, the new method of work was said to regress to the old artel method.[82]

Whatever the case, the assault on the artels had imperiled an important traditional function: transmission of skills. The artel usually accepted only "its own" people (children, relatives, and fellow countrymen of the members) as apprentices, and knowledge and skills were passed on from generation to generation rather exclusively.[83] This craft tradition had survived the 1917 revolution outside the exclusive artels as well. Master craftsmen in industry regarded their skills as a "production secret" that had to be kept from other workers and was to be passed on only to their children and apprentices.[84] Before the revolution, according to one account, this tradition worked so well, at least among construction workers, that other forms of training were not explored.[85] After the revolution, however, it appeared to the Bolsheviks as an undesirable legacy of the past that was both politically harmful (because it exploited the apprentices and socialized them in old values) and technologically obsolete (because mechanization would supersede craftsmanship). In the 1920s the Soviet Taylorist Gastev relentlessly attacked the "miserable private owners of craft secrets."[86] The removal of elders and the attack on craftsmen disrupted, at least partially, this traditional form of transmission of skills.

Many artels, deprived though they were of their elders and stripped of the transmission of skills and knowledge to the younger generations, survived "decapitated" or in disguise into the 1930s and influenced the way workers sought to protect their autonomy and security in production at a time when burning enthusiasm and immense privation lived side by side. It has yet to be carefully analyzed whether, as the contemporary press often reported, and contrary to their critics' claims, the egalitarian shock brigades actually attained high levels of labor productivity. If so, they, like some artels, may have reconciled the conflicting demands for equity and work motivation, whether their collective labor was based on collective security or on a noble "consciousness." Whatever the case, the attack on the egalitarian shock brigades launched in 1931 suggests that the Soviet political leadership came to consider them founded on an informal, grassroots collective security as much as on a misguided "consciousness."

Little information is available about what eventually became of the battered artels. No doubt, many survived in one form or another, particularly in areas where mechanization made little progress. What was proclaimed as socialist collective labor had much affinity with old artel labor, just as the new collective farm resembled the old village commune. The leap from modernity did not so much radically break with tradition as it continued to be influenced by it. However, the progress of mechanization and a series of productivity campaigns, particularly the individualistic Stakhanovite movement launched in 1935, almost certainly further isolated and undermined the foundations of the old artel traditions.[87]

The leap from tradition to modernity in Soviet industry sought to achieve overnight the same goal pursued by "advanced capitalist countries" over a much longer period: to maximize industrial efficiency. The leap was in fact even more ambitious: it was intended to "overtake and surpass the advanced capitalist countries," or to achieve supermodernity, as it were. Accordingly, the "scientific organization of labor," as Taylorism and Fordism were known in the Soviet Union, was carried to "super-Fordist" extremes.[88] Moreover, shock workers' "conscious" attitude toward production was optimistically assumed to supersede "capitalist" managerial supervision and differentiated incentive payments. In 1931, after much confusion, this assumption was largely abandoned; after 1931 and particularly after 1935, it gave way to the "capitalist" alternative, an alternative that appeared to Leon Trotsky and others as a betrayal of the revolution.

This analysis of the artel suggests two broad issues. First, despite their egalitarian and collectivist features, the artels appeared to the determined Bolshevik modernizers to be too traditional to fit their ideal of socialist labor. Their expedient use and emotional rejection of the artels was characteristic of their contradictory attitude toward NEP in general. Second, the eventual adoption of the "capitalist" alternative created new social hierarchies. Yet the adoption did not necessarily lead to its triumph over informal autonomy and collective security on the shop floor: even in the late 1930s and beyond, a complex web of informal relations persisted widely.[89] This phenomenon is usually attributed to the systemic problems of a centrally planned economy that relieved labor and management of the threat of unemployment and bankruptcy. It has yet to be examined in detail whether the old informal relations had survived to influence the new ones. If the artel did not exist in all industry, quasi-artel autonomy and collective security were widely observed on the shop floor during NEP.[90]

## NOTES

1. Russia's guilds had been created from above by Peter the Great in the eighteenth century. Unlike the Western European guilds, they "lacked the status of closed corporations and the exclusive authority over production and distribution"; their activities were "determined by state regulation, and they functioned under direct government supervision." Victoria E. Bonnell, *Roots of Rebellion: Workers' Politics and Organizations in St. Petersburg and Moscow, 1900–1914* (Berkeley and Los Angeles, 1983), p. 74. See also Reginald E. Zelnik, *Labor and Society in Tsarist Russia: The Factory Workers of St. Petersburg, 1855–1870* (Stanford, 1971), pp. 11–17.

2. See for the revolutionary period William G. Rosenberg, "Workers and Workers' Control in the Russian Revolution," *History Workshop*, 5 (Spring 1978), and his excellent case study "The Democratization of Russia's Railroads in 1917," *American Historical Review*, 1981, no. 5. The NEP period is a historiographical lacuna, but my study of the First Five-Year Plan period suggests that old craft hierarchies and sectarianisms persisted throughout NEP. See my *Stalin's Industrial Revolution: Politics and Workers, 1928–1932* (Cambridge, 1988), chap. 9.

3. See the case of Donbass coal miners' artels in *Sistema i organizatsiia*, 1925, no. 12, p. 31, and *Predpriiatie*, 1926, no. 6, pp. 31–32. Some artels consisted of as many as 70 to 80 members.

4 V. Maksimov (comp.), *Arteli birzhevye i trudovye* (Moscow, 1907), p. II.

5. S. Prokopovich, *Kooperativnoe dvizhenie v Rossii. Ego teoriia i praktika* (Moscow, 1913), p. 32.

6. Note, for example, that the word *artel* also became the standard term for Soviet collective farms. The word was widely applied to production or artisan artels (artels of cottage and handicraft workers), as well. These were cooperatives whose members jointly owned part or all of the equipment. Some of them worked in common workshops and sold the products of joint labor. After the revolution, these artels recovered their economic might much more quickly than the nationalized sector. They invited much suspicion because they owned capital and equipment.

7. K. A. Pazhitnov, *Iz istorii rabochikh artelei na Zapade i v Rossii. Ot utopistov do nashikh dnei* (Petrograd, 1924), p. 247.

8. As late as 1930, however, in Siberia the artel principle of labor was said to exist "in almost all factories (mining, glass, metalworking, and others)." *Za industrializatsiiu Sibiri*, 1930, no. 1, p. 12.

9. *Ugol' i zhelezo*, no. 29 (February 1928), p. 63, and *Ratsionalizatsiia promyshlennosti SSSR. Rabota komissii prezidiuma VSNKh SSSR* (Moscow-Leningrad, 1928), p. 344. In 1928, 63 percent of gold mining was done by the gold diggers' artels. *VI Vsesoiuznyi s"ezd gornorabochikh SSSR. Sten. otchet* (Moscow, 1928), p. 170.

10. For this law, see M. Bukhov and A. Lipets, *Trudovye arteli. Posobie po primeneniiu dekreta VTsIK i SNK ot 15 dekabria 1924 g.* (Moscow, 1926), and N. G. Berdichevskii, *Trudovye arteli. Prakticheskii postateinyi kommentarii k postanovleniiu VTsIK i SNK ot 15 dekabria 1924 goda o trudovykh arteliakh* (Moscow, 1925).

11. Iu. Milonov (ed.), *Rukovoditel' po Vserossiiskim s"ezdam i konferentsiiam professional'nykh soiuzov* (Moscow, 1924), pp. 171, 235–37, 436, 499, 544; M. Tomskii, *Izbrannye stat'i i rechi, 1917–1927* (Moscow, 1926), pp. 70, 213; and *V Vsesoiuznyi s"ezd gornorabochikh SSSR. Sten. otchet* (Moscow, 1926), p. 514.

12. *Vestnik truda*, 1927, no. 5, p. 26. See also *VII s"ezdu stroitelei. Otchet Ts.K. VSSR za 1926 i 1927 gg.* (Moscow, 1928), p. 52.

13. *Sobranie uzakonenii i rasporiazhenii Rabochego i Krest'ianskogo pravitel'stva RSFSR*, 1922, no. 70, art 903, clauses 29, 30, 33, 35.

14. Bukhov and Lipets, *Trudovye arteli*, p. 65.

15. *Sobranie uzakonenii i rasporiazhenii*, 1922, no. 70, art 903, clause 35. See also *Voprosy truda*, 1926, nos. 5–6, p. 107, discussing this issue.

16. Collective agreements tended to ignore artels, and how artels related to management and trade unions is unclear from reading them alone. See, for instance, *Kollektivnyi dogovor zakliuchennyi mezhdu Vseukrainskim Komitetom Soiuza Gornorabochikh—s odnoi storony i Pravleniem "Iugostali"—s drugoi s 1-go iiulia po 1-e oktiabria 1925 goda* (n.p., n.d.).

17. Robert E. Goffee, "The Butty System and the Kent Coalfield," *Society for the Study of Labour History Bulletin*, no. 34 (Spring 1977); and S. H. F. Hickey, *Workers in Imperial Germany: The Miners of the Ruhr* (Oxford, 1985), pp. 114 and 164.

18. *Vestnik Donuglia*, no. 1 (1 December 1926), p. 11. See also *Izvestiia Severo-Kavkazskogo kraikoma VKP(b)*, 1928, no. 3 (37), p. 4.

19. *Inzhenernyi rabotnik*, 1924, nos. 1–2, p. 66.

20. *Predpriiatie*, 1926, no. 6, pp. 31–32.

21. *Ugol' i zhelezo*, no. 26 (November 1927), pp. 73–74. After the revolution, workers were classified into skill ranks.

22. A. Perovskii, *Velikii perelom. Ot shakhtinskogo dela do udarnykh brigad* (Moscow, 1930), p. 32.

23. See, for example, N. Davydov and A. Ponomarev, *Velikii podvig. Bor'ba moskovskikh bol'shevikov za osushchestvlenie leninskogo plana sotsialisticheskoi industrializatsii* (Moscow, 1970), p. 153.

24. *Profsoiuz energetikov. Kratkii istoricheskii ocherk* (Moscow, 1964), p. 56.

25. Ibid., for example.

26. *Informatsionnyi biulleten' Ts.K. Vsesoiuznogo profsoiuza stroitel'nykh rabochikh*, 1927, no. 7 (23) (15 April 1927), pp. 17–18.

27. See G. I. Lifshits, *Usloviia truda stroitelei po novomu zakonu. S predisloviem zam. zav. OTE TsK stroitelei tov. G. A. Glozshteina* (Moscow, 1928), pp. 44–45; and A. F. Liakh, *Zakonodatel'stvo o trude na sezonnykh rabotakh. Prakticheskii kommentarii* (Moscow, 1928), pp. 64, 78–79.

28. *Rezoliutsiia II Vsesoiuznogo tarifno-ekonomicheskogo soveshchaniia VSSR s 10-go po 14-oe fevralia 1928 g.* (Moscow, 1928), p. 10; and *Postanovleniia i direktivy Komissii po stroitel'stvu pri Sovete Truda i Oborony. Sbornik 2* (Moscow, 1929), p. 28.

29. Resolution of 24 May 1928 by the All-Union Central Council of Trade Unions in *Trud*, 26 May 1928. See also *Spravochnik po voprosam soiuznoi raboty dlia rabochikh komitetov VSSR* (Moscow, 1929), pp. 161–62.

30. See, for example, G. F. Dakhshleiger, *Turksib—pervenets sotsialisticheskoi industrializatsii. Ocherki istorii postroiki Turksiba* (Alma Ata, 1953), p. 77.

31. *Pravda*, 28 August 1929.

32. Perovskii, *Velikii perelom*, p. 32; and P. B. Zil'bergleit, *Proizvoditel'nost' truda v kamennougol'noi promyshlennosti* (Kharkov, 1930). p. 39.

33. Zelnik, *Labor and Society in Tsarist Russia*, pp. 20–21.

34. N. F. Aristov, *Sezonnye raboty i trud sezonnykh rabochikh s obzorom deistvuiushchego zakonodatel'stva o trude sezonnykh rabochikh i kharakteristikoi proekta novogo zakona ob usloviiakh truda na sezonnykh rabotakh* (Moscow, 1926), p. 57. Because the Labor Commissariat organizations were weak in the provinces, artels were used widely as a means of recruitment of workers (construction workers in particular). *Dneprostroi*, 1927, no. 1, p. 158; *Trudy vtorogo Vsesoiuznogo soveshchaniia po stroitel'stvu i stroitel'nym materialam, 25–27-go marta 1929 g.* (Moscow, 1929), pp. 112–13; *Khoziaistvo Urala*, 1928, no. 7, p. 113; N. N. Vladimirskii, *Otkhod krest'ianskogo naseleniia kostromskoi gubernii na zarabotki* (Kostroma, 1927), p. 175, etc.

35. See, for example, Aristov, *Sezonnye raboty i trud sezonnykh rabochikh,* p. 36.
36. *Ustanovki rabochei sily,* 1927, nos. 3–4, p. 73. For Gastev, see Kendall E. Bailes, "Alexei Gastev and the Soviet Controversy over Taylorism, 1918–1924," *Soviet Studies,* 31, no. 3 (July 1979); and Zenovia A. Sochor, "Soviet Taylorism Revisited," ibid., 33, no. 2 (April 1981).
37. Pazhitnov, *Iz istorii rabochikh artelei na Zapade i v Rossii,* p. 186. See also idem, "Rabochie arteli," in *Arkhiv istorii truda v Rossii,* kn. 10 (1923), 65.
38. *Vestnik Donuglia,* no. 1 (1 December 1926), p. 11.
39. A. D. Ratner and V. P. Renke, *Kamennougol'naia i antratsitovaia promyshlennost' Donetskogo basseina. Obzor sovremennogo sostoianiia* (Kharkov, 1928), p. 21.
40. *Ugol' i zhelezo,* no. 26 (November 1927), p. 73.
41. *Vestnik Donuglia,* no. 1 (1 December 1926), p. 11.
42. Ibid., and *Sistema i organizatsiia,* 1925, no. 2, p. 32.
43. *Rezoliutsii II Vsesoiuznogo tarifno-ekonomicheskogo soveshchaniia VSSR,* p. 10, and *Spravochnik profrabotnika-stroitelia po voprosam tarifnym, ekonomicheskim, okhrany truda i sotsial'nogo strakhovaniia* (Moscow, 1928), p. 45.
44. See the case of the Stalingrad Tractor Plant construction project in Iurii Tepliakov, *Operatsiiu nachnem na rassvete . . . ,* 2nd ed. (Moscow, 1984), p. 23.
45. See, for example, N. A. Filimonov, *Vstrechi v puti. Vospominaniia* (Moscow, 1963), p. 24.
46. *Inzhenernyi rabotnik,* 1930, no. 10, p. 21.
47. For the Soviet scientific organization of labor in the 1920s and 1930s, see Melanie Tatur, *"Wissenschaftliche Arbeitsorganisation." Arbeitswissenschaften und Arbeitsorganisation in der Sowjetunion 1921–1935* (Wiesbaden, 1979).
48. F. W. Taylor, *Scientific Management, Comprising Shop Management, the Principles of Scientific Management, and Testimony before the Special House Committee* (New York, 1947), pp. 72–73.
49. Zil'bergleit, *Proizvoditel'nost' truda v kamennougol'noi promyshlennosti,* p. 80, and *Partiinoe rukovodstvo povysheniem tvorcheskoi aktivnosti trudiashchikhsia Sibiri v period stroitel'stva sotsializma i kommunizma* (Moscow, 1983), p. 49.
50. *Sistema i organizatsiia,* 1925, no. 12, pp. 30, 32; *IV plenum TsKK sozyva XIV s"ezda VKP(b), 21–22 oktiabria 1926 g.* (Moscow, 1926), p. 110; *Ocherednye problemy truda. Trudy I Vsesoiuznogo s"ezda otdelov ekonomiki truda i T.N.B. trestov i zavedenii* (Moscow-Leningrad, 1927), pp. 272, 344; *Vestnik Donuglia,* no. 22 (15 October 1927), pp. 8–11; no. 26 (15 December 1927), pp. 16–18.
51. *V Vsesoiuznyi s"ezd gornorabochikh SSSR,* p. 448. See also A. I. Segal', *Besedy po gornoi ekonomike. Ugol', neft', zhelezo, marganets* (Moscow-Leningrad, 1927), p. 273, and *Resheniia II plenuma Tsentral'nogo Komiteta Soiuza gornorabochikh SSSR shestogo sozyva (20–26 sentiabria 1928 goda)* (Moscow, 1928), pp. 26, 83, 150.
52. *Vestnik Soiuzuglia,* nos. 24–25 (99–100) (10 October 1930), p. 16.
53. *Ustanovki rabochei sily,* 1929, nos. 5–6, p. 17. See for an example of functional labor in construction *Organizatsiia truda,* 1930, no. 4, pp. 9–36.
54. *Trudy vtorogo Vsesoiuznogo soveshchaniia po stroitel'stvu i stroitel'nym materialam,* p. 130. For the dissolution of artels on the Dnepro Hydroelectric Dam construction site, see Anne D. Rassweiler, "Soviet Labor Policy in the First Five-Year Plan: The Dneprostroi Experience," *Slavic Review,* vol. 42, no. 2 (Summer 1983), p. 239.
55. *Sistema i organizatsiia,* 1925, no. 12, p. 32. See also *Predpriiatie,* 1926, no. 3, p. 81, and *Sistema i organizatsiia,* 1927, no. 4, p. 9.
56. *Vestnik Donuglia,* no. 64 (15 July 1929), p. 13.
57. *Inzhenernyi rabotnik,* 1929, nos. 11–12, p. 127; 1930, no. 10, pp. 17–26; and *Ugol' i zhelezo,* no. 22 (July 1927), p. 13.

58. *Piatyi Vsesoiuznyi s"ezd inzhenerno-tekhnicheskoi sektsii soiuza gornorabochikh SSSR, 3–9 aprelia 1928 g. Sokrashchennyi sten. otchet* (Moscow, 1928), p. 197; *Ugol' i zhelezo*, no. 29 (February 1928), p. 64; *Inzhenernyi rabotnik*, 1929, nos. 11–12, pp. 123–28; *Vestnik Soiuzuglia*, no. 1 (101), 10 October 1930, pp. 18–19. See also Petrovskii, *Velikii perelom*, p. 32. In September 1930 the highest industrial authority responsible for the coal-mining industry, the association Coal, issued an order to organize "production artels." *Za industrializatsiiu*, 20 September 1930.

59. *Vestnik Donuglia*, no. 64 (15 July 1929), p. 13; and *Pravda*, 5 October 1930. Experienced miners concerned with the underground order were reported to be willing to enter the artels still in existence. *Inzhenernyi rabotnik*, 1930, no. 10, p. 22.

60. *VIII s"ezd professional'nykh soiuzov SSSR, 10–24 dekabria 1928 g. Plenumy i sektsii. Polnyi sten. otchet* (Moscow, 1929), pp. 522 and 566. In Leningrad, as industrial modernization progressed in the late 1920s, collective, "artel" work increased in some factories but decreased in others. See *Zavershenie vosstanovleniia promyshlennosti i nachala industrializatsii Severo-Zapadnogo raiona (1925–1928 gg.)* (Leningrad, 1964), p. 342.

61. *Ustanovki rabochei sily*, 1929, nos. 11–12, p. 6. Unlike functional construction labor, which was still predominantly manual, functional textile labor was believed to be already controlled and regulated by the speed of the machine itself.

62. See Hiroaki Kuromiya, "The Crisis of Proletarian Identity in the Soviet Factory, 1928–1929," *Slavic Review*, vol. 44, no. 2 (Summer 1985).

63. Gastev, in introducing a functional organization of textile labor, placed this assumption on a technological basis. See *Ustanovki rabochei sily*, 1929, nos. 11–12 (November–December), pp. 6–7.

64. See, for example, *Trud*, 16 November 1929. In the Donbass and the Urals, this "autonomy" was characterized as "production syndicalism." Ibid., and *Partiinoe stroitel'stvo*, 1929, no. 2 (December), p. 19.

65. *Statistika i narodnoe khoziaistvo*, vyp. 4–5 (1930), p. 11. For a slightly higher figure (62.1 percent), see *Na fronte industrializatsii*, 1930, no. 11 (7 June), p. 9.

66. *Liudi stalingradskogo traktornogo*, 2nd ed. (Moscow, 1934), p. 195.

67. *VI Vsesoiuznaia konferentsiia VLKSM, 17–24 iiunia 1929 g. Sten. otchet* (Moscow, 1929), p. 459.

68. *Na fronte industrializatsii*, 1930, no. 6 (31 March), p. 61; 1931, nos. 13–14 (31 July), p. 5; nos. 15–16, pp. 42–43; *Koldogovor tret'ego goda piatiletki* (Leningrad, 1931), p. 12. For the egalitarian communes, see Lewis H. Siegelbaum, "Production Collectives and Communes and the 'Imperatives' of Soviet Industrialization, 1929–1931," *Slavic Review*, vol. 45, no. 1 (Spring 1986).

69. In 1930 in the Donbass coal mines, for example, old artels were said to have reemerged "under the guise of communes." *Na novom etape sotsialisticheskogo stroitel'stva. Sbornik statei* (Moscow, 1930), vol. 2, p. 224.

70. For example, see the case of Leningrad in *Partiinyi rabotnik*, 1930, nos. 19–20 (July–August), p. 46; 1931, no. 2 (January), p. 121. This phenomenon invites an important but difficult question concerning the interaction of artel and nonartel workers on the shop floor during the NEP period. It appears that artel workers tended to be looked down upon by those nonartel workers concerned with party and trade-union politics, while they were envied by those who received little assistance from the party and union organizations. In the Donbass, during NEP young miners organized "youth artels" to promote their particular interests in work. See, for example, M. I. Horlach, "Rozvytok tvorchovoi initsiatyvy robitnychoho klasu Ukrainy v period nastupu sotsializmu po vs'omu frontu," *Ukrains'kyi istorychnyi zhurnal*, 1961, no. 5, p. 67.

71. See Kuromiya, *Stalin's Industrial Revolution,* chap. 10.

72. *Voprosy truda,* 1932, no. 2, p. 3. For a similar assertion, see also V. Andrle, "How Backward Workers Became Soviet: Industrialization of Labor and the Politics of Efficiency under the Second Five Year Plan, 1933–1937," *Social History,* vol. 10, no. 2 (May 1985), p. 158.

73. *Nashe stroitel'stvo,* 1931, no. 15 (August), p. 612; *Pravda,* 1 May 1932; *Voprosy truda,* 1933, no. 7, pp. 46–55; *3 sessiia TsIK Soiuza SSR 6 sozyva. Sten. otchet,* 23–30 January 1933 (Moscow, 1933), bulletin 3, p. 31; *Nashe stroitel'stvo,* 1935, no. 7 (April), p. 29. In 1931 the legal category of labor artels was abolished and reincorporated into the category of production artels to tighten central control over them. *Sobranie uzakonenii i rasporiazhenii,* 1931, no. 9, st. 115. *Vestnik promyslovoi kooperatsii,* 1931, no. 3, pp. 21–23; no. 4, pp. 40–42. Presumably those labor artels which possessed no capital or equipment became "ordinary" artels.

74. See, for example, *Partiinoe stroitel'stvo,* 1931, nos. 9–10 (May), p. 44.

75. See, for example, *Profsoiuz energetikov,* p. 56; M. E. Raikher and L. A. Satanovskii, *Planovoe ispol'zovanie rabochei sily na shakhtakh Donbassa* (Moscow, 1930), p. 22; *Vestnik Donuglia,* no. 66 (15 August 1929), pp. 28–30; *Partiinoe stroitel'stvo,* 1931, no. 8 (April), p. 47.

76. *Za industrializatsiiu Sibiri,* 1930, no. 1 (4), p. 41.

77. *Planovoe khoziaistvo,* 1934, nos. 8–9, p. 52. Two years later, still only 20 percent of excavations were mechanized. *Sovetskie arkhivy,* 1967, no. 2, p. 44.

78. *Sotsialisticheskoe stroitel'stvo Soiuza SSR (1933–1938 gg.). Statisticheskii sbornik* (Moscow-Leningrad, 1939), p. 48. The corresponding figures for the U.S. were 78.4 in 1929 and 84.2 in 1935. *Proizvoditel'nost' truda v promyshlennosti SSSR* (Moscow-Leningrad, 1940), p. 134.

79. See, for example, *Sovetskaia Sibir',* 18 September 1932, concerning the Kuzbass coal mines.

80. *Pravda,* 21 April 1933, and N. Izotov, *Moia zhizn'—moia rabota* (Kharkov, 1934).

81. See *KPSS v rezoliutsiiakh i resheniiakh s"ezdov, konferentsii i plenumov TsK,* 8th ed., vol. 5 (Moscow, 1971), pp. 91–97.

82. See, for example, *Trud,* 29 March 1934.

83. V. Zaitsev, *Perspektivy iunosheskogo truda v svete piatiletnego plana razvitiia narodnogo khoziaistva* (Moscow-Leningrad, 1928), p. 161; V. P. Danilov, "Krest'ianskii otkhod na promysly v 1920-kh godakh," *Istoricheskie zapiski,* t. 94 (1974), p. 90; and *Inzhenernyi rabotnik,* 1930, no. 10, p. 27.

84. For this type of skilled workers, see *Komsomol'skaia pravda,* 21 March 1929, about a fitter in Leningrad, and M. Dubrov, *Pervaia udarnaia* (Leningrad, 1960), pp. 15–16, about an assistant foreman in a textile factory. See also V. Turov, *Na shturm uglia* (Moscow, 1931), p. 46, for senior miners who refused to teach their juniors mining skills.

85. *Organizatsiia truda,* 1930, no. 4 (October–December), p. 14.

86. See, for example, Aleksei Gastev, *Trudovye ustanovki* (Moscow, 1973), pp. 214, 287–88; and idem, *Kak nado rabotat',* 2nd ed. (Moscow, 1972), pp. 176–77. See also Kuromiya, "The Crisis of Proletarian Identity in the Soviet Factory," p. 292.

87. See Gastev's remark about miners' artels in *Organizatsiia truda,* 1934, no. 9 (November), p. 3; and his associate's in ibid., 1935, no. 11 (November), pp. 8–9.

88. The phrase "super-Fordism" is used in *Voprosy profdvizheniia,* 1935, nos. 5–6, p. 58.

89. See Joseph Berliner, *Factory and Manager in the USSR* (Cambridge, Mass., 1957), and Donald Filtzer, *Soviet Workers and Stalinist Industrialization: The Formation of Modern Soviet Production Relations, 1928–1941* (New York, 1986.)

90. In the mid-1920s artel labor was said to exist in the majority of metalworking factories (*Predpriiatie*, 1925, no. 5, p. 31). Even in the 1930s, so-called worker dynasties, close-knit gangs of workers operating independently of management, were observed in the electric and engineering industries. See the Semenovs, a dynasty of fitters in the Moscow Electric Factory (formerly Morze), in S. A. Antonov, *Svet ne v okne* (Moscow, 1977), pp. 87–91, and the Terentievs, a locomotive dynasty in the Kharkov Locomotive Plant, in Lev Kopelev, *The Education of a True Believer*, trans. from the Russian by Gary Kern (New York, 1980), pp. 201–202.

# VI

# PRIVATE TRADE AND TRADERS DURING NEP

## *Alan Ball*

The surge of private trade loosed in Soviet Russia by the New Economic Policy (NEP) amazed observers from one end of the political spectrum to the other. To some, the new wave of trade seemed a considerable improvement over the shortages and black market of War Communism. A few, including the American industrialist Armand Hammer, approached euphoria.

> Its [NEP's] immediate effect was to bring forth untold quantities of goods of every variety which suddenly appeared as if by magic. The shelves of stores formerly empty were overloaded with articles which had not been seen since the days of the Bolshevik revolution four years before. In addition to a great variety of food products and delicacies, one could buy the choicest French wines, liqueurs and the best of Havana cigars. The finest English cloth lay side by side with the most expensive French perfumes. It took the magic of the NEP to bring forth these goods from their hiding places in cellars, barns and secret hoards.[1]

The entrepreneurial revival also struck a young Bolshevik, though for different reasons.

> This policy [NEP] very soon showed its fruits in improved conditions of living. Food was better and more plentiful; the standards of production rose everywhere; there was, throughout the country, an undeniable sense of lessened tension. But money had reappeared; money was once more becoming the touchstone of social life. We young Communists had all grown up in the belief that money was done away with once and for all. . . .
>    If money was reappearing, wouldn't rich people reappear too? Weren't we on the slippery slope that led back to capitalism? We put these questions to ourselves with feelings of anxiety.[2]

For better or for worse, then, trade quickly became the most important of NEP's newly permitted occupations. Nor was it difficult to understand why. For one thing, petty trade required very little business experience and capital. Also, small-scale merchants enjoyed far greater mobility than, say, manufacturers and thus avoided more adroitly the brunt of state supervision and control. Finally, trade promised rapid return on investment—a common concern when long-term business prospects seemed most uncertain.[3]

During the early months of NEP, nearly all private trade took the form of petty transactions in the streets and market squares, hardly more sophisticated than the illegal peddling characteristic of War Communism.[4] People of all backgrounds—factory workers, intellectuals, demobilized soldiers, prewar merchants, artisans, invalids, peasants, and a large number of housewives—plunged into trade, often simply the barter of personal possessions.[5] Some, driven by acute shortages of food and clothing, sought mere survival, others an opportunity to profit from the demand for very scarce necessities.

Many petty traders of this sort worked irregularly, on time off from other occupations, traveling now and then to rural markets to barter with peasants for food. Given the inability of the state's distribution apparatus to supply the urban population with food at the beginning of NEP (and during War Communism), this type of trade, called "bagging" (meshochnichestvo), proved essential to urban residents. Bagging's small-scale itinerant nature, impossible for the fledgling government to monitor, ensured that few statistics on its extent exist. Nevertheless, many observers reported crowds of bagmen clogging trains to and from food-producing regions. They engulfed some trains so completely that no space remained even on the sides and roofs of cars. According to one source, over 200,000 bagmen flooded the rails in the Ukraine alone by the spring of 1921.[6]

Thus at the beginning of NEP virtually no private trade occured in large, permanent shops. In the wake of the preceding years' turmoil and destruction, relatively few individuals possessed the resources and experience necessary for such activity. Even more important, the uncertainty surrounding NEP itself left no one confident what sorts of private trade would now be tolerated. Initially, in the spring of 1921, the state had hoped to restrict private trade to local barter and only grudgingly relaxed the legal limits in the months thereafter. Furthermore, with the harsh experience of War Communism a very recent memory, potential traders found it difficult to control their skepticism and assume that NEP had indeed been adopted, as Lenin claimed, "seriously and for a long time." Restrained by such concerns, individuals capable of conducting large-scale trade generally did not rush to test the waters.[7]

However, as entrepreneurs gradually became convinced of War Communism's death during the course of 1922, the number of permanent private shops began to increase.[8] Some traders, still quite reluctant to thrust themselves out prominently into the new atmosphere of NEP, gave their businesses official, "Soviet" names such as Snabprodukt and tried to operate as discreetly as possible. It often took some time for them to acquire enough confidence to dispense with camouflage and conduct business more openly under their own names.[9]

Here and there, people in the state apparatus itself—especially economic agencies—began to take advantage of opportunities offered by the new business climate to move into private trading. Indeed, it was not unheard of at the beginning of NEP for a private trader to have a second "full-time" job in a government enterprise. The state trading agency Gostorg, for instance, employed a number of people who simultaneously operated private businesses well stocked with Gostorg's wares.[10] The temptation to take advantage of official access to scarce consumer goods overcame many government employees. With virtually all essential products in short supply following War Communism, occasions for profitable resale of these items could scarcely elude even the dimmest or most cautious operator.

Some of the very first sizable private stores opened during NEP were owned by former state employees who had used their official positions to acquire the goods they then sold on their own. Others remained in state service, registering their shops under someone else's name and then supplying the stores with products they controlled as government officials. An individual might also launch a private business counting on merchandise supplied by relatives holding jobs in the "socialist" (state and cooperative) sector. In 1922, for example, an agent of Gostorg at the Nizhnii Novgorod fair delivered supplies at low prices to the private firm Transtorg, whose director happened to be his brother. Nor did the ties between the two enterprises end there. A member of the board of directors of Transtorg also headed a division of Gostorg, and the founder of Transtorg served simultaneously as an agent for Gostorg—at the time, quite legally.[11]

Very few members of the prerevolutionary business elite—millionaire merchants, financiers, and industrial magnates—surfaced again in NEP's commercial arena. Nearly all these people lost or closed their businesses, emigrated, or perished during the onslaughts of the revolution and Civil War. A handful, however, landed on their feet when the whirlwind subsided at the beginning of the 1920s and exploited nimbly—at least for a time—the openings presented by NEP. Semen Pliatskii was one of these survivors. He had been a wealthy metal trader in St. Petersburg and elected to remain in Russia after the revolution to ride out the storm working for the state. Surviving two arrests by the Cheka during War Communism, he set out on his own following the introduction of NEP, profiting from transactions in a wide variety of wares. His many connections with state agencies, often established with bribes, enabled him to obtain even the scarcest commodities and soon amass another fortune.[12] But the ranks of the "new bourgeoisie" contained very few merchants who had occupied the upper reaches of the prewar business world. In the 1920s, nearly all the private traders with prerevolutionary business experience had toiled as small-scale entrepreneurs or shop employees prior to 1917.[13]

During NEP, certain regions of the country, most notably Belorussia and the Ukraine, contained unusually high concentrations of private traders with prerevolutionary business experience. Much of the explanation lies in the relatively large number of Jewish entrepreneurs in these areas—the old Jewish Pale. Approximately 60 percent of the Soviet Jewish population lived in the Ukraine and 17 percent in much smaller Belorussia. Thus, while only 1.8 percent of the Soviet Union's people were Jewish, Jews represented 5.4 and 8.2 percent respectively of the Ukrainian and Belorussian populations in 1927.[14] An unusually high percentage of Soviet Jews, compared to most of the other groups making up the country's population, had traditionally been traders and artisans. According to the census of 1897, for example, 31 percent of all "economically active" Jews were shopkeepers, hawkers, peddlers, and the like, with an additional 36 percent in "industry," mainly handicrafts (which often involved trading as well as producing).[15] The central point here is that, following the introduction of NEP, many Jews returned to these activities or emerged from the black market to practice them openly—thus helping to explain why private traders in Belorussia and the Ukraine in the 1920s were much more likely to have had prerevolutionary business experience than were merchants in the Russian Republic.[16]

As part of its effort to license and tax private traders, the state divided them into ranks according to the nature and size of their businesses. By the summer of 1921, only three rather broad trade ranks had been designated, but as the quantity and diversity of private traders increased, so too did the number of ranks. Two more were added in 1922, and all five ranks were redefined in greater detail the following year.[17] Much of the data available on private trade is expressed in terms of these ranks, making a brief definition of each essential before proceeding. Based on the decree of 1922, the activities assigned to the various ranks may be summarized as follows:

Rank I:    Trade (generally in market squares, in bazaars, or along streets) by an individual selling goods carried in his or her hands, a sack, a hawker's tray, etc.

Rank II:   Trade by an individual, or with help from one family member or hired worker, conducted from temporary facilities (stalls, tables, carts, etc.) at markets and bazaars; or trade by no more than two people from small permanent facilities (such as a kiosk) which the customer does not enter.

Rank III: Retail trade, by the owner of the business and no more than four hired workers or family members, conducted from a modest permanent shop designed for the customer to enter.

Rank IV: (a) Partial wholesale trade *(poluoptovaia torgovlia)*, i.e., the sale of small lots of goods (worth up to 300 rubles) from enterprises with no more than ten workers.
(b) Retail trade from permanent stores employing five to twenty workers or family members.

Rank V: (a) Wholesale trade.
(b) Partial wholesale trade by businesses with more than ten workers.
(c) Retail trade from large stores with more than twenty workers.

From 1922 through 1926, the distribution of entrepreneurs in the various trade ranks assumed the following proportions. Half of all licensed private traders belonged to rank II, numbering between 180,000 and 260,000 individuals, depending on the year and the season. Rank III traders held approximately one-quarter (90,000–140,000) of all private licenses, and slightly over one-fifth (70,000–120,000) belonged to rank I vendors. The remaining 3 or 4 percent were issued mainly to merchants in the fourth rank (8,000–18,000), with rank V private traders accounting for less than 1 percent (1,600–4,000) of the total during these years.[18] Thus, over 70 percent of all licensed private traders—ranks I and II—did not operate from facilities large enough for the customer to enter, but traded mainly in the streets, market squares, and bazaars, either from booths or stalls or out in the open. Since many small-scale traders avoided registration, their actual preponderance undoubtedly exceeded the figures presented.[19]

As one might expect, the larger the scale of a merchant's operation (i.e., the higher its rank), the more likely he or she was to have engaged in trade before NEP. The data in table 1 on the earlier occupations of private traders, collected by the Commissariat of Domestic Trade in 1927, underscore the dominance of experienced traders in the upper ranks.[20] At the other end of the scale, in ranks I and II, one is hardly surprised to find concentrated those vendors with little or no previous business experience, most often peasants, workers, and housewives.

The numerical predominance of small-scale trade stemmed from many factors. Even in the relatively prosperous middle years of NEP, most entrepreneurs found it impossible to raise the capital necessary for a large wholesale or retail firm. On the other hand, the expenses of modest vendors were minimal, because they did not have to maintain large inventories, permanent stores, or numerous employees. They also confronted the lowest tax brackets for private traders. Furthermore, petty

**TABLE 1**

Previous Occupations of Private Traders

| | Traders, store employees | Peasants | Workers | Handi-craftsmen | Office workers | House-wives | Other |
|---|---|---|---|---|---|---|---|
| Rank I | 20% | 31% | 10% | 4% | 5% | 18% | 12% |
| Rank II | 38% | 27% | 9% | 5% | 6% | 7% | 8% |
| Rank III | 59% | 15% | 5% | 6% | 5% | 2% | 8% |
| Rank IV | 67% | 6% | 3% | 3% | 6% | 1% | 14% |
| Rank V | 78% | 4% | 1% | 2% | 6% | 1% | 8% |

traders could avoid the attention of state tax officials, the police, and other inspectors more easily than could the proprietors of larger, permanent enterprises. These advantages became virtual necessities during the last years of NEP, when the state stepped up its campaign to "liquidate the Nepmen."

Still, the lopsided preponderance of licenses in ranks I and II should not suggest a role of insignificance for the upper ranks. The permanent shops in rank III conducted sales worth roughly twice those of rank II merchants in the open markets, according to data for the period 1923–26, despite the fact that rank II contained twice as many licensed traders as rank III. More striking still, entrepreneurs in ranks IV and V, who, taken together, numbered no more than 8 percent of the private traders in rank II, sold more goods than did these rank II vendors (from 16 to 77 percent more in the various six-month segments of the period).[21] Obviously, then, in the middle years of NEP the large permanent shops in the upper trade ranks balanced their numerical minority with an impressive sales volume.

The significance of private trade appears vividly in data gathered by various state agencies during NEP. Estimates place the private share of retail sales in 1922 at over 80 percent, and private retailers doubtless dominated the market just as completely the previous year, given the utter inadequacy of the state's distribution system following the Civil War. Even as late as 1926, by which point the state had been building up its own retail network for several years, the private share of total retail sales hovered around 40 percent (higher yet if illegal and unlicensed sales could be included).[22] The core of the Soviet state—government employees and the proletariat—made 36 to 40 percent of their purchases from private entrepreneurs, according to household budget studies conducted throughout the country in 1925 and 1926. A similar study in Kiev revealed that as late as 1928/29 these people obtained 44 percent of their food from private traders (51 percent in 1927/28).[23] Even in Moscow, where state and cooperative shops were comparatively numerous and well stocked, private merchants accounted for over half the volume of consumer goods sold in 1925.[24]

The Soviet urban population in general depended heavily on private entrepreneurs for many necessities. In the marketing of manufactured consumer goods, for instance, private retailers maintained a prominent position as purveyors of haberdashery, textiles, common hardware and other metal products, and leather goods. Urban merchants around the country frequently conducted at least half the sales of these items, and out in provincial towns their market share sometimes exceeded 90 percent.[25] The private share of food sales assumed even greater importance for urban consumers. Muscovites, for example, bought approximately 70 percent of their bread from private traders in 1924, and the figure at the beginning of NEP must have been higher still. Reports from various regions indicate that private merchants most commonly dominated the trade of dairy products, eggs, meat, fruits, and vegetables, often accounting for 80 percent or more of total retail sales even toward the end of the decade.[26]

Private vendors also played an important role out in the countryside, though the goods they sold to peasants naturally differed somewhat from the items most in demand in cities. According to data collected by the Central Statistical Bureau for the middle of NEP, slightly less than 60 percent of the manufactured goods (such as agricultural and construction tools, clothing, footwear, dishes, soap, and processed food products) bought by peasants were sold to them by private traders. Other studies of purchases made by peasants on shopping trips in local bazaars and larger cities and towns in the period 1925–27 support the Central Statistical Bureau's data.[27] All of this alarmed the Bolsheviks, given the importance they attached to forming an alliance *(smychka)* with the peasantry and driving private entrepreneurs out of the countryside. The peasantry seemed as inclined to form a *smychka* with private traders as with the proletariat.

Despite such concerns, Bolsheviks regarded the primary menace from private entrepreneurs to lie outside the realm of retail trade. Complaints and warnings in the press and at party meetings identified as a graver obstacle to socialism those individuals who purchased produce from the peasantry or acted as middlemen for state enterprises. In the countryside, the Bolsheviks had hoped to induce peasants to join cooperatives, through which the latter would market their produce and receive goods from the state. Relatively little progress took place on this front during NEP, however, and peasants remained an important source of goods for private traders. This held especially true at the beginning of the period (before consumer-goods industries had recovered from the devastation of the preceding years) and at the end (when the state tried to cut off the flow of its own manufactured goods to private merchants). Thus private buyers roamed the countryside in search of a wide variety of goods (ranging from grain, meat, vegetables, and eggs to hides, wool, and flax), which they then resold to other private entrepreneurs, to state agencies, or directly to consumers. The private procurement *(zagotovka)* of grain disturbed the party most of all. For one thing, bread was the staple of the population's diet. Just as important, the Bolsheviks' goal of industrialization required the government to secure a grain surplus—both to feed what would be a rapidly growing proletariat and to export for hard currency. The party found itself in the uncomfortable position of needing private entrepreneurs to help induce the peasantry to produce and market more grain, but fearing that private grain transactions would undermine the state's control of this vital sector of the economy.

Given the chaos plaguing the state's procurement efforts at the beginning of NEP, and the peasants' suspicion of state grain-collection campaigns in the wake of War Communism, the private share of the grain procurement must have been quite large early in the decade. During 1922/23 in Tambov province, for example, private buyers obtained over four times as much grain as state and cooperative procurement agencies combined, though the fragmentary information available for these early years does not permit confident estimates for the country as a whole.[28] The private percentage of grain procurement fell by the middle of NEP, but estimates continued to place it above negligible levels—roughly 30 percent in 1924/25, 20 percent in 1925/26, and 15 percent in 1926/27.[29] In 1924/25 Ukrainian peasants made approximately 40 percent of their grain sales to private middlemen, who accounted for over half the procurement in some regions of the country.[30]

Looking beyond grain, private traders in 1924/25 handled 40 to 50 percent of the procurement of all agricultural commodities taken together—30 to 40 percent in 1925/26, and in the neighborhood of 30 percent the next two years.[31] As shown in table 2, the private procurement share of many individual products far surpassed these averages.[32]

Part of the state's dilemma in confronting private purchases of this sort consisted in the fact that not only consumers but also some "socialist" agencies relied on them. According to one estimate, nearly half of all private traders' purchases in the countryside were resold to state and cooperative enterprises in 1926/27.[33] No one could be certain how much of the state's total procurement had passed first through the hands of private middlemen, especially since "socialist" procurement agents sometimes bought goods illegally—grain, for example—through the private procurement network.[34] Middlemen supplied roughly 40 percent of the state's procurement of hides and furs in 1925/26, and many other products followed similar paths to the "socialist" sector.[35] Considerable quantities were involved, and the government knew it.

**TABLE 2**

Percentage of Procurement Accounted for by Private Traders

|  | 1924/25 | 1925/26 |
|---|---|---|
| *Makhorka* | 30% | 20–40% |
| Hemp | 45% | 30–50% |
| Seeds (for oil) | 20% | 40–60% |
| Wool | no data | 50% |
| Hides | no data | 50% |
| Furs | 60% | 60% |
| Meat | no data | 67% |
| Flax | 9% | 3% |
| Cotton | 4% | 3% |
| Tobacco | 21% | 24% |
| Butter | 64% | 63% |
| Eggs | 54% | 61% |

The sizable role assumed by the private procurement network reflected in part the shortages of resources and buyers that plagued the "socialist" competition, especially in the first part of the decade.[36] But the main advantage enjoyed by private purchasers lay in their freedom to offer peasants higher prices than could state procurement agents, who were generally restricted by price ceilings. Private middlemen commonly outbid the state's buyers and still resold their acquisitions for a profit, relying on a demand that exceeded the supply of many farm products.[37]

Concern over this activity—especially private grain purchases—prompted the state in the second half of NEP to adopt a number of restrictive measures,[38] which helped reduce the private grain procurement share to the neighborhood of 15 percent by 1926/27. In the following years, however, the volume of grain marketed by peasants lagged farther behind demand, producing a larger gap between official prices and those offered by private buyers. As a result, the private portion of the grain procurement recovered to just under one-quarter by 1928/29.[39] The anxiety that this rally inspired in the party must be considered one of the factors that prompted Stalin and his allies to launch their momentous collectivization drive and ban the free trade of grain. The time had come, they concluded, to confront decisively the troubling state of affairs in the countryside which made it so difficult for the party to obtain a steady, reliable source of grain without having to pay free-market prices for it.[40]

State procurement agencies were not the only "socialist" operations to utilize the services of private middlemen. Many other government enterprises, thrust out into the marketplace during NEP and compelled to fend for themselves, had difficulty obtaining the products they needed. In such straits they frequently employed the services of private middlemen, at times to arrange deals with other state firms.[41] Data available for October 1922 indicate that nearly a third of state industry's purchases came from private suppliers (dropping to 11 percent in September of the following year). Even some state *stores* relied on private traders at the beginning of the decade for a portion of their merchandise.[42]

"Socialist" enterprises not only made purchases from private middlemen; they also sold to them. In some cases, desperation for cash to meet immediate needs prompted the transactions,[43] but not all state sales to private entrepreneurs reflected economic incompetence or crisis on the part of the state firm. Private traders as a rule operated more efficiently than the "socialist" retail system, and they could also charge higher prices to consumers than could their state and cooperative competitors. Consequently, private buyers often agreed to pay more (not to mention bribes) and accept harsher credit terms from state suppliers than could "socialist" enterprises in need of the same scarce goods. Many state officials, forced to navigate their factories and trusts profitably along the reefs of NEP, found it quite possible to overcome any ideological scruples they may have had concerning sales to the "new bourgeoisie." Although such sales occurred most frequently at the beginning of NEP, when the "socialist" retail network was rudimentary at best, they continued in later years as well. In 1926, the state salt syndicate announced its desire to sell to private traders 30 percent of the syndicate's output, precisely because private entrepreneurs could accept less credit and higher prices from the syndicate than could the cooperatives.[44]

Even when state and cooperative retail outlets functioned capably, their insufficient number served as another compelling reason for state suppliers to include private businessmen among their customers. Otherwise, goods simply would not reach a large portion of the market. Many officials in trusts, syndicates, and factories recognized this clearly. In the middle of NEP, for instance, the state sugar trust regarded it as essential to market 26 to 28 percent of its products through private traders, because of the inadequate development of the "socialist" trade network in the countryside. The division of the All-Russian Textile Syndicate headquartered in Rostov-on-Don stressed that early in NEP private traders were practically the *only* people available through whom textiles could reach consumers.[45]

Although chaotic bookkeeping and unrecorded shady transactions prevent a precise calculation of the volume of state goods that passed through the hands of private middlemen on the way to consumers or other state firms, the total was clearly very large. An extensive study of private capital in the USSR, prepared for the Supreme Council of the National Economy in 1927, estimated that close to half the output of state consumer-goods industry in the middle of NEP eventually reached the population through private traders.[46] Expressed in different terms, urban private traders received approximately 40 percent of their merchandise from state and cooperative factories, agencies, and stores in 1925/26—an estimate that fell to 33 percent in 1926/27, 25 percent in 1927/28, and 17 percent in 1928/29, as the state cracked down on the private sector.[47]

Beginning in the fiscal year 1926/27, the government mounted a campaign to restrict private trade, gradually at first, but with rapidly accelerating intensity from 1928 through the rest of the decade. Predictably, the number of private traders plunged, as the party had hoped.[48] However, this "elimination of the new bourgeoisie" took place more swiftly than the state planning agency (Gosplan) had anticipated and far exceeded the pace at which the "socialist" distribution system was growing.[49] By 1928 newspaper headlines such as "Private Entrepreneur Eliminated but Not Replaced" openly admitted as much.[50] "Trade deserts" *(torgovye pustyni)*, as Soviet correspondents dubbed them, dotted the countryside. Here, *no* "socialist" shops appeared to fill the void created by the retreating private sector. Peasants either had to do without or embark on shopping expeditions to neighboring towns. Even where state and cooperative stores existed, they frequently lacked desirable merchandise.[51] The alternative, available earlier in the decade, of purchasing a scarce item from a private trader—at a higher price, to be sure—proved increasingly difficult to exercise. Such supply and distribution breakdowns beleaguered the countryside most severely, but cities, too, witnessed worsening shortages and long lines. Moscow itself, far better supplied than provincial towns, did not escape the label "trade desert" in the Soviet press at the end of the 1920s.[52]

Not only did the drive to throttle private traders reduce their number; it also altered the nature of the remaining private sector. Virtually all operations able to survive the state's onslaught were very small-scale. Large, "permanent" private retail and wholesale operations, especially enterprises dependent on the state for much of their merchandise, found it impossible to escape the increasingly hostile attention of government officials. Private wholesale trade disappeared almost without a trace, for the proprietors of large firms could not pick up their businesses and elude a policeman or tax inspector in the manner of rank I and some rank II traders. Furthermore, taxes and fees levied on enterprises in the upper ranks soared far higher than those imposed on petty traders. In a nutshell, large businesses in permanent facilities were most visible, most obviously "capitalist," least mobile, and thus most vulnerable.[53]

Surviving private traders sometimes responded to higher taxes and more aggressive regulation by shifting their activities to the countryside, where it remained easier to avoid contact with state officials. Here such endeavors often resulted in the formation of so-called closed circles *(zamknutye krugi)*. Typically, private craftsmen would obtain raw materials from peasants (hides, clay, or hemp, for example), either directly or via private middlemen. They then sold their finished products to private traders, who retailed them to private customers. This, of course, was all quite primitive—recalling the "domestic system" prevalent in Europe prior to the Industrial Revolution. It represented a response to both increased taxes and regulation, on the one hand, and the state's reduction of supplies to the private sector, on the other. From 1927 to the end of the decade, these arrangements supported an ever larger share of private trade.[54]

The state's crackdown at the end of NEP also drove a larger percentage of remaining private traders outside the law. As taxes and harassment from local officials grew more onerous, survival for private entrepreneurs depended more often on an ability to conceal their activity. Some tried ruses, employed at times even in the middle of NEP, such as disguising their businesses as cooperatives.[55] But most traders who survived did so underground in the black market, or simply by selling goods without a license in the streets and running whenever the police approached.[56]

Thus private trade came full circle by the end of the decade. In 1918–20, it had been almost exclusively small-scale, unsophisticated, illegal (or barely tolerated) sales and barter, sometimes conducted by bagmen. Following the introduction of NEP, little changed immediately, except that this activity became less risky and attracted more people. Thereafter, the passage of months expanded the range of ventures permitted and convinced a wary population that NEP had indeed been adopted "seriously and for a long time." Responding to the new day, larger, permanent private shops opened their doors, and private traders continued to play an important role in supplying the population with essential products. As it turned out, the private sector reached its peak, in terms of the number of licensed traders and the volume of their sales, in 1926. Thereafter the environment changed, slowly at first, back in the direction of a climate bracing for Bolsheviks but bleak for merchants. By 1928 the campaign to "liquidate the Nepmen" recalled the War Communism years, in both its harshness and its results. Once again the state had elected to crack down on private entrepreneurs before it could fully replace them. The consequences, which appeared at once in the form of endless lines and "trade deserts," remain evident to this day and have spawned the Soviet Union's vast "second economy."

Mikhail Gorbachev's current efforts to resuscitate the Soviet economy feature numerous measures reminiscent of NEP, including the legalization of a wider range of private economic activity. Private undertakings—now usually constituted as "individual enterprises" and "cooperatives," thus avoiding ideologically unpalatable labels more freely applied in the 1920s, such as private, bourgeois, and capitalist—have already expanded the range of goods and services available to Soviet citizens. But they can hardly be regarded yet as a resounding success. Legal uncertainties, supply difficulties, hostile local officials, and even underworld extortion hamstring the operations of many. Furthermore, as letters to editors and recent public opinion surveys have emphasized, the high prices charged by numerous private operators have prompted a large portion of the citizenry to view them as speculators exploiting shortages to amass large profits. Some voices place partial blame for shortages themselves on private entrepreneurs, said to buy up raw materials and finished products for resale, thus preventing their appearance in state stores at lower prices. One did not have to strain during NEP to hear the same charges, expressed by many citizens without need of the encouragement they received nevertheless from official sources. In short, the view of private ventures widespread in the 1920s—better goods and better service, but at painful prices—remains common today.

Whether the parallel with NEP will extend to include a similarly short life span for Gorbachev's *perestroika* remains to be seen. Certainly, sentiment for tighter constraint of the private sector appears resilient not only in party ranks but in society at large. Should Gorbachev's reforms be discredited—even by events not directly related to the economy—it is difficult to imagine his successor promoting a new policy that embraces the wager placed by the present regime, and NEP, on private initiative.

## NOTES

1. Armand Hammer, *The Quest of the Romanoff Treasure* (New York, 1932), pp. 56–57.

2. Alexandre Barmine, *One Who Survived: The Life Story of a Russian under the Soviets* (New York, 1945), pp. 124–25.

3. A. M. Ginzburg, ed., *Chastnyi kapital v narodnom khoziaistve SSSR. Materialy komissii VSNKh SSSR* (Moscow-Leningrad, 1927), pp. 41, 69; V. M. Selunskaia, ed., *Izmeneniia sotsial'noi struktury sovetskogo obshchestva. 1921–seredina 30-kh godov* (Moscow, 1979), p. 114; Spektator [Miron Isaakovich Nachimson], *Russkii "Termidor"* (Kharbin, 1927), pp. 106–107; E. H. Carr and R. W. Davies, *Foundations of a Planned Economy, 1926–1929*, 2 vols. (London, 1969), vol. 1, part 2, p. 663; I. Ia. Trifonov, *Klassy i klassovaia bor'ba v SSSR v nachale nepa*, vol. 2: *Podgotovka ekonomicheskogo nastupleniia na novuiu burzhuaziiu* (Leningrad, 1969), pp. 49, 68; *Torgovo-promyshlennaia gazeta* [hereafter cited as *TPG*], 1922, no. 215 (November 25), p. 5; and I. Mingulin, *Puti razvitiia chastnogo kapitala* (Moscow-Leningrad, 1927), p. 86. Many people, especially small-scale artisans, engaged in both manufacturing and trade.

4. *Na novykh putiakh. Itogi novoi ekonomicheskoi politiki 1921–1922 g.g.* (Moscow, 1923), vyp. I, p. 175; *Ekonomicheskaia zhizn'*, 1921, no. 287 (December 21), p. 2; 1922, no. 92 (April 27), p. 4; I. A. Gladkov, ed., *Sovetskoe narodnoe khoziaistvo v 1921–1925 gg.* (Moscow, 1960), p. 449; *Ekonomicheskoe obozrenie*, 1925, April, p. 190; P. C. Hiebert and Orie O. Miller, *Feeding the Hungry: Russian Famine, 1919–1925* (Scottdale, Pa., 1929), p. 114; F. A. Mackenzie, *Russia before Dawn* (London, 1923), p. 18; and Ts. M. Kron, *Chastnaia torgovlia v SSSR* (Moscow, 1926), p. 10.

5. *Promyshlennost' i torgovlia*, 1922, no. 3, pp. 24–25; *Nashe khoziaistvo* (Vladimir), 1923, no. 7–9, pp. 42–43; V. P. Dmitrenko, *Torgovaia politika sovetskogo gosudarstva posle perekhoda k NEPu 1921–1924 gg.* (Moscow, 1971), pp. 143, 145; V. A. Arkhipov and L. F. Morozov, *Bor'ba protiv kapitalisticheskikh elementov v promyshlennosti i torgovle. 20-e–nachalo 30-kh godov* (Moscow, 1978), p. 39; *Ekonomicheskaia zhizn'*, 1921, no. 287 (December 21), p. 2; and *Mesiachnye obzory narodnogo khoziaistva*, 1922, March, p. 68; 1922, April, p. 60.

6. Dmitrenko, *Torgovaia politika*, pp. 57–58; Trifonov, *Klassy*, vol. 2, p. 47; and Arkhipov and Morozov, *Bor'ba*, p. 27.

7. *TPG*, 1924, no. 120 (May 29), p. 4; M. M. Zhirmunskii, *Chastnyi kapital v tovarooborote* (Moscow, 1924), p. 7; A. Zalkind, ed., *Chastnaia torgovlia Soiuza SSR* (Moscow, 1927), p. 157; Mackenzie, *Russia before Dawn*, p. 22; and Frank A. Golder and Lincoln Hutchinson, *On the Trail of the Russian Famine* (Stanford, 1927), p. 227.

8. Iu. S. Kondurushkin, *Chastnyi kapital pered sovetskim sudom* (Moscow-Leningrad, 1927), p. 59; *Mestnoe khoziaistvo* (Kiev), 1924, no. 6 (March), pp. 18–19; *TPG*, 1923, no. 45 (February 27), p. 2; 1923, no. 261 (November 18), p. 4; *Na novykh putiakh*, vyp. I, p. 183; and Paul Scheffer, *Seven Years in Soviet Russia* (New York, 1932), p. 4.

9. *Na novykh putiakh*, vyp. I, pp. 187, 236.

10. Kondurushkin, *Chastnyi kapital*, pp. 42, 100; Arkhipov and Morozov, *Bor'ba*, p. 78.

11. Kondurushkin, *Chastnyi kapital*, pp. 56, 59–60, 186.

12. Ibid., p. 70; Victor Serge, *Memoirs of a Revolutionary, 1901–1941* (London, 1967; Reprint, 1975), p. 201.

13. Trifonov, *Klassy*, vol. 2, p. 71; *Torgovye izvestiia*, 1925, no. 19 (May 21), p. 6; 1925, no. 45 (August 4), p. 6; *TPG*, 1924, no. 78 (April 5), p. 1; *Mestnoe khoziaistvo* (Kiev), 1924, no. 6 (March), p. 70.

14. Lionel Kochan, ed., *The Jews in Soviet Russia since 1917* (Oxford, 1978), pp. 92, 139.

15. Zvi Y. Gitelman, *Jewish Nationality and Soviet Politics: The Jewish Sections of the CPSU, 1917–1930* (Princeton, 1972), pp. 19–20.

16. The resumption by many Jews of their former occupations helps account for the fact that in 1927 nearly two-thirds of the private traders in Belorussia and over half in the Ukraine had prerevolutionary trading experience, while the corresponding figure for the RSFSR (where Jews were not as numerous) was only 38 percent. *Voprosy torgovli*, 1929, no. 15, p. 61. The figures for Transcaucasia and Central Asia were 57 and 32 percent respectively.

17. *Sobranie uzakonenii i rasporiazhenii. 1917–1949* (Moscow, 1920–50) [hereafter cited as *SU*], 1921, no. 56, art. 354; *SU*, 1922, no. 17, art. 180; *SU*, 1923, no. 5, art. 89. A sixth rank was added in 1926. *Sobranie zakonov i rasporiazhenii raboche-krest'ianskogo pravitel'stva SSSR. 1924–1949* (Moscow, 1925–50) [hereafter cited as *SZ*], 1926, no. 63, art. 474.

18. *Ekonomicheskoe obozrenie*, 1924, no. 6, pp. 46–47; 1925, October, pp. 162–64; Ginzburg, *Chastnyi kapital*, pp. 120–21, 200; and Zalkind, *Chastnaia torgovlia*, pp. 9, 11, 160. Figures for Moscow and a number of provinces concerning the distribution of private traders in the five trade ranks may be found in *Na novykh putiakh*, vyp. I, p. 184; *Finansy i narodnoe khoziaistvo*, 1928, no. 21, p. 26; *Severo-Kavkazskii krai* (Rostov-on-Don), 1925, no. 4–5, p. 107; 1925, no. 10, p. 54; *Ekonomicheskii vestnik Zakavkaz'ia* (Tiflis), 1926, no. 6, p. 22; *Nashe khoziaistvo* (Riazan'), 1924, no. 1, p. 38; and *Khoziaistvo Urala* (Sverdlovsk), 1925, no. 2 (July), p. 55.

19. It should be noted that the number of large shops (primarily businesses in ranks IV and V) was smaller than the number of merchants who operated them. As a general rule, the larger an enterprise, the likelier it had more than one owner.

This was due in part to the need for considerable quantities of capital in the upper ranks, but also to a desire to avoid or reduce the use of hired labor (the presence of which often brought additional taxes and regulation). *Finansy i narodnoe khoziaistvo*, 1927, no. 4, p. 10; *Torgovye izvestiia*, 1925, no. 45 (August 4), p. 6; 1926, no. 1 (January 5), p. 5; 1926, no. 59 (June 1), p. 4; *Mestnoe khoziaistvo* (Kiev), 1924, no. 6 (March), p. 70; and *Mestnoe khoziaistvo Ekaterinoslavshchiny* (Ekaterinoslav), 1924, no. 1 (October-December), p. 34.

20. *Voprosy torgovli*, 1929, no. 15, p. 65.

21. Ginzburg, *Chastnyi kapital*, p. 203; Zalkind, *Chastnaia torgovlia*, p. 18; and *Materialy po istorii SSSR. VII. Dokumenty po istorii sovetskogo obshchestva* (Moscow, 1959), p. 90.

22. In some sources the figures differ slightly. Trifonov, *Klassy*, vol. 2, p. 251; Carr, *Foundations*, vol. 1, part 2, p. 962; *Ekonomicheskaia zhizn' SSSR. Khronika sobytii i faktov 1917–1965*, 2 vols. (Moscow, 1967), vol. 1, pp. 163, 176, 189, 206, 221; and N. Riauzov, *Vytesnenie chastnogo posrednika iz tovarooborota* (Moscow, 1930), pp. 18, 21. Not surprisingly, private entrepreneurs played a less important role in wholesale trade. In 1926, the best year for private wholesale trade, retail sales represented approximately 80 percent of all private trade, and the percentage was even higher at the beginning and end of NEP. Less than 5 percent of private rural trade was wholesale. *Materialy, VII*, pp. 103, 150; L. N. Kritsman, *Tri goda novoi ekonomicheskoi politiki* (Moscow, 1924), p. 23; and *Vnutrenniaia torgovlia Soiuza SSR za X let* (Moscow, 1928), p. 259. Private merchants accounted for roughly 20 percent of all (state, cooperative, and private) wholesale trade in 1923/24, 10 percent in 1924/25, 9 percent in 1925/26, 5 percent in 1926/27, 2 percent in 1927/28, and 0.4 percent in 1928/29. Carr, *Foundations*, vol. 1, part 2, p. 961; Trifonov, *Klassy*, vol. 2, pp. 50, 248; and Riauzov, *Vytesnenie*, p. 18.

23. *Ekonomicheskoe obozrenie*, 1927, May, p. 160; 1929, no. 1, p. 66; *Finansy i narodnoe khoziaistvo*, 1930, no. 10, p. 19. Other studies of workers' budgets in various regions yielded similar findings. See, for example, A. Zlobin, *Gosudarstvennyi, kooperativnyi i chastnyi kapital v tovarooborote sibirskogo kraia* (Novosibirsk, 1927), p. 10; *Ekonomicheskaia zhizn'*, 1927, no. 236 (October 15), p. 3.

24. *Ekonomicheskoe stroitel'stvo*, 1926, no. 1, p. 31.

25. *Narodnoe khoziaistvo Srednei Azii* (Tashkent), 1927, no. 5, p. 53; *Torgovye izvestiia*, 1925, no. 34 (July 9), p. 6; *TPG*, 1928, no. 218 (September 19), p. 4; *Nash krai* (Astrakhan'), 1926, no. 8, p. 27; *Kooperativnoe stroitel'stvo*, 1926, no. 14, p. 54; and A. Kaktyn', *O podkhode k chastnomu torgovomu kapitalu* (Moscow, 1924), p. 10.

26. *TPG*, 1924, no. 56 (March 8), p. 2; 1927, no. 249 (October 30), p. 3; 1928, no. 266 (November 16), p. 6; 1928, no. 269 (November 20), p. 4; *Tverskoi krai* (Tver), 1926, no. 6, p. 39; *Sovetskaia torgovlia*, 1927, no. 7, p. 15; *Trud i khoziaistvo* (Kazan'), 1927, no. 1, p. 90; Selunskaia, *Izmeneniia sotsial'noi struktury*, p. 118; A. M. Lezhava, *Vnutrenniaia torgovlia 1923 g.* (Moscow, 1924), p. 12; *Kooperativnoe stroitel'stvo*, 1926, no. 9, pp. 54, 56; *Torgovye izvestiia*, 1925, no. 27 (June 13), p. 6; 1925, no. 34 (July 9), p. 6; *Nash krai* (Astrakhan'), 1926, no. 8, p. 27; and Kaktyn', *O podkhode*, p. 10.

27. *Torgovlia, promyshlennost' i finansy*, 1925, no. 5–6, p. 161; Vasil'kov, *Chastnyi kapital v khoziaistve orlovskoi gubernii. (Issledovatel'skaia rabota Gubplana pod rukovodstvom i redaktsiei Vasil'kova)* (Orel, 1928), p. 19; and *Ekonomicheskoe obozrenie*, 1927, May, p. 160.

28. *Na novykh putiakh*, vyp. I, pp. 207–208; Kron, *Chastnaia torgovlia*, pp. 16–17; *TPG*, 1923, no. 231 (October 12), p. 3; and *Trud i khoziaistvo* (Kazan'), 1927, no. 1, p. 84.

29. Estimates differ considerably. See, for example, *Ekonomicheskoe obozrenie*, 1926, August, p. 101; 1928, no. 9, p. 27; *TPG*, 1924, no. 126 (June 5), p. 2; and S. O. Zagorskii, *K sotsializmu ili k kapitalizmu?* (Paris, 1927), p. 150.

30. *Khoziaistvo Sev.-Zap. kraia* (Leningrad), 1924, no. 8, p. 51; Kron, *Chastnaia torgovlia*, p. 37; *Torgovye izvestiia*, 1925, no. 74 (October 10), p. 5; 1926, no. 108 (October 2), p. 4; and Ginzburg, *Chastnyi kapital*, p. 11.

31. *TPG*, 1927, no. 31 (February 8), p. 3; 1928, no. 283 (December 6), p. 4; *Ekonomicheskoe obozrenie*, 1928, no. 4, p. 161; and *Sovetskaia torgovlia*, 1926, no. 10, p. 3; 1927, no. 7, pp. 6–7. For more on the procurement of various products in different regions, see *Trud i khoziaistvo* (Kazan'), 1927, no. 1, pp. 88–89, 94; *TPG*, 1928, no. 229 (October 2), p. 5; 1928, no. 246 (October 21), p. 6; Vasil'kov, *Chastnyi kapital*, p. 33; Zlobin, *Gosudarstvennyi, kooperativnyi i chastnyi kapital*, p. 16; *Tverskoi krai* (Tver), 1926, no. 7–8, p. 17; and *Finansy i narodnoe khoziaistvo*, 1926, no. 6, p. 27.

32. *Sovetskaia torgovlia*, 1927, no. 7, pp. 7–8; *Torgovye izvestiia*, 1926, no. 99 (September 11), p. 2; *TPG*, 1928, no. 283 (December 6), p. 4; Zalkind, *Chastnaia torgovlia*, pp. 49, 62, 65; and Mingulin, *Puti razvitiia*, pp. 75–76.

33. *Materialy. VII*, p. 150.

34. *Torgovye izvestiia*, 1925, no. 72 (October 6), p. 5.

35. *Sovetskaia torgovlia*, 1926, no. 9, p. 9; 1927, no. 7, p. 7. See also *Na novykh putiakh*, vyp. I, p. 220; Zagorskii, *K sotsializmu*, pp. 123–24, 150.

36. *Kooperativnoe stroitel'stvo*, 1926, no. 14, p. 47; Zhirmunskii, *Chastnyi kapital*, p. 100; *TPG*, 1922, no. 127 (August 11), p. 2; 1923, no. 190 (August 25), p. 4; 1928, no. 225 (September 27), p. 4; Kron, *Chastnaia torgovlia*, p. 34; and *Materialy. VII*, p. 150.

37. Zalkind, *Chastnaia torgovlia*, pp. 66–67, 147; Ginzburg, *Chastnyi kapital*, p. 30; Zhirmunskii, *Chastnyi kapital*, p. 96; Nachimson, *Russkii "Termidor,"* pp. 133–34; Bernard Edelhertz, *The Russian Paradox: A First-hand Study of Life under the Soviets* (New York, 1930), p. 9; William C. White, *These Russians* (New York, 1931), pp. 68, 324, 337; Scheffer, *Seven Years*, p. 55; Karl Borders, *Village Life under the Soviets* (New York, 1927), pp. 102–103; and *Ekonomicheskaia zhizn'*, 1924, no. 306 (October 10), p. 4.

38. These included cutting off credit to private procurement operations, limiting the amount of privately owned grain that could be milled in "socialist" facilities, revoking the leases of many large private mills, forbidding state and cooperative agencies to conduct grain transactions with private traders, and restricting private grain shipments by rail.

39. G. A. Dikhtiar, *Sovetskaia torgovlia v period postroeniia sotsializma* (Moscow, 1961), p. 271; Moshe Lewin, *Russian Peasants and Soviet Power: A Study of Collectivization* (London, 1968; Reprint, New York, 1975), p. 389. A correspondent reported from the Ukraine that free-market grain prices, far above official prices, severely hampered the state's efforts to buy grain. *TPG*, 1928, no. 209 (September 8), p. 5. The Poltava correspondent sent a similar report concerning the procurement of hides. *TPG*, 1928, no. 257 (November 3), p. 4.

40. Measures taken against private grain trading have been described above. The state also issued decrees banning the private procurement of furs in many regions. See *Zakony o chastnom kapitale. Sbornik zakonov, instruktsii, prikazov i raz"iasnenii*, comp. B. S. Mal'tsman and B. E. Ratner (Moscow, 1928), pp. 159–60; *SU*, 1927, no. 77, art. 525; *SU*, 1927, no. 87, art. 579; *SU*, 1928, no. 99, art. 626; and *SU*, 1928, no. 101, art. 638. For more on efforts to reduce the private procurement of hides, see *TPG*, 1928, no. 283 (December 6), p. 4. Private procurement activity in general was undercut indirectly by the drastic reduction of the number of private retail traders in 1928 and 1929, which left private middlemen with few customers. See (concerning eggs and butter) *Ekonomicheskoe obozrenie*, 1928, no. 4, p. 164.

41. Trifonov, *Klassy*, vol. 2, p. 58; Kron, *Chastnaia torgovlia*, p. 15.

42. Dmitrenko, *Torgovaia politika*, p. 185; *TPG*, 1923, no. 1 (January 1), p. 2; and *Na novykh putiakh*, vyp. I, p. 235.

43. Zagorskii, *K sotsializmu*, p. 120; Iu. Larin, *Chastnyi kapital v SSSR* (Moscow-Leningrad, 1927), pp. 7, 12, 25–26; E. H. Carr, *The Bolshevik Revolution*, 3 vols. (London, 1950–53; Reprint, Harmondsworth, 1973), vol. 2, p. 312; Zhirmunskii, *Chastnyi kapital*, pp. 10–11, 23; Zalkind, *Chastnaia torgovlia*, p. 157; Kron, *Chastnaia torgovlia*, pp. 14, 113; *Iugo-Vostok* (Rostov-on-Don), 1922, no. 2, p. 164; and *TPG*, 1922, no. 150 (September 9), p. 1.

44. Nachimson, *Russkii "Termidor,"* p. 132; Zhirmunskii, *Chastnyi kapital*, pp. 22, 86; Ginzburg, *Chastnyi kapital*, pp. 18, 20; *TPG*, 1922, no. 124 (August 8), p. 4; 1922, no. 132 (August 17), p. 3; 1924, no. 79 (April 6), p. 1; *Iugo-Vostok* (Rostov-on-Don), 1924, no. 4, p. 64; *Na novykh putiakh*, vyp. I, p. 111; and *SU*, 1923, no. 29, art. 336.

45. Zhirmunskii, *Chastnyi kapital*, p. 24; Ginzburg, *Chastnyi kapital*, p. 19; Kron, *Chastnaia torgovlia*, p. 16; *Torgovye izvestiia*, 1925, no. 76 (October 15), p. 5; *Ekonomicheskii vestnik Zakavkaz'ia* (Tiflis), 1926, no. 2, p. 54; *Severo-Kavkazskii krai* (Rostov-on-Don), 1925, no. 4–5, p. 101; and *Ekonomicheskoe obozrenie*, 1925, April, p. 194.

46. Ginzburg, *Chastnyi kapital*, p. 14.

47. Riauzov, *Vytesnenie*, p. 35. See also *Mestnoe khoziaistvo* (Kiev), 1924, no. 6 (March), p. 72.

48. The number of licensed private traders (excluding rank I) decreased during the second half of NEP as follows: 1925/26—590,500; 1926/27—444,200; 1927/28—339,400; 1928/29—213,700. Riauzov, *Vytesnenie*, p. 17.

49. *Finansy i narodnoe khoziaistvo*, 1928, no. 39, pp. 2–3; 1929, no. 7, p. 16; Dikhtiar, *Sovetskaia torgovlia*, p. 335.

50. See, for example, *TPG*, 1928, no. 266 (November 16), p. 6; 1928, no. 293 (December 18), p. 4.

51. For a sampling of reports filed by *TPG*'s correspondents in Saratov, Tver, Poltava, Kiev, Sverdlovsk, Smolensk, and Penza, see ibid., 1927, no. 122 (June 1), p. 4; 1928, no. 225 (September 27), p. 4; 1928, no. 266 (November 16), p. 6; 1928, no. 267 (November 17), p. 4; and 1928, no. 269 (November 20), p. 4. See also *Ekonomicheskaia zhizn'*, 1928, no. 53 (March 2), p. 4; 1928, no. 113 (May 17), p. 5.

52. *TPG*, 1928, no. 177 (August 1), p. 4; 1928, no. 269 (November 20), p. 4.

53. Riauzov, *Vytesnenie*, p. 24; L. F. Morozov, *Reshaiushchii etap bor'by s nepmanskoi burzhuaziei (1926–1929)* (Moscow, 1960), pp. 47–48; *TPG*, 1928, no. 177 (August 1), p. 4; 1928, no. 218 (September 19), p. 4; 1928, no. 293 (December 18), p. 4; and *Finansy i narodnoe khoziaistvo*, 1928, no. 39, p. 3.

54. *TPG*, 1927, no. 31 (February 8), p. 2; *Materialy. VII*, p. 166; *Sovetskaia torgovlia*, 1927, no. 7, p. 15; 1927, no. 20, p. 8; I. Ia. Trifonov, *Ocherki istorii klassovoibor'by v SSSR v gody NEPa (1921–1937)* (Moscow, 1960), p. 131; and *Ekonomicheskoe stroitel'stvo*, 1926, no. 9, p. 21.

55. *TPG*, 1928, no. 95 (April 24), p. 4; 1928, no. 293 (December 18), p. 4; *Ekonomicheskaia zhizn'*, 1928, no. 67 (March 20), p. 5; 1928, no. 68 (March 21), p. 3; and *Finansy i narodnoe khoziaistvo*, 1928, no. 39, p. 17.

56. Anne O'Hare McCormick, *The Hammer and the Scythe* (New York, 1928), p. 24; Calvin B. Hoover, *The Economic Life of Soviet Russia* (New York, 1931), pp. 150–51; Alexander Wicksteed, *Life under the Soviets* (London, 1928), p. 17; Albert Muldavin, *The Red Fog Lifts* (New York, 1931), pp. 50, 112–13; *Sotsialisticheskii vestnik* (Berlin), 1929, no. 21, p. 7; H. J. Greenwall, *Mirrors of Moscow* (London, 1929), pp. 38–39; and Edelhertz, *Russian Paradox*, p. 9.

# VII

# FAMILY LIFE IN MOSCOW
# DURING NEP

## R. E. Johnson

In historical accounts of NEP, family life has received relatively little attention. Historians have acknowledged the disruption occasioned by civil war and economic collapse and the controversies engendered by radical social legislation in the fields of divorce and abortion. Most attention, however, has been focused on policy debates rather than on demographic analysis of family life. The picture of family relations that has emerged is one of sharp rural/urban contrasts, with the peasant population tending to uphold traditional patterns and the cities experiencing a range of social ills compounded by family instability.[1]

My purpose in the following pages is not to challenge this picture but to refine it. In particular, I will attempt to illuminate the interconnections between migration and family life in the urban and rural populations of a single region—Moscow and its hinterland—which in prerevolutionary times had developed distinctive patterns of family life based on temporary labor migration [otkhodnichestvo]. Using data from censuses and local statistical surveys, I will try to construct a fuller picture of family relations than has hitherto been available. Specifically, I will ask whether the age/sex composition of city and countryside changed as a result of new migration patterns in the 1920s: Were migrants in the NEP years more likely to establish new families in the city? How large were such families, and how were they organized? Did their patterns of birth and childrearing differ from those found in rural areas? What roles did men and women play in them? Having surveyed the data, I will try to place the demographic changes in a wider cultural and economic context and identify the causes of behavioral change.

## Ratio of Women to Men

In the latter half of the nineteenth century, Moscow was a city of peasant migrants. Males and females were drawn to the city in search of work, but in different proportions at different ages. On the one hand, young peasant males tended to move to the city in their teens and remain there for two or more decades, but without severing ties to their villages; they kept their wives and younger children in the countryside and maintained a claim to a land allotment despite spending most of every year in town. When they became too old or too ill to go on working in the city, male migrants [*otkhodniki*] tended to return permanently to the villages.

Female migrants, on the other hand, moved to the cities in two distinct waves. The first consisted of women in their teens, who came to work in factories, workshops, or domestic service but often departed after a few years to marry and raise children in the rural areas. Peasant women who remained in the city were more likely to remain unmarried; if they bore children, they sometimes sent them to the country to be raised by relatives. The second wave was made up of older women, often past childbearing age, who settled permanently in the cities for want of other alternatives. Women who were widowed or deserted and had no grown children to assist them might find themselves deprived of any claim to a communal land allotment. The city offered such women a meager existence at best, but this was often more than they could find in the countryside.[2]

The older system of migration was thus closely bound up with other cultural and economic variables such as the kinship system and the organization of the labor force. Any change in the ratio of the sexes in the city would therefore seem to imply broader trends in the reorganization of work and family life, as well as in the interrelation between the urban and rural populations.

Turning to data on the age/sex composition of Moscow's population, we find that dramatic changes did indeed occur in the first decades of the twentieth century. Between the general census of 1897 and that of 1926 (Table 1), the ratio of men to women fell from 132 : 100 to 95 : 100. Even greater changes were recorded among adolescents and young adults, who were conspicuously absent from Moscow in 1897; in the age group 15–19, the sex ratio fell from 194 : 100 to 87 : 100, and for ages 20–29 from 170 : 100 to 95 : 100.

One of the first questions that arise is whether the increase in Moscow's female population between the two general censuses was a consequence of the 1917 revolution and the establishment of Soviet power. Were women, in other words, migrating in response to new opportunities (and problems)

**TABLE 1**

Ratio of Men to Women in Moscow City

| Year | Sex ratio (Males per 100 Females) | | |
|---|---|---|---|
| | Overall | Ages 15–19 | Ages 20–29 |
| 1897 | 132 | 194 | 170 |
| 1912 | 119 | 130 | 141 |
| 1917 | 98 | 112 | 79 |
| 1920 | 94(81)* | 100(77)* | 99(62)* |
| 1923 | 99(93)** | 95 | 106 |
| 1926 | 95 | 87 | 95 |

Sources: *Pervaia vseobshchaia perepis' naseleniia Rossiiskoi imperii*, vol. 24, Table V, p. 32; *Statisticheskii ezhegodnik Moskovskoi gubernii i goroda Moskvy*, vyp. 2, otd. 2, Table V, p. 15; *Vsesoiuznaia perepis' naseleniia SSSR 1926 g.*, vol. 36, pp. 71–72.
*Itogi perepisi 1920 g.* (Moscow, 1928), Table 2.
***Polozhenie truda v Moskve*, p. 5.

that had arisen, or was their behavior part of a longer trend that predated 1917? This question can be answered, at least in part, by data from the various censuses that were taken in the years just before and after the revolution. Tables 1 and 2 describe the changing age-sex composition of Moscow from 1897 to 1926. The first reveals that the proportion female in the total population was rising sharply before the outbreak of war in 1914 and rose more rapidly between 1912 and 1917. This effect was undoubtedly exaggerated by the drop in male population, due to the mobilization of young men for military service. (The number of males aged 20–29 in Moscow decreased by a full 25 percent in these years.)

Table 2, which compares the number of women in each age group in successive censuses, demonstrates that adolescent and young adult women were the most volatile group in the female population; the age groups 15–19 and 20–29 grew more rapidly between 1897 and 1917 but also decreased more rapidly between 1917 and 1920.[3] Clearly the influx of women antedated the war and revolution, but the movement received an extra impetus during the first years of the war. Although the proportion female rose in all age groups (a result in part of the settlement of refugees in Moscow), the greatest rates of increase were among women of working age. After 1917, as jobs and food became scarce, women of all ages joined in the general exodus from Moscow, which reduced the city's population by almost 45 percent by 1920.[4] Among those who remained, however, women outnumbered men by at least a small margin, and possibly by as much as 25 percent. There seems to have been a core of urbanized women who were unable or unwilling to depart.

**TABLE 2**

Adult Female Population of Moscow City, by Age Cohort (showing rate of growth or decline from one census to the next)

| Age cohort | 1897 | 1912 | 1917 | 1920 | 1923 | 1926 | Overall increase 1897–1926 |
|---|---|---|---|---|---|---|---|
| 15–19: ttl | 42,692 | 76,898 | 118,985 | 53,033 | 75,386 | 102,809 | |
| % change | | +80% | +54% | −55% | +42% | +36% | 141% |
| 20–29: ttl | 101,303 | 173,553 | 230,262 | 121,939 | 205,958 | 272,314 | |
| % change | | +71% | +33% | −47% | +69% | +32% | 169% |
| 30–39: ttl | 81,140 | 123,779 | 151,972 | 84,261 | 126,199 | 182,675 | |
| % change | | +52% | +23% | −45% | +50% | +45% | 125% |
| 40–49: ttl | 54,396 | 80,615 | 99,400 | 65,918 | 84,079 | 104,992 | |
| % change | | +48% | +23% | −33% | +27% | +25% | 93% |
| 50–59: ttl | 36,004 | 50,047 | 62,113 | 46,681 | 57,732 | 72,172 | |
| % change | | +37% | +24% | −25% | +24% | +25% | 100% |
| 60 & over | 34,059 | 44,651 | 50,223 | 32,862 | 46,305 | 61,236 | |
| % change | | +31% | +12% | −35% | +41% | +32% | 80% |
| Total | 349,594 | 549,543 | 712,955 | 404,694 | 595,659 | 796,198 | |
| | | +57% | +30% | −44% | +47% | +34% | 127% |

Sources: Pervaia vseobshchaia perepis', vol. 24, Table V; Vsesoiuznaia perepis' . . . 1926 goda, vol. 2, Table IX; Statisticheskii ezhegodnik Moskovskoi gubernii i goroda Moskvy, vyp. 2, otd. 2, Table V, p. 15.

When Moscow's population revived after 1920, women again kept pace with men. The male/female ratio rose slightly, especially for ages 20–29, in the years when the greatest numbers of young men were being de- mobilized from military service, but it dropped again after 1923, with the result that women outnumbered men in most age groups by 1926. Com- paring Moscow's 1926 female population with that of 1897 (columns two and seven of Table 2), we find that the age group 20–29 grew by 169 percent and ages 15–19 by 141 percent, while the rest of the adult female population increased by 105 percent; for males the comparable figures were 50 percent, 8 percent, and 75 percent.[5]

Statistics on marital status illuminate urban life from another angle. In 1897, 44 percent of Moscow's female inhabitants were married and 22 percent were widows. In the 1926 census the proportion married had grown to 51 percent, while the proportion widowed shrank to 16.7 per- cent.[6] The changes are in part a reflection of the growing proportion of younger women, and in part a result of the 1926 census's looser definition of marriage.[7] They do, however, reinforce the suggestion that older pat- terns of behavior were changing, particularly where female migrants from the countryside were concerned.

Urban changes, of course, did not take place in a vacuum. Migration was a product of rural influences as well as urban ones, and in this context the sex ratios of the surrounding countryside offer an interesting counterpart to the trends in the city. As Table 3 indicates, in most of Moscow's hinter- land the ratio of men to women, and of married men to married women, actually rose from 1897 to 1926.[8] In other words, there were pro- portionately more adult males living in the peasant villages in the mid- 1920s than at the turn of the century. At first glance the changes in most provinces seem rather slight, but they must be seen in the context of an overall decline in the male population in the war years. In the USSR as a whole, the ratio of men to women in the adult population fell from 96 : 100 in 1897 to less than 90 : 100 in 1926,[9] but in Moscow's peasant hinterland it remained stable or rose. In both city and countryside the ratio between the sexes became more even, and the number of married persons living apart from their spouses appears to have declined. The evident cause was the departure of married women from the countryside, though it is also possi- ble that some men who would formerly have migrated were now remaining in the village.

To summarize: The age/sex profile of Moscow's population in 1926 was quite different from that of 1897. The changes began before 1914 and cannot be attributed solely to the effects of war, revolution, or the other disruptive forces of the period 1914–21. The increase in the city's female population—and most particularly the young adult female population— did, however, accelerate sharply after 1914, and this influx was not re-

**TABLE 3**

Sex Ratio (Males per 100 Females) in Rural Population of Provinces
Surrounding Moscow

| Province | 1897 Ratio | | 1926 Ratio |
|---|---|---|---|
| Yaroslavl: adults (ages 15+) | 58 | | 70 |
| Yaroslavl: married | 83 | | 89 |
| Ivanovo: adults | | [73]* | 74 |
| Ivanovo: married | | [85.5]* | 89 |
| Kaluga: adults | 67 | | 68 |
| Kaluga: married | 85 | | 82 |
| Kostroma: adults | 73 | | 70 |
| Kostroma: married | 86 | | 88 |
| Moscow: adults | 73 | | 75 |
| Moscow: married | 85 | | 91 |
| Riazan': adults | 79 | | 79 |
| Riazan': married | 85 | | 89 |
| Tula: adults | 74 | | 80 |
| Tula: married | 82 | | 88 |
| Tver: adults | 74 | | 75 |
| Tver: married | 83 | | 91 |
| Vladimir: adults | 73 | | 77 |
| Vladimir: married | 85 | | 91 |
| Regional Total: adults | 73 | | 73 |
| Regional Total: married | 86 | | 89 |

*Sources: Pervaia vseobschaia perepis'*, vol. 6, 15, 18, 24, 35, 43, 44, 50, Table V;
*Perepis . . . 1926 goda*, vol. 36, Table I, pp. 72ff.
*Ivanovo was not a province in 1897. Bracketed figures represent the combined averages of Vladimir and Kostroma provinces, from which Ivanovo province was later created.

versed in the early 1920s. On the contrary, female in-migrants outnumbered males after 1923, raising the possibility that work and family life were also changing.

## Women as Wage Earners and Dependents

Although Moscow's female workforce was growing through most of the NEP period, it barely kept pace with the growth in the female population as a whole. A substantial proportion of adult women came to live in the city without entering into wage labor. Those who were actively looking for work often found themselves at a disadvantage vis-à-vis males.

Before and after the revolution, the city's principal attraction for migrants was wage employment. At the turn of the century a sizable majority

of migrant women were listed by census takers as self-supporting or economically independent [*samodeiatel'nye*],[10] working mainly in domestic service, handcraft industries, and certain branches of factory industry such as
textiles and food processing. Their numbers increased sharply during the
years 1914–17; over the next five years they shrank in absolute terms, but
the proportion of women in the workforce did not decline. With the end of
the Civil War and the restoration of urban and industrial activity, however,
female job seekers found the labor market flooded with males returning
from military service or from the countryside. Many of these men could
claim prerevolutionary work experience [*stazh*] and specialized skills and
were more likely to be hired in the early days of industrial recovery.

The extent to which female wage earners were displaced by males in the
early years of the NEP is unclear. Some observers were convinced that the
proportion of women in the industrial workforce was lower in 1926 than it
had been in 1913, but others disputed this conclusion. The statistician A. G.
Rashin produced an industry-by-industry comparison which pointed to a
modest increase in the percentage of women from 31.2 to 34.7
nationwide.[11] A similar calculation using 1917 as the base year, however,
would undoubtedly have produced different results.

Labor force statistics from Moscow indicate that there was indeed a
major influx of women in the period 1920–23, but the number who were
economically independent showed hardly any increase: altogether the
number of *samodeiatel'nye* grew by some 18,000, while the total female
population increased by 244,000. Over the same period the number of
independent males in Moscow grew by 211,000, while the total male population rose by 285,000.[12] In other words, at a time when 75 percent of
male in-migrants were described as working or seeking work, the number
of women wage earners showed almost no increase. Meanwhile, the number of female Muscovites who were counted as dependent on someone
else's earnings grew by 74 percent. Three years later the national census of
1926 showed just over half of all adult women (ages 15 and above) in
Moscow city as economically dependent, compared to 7.7 percent of males.
Dependent women were mainly the spouses (65 percent) and children (20
percent) of self-supporting individuals, with widows and divorced women
accounting for the remaining 15 percent.[13]

Nationwide statistics from the same census suggest that the proportion of
female dependents in the urban population was three times greater than in
rural areas.[14] In part this statistic reflects the census takers' conventions,
which defined unpaid rural household labor as work but excluded unpaid
urban housework. Even so, it raises questions about the nature of urban
family life. Were half the women in Moscow and other cities truly dependent, or were they really an unregistered population of wage earners or
job seekers? Were they merely waiting for an appropriate opportunity to

enter the paid workforce?[15] To reconstruct the motives and wishes of these nameless individuals is not possible from the available records, but nation-wide statistics from a slightly later period do cast one ray of light. In 1931, when the workforce was expanding rapidly in the midst of the First Five-Year Plan, fully 54 percent of urban women of working age were still counted as dependents, as compared to just 4.5 percent of men.[16] For whatever reason—lack of marketable skills, shortage of social supports such as child-care centers, bias in hiring, or traditional conceptions of sex roles—urban women were more likely to remain outside the category of *samodeiatel'nye*, even when jobs were more available.

What about the other half of the female population? This total included not only those who had successfully found employment but also the reg-istered unemployed. As noted above, the influx of women into these two categories fell sharply between 1920 and 1923, but after that date it began to rise again, not just in Moscow but nationwide, keeping pace with the overall growth of cities. The number of women in the Soviet workforce grew slowly from 1923 to 1929, approaching 30 percent by the end of the period. Growth was recorded even in metalworking and other traditionally male occupations, but the great majority of working women remained in textiles and a few other traditionally female industries.[17]

In the specific case of Moscow city, several conditions seemed likely to favor women's employment in the early years of the NEP. The city was a major center of the textile industry, which had been the largest single industrial employer of women in earlier times and was also one of the first industries to revive after the end of the Civil War.[18] The shift of the seat of government from Petrograd to Moscow, together with the reorganization of everyday life and public services, also created a range of new clerical and service positions—fields in which female labor had traditionally flourished. In 1926, women were almost 36 percent of the city's economically in-dependent population: 25 percent of workers, 41 percent of servants and clerks, and 29 percent of all other occupations.[19]

Data on wages, skill, and previous work experience reveal important differences between men and women in these years. According to Rashin's nationwide statistics, although women worked on average almost exactly the same number of hours per day and the same number of days per month as men, they received only 65 percent of the wages of males. When comparison was restricted to specific occupational subgroups, the differ-ences were substantially reduced but not altogether eliminated. Women in almost all occupations were concentrated in the least-skilled, lowest-paid ranks; in the entire country, 80 percent (compared to 41.5 percent of males) were in the five lowest wage categories, while in textiles 24.5 percent of women and 7.5 percent of men were in the lowest three.[20] In all these respects Moscow seems to have followed national trends.

The women who sought employment in this period were not, for the most part, coming to the city or factory for the first time,[21] but their prior work experience was less on average than men's. Many had first entered the workforce during the war years and had spent some part of the Civil War in the countryside.[22] If we compare the age profiles of 1897 and 1926, Moscow's female workforce in the latter year had grown the most in ages 20–39, while the proportions of adolescents and older women had declined.[23] The movement of young adult women into the workforce in the 1920s represented a break with tradition, for in prerevolutionary times such individuals, even if they spent their adolescence working in towns or factories, tended to move back to the villages once they were ready to marry and raise families. Now, it seems, a greater proportion of them were prepared to spend their whole adult lives in the city.

Statistics on *un*employment can illuminate women's work experience from a different angle. Nationwide, the average length of unemployment among women was consistently greater than among men. In Leningrad in 1923, women who were registered as unemployed remained so for an average of ten months, while for men the average was five. Elsewhere in the USSR the difference was sometimes less; Moscow's averages of 5.2 months for women and 4 for men were close to the national mean.[24] Even so, there seems to have been a hard core of women who remained unemployed for significantly longer periods. A 1926 study found that 43 percent of Moscow's unemployed women had been out of work for one full year or more, but only 17 percent of unemployed men had been seeking work for such a term.[25]

Another male-female contrast is found in the ratio of job placements to applicants in the labor bureaus [*birzhi truda*], where 81 jobs were found for every 100 males registered, but only 42.4 per 100 females. Reports of the unemployed workers' previous work experience may well exaggerate the applicants' background and skills, but they also show a sharp male-female differential. Unemployed men are reported as having worked for wages for an average of eight to nine years, while unemployed women's experience averaged between five and six years.[26]

The different experiences of men and women who were seeking work in the early 1920s can be explained in several ways. Women were at a competitive disadvantage with regard to skill and previous work experience, but other factors may also have influenced their quest for employment. In particular, the duration of the search for work was affected by an individual's family circumstances and background. Since most new job seekers came to the cities from rural areas, marital status and family landholding helped to determine how long they continued to look for work in the city. On the one hand, an unemployed person whose spouse was already earning an income may have been in a better position to keep on looking for a job. Moscow women whose husbands were wage earners had the option of squeezing by on a single income, inadequate though it might be. A spouse's job could also keep unemployed women from moving elsewhere in search of work, whereas unattached individuals, as well as couples in which both partners were unemployed, were probably more mobile.

On the other hand, individuals with land and/or close relatives in the countryside may have been more inclined to quit the city after a few months of unemployment. In general, female workers were reported as having weaker ties to the land than males,[27] and those who stayed longer on the unemployment rolls may have done so from a lack of alternatives. For widows, orphans, divorcees, and others whose rural households were no longer viable (e.g., because of inadequate land or loss of livestock), the city was probably a last resort.

The greatest contrast between the pre- and postrevolutionary eras, however, was not in the numbers of widows and other outcasts from the countryside who moved to the city, or in the lower wages or longer unemployment that women workers experienced. Rather, it was in the greater proportion of economically dependent women who spent their young adulthood in cities instead of rural areas.

### The Role of the Breadwinner

Statistics on urban household composition offer another perspective on women's lives and family relations. They suggest that family life in Moscow in the 1920s was tending toward a nuclear pattern in which small households, consisting mainly of parents and underage children, were predominant. Such families were most often supported by one person's wages.

The fullest statistics on Moscow households are found in the general censuses of 1897 and 1926, and the contrast between the two sets of figures is sufficiently great to raise a number of questions about the organization of urban life. In 1897, roughly 25 percent of the population of Moscow lived in factory barracks, hostels, and other nonfamilial units. Six percent lived as solitaries [*odinochki*], and the remaining 69 percent resided in family-based households.[28] In the latter category, the census takers counted 717,000 persons in 87,900 households, for an average of more than 8 persons per family. This large figure can be explained by the fact that many households included boarders, servants, and resident employees, who taken together made up 48 percent of their inhabitants. In other words, just over half of the residents of "family" households, or 36 percent of Moscow's total population, were in fact family members.[29]

Moscow's 1926 census results reveal a substantially different pattern. The number of persons living in family-based units was now 83 percent of the entire urban population, with solitaries accounting for an additional 13 percent and inhabitants of institutions and other nonfamilial units making up the remaining 4 percent. In addition, the number of family households had increased to 482,000, with an average membership of 3.5.[30] The number of households, in other words, had grown by almost 550 percent in thirty years, in a period when the urban population barely doubled. Without additional evidence, we cannot be certain how the membership of households was changing, but it seems probable that the proportion of servants and resident employees dropped drastically; the number of lateral relatives and boarders would also be expected to go down. The city, in other words, shifted toward a pattern in which small nuclear units were predominant. This seems consistent with data from other regions of the USSR, in which the mean household size of industrial workers ranged between 3 and 4.5.[31]

One should not automatically assume that all these new households were kinship-based. Given the shortage of housing in Moscow, unrelated individuals sometimes found themselves sharing quarters, and even divorced couples might continue to cohabit because other living accommodations could not be obtained. Data on the sex ratio (discussed above) and on the proportion of children in the population (discussed in the next section) do, however, imply a trend toward family living. In addition, the 1926 census provided a breakdown of the economic status of household members: 72 percent of all Moscow households had only one member who was working or seeking work, and 80 percent were headed by males.[32] The household tables provide only sketchy information about the other members of these households, but their gender can be extrapolated from other parts of the census, leading to the conclusion that roughly 45 percent of working women lived in a household headed by someone else.[33]

Household budgets are another source of clues to family composition, for they also indicate how many members of a family were working, and what proportion of the household budget came from their earnings. According to survey data from 1925, an average of 70 percent of the household income of Moscow workers came from the earnings of one principal wage earner, as compared to 18.6 percent from the earnings of all other family members. For 1926 the comparable figures were 73 percent and 16.2 percent.[34] A more detailed study of ninety-six households over a three-year period reached similar totals—74 percent for the head, and 22 percent for the earnings of spouses and children—but commented that these figures could not be taken as typical of the entire workforce; the sample included a large proportion of textile workers, "among [whom], when wages are comparatively low, many members of a family work."[35] Without this group the head's contribution to family earnings would have been even greater.

Statistics from other localities show a positive correlation between the level of a family's earnings and the number of members working, but describe the "typical worker family" as one with a single (male) wage earner.[36] (Households with a lone female breadwinner were relatively rare in Moscow, and rarer still in other parts of the USSR.[37] Those that existed tended to be at the bottom of the scale in their total income and often found it difficult to make ends meet; their poverty sometimes led to criminal behavior and child abandonment.)[38]

As noted above, the influx of younger women and the increase in the proportion of dependents in the total urban population seem to point to a reorganization of family life in the cities. A steep rise in the number of family units, coupled with a sharp drop in the average size of households, implies that female migrants were settling into nuclear family units. Non-familial patterns of residence had virtually disappeared from Moscow by 1926, and although the proportion of solitaries in the population had doubled since 1897, this group could account for only a small minority of female Muscovites. The apparent trend toward smaller, family-based households, however, need not imply an equality between the sexes. On the contrary, families of city dwellers and industrial workers—not just in Moscow but in many parts of the USSR—seemed to be following a pattern in which one wage earner was the main source of support. The picture of female dependency that was drawn in Section 2 is reinforced by this discussion.

### Mothers and Children

One further aspect of family life that can be traced through the censuses is the proportion of dependent children in the population. In 1897 children under age 10 were 12.5 percent of Moscow's population, whereas by 1926 the figure had risen to almost 17 percent. In view of the sharp increase in the number of women of childbearing age, it seems reasonable to compare trends in the numbers of children and adult women in the total population. Table 4 presents ratios of children to potential mothers, calculated from seven censuses from 1897 to 1926. (For purposes of this calculation, ages 15–40 were taken to be the years of female fertility.)

The first ratio presented is that of children under age 1 to potential mothers. Beginning at 8.7 children per 100 women in 1897, it rises slightly by 1912, then drops by more than 50 percent in 1917–18. It should be noted that three different forces may be at work here—reduced fertility, increased mortality, and removal of infants from the city by mothers who had relatives in the countryside. By 1920 the proportion of infants showed a moderate increase, and by 1926 the ratio of 1897 had been surpassed.

**TABLE 4**

Child/Mother Ratios, Moscow City, 1897–1926

| Year | Women Ages 15–39 | Children Under 1 yr | Children Ages 0–9 | Infant/Woman Ratio | Child/Woman Ratio |
|------|------|------|------|------|------|
| 1897 | 255,135 | 21,206 | 129,439 | .083 | .507 |
| 1912 | 374,230 | 37,608 | 255,969 | .100 | .684 |
| 1917 | 501,219 | 20,991 | 264,705 | .041 | .528 |
| 1918 | 459,416 | 19,573 | 245,746 | .042 | .534 |
| 1920 | 259,233 | 15,093 | 146,608 | .058 | .565 |
| 1923 | 407,543 | 33,219 | 217,570 | .081 | .534 |
| 1926 | 557,778 | 48,876 | 341,415 | .088 | .612 |

*Sources: Pervaia vseobshchaia perepis', vol. 24, Table V, p. 32; Statisticheskii ezhegodnik Moskovskoi gubernii i goroda Moskvy, vyp. 2, otd. 2, Table V, p. 15; Vsesoiuznaia perepis' . . . 1926 goda, vol. 36, pp. 71–72.*

When the female population is compared to the number of children under age 10, a somewhat different pattern emerges. The 1897 ratio of 48 children per 100 "mothers" is the lowest on the table. The figure rises sharply by 1913, declines somewhat by 1917, and remains steady through the years of the Civil War, rising again between 1923 and 1926 but not quite recovering its 1913 level.

Taken by themselves, these figures would suggest that, apart from a drop in the proportion of newborn children during the years of war and hardship, the women who lived in Moscow in 1926 were raising (or not raising) children much as their immediate forebears had done. The proportion of children in Moscow kept pace with the growing female population, but on a per capita basis the women of 1926 had barely more children than those of 1897.

The ratios take on a somewhat different meaning when they are compared to those in the rural population. In the nonurban territories of central Russia, the child/woman ratio in 1926 was approximately 18 infants or 140 children of ages 0–9 per 100 women of childbearing age—roughly double the figures for Moscow. The rural ratios, it should be noted, declined noticeably from 1897 to 1926.[39]

In 1897 the small proportion of young children in Moscow could be attributed to the rural-urban migration patterns, which either kept young mothers in the country or allowed them to send their children away from the city to be raised by relatives. In 1926, when the proportion of young women in the city had risen and the nuclear family unit had apparently become the norm, one might expect to find the proportion of children in the urban population rising rapidly. It did rise, but the change was hardly dramatic, and the city's child/woman ratios continued to trail far behind those of the country. The likeliest explanation is that urban women were practicing some form of fertility control, through abortion, contraception, or abstinence. Less likely, in view of the declining ratios in the countryside, is the suggestion that numbers of NEP urban women were sending their children away to relatives in the villages.

### Implications

The evidence reviewed here seems to point in two directions. On the one hand, some of the contrasts between population patterns of 1897 and 1926 diminish when data from the intervening years are reviewed. The rising proportion of women in Moscow's population, for example, was a trend that was well under way before the outbreak of World War I, and the ratio of potential mothers to children did not change very much even in the most difficult years of civil war and deurbanization.

On the other hand, the increased in-migration of young adult women, the growth of city-based family units, and the rise in the proportion of adult female dependents seem to point in another direction, and to set the years of the NEP apart from those that came before. The women who remained in the city—some of them with children—throughout the years of warfare, unemployment, and desperate shortages probably did so because they had nowhere else to go. Those who moved to the city in the NEP years may have been fleeing from a countryside where they were no longer welcome.

This is not to deny that the older patterns associated with *otkhodnichestvo* reappeared in the 1920s. Divided households and two-way migration were undoubtedly part of the picture. The evidence discussed in the previous sections, however, suggests that their importance was diminishing, and that much of the movement from the countryside to Moscow was differently organized. One must ask how many of the new migrants could really be termed *otkhodniki*, how many really had a place in the village to which they could return. The social difficulties described in Douglas Weiner's essay in this volume take on a different meaning if peasant job seekers were already effectively uprooted from the countryside.

The disruption of family life was conspicuous in the lives of widowed, divorced, and abandoned women, whose experience is treated more fully in Wendy Goldman's essay. The proportion of widows in the city, however, was declining in the early years of the NEP, and the number of divorcees was still minuscule, a mere 3.2 percent of adult women. Statistics on dependency and household composition, on the other hand, point to a different kind of disruption. Migrants were settling into Moscow as families—either by departing with their spouses and children from the villages or by marrying after arrival in the city. Whether they intended to sever their ties to the land cannot be determined directly, but the evidence seems to point in that direction.[40]

The greatest changes were occurring in the lives of younger women, who were leaving the countryside in unprecedented numbers. Unlike most female migrants of earlier decades, those of the NEP years often came to Moscow as wives and dependents. The family life that they established in the city may have been a liberating experience in one sense, allowing an escape from the restrictions of the patriarchal village. In other ways, however, it introduced new problems and uncertainties. Divorce, unemployment, housing shortages, and inadequate wages darkened the picture of family living. The nuclear family in NEP Moscow was in many cases less stable and secure than the extended patriarchal household of earlier times.

Technically this was proletarianization, the establishment of a class of wageworkers who owned no land or tools and had no way of supporting themselves except by sale of their own labor. The people I have been describing, however, seem unlikely candidates to play the creative and progressive role that has often been ascribed to a proletariat, or to fulfill the expectations of Bolshevik leaders. Proletarianization as they experienced it was a disruption of established patterns of living, but not yet the substitution of a new identity.

The process of change was influenced but not fully determined by policy decisions of Lenin and his associates. The Land Decree of 1917, the proclamation of War Communism, and the institution of the NEP three years later—all these had enormous social consequences, but their effects on family life, migration, and urbanization were indirect and, one suspects, unanticipated. Legislation dealing with women's rights and family law also produced unpredicted results.[41] The revolution and Civil War and the economic upheavals that followed created a new economic and social environment for Russian peasants, a new set of problems, obstacles, and opportunities that brought hundreds of thousands of individuals to Moscow in the early 1920s. In all likelihood, many who migrated in those years would have preferred to reestablish the older to-and-fro system of *otkhodnichestvo*, but in the changed circumstances of those years they found it much harder to do so. Among the factors which restricted them, one set is a direct result of warfare: numbers of widows and orphans, and of disabled adult males who were no longer fit for agricultural labor; loss of livestock and inventory. A second set can be attributed to the revolutionary land settlement, which provided more households with land but also encouraged household fissions: the results included smaller agricultural units, many of them ill supplied with animals or tools; a decline in the amount of surplus labor available for *otkhodnichestvo;* and the possible stigma associated with the use of hired labor, which in prerevolutionary times had been used to replace absent *otkhodniki.*[42]

A third influence, hardest to measure, would be the tensions generated in rural households and villages by the exodus from the cities after 1918. The "safety net" that the countryside had provided to urban kin was for a time stretched to its limits and beyond. Villages were flooded with half-urban refugees who knew little about agriculture and who may have worn out their welcome during the years of civil war and famine.

All these factors taken together would have led a substantial number of rural men and women to conclude that their future lay in the city. They were not simply reverting to older patterns of behavior but rather were groping their way toward different arrangements that would suit the new conditions in which they were living. Relations between city and countryside were still reciprocal, but the social results were unlike those of prerevolutionary times.

NEP society has sometimes been seen as the product of a tug of war between a tradition-minded peasantry and an innovative state. The evidence presented here suggests that peasants were not all pulling in the same direction. For many, family life was a product of innovations, adaptations, and improvisations in a changing rural and urban environment. We should not be surprised if these changes were poorly understood by contemporaries or received little attention from historians. Still, their influence should be seen as a major undercurrent of the NEP period, creating additional problems and constraints, and possibly new opportunities, for those who sought to set a new course for the young socialist society.

## NOTES

1. See, for example, Gail Lapidus, *Women in Soviet Society* (Berkeley, 1978), pp. 54–94; E. H. Carr, *Socialism in One Country*, vol. 1 (London, 1958), pp. 27–37; H. Kent Geiger, *The Family in Soviet Russia* (Cambridge, Mass., 1968), pp. 43–75. William Chase's *Workers, Society, and the Soviet State: Labor and Life in Moscow, 1918–1929* (Urbana, 1987), pp. 73–102, offers a more nuanced interpretation based in part on quantitative evidence.

2. For a fuller discussion see R. E. Johnson, "Mothers and Daughters in Urban Russia: A Research Note," *Canadian Slavonic Papers*, vol. 30, no. 3 (September 1988), pp. 363–73. Cf. Barbara Engel, "The Woman's Side: Male Out-migration and the Family Economy in Kostroma Province," *Slavic Review*, vol. 45 (1986), pp. 262–63.

3. Evidence for this latter period is contradictory. The national census of 1920 suggests that the female population of Moscow remained stable while the number of males dropped sharply; evidence presented by local statistical authorities points to a much smaller drop in the number of males and a higher overall ratio of men to women.

4. Mortality and reduced fertility also played a part in reducing the city's population, but their effects were greatest among the very old and the very young.

5. *Pervaia vseobshchaia perepis' naseleniia Rossiiskoi imperii* (St. Petersburg, 1899–1905), vol. 24, Table V, p. 32; *Vsesoiuznaia perepis' naseleniia SSSR 1926 goda* (Moscow, 1928–33), vol. 36, Table I, pp. 71–72.

6. *Pervaia vseobshchaia perepis'*, vol. 24, p. 32; *Vsesoiuznaia perepis' . . . 1926 goda*, vol. 36, p. 72. These data pertain to the adult population (ages 15 and above).

7. *Vsesoiuznaia perepis' . . . 1926 goda*, vol. 35, p. v: all persons who considered themselves married were so listed, regardless of whether the marriage had been legally registered.

8. The provinces listed in Table 3 were the closest to the city and accounted for over 60 percent of in-migration to Moscow in the years before the 1926 census.

9. Norton Dodge, *Women in the Soviet Economy* (Baltimore, 1966), p. 6, presents age-specific ratios: for ages 16–34, the ratio fell from 96.9 to 89.8; for ages 35–59, from 100.7 to 90.4; and for ages 60 and above, from 95.5 to 78.8.

10. Census takers used the term *samodeiatel'nyi*, which can be translated as independent or gainfully employed, but the category was defined to include anyone who was not dependent on another person's earnings. Pensioners, persons living at the expense of state or public institutions, and the unemployed were all considered *samodeiatel'nye* even though they were not currently earning an income from their own labor (*Vsesoiuznaia perepis' . . . 1926 goda*, vol. 18, p. v).

11. A. G. Rashin, *Zhenskii trud v SSSR* (Moscow, 1928), p. 10.

12. Moskovskii gubernskii sovet professional'nykh soiuzov, *Polozhenie truda v Moskovskoi gubernii v 1922–23 gg. Sbornik materialov,* ed. F. D. Markuzov (Moscow, 1923), p. 5.

13. *Vsesoiuznaia perepis' . . . 1926 goda*, vol. 19, p. 144.

14. L. I. Vas'kina, "Gorodskoe naselenie SSSR v kanun sotsialisticheskoi industrializatsii (po materialam Vsesoiuznoi perepisi naseleniia 1926 g.)," *Vestnik Moskovskogo universiteta,* ser. IX, 1971, no. 4, pp. 5–6.

15. After reviewing statistics on unemployment in Moscow in 1926, S. Uspenskii reached the opposite conclusion: that a significant number of married women who were listed as long-term unemployed had in fact given up the search, and were more appropriately regarded as dependents (S. Uspenskii, "Bezrabotnye goroda Moskvy po perepisi 1926 g.," *Statisticheskoe obozrenie,* 1927, no. 8, p. 107).

16. *Sostav novykh millionov chlenov profsoiuzov* (Moscow, 1933), p. 21.

17. A. G. Rashin, "Dinamika promyshlennykh kadrov SSSR za 1917–1958 gg.," in *Izmeneniia v chislennosti i sostave sovetskogo rabochego klassa* (Moscow, 1961), p. 57. By 1929, 55 percent of all female factory workers in the USSR were working in textile mills, where they made up 65 percent of the industry's labor force. TsUNKhU SSSR, *Biulleten' po uchetu truda, Itogi 1931 goda* (Moscow, 1932), p. 25, Table 10.

18. A. A. Matiugin, *Rabochii klass SSSR v gody vosstanovleniia narodnogo khoziaistva* (Moscow, 1961), pp. 197–207: in the period 1920–23, the number of textile workers in Moscow grew by 63 percent, while the total in metalworking rose by only 17 percent (*Polozhenie truda v Moskovskoi gubernii,* pp. 9–10).

19. *Vsesoiuznaia perepis' . . . 1926 goda*, vol. 19, pp. 144ff.

20. Rashin, *Zhenskii trud,* pp. 13, 18.

21. According to Rashin, the proportion of adolescents among female textile workers declined from 25.5 percent in 1897 to 13.6 percent in 1926; in heavy industry, on the other hand, younger women were more likely than older ones to be hired (Rashin, *Zhenskii trud,* pp. 15–18).

22. This is a recurring theme in the life histories of industrial workers described in E. O. Kabo, *Ocherki rabochego byta* (Moscow, 1928).

23. In 1897, 48 percent of female *samodeiatel'nye* were between ages 20 and 39; in the 1926 census this figure had risen to 63 percent. *Pervaia vseobshchaia perepis'*, vol. 24, pp. 168–69; *Vsesoiuznaia perepis' . . . 1926 goda*, vol. 19, p. 144.

24. L. E. Mints, *Materialy po statistike truda* (Petrograd, 1924), vyp. 15, p. 199.

25. Uspenskii, "Bezrabotnye goroda," p. 107. In all, the census counted 66,209 women as unemployed, accounting for more than 16 percent of female *samodeiatel'-nye*. Among males, just over 10 percent of the economically active population was unemployed. *Vsesoiuznaia perepis' . . . 1926 goda*, vol. 19, pp. 144, 155.

26. Mints, *Materialy*, pp. 202–206. Cf. Chase, *Workers*, pp. 149–50.

27. Ia. Kvasha and F. Shofman, "K kharakteristike sotsial'nogo sostava fabrich-no-zavodskikh rabochikh SSSR," *Puti industrializatsii*, 1930, no. 1, pp. 40–41.

28. *Pervaia vseobshchaia' perepis'*, vol. 24, Table 2.

29. A previous municipal census offered a fuller breakdown of residential patterns in 1882, and suggested that only one-third of all Muscovites were members of nuclear families. An additional 6 percent were lateral relatives of heads of households (e.g., cousins and aunts), while the remaining 60 percent were servants, workers, clerks, and occupants of group living units. *Perepis' Moskvy 1882 goda* (Moscow, 1885), pt. 1, sec. 1, pp. 73–76.

30. *Vsesoiuznaia perepis' . . . 1926 goda*, vol. 55, Table IV, p. 172.

31. See, for example, Severo-Kavkazskoe kraevoe statisticheskoe upravlenie, *Biudzhety rabochikh obsledovannye 1925 g.* (Rostov-on-Don, 1926), pp. 2–6; I. N. Dubinskaia, "Biudzhety rabochikh Donbassa zimoi 1922 g.," *Materialy po statistike truda na Ukraine*, vyp. 4 (1922), pt. 1, p. 125.

32. *Vsesoiuznaia perepis' . . . 1926 goda*, vol. 55, Table 2, p. 128. Of all two-person households, just over 80 percent had only one working member; of three-person households, 76 percent; and in households with more than three members, 64 percent.

33. *Vsesoiuznaia perepis' . . . 1926 goda*, vol. 19, p. 144, and vol. 55, p. 128. Of 350,000 economically active women, 30 percent lived alone, 25 percent were heads of households, and the remainder lived in family households headed by some other person. Among males, the equivalent percentages were 21, 56, and 23.

34. G. Polliak, "Dinamika rabochego biudzheta," *Statisticheskoe obozrenie*, 1929, no. 12, pp. 37–46.

35. Moskovskii oblastnoi sovet professional'nykh soiuzov, Biuro statistiki truda, *Biudzhety Moskovskikh rabochikh; populiarnyi ocherk* (Moscow, 1929), p. 22.

36. Dnepropetrovskoe okruzhnoe statisticheskoe biuro, *Rabochie biudzhety g. Ekaterinoslava v 1925 g.* (Dnepropetrovsk, 1926), p. 3. Among mining and metallurgical workers in the Ural and Ukrainian industrial regions, the head's earnings ranged from 70 to well over 80 percent, while those of other family members rarely exceeded 8.5 percent of household income except in the worst years of economic disruption and depression (ibid., pp. 3–4, 21, 25; TsSU SSSR, Sektor statistiki truda, sektsiia obshchei statistiki, *Biudzhety rabochikh i sluzhashchikh v 1922 g.* [Moscow, 1929], vyp. 1, pp. 14ff.; Ural'skii oblastnoi sovet profsoiuzov, statisticheskoe biuro, *Polozhenie truda na Urale v 1923 g.* [Ekaterinburg, 1924], p. 56; *Biulleten' Ivanovo-Voznesenskogo gubernskogo statisticheskogo biuro*, 13 [1927]; on Moscow earnings cf. Chase, *Workers*, p. 177 and n. 16).

37. In the Donbass region, where mining and metallurgy were the predominant industries, only 7 percent of households were headed by women (I. Dubinskaia, "Material'nye usloviia zhizni rabochikh Donbassa letom 1922 goda," *Materialy po statistike truda na Ukraine*, vyp. 3 [1922], p. 55). In Moscow, as noted above, the figure approached 20 percent, but some proportion of these (not indicated in the 1926 census) included more than one wage earner.

38. Louise Shelley has identified impoverished urban women of rural background, especially widows and single parents, as accounting for a disproportionate share of female criminal behavior in the 1920s (Louise Shelley, "Female Criminality in the 1920s: A Consequence of Inadvertent and Deliberate Social Change," *Russian History/Histoire russe*, vol. 9, no. 2–3 [1982], pp. 270ff.). According to Jennie A. Stevens, roughly 30 percent of the homeless children of Moscow in this period were the offspring of sole-support mothers who were unable to care for them (Jennie A. Stevens, "Children of the Revolution: Soviet Russia's Homeless Children [*Besprizorniki*] in the 1920s," ibid., pp. 244–46).

39. Calculated from *Pervaia vseobshchaia perepis'*, Table V of individual volumes, and *Vsesoiuznaia perepis' . . . 1926 goda*, vol. 36, Table I, pp. 71ff. The following provinces were included in the calculation: Yaroslavl, Ivanovo, Kaluga, Moscow, Riazan', Tula, Tver, Vladimir.

40. Worker budgets provide one more indication of NEP migrants' ties to the countryside. Monetary contributions to relatives in the countryside, which in prerevolutionary times had amounted to as much as 25 percent of annual earnings, now amounted to well under 2 percent of worker income (N. Filippova, "Dinamika biudzheta rabochei sem'i v 1928 g.," *Statisticheskoe obozrenie*, 1929, no. 12, pp. 35–49).

41. Cf. Shelley, "Female Criminality," esp. p. 284.

42. These factors help to explain the sex ratios in Table 3, in which the proportion of adult males in Moscow's hinterland rose in spite of the nationwide decline in the male population. In the smaller agricultural households of postrevolutionary Russia, the average number of adult workers was lower than it had been; a male's departure might leave the household incapable of working the land. Two other alternatives remained: those who had formerly migrated could remain in the village, or else the entire family could depart in search of a better life in the city.

# VIII

# WORKING-CLASS WOMEN AND THE "WITHERING AWAY" OF THE FAMILY

## POPULAR RESPONSES TO FAMILY POLICY

*Wendy Z. Goldman*

In 1926 the Central Executive Committee (VTsIK) of the Soviet, Russia's highest elected legislative body, met in Moscow in the former palace of the tsar. More than three hundred delegates gathered in the Great Kremlin Palace. Ablaze with light and decorated with gold, the meeting place resembled the inside of a magnificent cathedral. Beneath the crystal chandeliers, women workers and peasants in their ragged coats and red armbands mingled in the crowd. Workers in old felt boots, peasants in bast sandals, and foreigners in smart leather shoes moved across the inlaid marble floors.[1] Here, in 1926, after more than a year of intense nationwide discussion, the delegates finally ratified the new Code on Marriage, the Family, and Guardianship.

The debate over the new code had been far-reaching and democratic.[2] Peasants, workers, jurists, sociologists, women, and young people had met in the towns and in the country, in conventions ranging from the VTsIK to six thousand village meetings, to dispute the very meaning and purpose of marriage. The broad debate involved sections of the population whose ideas might otherwise have gone unrecorded. Peasants and workers, although often unaware of the technicalities of family law, did not hesitate to state their strongly held views of Soviet social life.

Working-class women played a significant role in the discussion, and their opinions are particularly important, for they reveal how women themselves viewed the juridical attempts to transform the family and facilitate women's liberation. The debate over the 1926 code offers a unique

125

opportunity to discover how working-class women perceived marriage, divorce, sexuality, and the socialist experiments in family law.

The Bolsheviks came to power with a vision of family relations based on the ideas of Karl Marx, Frederick Engels, and August Bebel.[3] The Marxist tradition held that capitalism itself gradually undermined the family by involving women in production outside the home. Under socialism, the state would assume the basic functions of the family. Communal laundries, dining rooms, and daycare centers, staffed by paid workers, would minimize or eliminate women's labor in the home. Women would enter the world of waged work on an equal footing with men. The state would cease to interfere in the union of the sexes, marriage would become superfluous, and the family itself would eventually "wither away."[4]

The Bolsheviks recognized that the family could not be abolished immediately. Civil marriage was needed to combat the reactionary influence of the Church, and parental obligations were important as long as the state could not assume the upbringing of children. Yet family law in the transition period was geared to the realization of the vision of free union. The Bolsheviks believed that the freedom to divorce—to dissolve a union no longer founded on love—was essential to the freedom of the individual. The right to divorce was considered particularly important to women, whose true feelings and abilities were often stifled by the unbreakable bonds of marriage. The Soviet jurist I. A. Rostovskii explained in his popular handbook on family law that divorce was crucial for "the emancipation of the individual in general, and in particular, the emancipation of women."[5] In the words of the jurist A. T. Stel'makhovich, "the revolutionary freedom of divorce" was "the best regulator of marital relations."[6]

The first family code, issued in 1918, substituted civil for religious marriage and set up local bureaus of vital statistics (ZAGS) to register births, deaths, marriages, divorces, paternity, and name changes. It established the right of divorce at the request of either spouse. No grounds were necessary. If the break-up was mutually acceptable, the spouses registered their decision in ZAGS; if only one party wished to divorce, he or she submitted a petition to a people's court. In either case, divorce, like marriage, became a simple civil procedure. The duties and responsibilities imposed by the marriage contract were sharply restricted in accordance with the prevailing idea of marriage as a union between equals. A. G. Goikhbarg, one of the jurists who drafted the 1918 code, stressed that the code "establishes absolute equality of men and women before the law." Marriage did not create community of property between spouses: neither the husband nor the wife had any claim on the property of the other. As the introduction to the code explained, "The woman's economic rights and her private possessions are carefully protected against any operation of bourgeois and feudal discriminations and usurpations."[7] Among the few concessions the code made to the marital bond was the guarantee, upon divorce, of alimony for a needy, disabled spouse. All children were entitled to parental support regardless of whether they were born within or outside a registered marriage. The new code thus obliterated the legal distinction between legitimate and illegitimate children.[8]

The 1918 code was remarkably ahead of its time. Similar legislation concerning divorce and legitimacy has yet to be passed in any of the major European countries.[9] Yet in the debate over the new Soviet code, at least one delegate to the VTsIK, a Ukrainian woman named Roslavets, argued that it did not go far enough. She said, "I cannot reconcile the section on marriage law with my socialist consciousness." Roslavets believed that marriage registration should have been abolished altogether. In her words, "the freedom of marriage relations" was one of the conditions for "the freedom of the individual," and marriage registration undermined both of these freedoms. Arguing strongly for "free union," Roslavets declared: "For me, marriage can only be a personal and private affair. . . . I cannot understand why this code establishes compulsory monogamy. This, it seems, is some kind of bourgeois survival." Roslavets also contemptuously dismissed the provision on alimony as "nothing more than payments for love." She insisted that alimony not only enslaved women but encouraged "the view that girls should attach themselves to a marriageable man and not develop themselves as people."[10]

Most jurists, however, considered alimony necessary in the transitional period. As Dmitrii Kurskii, people's commissar of justice, explained, "We still have not reached the point where each person can contribute his or her labor so that even the disabled will be supported by society. We still have not reached the point where a child, from the first day of birth, will be cared for by our motherland. For this reason, we are compelled to establish a position on alimony."[11] Kurskii and others realized that the state was too poor to create a comprehensive social welfare system that could eliminate women's dependence on men. Alimony was "a frank and sensible acknowledgment of the existence of certain economic and psychological conditions" that, hopefully, would soon "be overcome." Jurists expected the "transitional" provisions on alimony and child support to solve any problems that the freedom to divorce might create.[12] Roslavets thus found herself in a minority. The VTsIK ratified the family code in 1918, and the Civil War soon put a moratorium on further debates.

Yet arguments in favor of free union quickly resurfaced in 1921 with the end of the Civil War. The proponents of free union were soon joined by others seeking reform of the 1918 family code.[13] The reformers argued that the code did not address the social problems created by the recent years of war, famine, and economic ruin. Millions of homeless children roamed the streets. Thousands of families had fallen apart under the strains of survival. With the onset of the New Economic Policy in 1921 and the partial restoration of free market conditions, many state enterprises closed. Women figured prominently in the ranks of the unemployed. Impoverished widows and *batrachki* (landless peasant women), unable to survive in the countryside, swelled the ranks of the female unemployed in the cities. Between 70,000 and 100,000 women lived with men in de facto unions without the legal protection of registered marriage.[14] Such women were frequently abandoned as soon as they became pregnant. With few opportunities for employment and no recourse to alimony, many turned to prostitution.

In 1925, jurists drafted a new family code designed to address both the new social problems and the old demands for free union. The new code would extend the legal rights of marriage to de facto unions, further simplify the divorce procedure, and give both the married and the unmarried a claim on the earnings of their partners.[15]

During the nationwide debate that followed publication of the draft code, several positions emerged. Many jurists argued that recognition of de facto marriage would protect women. Others applauded the new code as a proper step in the direction of free union. Party officials and jurists opposed to the code argued that recognition of de facto marriage undermined the stability of registered marriage and placed women in a vulnerable position. Peasant men argued that easy divorce and de facto marriage spelled the ruin of the peasant household. But what did working-class women think of the new family legislation? How did they regard the freedom to divorce and the idea of free union?

Although women were divided in their opinions of the new legislation, they were united in their critique of existing social relations. They passionately opposed the practice of frequent divorce and repeatedly stressed that men should take more responsibility for their sexual behavior. Pasynkova, a delegate to the VTsIK from Viatka province, spoke for many women in her angry condemnation of male irresponsibility. "Some men have twenty wives," she said; "they live with one for a week, another for two, and leave each one with a child. Indeed, this should not be allowed!" Denouncing men's lack of commitment to marriage, she noted with sarcasm: "Men always say that women are guilty; they swear they have nothing in common with their wives. This is completely ridiculous: is it really possible to marry so many times and never to have anything in common? They themselves don't want to live together."[16]

Kapustina, a delegate to the VTsIK who worked in a textile factory in Kostroma province, deplored the disintegration of family life she saw all around her. She said, "A girl marries, a year or so passes—her husband abandons her, she goes to another, more children result." "What kind of life is this?" she asked her fellow delegates. She called attention to a widespread phenomenon wreaking havoc with working-class marriages. As men took advantage of the opportunities for social mobility created by the revolution, some began to regard their wives as backward and uneducated. "When you are working in a factory, you note a very unpleasant picture," Kapustina explained. "As long as a guy doesn't participate in political work, he works and respects his wife as he should. But just a little promotion and already something stands between them. He begins to stay away from his family and his wife: already she doesn't please him."[17]

Gnipova, an older delegate from Kursk province who worked in a local branch of the Commissariat of Land, agreed. Born into a family of poor peasants, Gnipova lived on a gentry estate until the revolution. Her first husband, arrested for political activity in 1905, died in prison. Her second husband, a Red Army soldier, was killed in the Civil War. Illiterate at the outbreak of the October Revolution, Gnipova had recently learned to read and carried a handbook on women's rights to the sessions of the VTsIK.[18] Having put two husbands and two revolutions behind her, Gnipova did not hesitate to speak her mind. She said she could understand a man who married for a short time and then divorced his wife because the two were incompatible. But, she added angrily, "I can't forgive a man who lives with a woman for twenty years, has five kids, and then decides his wife no longer pleases him. Why did she please him before, but now she doesn't? Shame on you, comrade men." Gnipova accused men of using women, benefitting from their labor and then discarding them as they grew older and less attractive. "He doesn't understand why she is ugly now," Gnipova scolded. "It's because she is worn out on his behalf." Gnipova castigated those men who betrayed their wives and justified their actions in terms of "love." "This isn't love," she said firmly, "this is swinishness." Such swine took advantage of the easy divorce law to abandon their wives and families. Gnipova mimicked the popular male mentality: "Here is freedom. I feel free. Give me a divorce."[19]

Women's subjective assessments of social life were objectively confirmed by the statistics on divorce. The Central Statistical Bureau noted "an extraordinary growth of divorce" in the 1920s.[20] The Soviet divorce rate was higher than that of any other European country: almost 3 times as high as in Germany, 3.5 times as high as in France, and 26 times that of England and Wales.[21] Moreover, the divorce rate in Soviet cities and towns far surpassed even the national average. The rate in the towns was nearly twice as high as in the rural areas, and more than 1.5 times as high as the national average.[22]

The divorce rate was correlated to the degree of urbanization. Cities with populations over 50,000 had the highest rates, 3.6 divorces per 1,000 people, while the rural areas had only 1.3 divorces per 1,000 people. The divorce rate was higher in the urbanized districts (1.8 per 1,000 people), higher still in the towns (2.8), and highest in the cities (3.6). Moscow's divorce rate in 1926 was highest of all: 6.1 divorces per 1,000 people, followed by Tver, 4.8; Yaroslavl, 4.0; and Leningrad, 3.6. Moscow had 477.1 divorces for every 1,000 marriages; Tver, 359; Yaroslavl, 279; and Leningrad, 265.[23] In Moscow there was almost 1 divorce for every 2 marriages!

In 1927 the rate jumped even higher, reflecting the new simplified divorce procedure in the 1926 family code. Spouses no longer had to go to court for a contested divorce but could simply pop into their local registry office (ZAGS) and fill out a form. If one spouse was not present when the other registered the divorce, he or she would be informed by postcard. Thousands of Soviet citizens availed themselves of the new procedure. In Moscow, the divorce rate shot up to 9.3 per 1,000 people in 1927; in Tver, to 7.6; Yaroslavl, 7.8; and Leningrad, 9.8. By 1927, more than two-thirds of the marriages in Moscow and one-half of the marriages in Leningrad ended in divorce.[24]

The new law reflected the Bolshevik ideal of marriage as a partnership of equals founded on mutual affection and united by common interests. In place of traditional marriage constructed by law, bound by economic exigency, and stabilized by a clear division of labor, Soviet jurists posited a highly modern notion of a companionate union. In their view, there was no basis for marriage without love.[25] The divorce statistics were the result of choices that were the right of every individual.

Yet the women delegates to the VTsIK were suspicious of this new "modern" model of marriage. They expressed special bitterness toward men who left their marriages to pursue a new "commonality" with younger, less burdened women. These women and thousands like them valued a different commonality in marriage, based on a shared economy, a working partnership, and mutual commitment to children. Relationships based on personal inclination and sexual attraction were extremely threatening to women who had labored all their lives in the narrow confines of household or factory, and who in many ways depended economically on their husbands. The fears of such women were further exacerbated by the imbalance of the sex ratio in the 1920s. As a result of the war losses, women outnumbered men by roughly 10 percent, increasing the competition for a male partner and provider.[26] While the law embodied the companionate ideal, women like Gnipova quickly perceived that "commonality" as expressed by men frequently masked an attraction to a younger, prettier, less careworn face and figure.

None of the women in the debate argued that women should imitate male sexual behavior. On the contrary, many called for a stricter, more repressive approach to sexuality. They invoked older strategies of sexual restraint, and they urged both men and women to take a more serious and responsible approach toward sex and marriage. In an age-old appeal to women's power to withhold their sexual favors, Gnipova criticized women for contributing to their own sexual exploitation. "Who permitted this?" she asked. "You permitted this yourselves, comrade women. . . . We value ourselves too cheaply." "One man should not have four women," she argued, "but should wait two months for one. The question is, how can we avoid being exchanged like gypsies?" Gnipova pleaded for an end to male promiscuity so that "our children will not suffer and our households will not be ruined."[27]

The economic and social consequences of divorce were a recurring theme in the discussions of the new family code. One of the main underlying assumptions of Soviet divorce law was that both spouses were independent individuals, free to make decisions on the basis of personal choice rather than economic necessity. Yet unemployment, especially for women, proved a serious problem throughout the 1920s.[28] Large numbers of women were forced to leave the workforce after the Civil War, and entire branches of industry closed in the shift to cost accounting under NEP. Sharp cutbacks in spending hurt social welfare agencies and state industries, sectors where women workers predominated. Thousands of medical personnel, state employees, daycare staffers, and Narpit (People's Feeding) and communications employees lost their jobs. The Petrograd Bureau of Labor announced in 1922 that 67 percent of the 27,000 registered unemployed in the city were women.[29] NKTrud investigated twelve provinces and found that women constituted 61.7 percent of the registered unemployed.[30] The small industries that sprang up under private management could not rehire all the workers who had lost their jobs. One critic of NEP angrily described the reappearance of labor competition, a feature of capitalism often criticized in Marx and Engels's writings on women: "The reconstruction of enterprises on the basis of cost accounting and the development of privately owned enterprises have inevitably created the disgusting phenomenon of capitalist thriftiness, giving rise to the competition between male and female labor."[31] Men and women competed for jobs in a tight labor market, and women invariably lost. Organizers for the Petrograd Soviet of Unions (Petrogubprofsoveta) noted in 1922 that conditions for women were "extraordinarily difficult" as a result of the mass layoffs of staff.[32] In Petrograd and the textile center of Ivanovo-Voznesensk, women accounted for 58.7 percent and 63.3 percent of all unemployed, respectively.[33]

The number of unemployed women continued to rise throughout the mid-twenties, although the percentage of female unemployed dropped. In July 1923 an estimated 154,578 women (41.4 percent of the total) were unemployed. By July 1925, the number of unemployed women had risen to 232,422, although their percentage dropped to 35.4 percent.[34]

After the mass layoffs in 1921–22, women continued to face severe disadvantages at work. Many women were fired by managers who considered them more costly to employ than men. One delegate to the All-Union Congress of Working and Peasant Women in 1927 complained that managers fired women without considering their family responsibilities. "Often they terminate those who have three or four children and no husbands or relations," she said.[35] Conditions were even more difficult for divorced housewives, peasant women who migrated to the cities in search of work, or any other women entering the labor force for the first time. These women had no skills, no unemployment insurance, and no access to factory daycare. A. V. Artiukhina, the head of the Zhenotdel in 1927, argued that 84 percent of the women who needed jobs had never worked for wages.[36]

Robert Johnson's essay in this volume posits a new trend in migration patterns involving entire families in the move from country to city. Female family members came to the cities as wives and dependents and were less likely to have a place in the village to return to.[37] Such circumstances made women especially vulnerable in the face of divorce. As one delegate to the Congress of Working and Peasant Women explained, "If a woman worker leaves her husband, she only loses a husband, she has an independent source of income. But when the wife of a worker leaves her husband, she is considered a nonlaboring [netrudnyi] element, abandoned in the street, homeless and alone [besprizornoi]. There is nowhere for her to turn, all is closed, and everyone turns away from her."[38]

Given the problems of female unemployment and dependency, the rocketing divorce rate had a special significance for working-class women. Almost 45 percent of the urban women who divorced in the 1920s were unemployed and economically dependent on their husbands.[39] Without an independent wage, women were in no position to exercise their right to free union. Vera Lebedeva, the head of the Department for the Protection of Maternity and Infancy (OMM), grimly summed up the future of many divorced women:

> The weakness of the marital tie and divorce create masses of single women who carry the burden of childcare alone. Imagine yourself such a woman, without support from your husband, with a child on your hands, laid off because of a reduction in staff, and thrown out of the dormitory . . . with no possibility to continue supporting yourself.

"Where do these thousands go?" Lebedeva asked. "There is one exit—the street."[40]

The contrast between the socialist ideal of free union and the conditions of the time was nowhere so painfully depicted as in the spectacle of women selling themselves on the streets. Women solicited in the public toilets and "nestled in front doors, in passenger and freight cars, in alleys, in baths, and in other places."[41] Abandoned women, peasant widows, mothers with small children sold sex for six kopeks, for five rubles, for ten rubles for the night. Homeless girls, the female *besprizorniki,* slept in train cars. Many women, desperate for money, turned to prostitution. A. Irving, a sociologist who published a study of prostitution in 1925, concluded that "the main factors in prostitution are NEP and its temptations and the unemployment of women workers."[42] Prostitution represented the most painful, but not the most improbable, fate of the husbandless woman under NEP.

While unemployment stood as an unmistakable barrier to women's independence, the concentration of women in poorly paid, unskilled jobs also reinforced their dependence on men. Women earned only 65 percent of what men earned in the mid-twenties. In 1925, the average salary of women workers in various branches of industry nationwide was 32.60 rubles a month. The majority of women workers earned between 20 and 40 rubles; about 20 percent of women made less than 20 rubles, and only about 4 percent earned more than 60.[43] However meager the pooled salaries of the working-class family, the man's higher wages ensured a better standard of living for his wife and children. Even if a woman worked, divorce entailed a substantial drop in her material well-being.

Shurupova, an older delegate from the executive committee of Biisk district in Siberia, stood before the VTsIK wrapped in a dark crimson shawl and stressed the different consequences divorce had for men and women.[44] "There is no danger for the man," she declared, for "he meets another and will live with her. But for the woman it is horribly difficult to live under such conditions. All she gets is poverty, and poverty gets you nowhere." She noted that the country desperately needed children's homes, but added, "If the state took responsibility for this now, it would fail." In the absence of adequate state resources, Shurupova placed the blame on men. "Our side makes mistakes," she said, "but all the same, the majority of the guilty ones are men." Shurupova argued that a man should support his children no matter how many ex-wives he had. She flatly told the male delegates, "If you love tobogganing, then you have to pull your sled uphill."[45]

Unfortunately, even if a man harnessed himself to the family sled and trudged responsibly uphill, he confronted insurmountable obstacles in his path. Even with the best intentions, the average Soviet workingman could not support two families on his wages. In Moscow, the average worker heading a family in 1924 earned about 82 rubles a month. A second income from a working wife or teenager brought the monthly family earnings to about 125 rubles. The monthly expenses for this average family of three people were 107 rubles.[46] If the male worker became involved with another woman and had a child by her, the court was likely to order him to pay one-third of his wages in child support. This left his original family in serious financial trouble: almost 10 rubles short of meeting their monthly expenses. If the same male worker left his wife and children for the other

woman, the court would have ordered him to pay one-third of his income
to his former wife. Without the male wage, the family's income amounted
to only 43 rubles a month; and with child support, 70 rubles. Yet the
monthly expenses for a woman with one child amounted to about 72
rubles: her earnings and her former husband's payments could not cover
the family's basic expenses. And if a woman did not work, or worked only
part-time, or had more than one child, the family's financial prospects were
even more dismal. But regardless of circumstances, the result was unambiguous: given the high level of female unemployment, the low level of
wages in general, the concentration of women workers in unskilled, low-
paying jobs, and the lack of adequate daycare, the progressive legislation
on divorce was sharply at odds with the economic facts of working-class life.

Working-class wives did not need training in statistics to grasp this point.
Several women discussed the problems of divorce, alimony, and child
support in precise budgetary terms. Offering their own modest family
budgets as examples, they told the jurists that the average male wage could
support no more than one family. Turenkova, a woman worker from the
Urals, argued that divorce had economic as well as emotional consequences. "A man is registered with one women and lives with another,"
she explained.

> One has his children and a child is born to the other; the point is not only
> that he is the father of that other child, or that the registered wife is insulted.
> The main thing is that often the husband receives sixty-five rubles of pay;
> thirty rubles go to the apartment, firewood, and light, and thirty-five rubles
> is all that is left. Clearly, a family of six people can buy hardly anything. And
> according to the court, the husband must tear away part of his salary from
> the family to pay another wife.[47]

If a man married several times—as many did—it was even more difficult
for women to collect adequate child support. Tormazova, a delegate to the
VTsIK from Samara province, remarked, "We know of cases in which boys
eighteen to twenty years old have registered fifteen times, and in ten of
these marriages there were consequences. What can the court take from
him? Nothing."[48]

Tormazova's bitter assessment of the courts' ability to solve the problems
created by divorce was entirely accurate. Although the courts were lenient
in their awards to women and employed a loose standard of proof in
paternity cases, the awards were pitifully small. A typical case concerned a
woman worker who earned twenty-four rubles a month. She went to court
to get her ex-husband, who earned eighty rubles a month, to support their
seven-year-old daughter. But the man had remarried and now had four
children to support. He asked the court to award him custody of his
daughter because he simply could not afford to give up any of his income.

The court ordered him to pay twelve rubles a month,[49] leaving him and his four children even poorer than before and providing his ex-wife and daughter with roughly half of what they needed to survive.

In another case, a forty-five-year-old woman with a small child was divorced by her husband of twenty-one years. He remarried and had five children to support. The ex-wife, sick and unemployed, asked the court for thirty-five rubles a month to support her and the child. The court awarded her twenty rubles.[50] The spectacle of men and women haggling over petty sums before the judges revealed a painful truth. Women could not live on the court-ordered awards, and men could not afford to pay them. Poverty coupled with female dependence produced a situation that even King Solomon could not have resolved.

Given the great financial obstacles to divorce, men and women tended to blame each other for their hardships. Judges received "venomous notes" from men, complaining about court settlements. Men grumbled that alimony led to "unfree Soviet marriage," that it interfered with their freedom, that women were liberated at the expense of men. They claimed that the courts were unfair, always threatening "to swoop down on 'the third.'" Women, they insisted, used the courts to trap and blackmail men. Alimony was "punishment without a crime."[51]

Women blamed men, pointing to their promiscuity and irresponsibility. Delegate Pasynkova, infuriated by a man's charge that women used alimony to ensure a prosperous income, snapped back, "I categorically object to this comrade's attitude. Where is this man's head? He should understand that a child must be supported."[52] Baskakova, another delegate, retorted that such charges were "offensive to me and to all women." She said, "Men do not want to pay for their children because they do not feel the pains that a mother feels with a child. There is not a single woman who profits from alimony, and if there are such cases, they are compelled by bitter need."[53]

Moreover, women repeatedly pointed out that even if a woman received an alimony award, there was no guarantee the man would pay. A woman from a rural area wrote: "In the towns and in the countryside it is possible to find no small number of families abandoned by husbands. Although they sometimes pay child support, it is not enough to live on, and often they simply stop paying. This affects children most painfully of all. . . . In some cases, women are responsible for these tragedies, but mainly it is men."[54]

Thousands of men simply refused to pay the court-ordered awards. They left town or changed jobs. Sofia Smidovich, the head of the Zhenotdel, observed in 1926 that there were "a hundred subterfuges to avoid paying alimony." "Even on the occasion of a favorable settlement," Smidovich asserted angrily, "the woman (and practice shows that it always is the wretched woman who is importuning the courts for alimony) vainly strives to collect it. Her former spouse either leaves for the North Pole or claims he is unemployed, orphaned, etc."[55] The bailiffs had great difficulty collecting from such men, apprehending only about half of the men on their lists.[56]

Although women agreed on the main problems of social life—the high divorce rate, male irresponsibility, and inadequate child-support payments—they differed in their solutions. Some were willing to accept a freer vision of social life if the state would ensure that women and children would not suffer. A local meeting of women workers stressed that the material side of marriage was more important than the legal side. They resolved, "For us it is not important whether we are registered in ZAGS or not, it is important only that our children have the chance to be raised properly."[57] One of the VTsIK delegates who favored ratification of the new code suggested that the recognition of de facto marriage offered an excellent means for protecting needy women at a time when the state could not.[58] Another delegate favored recognition of de facto marriage but doubted that the law alone could resolve the problems of social life. Although men should pay alimony if they abandoned the women they lived with, the country really needed children's homes, "not court procedures."[59] A woman worker in a spirits factory wrote: "I think it is necessary to increase the number of childcare institutions so that women can stop fearing divorce and running after alimony."[60] And women needed jobs as well as childcare. Chernysheva, a delegate to the VTsIK, argued that waged work was essential to independence. She offered the example of a divorced housewife who remained unemployed because she had no skills. "What will be?" Chernysheva asked; her husband "can't support her and feed her for eternity." Chernysheva argued that women needed to acquire skills and become self-supporting. Only in this way could they escape their demeaning dependence on men.[61]

Yet many working-class women responded negatively to the permissive aspects of Soviet law. Regarding their dependence on men as a fact of life, they sought to strengthen, not loosen, the bonds of marriage. In their view, the "withering away" of the family did not represent an abstract restructuring of gender relations but the ever-present possibility that they would be unable to feed their children. Their opposition to divorce and free union was based on their desperate need for full access to their husbands' wages in order to support themselves and their children. One working-class housewife noted with grim honesty, "Women, in the majority of cases, are more backward, less qualified, and therefore less independent than men. . . . To marry, to bear children, to be enslaved by the kitchen, and then to be thrown aside by your husband—this is very painful for women. This is why I am against easy divorce."[62] Another woman, working in the Zhenotdel in a rural area, read an article by Aleksandra Kollontai in her local paper and expressed similar disapproval. She wrote,

It seems to me that her [Kollontai's] view is directed toward the destruction of the family. She proposes "free love" and "free union." Her opinion is that the spiritual life of a person, insofar as it is vast and complex, cannot be satisfied by union with one, but that a person needs several "partners." . . . In our opinion in the countryside this is simply called debauchery.

She concluded, "We need to struggle for the preservation of the family. Alimony is necessary as long as the state cannot take all children under its protection."[63]

Many women spoke directly against free union, insisting that the right to divorce be limited by law. Gnipova unconsciously appealed to a modified version of tsarist law when she suggested, "We must establish how many times it is possible to remarry—one, two, or three times."[64] A woman from Siberia emphasized that marriage was a social as well as an individual affair. She suggested that a formal meeting of friends and neighbors should decide whether a couple had the right to divorce. She wrote,

I consider the wishes of quarreling spouses, when they are in the thick of a fight, to be an insufficient reason for divorce, particularly if they have children. In the interests of the family, it is first necessary to ascertain if there is no chance for a mutual life. (This should be ascertained through a collective or formal meeting of citizens who know the life of the divorcing couple.) One must remember that divorce is painful for children and its consequences are often bad, not only for the family but for all of society (*besprizornost'*, promiscuity, etc.)[65]

Kapustina, a textile worker, said: "My request from the other women workers is to pass a decree ending serial marriages."[66] And a cleaning woman in Moscow wrote a letter expressing the same sentiment: "We must restrict divorce because it damages the state and the mother."[67]

Given the state's inability to shoulder the burden of childrearing, many working-class women feared divorce and regarded recognition of de facto marriage as a direct threat to their own economic security. If the mistress of a married man could sue for alimony, his wife and entire family would suffer a serious loss of income. Some women even opposed the provisions in the 1918 code that entitled all children to parental support whether they were born within or outside a registered marriage. Ten women factory workers wrote a joint letter suggesting that only two types of women should have the right to child support: the legal ex-wife and the woman living openly with a man who did not have another family. Any woman who knowingly got involved with a married man did not deserve support. Women who had sexual relations with many men did not deserve even a "scrap of bread."[68] One woman worker in a sawmill factory wrote: "I think that a woman who has relations with several individuals should not be awarded alimony. If she doesn't know who the father of her child is, let her bring it up herself." She added, "Such women are no better than street prostitutes, and alimony would only corrupt them even more."[69] Other women went even further, demanding that people who had extramarital affairs should be punished. A group of ten housewives argued that the government should "strengthen the punishment for husbands who get involved with other women, and also establish punishment for these women."[70]

These suggestions showed that not all women had the same economic and legal interests. The interests of single and married women frequently diverged as a result of their different relationships to the male wage earner. Just as the low level of the working-class wage led men and women to blame each other for the problems of divorce, married women saw sexually active single women as a threat to their families' income. While recognition of de facto marriage benefited the single woman, it directly threatened the wife. It is not surprising, then, that housewives were often the sharpest critics of sexual freedom and the strongest opponents of the recognition of de facto marriage. Their economic dependence undoubtedly conditioned their ideas about family and sexuality.

These working-class women fiercely defended a strict sexual morality, and they were willing to enforce it by repressive measures against both men and women. In contrast to the jurists who promoted free union, many working-class women mistrusted the "freedom" embodied in Soviet family law. Even if they favored the new code, they unanimously opposed frequent divorce and the break-up of the family. Rejecting the more permissive features of Soviet family law, they sought to limit divorce, establish punitive measures for extramarital relations, and limit men's responsibility for children born out of wedlock. Ironically, they sought to reestablish many features of a more patriarchal system of family law.

Working-class women did not put forward these ideas because of ignorance, backwardness, or irrational attachments to traditional social forms. On the contrary, their ideas were a direct expression of their own interests in the context of contemporary social conditions.[71] They quickly perceived that freedom was not an abstract concept but was grounded in the harsh material realities of everyday life. High female unemployment, the low level of the working-class wage, and the paucity of state resources undermined the socialist vision of free union. Women were dependent on men, and it was almost impossible for the male wage earner to support two families. In this context, free divorce could not be realized without a profoundly negative impact on women and children.

The very idea of marriage embedded in Soviet family legislation was sharply at odds with the idea of marriage expressed by working-class women. The law was premised on the socialist vision of marriage as a freely chosen, freely dissolved companionate bond between two equal individuals. But working-class women did not see marriage in primarily companionate or individual terms. Wages were not set equally, responsibility for children was not shared equally, and household labor was not equally apportioned. How could marriage be a union of two equal comrades? Marriage was a working partnership, a joint commitment to the economic survival of the family.

Women's sexual conservatism was a direct result of the gap between law and life. Their financial positions were so precarious that they could ill afford the personal freedom inherent in Soviet divorce law. Their own family incomes, shakily balanced on a thin line separating subsistence from ruin, could not withstand the loss of the male wage. Under these circumstances, the suppression of female sexuality outside marriage served not only male interests but the economic interests of the entire family. Women's sexual conservatism served as a strategy to preserve the family as an economic unit.

Marx and Engels wrote that in the early stages of capitalist development, the worker's wage was determined by the cost of the existence and reproduction of the worker.[72] In other words, the wage covered the bare costs of survival, childrearing, and little more. The economic facts of working-class life in the 1920s illustrated this stark proposition. The average working-class family's income barely covered the costs of housing, food, clothing, and childrearing. Soviet law, introducing a freer vision of social relations in an underdeveloped country, disrupted the fragile "economy of reproduction," setting men against women, and women against women, in competition over the wage. The collision of law and life resulted in social chaos, which hurt the most vulnerable groups in the population: women and children. Soviet jurists, strongly committed to women's equality, produced unforeseen consequences by their efforts to recast family relations.[73]

In 1936, the state instituted new laws that made divorce more difficult to obtain, increased the punishment for men who refused to pay alimony, and outlawed abortion. Historians have frequently seen these legal changes as part of a larger "retreat" designed by Stalin to increase the power of the state.[74] Yet it is clear that many working-class women—with little interest in increasing the birthrate or creating an obedient citizenry—would have ardently supported certain parts of this legislation.[75] The resurrection of the family may have been designed to serve industrial "order," but it also served social order as defined by the women who experienced the chaos and the difficulties of the NEP years. Indeed, social pressure from below must be counted as a factor in the change in family policy.[76] During the debate on the "progressive" family legislation implemented after the revolution, the working-class women of the twenties proclaimed their message clearly and firmly: painful problems ensued from applying a vision of legal freedom to an economic structure ill designed to support it.[77]

## NOTES

1. Ia. Kirpichov, "III Sessiia VTsIK," *Krestianka*, 23 (1926), p. 1.

2. Treatments of the 1925–26 debate over family law include Harold Berman, "Soviet Family Law in the Light of Russian History and Marxist Theory," *Yale Law Journal*, Vol. 56, no. 1 (1946), pp. 25–57; Beatrice Farnsworth, "Bolshevik Alternatives and Soviet Family Law: The 1926 Marriage Law Debate," in D. Atkinson, A. Dallin, and G. Lapidus, eds., *Women in Russia* (Sussex, 1978); Kent Geiger, *The Family in Soviet Russia* (Cambridge, 1968); Wendy Z. Goldman, "Freedom and Its Consequences: The Debate on the Soviet Family Code of 1926," *Russian History*, Vol. 11, no. 4 (1984), pp. 362–88; John Quigley, "The 1926 Soviet Family Code: Retreat from Free Love," *Soviet Union*, 6, part 2 (1979); and Sheila Rowbotham, *Women, Resistance and Revolution* (Harmondsworth, 1974), pp. 134–70.

3. Bolshevik attitudes toward the family had Russian as well as Marxist roots. See Barbara Engel's *Mothers and Daughters: Women of the Intelligentsia in Nineteenth-century Russia* (Cambridge, 1983), pp. 80–82, 140, 191–97, for the views of Russian radical women toward marriage and the family. See also Richard Stites, *The Women's Liberation Movement in Russia: Feminism, Nihilism, and Bolshevism, 1860–1930* (Princeton, 1978), pp. 366–71.

4. See August Bebel, *Women under Socialism* (New York, 1910); Frederick Engels, *The Origin of the Family, Private Property and the State* (New York, 1972); idem, *The Condition of the Working Class in England* (London, 1969); Karl Marx, *Capital: A Critique of Political Economy*, trans. Ben Fowkes (New York, 1977), Vol. I, pp. 620–21, and "The German Ideology," in Karl Marx and Friedrich Engels, *Selected Works* (Moscow, 1969), Vol. I, pp. 63–64.

5. I. A. Rostovskii, *Sovetskii zakon o brake i sem'e* (Moscow, 1926), p. 23.

6. A. T. Stel'makhovich, *Dela ob alimentakh* (Moscow, 1926), p. 3.

7. *The Marriage Laws of Soviet Russia: The Complete Text of the First Code of the RSFSR Dealing with Civil Status and Domestic Relations, Marriage, the Family, and Guardianship* (New York, 1921), pp. 11, 12 (hereafter cited as 1918 Code).

8. 1918 Code. See articles 52, 87–91, 107, 130–33, 155, 161, 162, 166–68, pp. 35, 41–43, 50, 51, 59–62.

9. For the history of European family law see Mary Ann Glendon, *State, Law and Family* (New York and Amsterdam, 1977).

10. *Piatyi sozyv vserossiiskogo tsentral'nogo ispolnitel'nogo komiteta. Stenograficheskii otchet* (Moscow, 1919), pp. 150–51.

11. Ibid., p. 146.

12. See 1918 Code, p. 8, and A. Stel'makhovich, "Alimentnye dela," *Proletarskii sud*, 12 (1925), p. 2.

13. Policy differences between advocates of individual freedom and proponents of family stability were evident throughout the twenties and emerged again after Stalin's death. Peter Juviler notes that reformers tried to restore the "Leninist" freedom of divorce and abolish the distinction between legitimate and illegitimate children from 1954 until the early sixties. See his "Family Reforms on the Road to Communism," in Peter H. Juviler and Henry W. Morton, eds., *Soviet Policy-making: Studies of Communism in Transition* (London, 1967).

14. These figures were cited by Dmitrii Kurskii, people's commissar of justice, in his speech to the VTsIK in 1925. See "Stenograficheskii otchet. Zasedaniia 2 sessii Vserossiiskogo Tsentral'nogo Ispolnitel'nogo Komiteta, XII sozyva, 17 i 19 oktiabria 1925 goda po proektu kodeksa zakonov o brake, sem'e i opeke," in *Sbornik statei i materialov po brachnomu i semeinomu pravu* (Moscow, 1926), p. 136 (hereafter cited as 1925 VTsIK).

15. For the 1925 draft of the family code see "Kodeks zakonov o brake, sem'e i opeke," in *Sbornik statei i materialov po brachnomu i semeinomu pravu* (Moscow, 1926).

16. 1925 VTsIK, p. 136.

17. Ibid., p. 142.

18. "III sessiia VTsIK XII sozyva," *Izvestiia*, November 12, 1926, p. 3.

19. 1925 VTsIK, p. 169.

20. *Estestvennoe dvizhenie naseleniia RSFSR za 1926 god* (Moscow, 1928), pp. XLVIII, LII. Russia had 1.6 divorces per 1,000 people, France, .46, and England, .06.

21. L. Lubnyi-Gertsyk, "Estestvennoe dvizhenie naseleniia SSSR za 1926," *Statisticheskoe obozrenie*, 8 (1928), p. 89.

22. *Estestvennoe dvizhenie naseleniia RSFSR za 1926 god* (Moscow, 1928), p. LIV.

23. Ibid., and Lubnyi-Gertsyk, p. 88.

24. M. Kaplun, "Brachnost' naseleniia RSFSR," *Statisticheskoe obozrenie*, 7 (1929), pp. 95–97.

25. For a discussion of the changing models of Soviet marriage, see Vladimir Shlapentokh, *Love, Marriage and Friendship in the Soviet Union: Ideals and Practices* (New York, 1984). Shlapentokh terms the Soviet model of marriage in the 1920s "romantic marriage" and notes that Lenin's view of marriage was similiar to Engels's: "If only marriage based on love is moral, it lasts only as long as love continues. But the duration of the feeling of individual sexual love of different individuals is very different, and once this feeling has withered, or is replaced by new, passionate love, divorce comes to be good for both partners as well as society." See Marx and Engels, *Sobranie sochinenii*, vol. 21, p. 85, quoted by Shlapentokh, p. 20.

26. Frank Lorimer, *Population of the Soviet Union* (Geneva, 1946), pp. 231–33.

27. 1925 VTsIK, p. 169.

28. The problem of female unemployment during NEP is treated by Carol Hayden, "The Zhenotdel and the Bolshevik Party," *Russian History*, Vol. 3, part II (1976); Elizabeth Waters, "From the Old Family to the New: Work, Marriage and Motherhood in Urban Soviet Russia, 1917–1931," Ph.D. dissertation, Centre for Russian and East European Studies, University of Birmingham (1985), pp. 82–136; and William J. Chase, "Moscow and Its Working Class: A Social Analysis," Ph.D. dissertation, Boston College (1979), pp. 287–316.

29. V. L., "Vliianie novoi ekonomicheskoi politiki na byt trudiashchikhsia zhenshchin," *Kommunistka*, 3–5 (1922), p. 15.

30. A. Anikst, "Bezrabotnitsa i zhenskii trud v Rossii," *Kommunistka*, 2 (1922), p. 38. The twelve provinces are Vladimir, Voronezh, Viatka, Kostroma, Moscow, Nizhegorod, Penza, Samara, Smolensk, Ufa, Ural'sk, and Yaroslavl.

31. Ibid.

32. GAORSSLO, fond 6262, op. 5, d. 9, p. 2.

33. Hayden, p. 169.

34. G. Pavliuchenko, "Bezrabotnitsa sredi zhenschin," *Kommunistka*, 5 (1925), p. 39. The percentage of unemployed women dropped while their absolute numbers increased, as peasant men, migrating to the cities in search of work, added to the numbers of unemployed males.

35. *Vsesoiuznyi s"ezd rabotnits i krest'ianok. Stenograficheskii otchet* (Moscow, 1927), p. 220.

36. Ibid., p. 237.

37. R. E. Johnson, "Family Life in Moscow during NEP," above.

38. *Vsesoiuznyi s"ezd rabotnits i krest'ianok*, p. 452.

39. M. Kaplun, "Brachnost' naseleniia RSFSR," *Statisticheskoe obozrenie*, 7 (1929), p. 47.

40. V. L., "Vliianie novoi ekonomicheskoi politiki na byt trudiashchikhsia zhenshchin," *Kommunistka*, 3–5 (1922), pp. 15–16.

41. A. Uchevatov, "Iz byta prostitutsii nashikh dnei," *Pravo i zhizn'*, 1 (1928), p. 52.

42. A. Irving, "Vozrastnyi i natsional'nyi sostav prostitutsii," *Rabochii sud*, 5–6 (1925), p. 209.

43. B. Markus, "Zhenskii trud v SSSR v 1924 godu," *Kommunistka*, 4 (1925), p. 49; and A. G. Rashin, *Zhenskii trud v SSSR* (Moscow, 1928), pp. 39, 37.

44. "III sessiia VTsIK 12 sozyva," *Izvestiia*, November 17, 1926, p. 4.

45. 1925 VTsIK, pp. 138–39.

46. E. O. Kabo, *Ocherki rabochego byta* (Moscow, 1928), p. 19. Kabo's figures for income and expenses are drawn from a sample of Moscow workers and may be somewhat higher than national figures. William Chase, citing several case studies from Kabo's work, notes that the wages of many unskilled or semiskilled workers were insufficient to support a family (Chase, pp. 199–200). Thus, many workers were barely able to support one family. Supporting the two or more families engendered by divorce was clearly impossible.

47. "Chto predlagaiut rabotnitsy," *Rabotnitsa*, 15 (1926), p. 16.

48. *III Sessiia vserossiiskogo tsentral'nogo ispolnitel'nogo komiteta XII sozyva. Stenograficheskii otchet* (Moscow, 1926), pp. 613–14 (hereafter cited as 1926 VTsIK).

49. Stel'makhovich, *Dela ob alimentakh*, p. 15.

50. Ibid. The problem of alimony, complicated by low wages, was further exacerbated by the rural-urban nexus. Robert Johnson notes the importance of the interaction between town and country in prerevolutionary Russia in "Family Relations and the Rural-Urban Nexus: Patterns in the Hinterland of Moscow, 1800–1900," in David L. Ransel, *The Family in Imperial Russia* (Urbana, 1978), pp. 263–80. The division of the family between two labor systems greatly complicated the question of divorce. Examples abound of peasants' paying alimony in kind. Stel'-makhovich discusses the case of a peasant woman who left her husband in the countryside and moved to Moscow with their child. She went to court to demand twenty-five rubles a month in lieu of the sack of flour she was receiving for child support. She claimed that the flour was useless in the city, and her ex-husband claimed he had no money. See Stel'makhovich, *Dela ob alimentakh*, p. 20.

51. A. Stel'makhovich, "Alimentnye dela," *Proletarskii sud*, 12 (1925), p. 1.

52. 1925 VTsIK, p. 137.

53. 1926 VTsIK, p. 631.

54. "Mysli krest'ianki," *Krest'ianka*, 6 (1926), p. 7.

55. S. Smidovich, "O novom kodekse zakonov o brake i sem'e," *Kommunistka*, 1 (1926), pp. 49–50.

56. "Diskussiia po povodu proekta kodeksa zakonov o brake, sem'e i opeke," *Rabochii sud*, 3 (1926), p. 233.

57. As quoted by the delegate Tormazova, who represented views expressed in local women's meetings at the 1926 VTsIK, p. 613.

58. 1926 VTsIK, p. 593.

59. Ibid., p. 605.

60. "Chto predlagaiut rabotnitsy," *Rabotnitsa*, 15 (1926), p. 16.

61. 1925 VTsIK, p. 181.

62. "Chto predlagaiut rabotnitsy," *Rabotnitsa*, 13 (1926), p. 14.

63. "Mysli Krest'ianki," *Krest'ianka*, 6 (1926), p. 7.

64. 1926 VTsIK, p. 656.

65. "Chto predlagaiut rabotnitsy," *Rabotnitsa*, 15 (1926), p. 16.

66. 1925 VTsIK, p. 143.

67. "Chto predlagaiut rabotnitsy," *Rabotnitsa,* 13 (1926), p. 14.
68. Ibid.
69. "Chto predlagaiut rabotnitsy," *Rabotnitsa,* 15 (1926), p. 16.
70. Ibid.
71. Barbara Clements uses a similar argument to explain working-class and peasant women's attitudes toward the family and other traditional institutions in the years immediately following the revolution in "Working-class and Peasant Women in the Russian Revolution, 1917–1923," *Signs,* Vol. 8, no. 2 (1982).
72. Karl Marx and Frederick Engels, "Wage Labor and Capital," in *Selected Works* (London, 1968), pp. 66, 79–80; Karl Marx, *Capital,* Vol. 1 (New York, 1977), p. 274.
73. For an opposing view of the Bolsheviks' attitude toward women's liberation, see Anne Bobroff, "The Bolsheviks and Working Women, 1905–1920," *Soviet Studies,* Vol. 26, no. 4 (1974), pp. 540–67. Bobroff argues that the Bolsheviks never had an independent commitment to women's rights but were primarily interested in women's "willingness to carry out the tasks determined by the state as necessary for collective well-being" (p. 563).
74. See Kent Geiger, *The Family in Soviet Russia;* Alex Inkeles, *Social Change in Soviet Russia* (Cambridge, 1968); Nicholas Timasheff, *The Great Retreat* (New York, 1946); John Hazard, *Law and Social Change in the USSR* (Toronto, 1953).
75. For a similiar argument about students' attitudes toward marriage and family, see Sheila Fitzpatrick, "Sex and Revolution: An Examination of Literary and Statistical Data on the Mores of Soviet Students in the 1920's," *The Journal of Modern History,* Vol. 50, no. 2 (June, 1978), pp. 252–78.
76. Roger Pethybridge argues in *The Social Prelude to Stalinism* (New York, 1974), p. 46, that "social recalcitrance on the part of the masses" contributed to the change in family policy in the 1930s, but he offers little evidence to support his contention. Janet Evans notes that women's reactions to the 1936 legislation were mixed: many favored stricter laws on alimony and divorce but opposed the prohibition on abortion. Evans writes, "The literature does suggest that women felt exploited by the change in sexual attitudes after the Revolution and that many were fairly enthusiastic about the package as a whole, which offered a hope of curbing male irresponsibility and of improving the status of women in personal relationships in the family." See "The Communist Party of the Soviet Union and the Women's Question: The Case of the 1936 Decree 'In Defense of Mother and Child,' " *Journal of Contemporary History,* 16 (1981), p. 770.
77. Moshe Lewin notes more generally that Lenin's "superstructure" was "suspended temporarily in a kind of vacuum." "The problem consisted not, as it was hoped, in adapting the recalcitrant 'superstructure' to the basis, but in first creating and then lifting up the basis to the lofty heights of the most advanced political superstructure." See "The Social Background of Stalinism," in *The Making of the Soviet System: Essays in the Social History of Interwar Russia* (New York, 1985), p. 260.

# IX

## "RAZMYCHKA?"

### URBAN UNEMPLOYMENT AND
### PEASANT IN-MIGRATION AS
### SOURCES OF SOCIAL CONFLICT

*Douglas R. Weiner*

An unwary traveler in Moscow in the late 1920s, turning the corner onto the street housing the Moscow Labor Exchange, might have encountered the following scene:

> For the entire width of the sidewalk, on the pavement, along the walls, in the doorways of nearby houses in a dense human agglomeration, the doors are opening by the minute, people crowd around. They are dressed almost identically—in *valenki*, worn-out *sapogi*, some in *lapti* . . . in thick coats or *polushubki* . . . many with a set of tools. . . . Here is where the construction section of the Moscow Labor Exchange is congregating.[1]

The above scene, so typical of the peasant inundation of the labor market in the cities during those years, was symbolic of the structural upheaval that was occurring in the Soviet labor force: the rustification of the urban workforce. Such scenes bore witness not only to the relative (and absolute) poverty and relative overpopulation of the Soviet countryside under the NEP, impelling millions of rural folk to seek sustenance and a better life through seasonal or permanent labor in the towns and cities, but also to the growing problem of urban unemployment, a problem exacerbated by the vast peasant in-migration.

Unemployment and its concomitant social dislocation reached serious proportions in the Soviet Union during the 1920s. Its causes were rooted in agrarian backwardness, the relative wealth of the cities, and lack of investment capital for both the agricultural and industrial sectors rather than in business cycles gone awry, giving unemployment a specific, chronic character. At times, it almost seemed intractable. This essay argues that urban unemployment during the NEP engendered or deepened urban workers' hostility toward peasant in-migrants, who competed with them for jobs. Evidence of such attitudes may be located in the statements of rank-and-file union members and their leaders and in the official policies of trade unions, especially in the years immediately preceding the collectivization drive. The existence of such an antagonistic relationship between these two social groups, if borne out by further research, would help to explain worker participation—or at least acquiescence—in Stalin's conflict-scarred collectivization campaign. As Lynn Viola has noted, the implication in traditional accounts of those years "that the Stalin faction acted without the support or encouragement of society"[2] is hardly plausible; industrial workers, she goes on to assert, "demonstrated support for collectivization and participated in its implementation both before and after the November [1929] Plenum decision."[3]

## A Question of Statistics

By any standard, unemployment by the mid-1920s had attained serious proportions. By 1924, according to L. S. Rogachevskaia, the unemployment rate among all workers was 18 percent, and by 1928/29 it was still a disturbing 12 percent.[4] The trade unions, maintaining their own records, recorded a rate of 19.62 percent for their membership on January 1, 1928.[5] Whatever the exact percentage, and it is doubtful that such a figure could now be computed, the scale of urban unemployment approached that of many countries of the West during the Great Depression.

Soviet statistical records from the period are fragmentary and frequently noncomparable: no one set of data embraces the total spectrum of unemployed workers. The best source of data are the records of the Commissariat of Labor's labor exchanges (*birzhi truda*), whose 281 local branches published monthly summaries, with detailed breakdowns, of all their registered unemployed. Regrettably, owing to the fact that a significant number of unemployed did not register at the exchanges, these data are incomplete.

The records of the trade unions constitute a second useful source. However, these figures do not include the vast army of nonunion unemployed: peasant in-migrants, seasonals, and adolescents offering their labor for the first time. We are thus condemned to work with approximations.

## The Emergence of a Problem

The disruption of production accompanying the political events of 1917 precipitated the first wave of unemployment, which reached its peak in the summer of 1918: between 500,000 and 800,000 were out of work, according to a range of sources.[6] The Civil War quickly put an end to that state of affairs, and with 5,000,000 men under arms under the Red banner alone, Russia quickly exhausted its reserves of adult male labor. Women and adolescents were drawn into the economy to fill the places of the men who left for the front. Although overt unemployment had vanished, absolute employment by January 1922 had declined to its modern historical nadir: 1,096,000.[7] The billowing demobilization of the Red Army, the revival of the *otkhod* (the exodus from the villages to towns and factories in search of work during the agricultural off-season), the ruin of much of the Soviet Union's industrial plant, and critical shortages of resources of all kinds all quickly made the previous hidden unemployment painfully manifest. By January 1923 registered unemployed totaled 641,000, and by the following January, 1,344,000.[8] By January 1927, the labor exchanges reported 1,350,000 on their rolls, including 90,000 metalworkers, of whom 67,000 were union members and 46,000 were classified as skilled. Of the 293,000 industrial workers, exactly 50 percent were classed as skilled, while an additional 77,000 were semiskilled. About 70 percent of both groups were members of unions. Of the registered unemployed as a whole, 743,000, or slightly more than half, claimed union affiliation.[9]

The trade unions also provide data for the same time period, which is valuable since not all union members sought work through the exchanges. For January 1927, the unions list 1,667,600—or 17.3 percent of their membership—as out of work.[10] If we add the labor exchanges' nonunion contingent of 608,000 to the totals offered by the VTsSPS, we arrive at a subtotal of 2,275,381 union and nonunion unemployed who found their way onto one or another registry. This, of course, does not include those job seekers who fell outside the statistical net of either bureaucracy. With all the reservations that attend playing with statistics, the claims of Trotsky's followers in 1927 that unemployment was heading toward the 3,000,000 mark may not be as far-fetched as they might seem at first glance. Official unemployment, as calculated by the exchanges, peaked in April 1929 (1,741,000); nevertheless, it remained at well over 1,000,000 beyond the end of the year and was "liquidated" (as the Soviets describe it) only by late 1930 (or 1931, depending on the account).

Lack of job opportunities in the 1920s particularly afflicted urban young adults and women. One despairing group of young graduates of the Dmitrov School for Locksmiths and Carpenters pleaded, after a vain job search of eighteen months, "We do not want to join the ranks of the *besprizornye* [homeless orphans and runaways]. We want to be active and useful citizens. Give us work and help us!"[11] Equally urgent was the complaint from a factory worker, Fedorova, of Ivanovo-Voznesensk, to the 13th Congress of Soviets: "We have 25,000 unemployed in the province. . . . This unemployment embraces mainly the children of workers, even of those who served in the Red Army. There are twenty-two-year-old un-employed who are falling into hooliganism and prostitution."[12] The report of a party official from that province noted that workers of retirement age were compelled to keep working only because they could not find work for their adult children.[13] At the 7th All-Union Congress of Trade Unions, V. V. Shmidt, the commissar of labor, even spoke of "an entire generation of workers [which was] growing up [without] the opportunity . . . to find employment."[14] Women, too, found their opportunities sharply curtailed. Shmidt even admitted that "women are the first to be fired,"[15] while his commissariat's house organ, *Izvestiia Narkomtruda*, conceded in 1925 that "the dislodgment of female labor from almost all branches of the economy is a fact . . . which cannot elicit any doubt."[16]

Social dislocation generated by unemployment took on more lurid hues as well. "The absence of discipline among the unemployed brought in its wake hooliganistic outbreaks," complained a report in *Voprosy truda*. "An almost daily occurrence was the appearance of the unemployed at the labor exchange in a drunken state . . . [as well as] their humiliation of women and girls. . . . Several exchanges, located near bazaars, turned into meeting places for recidivists, where they made plans for their felonies. Prostitution had woven itself a nest even within the walls of the exchanges."[17]

More disturbing still were the threats to public order and the political alienation of the unemployed. Demobilized Red Army men, for example, often demanded immediate referral to work. Their discontent sometimes even "went as far as demonstrations," according to one recent Soviet account.[18] Unemployed Moscow metalworkers rallied three thousand for a mass meeting, while in Odessa disturbances culminated in the murders of the assistant director of the labor exchange and of other functionaries.[19] OGPU deputy chief V. P. Menzhinskii wrote to the Central Committee on June 6, 1924, of evidence indicating "a growing movement among the unemployed with a definite anti-Soviet cast."[20] Most alarming, perhaps, for thoughtful Bolsheviks and, in particular, for those sympathetic with Bukharin's positions, unemployment increasingly loomed as a major ele-ment of structural instability in the NEP and as a source of a growing rift between the urban workers and the peasantry.

## The *Otkhod*

Although sources of unemployment included demobilization of the Red Army, several campaigns to streamline the administrative bureaucracies (*ratsionalizatsiia*), and factors mentioned earlier, its preeminent source was the irrepressible tide of poor peasants streaming to the cities in search of work and a better life: the *otkhod*.[21] During the Civil War, the *otkhod* was a meager 200,000 to 250,000[22] annually as compared with the annual average of almost 9 million in the period 1906–10.[23] Famine and devastation often sent urbanites fleeing in the reverse direction, to the countryside. With the restoration of civil peace, the great mass of "surplus agrarian population," variously estimated at from 8 to 19 million souls,[24] once again began its elemental surge toward the metropolis. For the poor peasant, whose household was not sufficiently diversified to guarantee work and income during the nongrowing season, and whose average annual income of 128 rubles in 1927 was only 35 percent of the average urban worker's, there was much logic in the *otkhod*. NEP agricultural policies, which now favored the more prosperous and "middle" peasants capable of exploiting the freer market conditions, simultaneously consigned the numerous poor peasantry *(bednota)* to the status of rural semiproletarians and tenant farmers, working with rented tools and livestock. On the margins of subsistence, this group had little to bind it to the countryside once other options presented themselves.[25]

Lenin was one who saw merit in the *otkhod* as an integral part of NEP—a positive step in the transformation of the peasantry. "It tears the population away from the outmoded, backward *zakholust'e* . . . and drags it into the whirl of modern social life. It raises the literacy and the consciousness of the population, habituates it to cultural mores and requirements."[26] Even within the agricultural world itself, Lenin believed, the *otkhod* effected a kind of cultural revolution right down to the family level: "The *otkhod* to the cities weakens the old, patriarchal family, puts the woman in a more independent position, gives her equality with the male. . . . Finally, 'last but not least,' the nonagricultural *otkhod* raises the wage level not only of those who go off to hired labor but *also of those who remain*."[27]

Lenin's views on the *otkhod* were formed at a time when the problem of the transformation of the peasantry's consciousness was uppermost in his mind, and when the problem of urban unemployment was virtually nonexistent. By the mid-1920s, however, the *otkhod* was almost universally implicated in the unemployment crisis, and it was increasingly regarded as a socially and economically pathological phenomenon.

From 1.5 million in 1923/24, the *otkhod* involved 3.25 million individuals in 1925/26, 1 million greater than the total number of blue-collar workers, and almost 40 percent of the total number of blue- and white-collar workers combined.[28] More than 2 million settled permanently in the cities during the fiscal year 1926/27,[29] with an additional 1 million *otkhodniki* remaining in the towns the following year.[30]

One by-product of this countrification of the cities was accelerating peasant representation in urban industry. As L. E. Mints of the Commissariat of Labor concluded in his monumental *Agrarnoe perenaselenie i rynok truda SSSR* (1929), peasant in-migrants actually enjoyed a privileged position in the urban labor market of the late NEP period.[31] One contributing factor was the extension of NEP "free market" principles to the arena of hiring. From mid-1924, the labor exchanges lost their monopoly role in the hiring of labor. Thenceforth, neither employers nor job seekers were *obliged* to register with the exchanges and could operate as independent agents via the newspapers or even through enterprises' personnel offices. This opened the doors to a whole group of rural laborers who previously would have been excluded from registering at the exchanges for want of a union card or previous work experience.

In addition to outcompeting union workers for jobs available through the exchanges—owing to employers' historic preference for pliant peasant labor—*otkhodniki* served to assist employers, both state agencies and private, in shifting production from union to nonunion shops. The way this was done, explained at great length in a number of articles by G. Belkin, among others, was through the creation of fraudulent artels.[32] Although these artels, by law exempt from the Labor Code, were supposed to be cooperative workshops of equals, in fact their workplans, materials, and salaries were all provided by the de facto employer. "As a consequence of this," wrote Belkin, "from 1924 on . . . we observe a crescendoing process of the liquidation of enterprises and the laying off of organized . . . workers. The unions were helpless to stop the process by which union members were being replaced by unorganized cottage industry, both urban and rural."[33]

### The Reaction to the *Otkhod*

Antagonism to the *otkhod* among urban workers seemed to begin in spontaneous fashion—in the factories, at the labor exchanges, in the unions. Konstantin I. Suvorov writes:

> In conditions of unemployment, rivalry inevitably arose among the workers. . . . The Bureau of the Communist Fraction of the Central Committee of the Construction Workers' Union noted in 1925, for example, that urban workers viewed the unemployed who came from the countryside as dangerous competitors who were taking away their earnings, and when the volume of work was reduced, the urban workers insisted on laying off the seasonals first, without regard to their qualifications. Inasmuch as the seasonals were peasants, rivalry between them and urban workers spoke negatively on the solidification of the union of the working class and the peasantry.[34]

The feelings of the urban construction workers gradually began to be echoed by the leaders of the trade union hierarchy, and even by those of the Labor Commissariat. Indeed, in a speech to the unemployment-ravaged union of Soviet Trade and Clerical Workers, V. V. Shmidt declared his intention of replacing the *otkhodniki* in construction work with unemployed office workers who would be retrained:

> Up to now, peasant, migrant labor has predominated . . . in the labor market for construction. We must change this situation. We have before us the inescapable question (. . . so as not to neglect the growing urban mass which adds to the ranks of the unemployed) . . . of how to adapt them for work. . . . Here the unemployed labor force of the city, including youth, too, . . . could successfully replace [peasant] construction laborers, and they would carry out their work substantially better than arrivals from the countryside.[35]

Between its 7th and 8th congresses, the VTsSPS (All-Union Central Council of Trade Unions) undertook a broad study of the unemployment question and identified yet another process whereby the *otkhod* translated into unemployment among industrial union members. In this two-stage scenario, migrants first entered the "agricultural" trade unions—Food Workers, Sugar Workers, Agricultural and Forest Industries Workers, or Construction Workers. Using these as "ports of entry," these "quasi-peasant elements, taking advantage of their rights as union members . . . infiltrate into production as . . . low-skilled workers, and in so doing create unemployment among the urban proletariat."[36]

Membership breakdowns gave credence to the sense of alarm. From January 1927 to January 1928, seasonal membership in the Sugar Workers climbed from 53 percent to 63 percent. In the Construction Workers in 1927, seasonals accounted for no less than 46.5 percent, a gain of 15 percent in a year.[37]

At union gatherings large and small there was a rising clamor to close the union portcullis on the peasant hordes. Thus, at the 4th Plenum of the VTsSPS, held on June 14, 1928, L. Ginzburg, a high official in the unions, pointedly noted that several unions have "*excessively easy entry for peasants*. In this way," he argued, "a stimulus is created for their migration to the city. We must decisively terminate this," he appealed, "since the chaotic inundation of workers from the countryside is already too big without [easy entry]."[38] Many felt that the measures confined to limiting peasant entry to the "agricultural" unions did not go far enough, and argued that barriers should be extended to other unions, such as the Food Workers and Local Transport Workers, "which also serve as 'open doors' for [peasant] infestation of the industrial unions."[39]

Against this backdrop, the VTsSPS announced a series of new regulations on June 24, 1928, specifically designed to tighten entry for peasant labor into the unions. They provided for a minimum work record of two months in order to qualify for membership in a union, providing hired work was the seasonal's sole means of support. All other seasonals would be considered for entry based on the number of seasons they had already worked, to be fixed by the individual unions, with documentary proof of work history required.[40]

Individual unions were, if anything, more militant than the central body. Citing the "infestation of the union by nonproletarian elements and individuals, for whom hired labor is not a natural or basic form of sustenance,"[41] the Central Committee of the Marine Transport Workers adopted a number of measures to preserve what it felt was the threatened integrity of its membership. First, it ordered a reregistration of all members on inland waterways and tightened up procedures for issuance of new cards. Rank-and-file members pressed the leadership to extend this weeding out to cold-water seas as well, but that was vetoed by the leadership, which feared a complete breakdown in work discipline and the union's system of work sharing. Second, in line with the new VTsSPS directive, the union established as a precondition of membership a term of service of no less than six months on ships of the line. Finally, it enjoined a specially formed commission to "conduct an investigation into the social status of the union membership, especially those who live in the countryside, and take the measures incumbent upon it to safeguard the union from infestation . . . by nonproletarian elements and elements alien to the working class."[42]

The unions also moved into opposition concerning the laws providing for "free hire." Forced to go along with the legislation in late 1924, by October 1926, at its 7th Plenum, the VTsSPS had withdrawn its support, demanding restoration of the labor exchanges' monopoly on placement. Even representatives of the Labor Commissariat, such as Ia. I. Gindin, made it known that free hire had led only to disorganization in the labor market and the substitution of nonunion for union labor, taking particular aim at the growing practice by employers of dispatching agents to recruit whole villages for work in the cities.[43]

Acting in response to pressure from the VTsSPS, the government began an energetic program of peasant resettlement,[44] established a network of 650 labor correspondence points, and enacted three new decrees limiting the latitude of employers to recruit workers from outside the locality by mandating prior authorization by the Labor Commissariat.[45]

In light of the above, it seems a bit oversimplified to state, as does E. H. Carr, that "the trade unions were no longer organizations representative of the special interests of the working class (since no such special interests were recognized), but organs for the performance of certain specific functions within a governmental machine which identified the interests of the working class with those of the community as a whole."[46]

In the intraparty cleavages of the 1920s, the unions are generally placed in the camp of the Right Opposition, owing to Tomskii's alliance with Rykov and Bukharin. Yet, the whole relationship of the unions toward the *otkhod* reveals an important shared value with the Trotsky perspective: a belief in the ontological superiority of the proletariat over the peasantry. In their defensive, conservative way, the unions reflected the growing fears of their basic constituency—the urban proletariat—fears which ran along sociological rather than along ideological lines. Even such a stalwart Bukharin supporter as Uglanov concurred with the Left that it was necessary to stem the gushing human tide from the countryside.[47]

In their desperate, belated bid for working-class support, the various Left Oppositions repeatedly spotlighted the problem of unemployment. As early as 1925, Zinoviev was decrying half-measures, stating, "You cannot empty this sea of unemployment with a teaspoon."[48] One of the most fascinating and extreme of the Left's critiques were the countertheses to the 15th Party Congress, published on November 17, 1927, in *Pravda* by the Joint Opposition. The most furious attacks were loosed at the treatment by the party majority of unemployment. Momentously, the countertheses were first to suggest an offensive against the countryside: "Two million unemployed in the cities and one billion poods of unused grain stores in the countryside—this is the clearest and most graphic picture of those contradictions . . . which in huge measure have accumulated as a result of the errors of the current leadership."[49] The Opposition proclaimed that "it would not hesitate for one moment to assume responsibility" for putting that "dead capital" to work creating jobs. Significantly, too, the Opposition stressed that they would outlaw the "backseating of permanent workers in favor of seasonals in hiring," raise unemployment benefits and extend benefit terms, initiate massive public-works projects, halt the attachment of property of unemployed workers, abolish unpaid apprenticeships among adolescents, raise the youth job quotas, build more schools for working-class children, and give everyone pay raises.[50] Women, shown to have been receiving less than equal pay for equal work in at least one study,[51] were promised an end to all inequities.

Every major disaffected urban group was the target of the Left's final search for support. Were it not for a number of specific factors, including the rather important one of worker mistrust of the leaders of the Opposition, their appeal might have succeeded. That the appeal was a potent one was demonstrated soon afterward by Stalin, in my opinion, who was able to use it to good advantage against the Right. The appeal to workers, in contrast to that made to the Communist intelligentsia, was less an appeal to hopes than to fears of the future. Whereas the Communist intelligentsia was lured by the prospect of a "second," decisive "revolution," it seems likely that workers were drawn into the war against the countryside by a perception that they were defending the conditions of their very existence: their wages, their preeminence in the social hierarchy (or, more exactly, social mythology), their right to food and housing, and their right to work—their very turf. In light of this hypothesis, the mass withdrawals of worker-members of the various rural-assistance *"shefstvo"* societies *(obshchestva smychki)* from 1927 may arguably be regarded as another indication of this sociological *"razmychka"* or schism.[52]

In a truculent article in *Trud* (April 3, 1929), the Stalinist B. L. Markus announced "the political task of giving top priority in hiring to none other than proletarians." Asserting that "Mensheviks . . . heap mounds of abuse . . . in their *Sotsialisticheskii vestnik* on our policy of 'obstructing the inmigration of workers from the countryside to the cities,' " Markus stoutly defended what he called the policy of "governmental nepotism" toward the unemployed proletarian. "The presence of peasant infestation at the labor exchange despite existing limitations on alien elements," he continued ominously, "suggests to us not a retreat from our political line but the necessity of reevaluating its implementation."[53]

As I have tried to suggest, Markus's attitudes, now given official voice on the eve of collectivization, had been taking shape years earlier among the rank and file of urban workers. In their bid for urban working-class support for collectivization, Stalin and his faction, it seems, were perhaps able to mobilize those attitudes to a greater extent than we have heretofore suspected. Lynn Viola has observed à propos the "Twenty-five Thousanders," workers' brigades that went off to rural Russia to enforce collectivization, "A survey of recruitment pledges and letters, along with other types of evidence, indicates that many workers volunteered to serve in the countryside because they perceived the nation to be at war and because they believed that collectivization was necessary to the survival . . . of the nation."[54] This conviction, we may surmise, was strongly nourished by the bruising experiences of urban workers in the job market of NEP Russia.

## NOTES

1. K. I. Suvorov, *Istoricheskii opyt KPSS po likvidatsii bezrabotitsy (1917–1930 gg.)* (Moscow, 1968), p. 73.

2. Lynn Viola, "Notes on the Background of Soviet Collectivization: Metal Worker Brigades in the Countryside, Autumn, 1929," *Soviet Studies,* 36 (April 1984), p. 205.

3. Ibid.

4. L. S. Rogachevskaia, *Likvidatsiia bezrabotitsy v SSSR, 1917–1930 gg.* (Moscow, 1973), pp. 76, 399.

5. *Professional'nye soiuzy SSSR za 1926–1928 gg.* (Moscow, 1928), p. 394.

6. Suvorov, *Istoricheskii opyt,* p. 49; Rogachevskaia, *Likvidatsiia,* p. 70.

7. A. A. Matiugin, *Rabochii klass SSSR v gody vosstanovleniia narodnogo khoziaistva (1921–1925)* (Moscow, 1962), p. 208.

8. Suvorov, *Istoricheskii opyt,* p. 77.

9. *Voprosy truda*, 1927, no. 4, pp. 172–75.
10. *Professional'nye soiuzy*, p. 394.
11. *Pravda*, October 22, 1926.
12. Suvorov, *Istoricheskii opyt*, p. 126.
13. Ibid., p. 125.
14. V. V. Shmidt, "Nashi dostizheniia i nedostatki v oblasti regulirovaniia truda i ocherednye zadachi nashei trudovoi politiki," *Voprosy truda*, 1927, no. 1, pp. 22–23.
15. E. H. Carr, *Socialism in One Country*, vol. 1 (Baltimore, 1958), p. 393.
16. *Izvestiia Narkomtruda*, 1925, no. 6, p. 27.
17. S. Tarasov and D. Lediaev, "Puti ozdorovleniia raboty birzh truda," *Voprosy truda*, 1929, no. 3, p. 96.
18. Suvorov, *Istoricheskii opyt*, p. 83.
19. Rogachevskaia, *Likvidatsiia*, p. 80.
20. Ibid.
21. Strictly speaking, the *otkhod* was a *temporary* exodus from the villages during the nongrowing season in search of supplementary income—in construction, factory work, logging, and other activities. The fact of the matter was, however, that, especially from the mid-1920s, many *otkhodniki* never returned to their villages but stayed on as permanent residents of the cities and towns where they had been seeking seasonal work. Because a distinct term indicating *permanent* peasant in-migration to urban areas was never coined, *otkhod* came to designate that meaning as well.
22. V. P. Danilov, "Krest'ianskii otkhod na promysly v 1920-kh godakh," *Istoricheskie zapiski*, 1974, no. 94, p. 73.
23. Ibid., p. 71.
24. Ibid., p. 63, and Rogachevskaia, *Likvidatsiia*, p. 84.
25. See the discussion on peasant stratification and agrarian overpopulation in Moshe Lewin, *Russian Peasants and Soviet Power: A Study of Collectivization* (New York, 1968), chapter 2, pp. 41–64.
26. Danilov, *Krest'ianskii otkhod*, p. 56.
27. Ibid.
28. Carr, *Socialism*, p. 388.
29. Rogachevskaia, *Likvidatsiia*, p. 84.
30. L. S. Rogachevskaia, "K voprosu o sotsial'nom preobrazhenii sel'skogo khoziaistva i likvidatsiia bezrabotitsy v SSSR," *Rol' rabochego klassa v sotsialisticheskom preobrazovanii derevni v SSSR* (sbornik) (Moscow, 1968), p. 235.
31. L. E. Mints, *Agrarnoe perenaselenie i rynok truda SSSR* (Moscow, 1929), p. 459.
32. See G. Belkin, "Bezrabotitsa i neorganizovannyi trud," *Vestnik truda*, 1927, no. 12, pp. 38–43; also his "K voprosu o trudovykh arteliakh," *Bol'shevik*, 1926, no. 4 (Feb. 28), pp. 75–84; "O trudovykh arteliakh," *Vestnik truda*, 1927, no. 5, pp. 22–29; "Profsoiuz i neorganizovannye rabochie," *Vestnik truda*, 1926, no. 12, pp. 31–35; and "Zakonodatel'noe regulirovanie uslovii truda kvartirnikov," *Vestnik truda*, 1927, nos. 6–7, pp. 60–65.
33. Belkin, "Bezrabotitsa," p. 40.
34. Suvorov, *Istoricheskii opyt*, pp. 82–83.
35. V. V. Shmidt, "Voprosy bezrabotitsy, gosnormirovaniia, i okhrany truda sovtorgsluzhashchikh," *Voprosy truda*, 1927, no. 6, p. 5.
36. *Professional'nye soiuzy*, p. 395.
37. Ibid., p. 90.
38. *Trud*, June 15, 1928.
39. Ibid.
40. *Professional'nye soiuzy*, p. 90.

41. *Otchet tsentral'nogo komiteta profsoiuza rabochikh vodnogo transporta SSSR (avgust 1927 g.–avgust 1928 g.) k deviatomu kongressu* (Moscow, 1929), pp. 9–10.

42. Ibid., and p. 138.

43. Ia. I. Gindin, "Naem rabochikh v promyshlennosti i v sezonnoi rabote," *Vsesoiuznyi s"ezd otdelov ekonomiki truda VSNKh'a SSSR* (Moscow-Leningrad, 1927), p. 80.

44. Danilov, *Krest'ianskii otkhod*, p. 105. See also P. P. Maslov's recommendations in "Problemy bezrabotitsy," *Ekonomicheskoe obozrenie*, 1924, no. 16, pp. 13–22; and A. N. Isaev, "VII Vsesoiuznyi s"ezd professional'nykh soiuzov i voprosy bezrabotitsy," *Voprosy truda*, 1927, no. 1.

45. Svod Zakonov SSSR, SZ 13./139 1927 st. 3; SZ 13./132 1927 st. 2; SZ 13./132 1-10. "On regulating the labor market for construction workers for the 1927 season"; "On measures of regulating recruitment"; "On measures for regulating the labor market."

46. Carr, *Socialism*, p. 441.

47. *Vsesoiuznyi s"ezd professional'nykh soiuzov, Vos'moi, Stenograficheskii otchet* (Moscow, 1928), p. 363.

48. *Leningradskaia pravda*, April 15, 1925.

49. *Pravda*, November 17, 1927.

50. Ibid.

51. A. G. Rashin, *Zhenskii trud v SSSR, 1924–1926 gg.* (Moscow, 1926).

52. On this, see A. S. Siluianov, "Shefskaia pomoshch' rabochego klassa derevne v podgotovke sotsialisticheskogo preobrazovaniia sel'skogo khoziaistva, 1925–1929 gg.," in *Rol' rabochego klassa*, pp. 5–61; and V. Smyshliaev, *Po Leninskim zavetam* (Leningrad, 1969).

53. B. L. Markus, "Burzhuaznye i melkoburzhuaznye ustanovki v voprosakh truda," *Trud*, April 3, 1929.

54. Lynn Viola, "The '25,000ers': A Study in a Soviet Recruitment Campaign during the First Five Year Plan," *Russian History/Histoire Russe*, 10, part 1 (1983), p. 23. For an extended treatment, see her *The Best Sons of the Fatherland: Workers in the Vanguard of Soviet Collectivization* (New York and Oxford, 1987).

# X

# SOLDIERS IN THE PROLETARIAN DICTATORSHIP

## FROM DEFENDING THE REVOLUTION TO BUILDING SOCIALISM

*Mark von Hagen*

In the late 1920s the Bolshevik leadership launched a new revolution which it defined as the building of socialism. By this it meant the creation of a state that could survive in the international arena by means of a powerful army, a state that could rely upon a prosperous economy after a program of crash industrialization and collectivization pursued along an explicitly noncapitalist path.[1] The new order that emerged from the second revolution was declared to be "socialism," and it certainly appeared to have met some of the formal requirements established by the socialist movement since its inception. But the new order also had characteristics that many socialists, both in and outside Russia, found repulsive. Many of those characteristics could be summarized as militarism.[2] Indeed, one way of understanding the new order that coalesced under Stalin is as an uneasy mix of socialism and militarism that permeated all levels of political, social, economic, and cultural life. The Bolsheviks' political rhetoric was replete with war imagery and appeals to fight. The defense economy won a preponderant role in the nation's economic planning by the end of the First Five-Year Plan. Soldiers and officers came to enjoy a semiprivileged status, and military values helped shape much of education and popular culture.[3] Moreover, by the mid-1920s a vocal segment of the military leadership exhibited features of what William Fuller has called "negative corporatism," a contempt for civilians and civilian institutions and a preference for military solutions to political and social problems.[4]

Between 1917 and 1930, Russian society and state were transformed through intended and unintended consequences of the revolution, as the revolution itself came to be differently perceived by diverse groups throughout the former empire. Within the larger changes, the status and role of soldiers also evolved through distinct stages. How did these transformations occur? Why, especially, did aspects of militarism come to play such an important role in reshaping the revolutionary political order? Although the legacy of the years of the Civil War was very important, the changes cannot be reduced to "civil war determinism."[5] The transformation began with the collapse of the autocracy well before the Bolsheviks came to power in late 1917 and was shaped as much by the dilemmas of NEP society as it was by the Civil War itself. During all these years soldiers were key actors, and the Red Army at all levels—from the soldiers to the political officers and commissars, to the military specialists and Red Commanders, to the strategists and commanders-in-chief at the very top of the military hierarchy—played a crucial role in the transformation.

The army is important, however, not only because it played a key role in the emergence of the postrevolutionary order. Leon Trotsky quipped that "the Army is a copy of society and suffers from all its diseases, usually at a higher temperature."[6] Indeed, the army offers a particularly revealing window on Soviet society and politics during these crucial formative years because military men occupied a vantage point from which they had to constantly balance the imperatives of the international political struggle with the intractable dilemmas posed by Russia's economic and social structures, all the while considering alternatives and options that were in large measure shaped and limited by Bolshevik ideology. Importantly, the regime came to rely on the army to broaden its political hegemony in postrevolutionary society by disseminating the values of a national defense-welfare state among its soldiers, who would leave the army for careers in the civilian urban and rural bureaucracies. In this sense, the Bolsheviks acted as a "historical bloc" and sought to become hegemonic by winning assent to their claims that their particular interests were those of society at large.[7] Army service became a key component in defining citizenship in the new state; but the army also shaped the state's own self-identity in crucial ways.[8] By the end of the Civil War, the army was the largest national institution that the new state could claim, and the one through which the political elite maintained constant relations with the majority of the population—peasants, blue- and white-collar workers alike. In particular, soldiers occupied a position between the ideal proletariat and the suspect peasantry.

Despite the prominent place that the party and the Soviet state accorded soldiers in the founding documents of the new regime,[9] the social origins of the soldiers continued to trouble influential party figures in the military organization. When the newly formed Soviet government began to debate plans for an armed force, prominent Bolsheviks called for a militia made up exclusively of industrial workers.[10] By contrast, the imperial military establishment had regarded peasants as the most reliable fighting men and considered urban elements, especially workers and students, potential revolutionary leaven.[11] The Bolsheviks reversed this evaluation of political and military reliability, considering urban citizens to be far more reliable soldiers than peasants. Undoubtedly, a great deal of the prominence that soldiers occupied in early Bolshevik political hierarchies can be attributed to the leaders' naive expectations that theirs would be a socialist militia composed mostly of urban citizens with the requisite political consciousness and loyalty to the new regime. By the end of 1918, and certainly by early 1919, however, it became unmistakably clear that an overwhelmingly peasant army would be defending the dictatorship of the proletariat for the foreseeable future.

The same constitution that affirmed the exceptional status of soldiers in the new political order also erected an electoral system that consciously discriminated against the rural population by giving urban soviets greater proportional weight than rural soviets.[12] This uneven franchise was the context for the soldiers' political and legal existence as a halfway house between their peasant origins and their peculiar "proletarian consciousness." The new leaders remembered all along that soldiers were from the countryside and that the military survival of the regime was inextricably bound up with the problems of that countryside. At the same time, soldiers' behavior during 1917 and even afterward sustained the leaders' hopes that soldiers did stand apart in fundamental ways from their nonuniformed fellow villagers. And the regime continually made appeals and concessions to soldiers and their families that contributed to the emergence of a new social and political category—the Red Army man—that remained one of the most important legacies of the Civil War for later years.

The "social contract" with the soldiers took many forms. Besides the constitutional and moral status of military men discussed above, the three other most important indices of their prominence in the new order in-cluded Bolshevik Party membership policies, opportunities for upward mobility in the army itself, and education and welfare benefits. Following the 8th Party Congress in March 1919, the Central Committee ordered the first major purge of the party membership by means of a reregistration.[13] After the purge, the party resolved "to open wide its doors to healthy proletarian and peasant elements." During the party recruitment week, Red Army men were granted a special status that exempted them from the usual requirement of two recommendations in writing and, importantly, recognized them to be as worthy of party membership as were workers. Nationwide, the membership drive fell short of the leaders' ambitious targets, but the army alone contributed 40 percent of the new Communists. After 1919 the army's party organizations grew at a faster pace than those of the party at large. Rank-and-file soldiers made up between one-half and three-quarters of the new members. In the towns, 47 percent of the new party members were workers and 53 percent Red Army men, again demonstrating that soldiers were at least as loyal to the new regime as, if not more loyal than, "real" proletarians. Moreover, it was largely through the army's party organizations that most peasants and many white-collar workers gained access to the most important political organization in the country, the Communist Party.[14]

The second important policy that guaranteed rank-and-file soldiers a claim on the regime's power was the army's practice of promoting soldiers of worker and peasant origins to officer and political-officer ranks. Although the officer ranks of the Imperial Army certainly had become more open to nonnoble subjects by the end of the Romanov dynasty, and the Great War probably unwittingly served as a force of democratization, the military elite continued to be viewed as a preserve of the privileged classes of imperial Russian society. The exigencies of national defense after 1917 overturned this order as well. Because the new government was short on reliable and experienced officers, it turned reluctantly to the military specialists—as former imperial officers and military bureaucrats were branded—to staff its first commands. By the end of the Civil War, 48,500 officers, 10,300 bureaucrats, and 14,000 military doctors had been called up for service in the Red Army. The presence of the "class-alien elements," however, remained a sensitive and controversial issue throughout the Civil War and even well into the 1920s. From the beginning, the new military leadership committed itself to creating its own "Red" officer corps. The first schools to train Red Commanders opened in December 1917. The crash military courses turned out nearly 65,000 commanders, whose class origins were testimony to the policies of proworker and propeasant discrimination in promotion to officer rank. Of the new commanders, 12 percent claimed working-class origin, 67.3 percent peasant origin, and 20.7 percent intelligentsia origin (mostly Old Bolsheviks). By the end of the Civil War, the military specialists constituted only 34 percent of the total officer corps.[15]

The third important part of the social contract between the regime and its soldier constituency was the enactment of a wide panoply of education and welfare benefits for soldiers and their families. In part, these measures were intended to win the loyalty of the soldiers, who had demanded improved living conditions and more access to benefits in the Imperial Army in 1905, and again with more fervor in 1917; but the policies were also a reflection of the regime's self-image as a socialist state that was committed to bettering its citizens' welfare. Any casual survey of early Soviet decrees reveals how often soldiers' benefits occupied the leaders' attentions.[16] The Red Army, through its Political Administration (PUR), spent large sums on educational programs: literacy courses, political education, and even farming techniques. By no means were the new regime's relations with the soldiers free of conflicts and tensions; but soldiers did increasingly look to the regime to defend their economic and political interests in the towns and especially in the countryside in exchange for combat service against the regime's enemies.

Finally, the regime, through its army, adapted itself to accommodate and shape a constituency that its formal ideology did not allow it to accommodate per se in other important ways that would play a role in shaping the post–Civil War political settlement. Not only were soldiers granted a privileged status in revolutionary society, but workers were rendered closer to soldiers in their daily life. The entire republic was subject to labor conscription by the same "Declaration of Rights" that proclaimed the new government's first principles. During the Civil War the status of workers and soldiers became further conflated in the formation of labor armies, most often associated with Trotsky but in fact enjoying widespread support among the party's leadership, including Lenin's enthusiastic endorsement. The labor armies provisionally erased all status markers that distinguished workers from soldiers and placed demobilized units on labor conscription status for economic tasks. Based on the relatively successful experience with the armies, at least in the eyes of their advocates, the party's Central Committee submitted theses on the economic reconstruction of the nation to the delegates of the 9th Congress in March and April 1920 that recommended securing a prominent role in the necessary "militarization of the economy" to "the best workers who had completed the military school"; furthermore, as a model of how to structure labor in the postwar period, the Central Committee recommended the organization and principles according to which the Red Army was created, precisely because the army was the most important example of a mass Soviet organization of the type that "guaranteed for the less conscious, more backward peasant masses the natural leaders and organizers in the person of the most conscious, in their overwhelming majority professionally skilled, proletarians."[17] Although eventually the labor armies lost their supporters and were dismantled (the last ones, however, only in 1922), military experience still played a large role in the formulation of plans for economic reconstruction. The Council for Labor and Defense (created after a reorganization of the Council of Workers'-Peasants' Defense in April 1920), even after it was demoted to a commission subordinate to Sovnarkom, had primary responsibility for drafting a unified plan for economic reconstruction.[18]

Just how fragile the wartime settlement had been became unmistakably clear once the populace understood that the White armies had been defeated and the fighting might soon come to an end. Soldiers, workers, and peasants alike had been willing—to varying degrees—to suffer considerable material deprivations as long as the fate of the regime truly hung in the balance. But as soon as the Red Army pushed Wrangel's troops out of the Crimea, a new wave of mutinies, strikes, and peasant rebellions swept the country with a ferocity that caught the regime by surprise. Army conditions quickly came to resemble the situation in the Imperial Army during late 1917 when soldiers demanded to be demobilized and protested the shortages of food and supplies.[19] The breakdown in discipline and morale, desertions, and high crime rates among soldiers rendered many fighting units virtually useless, and Cheka troops were called in to put down domestic unrest.[20] Soldiers made clear to the regime that they had fulfilled their obligations to defend the state and would fight no more, especially in such terrible conditions.

All the tensions of the wartime compromises burst forth. The soldiers' discontent gave new life to all those men and women who had come to resent the army's privileged place in the regime's priorities; they too demanded a rapid demobilization of the army and that the regime begin the long-promised but repeatedly postponed transfer of its armed forces to a socialist militia. The army's enemies throughout the party resented not only the way in which the military machine had gobbled up inordinate resources during the recent fighting. They also attacked what they considered to be the military's pernicious influence on party politics. Members of both the Workers' Opposition and the Democratic Centralist group, as well as such prominent party leaders as Nikolai Bukharin, insisted that the military return to more democratic principles—including a renewed political role for soldiers' committees and a corresponding limitation of the powers of the commissar—and that the regime itself thoroughly demilitarize its own institutions.[21]

Among the most prominent of the army's critics, besides the Workers' Oppositionists and Democratic Centralists, were Nikolai Podvoiskii as head of the Universal Military Training Administration *(Vsevobuch)*, who envisioned himself as the head of the new militia forces; Anatolii Lunacharskii, commissar of enlightenment, and Nadezhda Krupskaia, director of the Main Political Enlightenment Administration *(Glavpolitprosvet)* and wife of Lenin, both of whom wanted to dismantle the army's Political Administration (PUR) and take over all enlightenment programs for soldiers; the Commissariat of Justice, which sought to restore its own control over the nation's judicial system and to abolish the revolutionary military tribunals; and most civilian provincial party committee chairmen, who were smarting from their subordination to the military authorities under the long periods of martial law during the Civil War.

The Revolutionary Military Council responded to the pressures by ordering a first demobilization in late 1920; within twenty days of the demobilization order, the army fell from second to sixth place in priority for food rations.[22] Another clear sign that the army had fallen in importance to the regime was the mass exodus of commissars and party members from military to civilian assignments. Just when the army most needed competent and experienced personnel to bring the nightmarish situation under control, it found itself desperately short of political commissars. Army leaders (especially Mikhail Frunze, Ivar Smilga, and Sergei Gusev), in defense of their institution, warned their political enemies that even the current seeming peace was only temporary because world capitalism was regrouping for its next assault on the Soviet republic. They enunciated—somewhat hesitatingly for the time being—the doctrine that the proletarian dictatorship must remain on a constant footing of wartime preparation because it was encircled by hostile capitalist powers. Later in the 1920s the doctrine of "capitalist encirclement" gained greater acceptance among the party leadership.[23] In any event, the army itself continued to undergo a prolonged siege from its many and influential civilian enemies until mid-1923.

The introduction of the NEP was, in an important sense, the first attempt to remake a contract with the soldiers; the news of the replacement of grain requisitioning by a tax in kind produced a "radical change in the mood of the Red Army men."[24] Moreover, soldiers were granted priority equal to trade union members in seeking employment upon demobilization, thereby reaffirming the leadership's commitment to treating soldiers as a form of proletariat to whom it pledged certain obligations.[25] Still, for those soldiers who remained in the army, life became even more unbearable as they endured the famine of 1921, the bitter winter of 1921–22, and continued hardships until the end of 1923. Despite a call at the 11th Party Congress in 1922 for party organizations to devote greater attention to the needs of Red Army households, soldiers' families found themselves exceedingly vulnerable to economic hardship. Desertion rates remained high; turnover among officers and political workers became a chronic problem. For those who once thought that nothing could be worse than the conditions of the Civil War, the first years of NEP brought waves of nostalgia for the "better days."[26]

For a variety of reasons—especially the nationwide economic recovery of 1923, the succession struggle for the ailing Lenin's mantle of party leadership, and new foreign threats and opportunities—the central leadership turned its attention to the disastrous state of the Red Army in June 1923. The Central Committee appointed an investigatory commission that subsequently proposed a series of reforms and began a turnabout in the army's failing fortunes. The primary aims of the reformers were to restore the military organization to stable and regular operations, to standardize service manuals and disciplinary policy, to place the army on a firm and adequate annual budget, and to raise morale and ensure soldiers' and officers' political loyalty to party and state leaders and their policies. Under the banner of "militarization" the reformers, who were the same men who had been defending the army from its civilian critics since the Civil War, and a few others who later were persuaded that the army deserved the state's most urgent attention, declared that they were seeking to remilitarize an institution that had fallen prey to harmful influences and was no longer suitable as a combat organization. The reform met considerable resistance from the groups in the army who stood to lose the most—the commissars and the military specialists—and these groups slowed down the military command's program to implement the changes. Nevertheless, by the end of 1925, the army was deemed a healthy institution. It changed very little again, except for a steady growth in numbers, until the late 1930s.

A very significant component of the reforms was the regime's remaking of its contract with officers and soldiers in ways that shaped much of subsequent NEP politics in the late 1920s. Significantly, an officer's career once again became a respectable and desirable option for young men. Because of the budget increases that Army Commissar Mikhail Frunze, Trotsky's successor, had won from the central leadership (Frunze had Stalin's influential support on this issue),[27] officers received large pay raises, improved living quarters, and a generous pension system. The military leadership began a gradual transition to one-man command, by which the commissar was effectively demoted to the officer's assistant for political affairs and troop morale. To assuage the injured feelings of loyal commissars, military schools accepted hundreds of commissars who were willing to undergo advanced military training and thereby earn the right to become officers themselves. Andrei Andreev, a Central Committee secretary, acknowledged in a letter explaining the reform that "there is no doubt that the transition to one-man command will increase the social and political weight of the command staff."[28] As a sign of that increased political weight, admission to party membership was made easier for officers than it had been previously. By autumn 1927, "party saturation" of the army (ratio of party members to total military personnel) attained a remarkably high 16.1 percent, a figure twenty times greater than that of the population at large and even several times greater than the party saturation of the proletariat itself. Among that large number of party members in the army, officers and political workers made up well over half the membership.[29] The most practical benefit derived by the state from the elevation of the officer's status in society was the end of the debilitatingly high turnover among officers that had plagued the army in the early 1920s. Now officers chose to stay in their military careers, and rank-and-file soldiers increasingly sought to enter higher military schools upon completion of their obligatory two-year service term.[30]

For soldiers the benefits of the reform were not so immediately obvious. Of course, they too enjoyed considerably improved material conditions and fulfilled their service obligations in an army much more stable than it had ever been before. By 1925, after a series of experiments with terms of duty and schemes for conscription, the political and military leadership settled on a procedure that guaranteed a consistent and comprehensive process of call-up and release. Again, as in 1918, the "class principle" dictated service obligations: all male citizens had the right and obligation to bear arms in defense of the republic, while disfranchised persons were obliged to perform support duties or pay a special military tax.[31]

Still, the new disciplinary policy sanctioned a return to harsher punishments for infractions and punishments which markedly differed from those which officers faced if they violated regulations. At least the soldiers now had a better idea of what to expect because the reforms introduced system into what had been arbitrary measures that soldiers perceived to be very unjust. The fact that soldiers felt the punishments were being more fairly administered partially defused their initial resistance to the reforms. According to army statistics, the tougher and fairer disciplinary policy reduced the incidence of military crimes as well as the frequency with which military authorities resorted to arrest instead of less severe punishments.[32]

The army command also restored its self-image as a welfare agency and school during the reform period. In 1925 Sovnarkom reorganized the structures responsible for dispensing the panoply of benefits promised to soldiers and veterans into the All-Russian Committee for Aid to Invalid, Sick, and Wounded Red Army Men and to the Families of Soldiers Killed in Action. Among the new agency's responsibilities were credits for Red Army households, forest allotments, free acquisition of horses rejected by the army, housing privileges, special employment opportunities and social insurance, health benefits, education quotas, and a series of deductions or exemptions from taxes on agriculture, rent, income, government seals, and hunting licenses. These welfare measures were at the center of soldiers' concerns in the thousands of letters they wrote to the consultative bureaus that PUR set up in 1923. Most of the letters addressed to the Central Bureau of Red Army Letters focused on tax benefits, aid provisions for servicemen and their families, and postservice educational opportunities.[33] Unfortunately for the soldiers, the local agencies that were responsible for dispensing the benefits were notoriously delinquent in fulfilling all the tasks that the center assigned to them. Political officers enthusiastically backed up soldiers' complaints with letters to local prosecutors and, in extreme cases of persistent neglect or obstinacy, sent plenipotentiaries to the villages to put direct pressure on delinquent officials. "As a rule," one political worker observed, "the soldiers and even the average peasants consider military [officials] better than their own."[34]

In several surveys that the army conducted among soldiers about their preservice impressions of army life, political workers reported that nearly two-thirds claimed to have joined the army willingly, one-half had had positive impressions of army life before they entered, and 12.7 percent answered that they had viewed the army as a school for workers and peasants.[35] Deputy Army Commissar Iosif Unshlikht boasted that the army was "a second Commissariat of Enlightenment"; indeed, per capita expenditures for education in the army outpaced the civilian commissariat's throughout the 1920s.[36] Military service provided the recruits with new cultural experiences ranging from the ever more popular mass sports programs, to musical, theatrical, and agronomic circles, to libraries, lectures, and cinemas. As the surveys discussed above suggested, growing numbers of soldiers now looked on the military as a desirable career and sought admission to military schools in order to enter the officer corps of the Red Army. Once the reformers purged most of the military specialists, military men of working-class and peasant origin began to fill their places.

Finally, and perhaps most important for the fate of the political compromise that framed state policies during the NEP, the central leadership and army command promised soldiers and officers prominent roles in the new "socialist" countryside. Most soldiers could not enter military schools because of the small number of places available. Many other thousands of peasant soldiers chose to try their luck in the cities and increasingly joined the lines of the urban unemployed. Army newspapers warned soldiers who were undecided about what to do after demobilization to return to the countryside because enterprises were refusing to hire former soldiers, despite laws that had been on the books since 1921 giving soldiers equal priority with trade-union members.[37] Unfortunately, one of the major reasons that soldiers chose to remain in the cities was their conviction that they had no opportunities to advance back home in the country. In this sense, they were little different from the thousands of other peasant men and women who were adding to what was becoming a chronic high unemployment problem in the major cities.[38] The problems soldiers faced were part of the larger dilemmas of NEP society—dilemmas of economic structure that the Bolsheviks had inherited from their tsarist and liberal predecessors, combined with dilemmas left by the dislocation and devastation of the Civil War and those that were of the Bolsheviks' own making since 1917.

Partially in response to frustrations that many soldiers were facing because of the limited opportunities that awaited them both in the cities and in returning to agricultural occupations at home, partially in response to the military leadership's call for a "militarization of the civilian populace" as part of the reform programs implemented under Frunze, but also because the regime continued to sense that its political support in the countryside was thin and volatile, the state and party began looking to soldiers as "builders of socialism" among the rural population. As early as 1923 the Commissariat of Internal Affairs had recommended former soldiers to their local agencies as reliable and healthy elements.[39] Since the Civil War the army's Political Administration had urged soldiers, upon returning home, "to take a quick look around, determine the major needs in their village," and call together the Communists, Komsomol members, and other demobilized soldiers to "create a nucleus for the struggle with the sores of rural life."[40] Until 1925, however, these men were given no more systematic preparation in reconstructing life in the village than a package of literature and a subscription to one or more newspapers. Yet despite their lack of preparation, many soldiers returned home eager to "turn everything upside down" and restore decent local government, claiming that they would turn out the village priests, kulaks, and moonshine-brewers.[41]

Certainly not all soldiers returned to such activist roles, perhaps not even a majority. And many of those who immediately after their demobilization were eager to remake their villages lost their enthusiasm after meeting the first resistance from traditional village elites. Especially the soldiers who returned home alone to the village or whose villages had no Komsomol or party cells to turn to for solidarity were, in the words of a frequent and authoritative writer on rural life, "eaten up by the countryside. Its inertia sucks them dry."[42] Still, enough soldiers were returning as agents of some sorts of change to win the attention of the central press and the party's leadership. Not only were soldiers in many villages forming their own communes after they had been excluded from the existing village structures, but they reported back to their former units that, in the face of village opposition to their attempts to "strengthen soviet power," they set up their own party and Komsomol cells and rural soviets, sometimes published their own newspapers, and even submitted separate candidates' slates for the elections to the soviets. One alarmed observer noted that particularly the separate candidates' slates made it look as if the soldiers had formed their own political parties, a clearly impermissible development.[43]

In July 1925 the party's Central Committee resolved to capitalize on this underutilized rural force and ordered all army political departments to organize courses for those soldiers scheduled for demobilization in September. The Political Administration allocated funds for the new programs, which trained soldiers in a wide variety of occupations, including cooperative workers, policemen, tractor operators, lower-level soviet employees, directors of reading rooms, and even film projectionists. After the 15th Party Congress in December 1927, when the party leadership announced its commitment to collectivization and assigned the army a major role in the upcoming "socialist restructuring" of the village, the army expanded its programs.[44] When the central leaders expressed alarm over the condition of local soviets, which had fallen into the hands of "bourgeois elements," that is, peasants who refused to obey the center's dictates, army political departments prepared soldiers to take an active part in the reelections that were called for the spring of 1926. As a rehearsal for the campaigns, soldiers participated in mock elections to fictional congresses from the volost to the national level.[45] Former soldiers won over half the seats in the volost-level executive committees and one-third in rural soviets. Veterans also won positions as chairmen in 53 percent of the rural soviets and 70 percent of the executive committees.[46]

The success that former soldiers had in challenging established elites in the village, even if it was—for the moment—in the relatively ineffective soviet structure, spurred the regime to demand even more from the political and educational organizations of the army. In late 1929 the Commissariat of Agriculture, because it was short of experienced personnel to implement the increasingly ambitious collectivization plans, called on the army to prepare 100,000 cadres a year for the collective farm system. On January 30, 1930, Army Commissar Klim Voroshilov announced the plan for 100,000 cadres.[47]

Voroshilov's decision to involve the army in the center's plans to "remake the countryside" was a severe test for the social contract the leadership had fashioned with its mostly peasant soldiers. The officers, though they appear to have more or less acquiesced to collectivization as a necessary policy, resisted efforts to involve the army in what they perceived to be a clearly "nonmilitary" and "nonprofessional" mission. Almost from the beginning of the collectivization campaign, officers' journals protested against the unwarranted diversion of army resources to the civilian campaigns and warned that the distractions threatened to undermine combat readiness.[48]

But officers had far more urgent concerns about collectivization than the potential damage to their professional mission. They were justifiably concerned that soldiers' morale would be affected by a campaign that threatened to provoke widespread resistance and armed violence in the countryside. In fact, some historians recently have revived an earlier argument that pressures from the military command forced Stalin into the temporary retreat that was signaled by his "Dizziness from Success" speech in March 1930.[49] The recent argument is based largely on diplomatic correspondence, but it can be confirmed by analyzing resolutions from the army's political administration and reports of soldier discontent in military archives.

Certainly, soldiers' morale was high among the priorities of the central leadership as it conducted the collectivization campaign. Soldiers who protested against collectivization were arrested and sentenced; military authorities forbade peasants from visiting soldiers on the grounds that "kulak elements" were disseminating anti-Soviet propaganda in the barracks and summer camps.[50] As had been the practice beginning in 1918, Red Army families were once again singled out for special treatment in the first decrees of 1930. The Central Committee, in its special resolution on "the struggle with distortions of the party's line on the collectivization movement," singled out the protection of Red Army families and their property as a priority of the highest urgency. The activists sent out from the center to ensure the success of the collectivization drive, including many soldiers among the 100,000-ers, had been applying the policy of dekulakization to families of soldiers and officers in the villages.[51] In a remarkable exemption from the otherwise "strict regulations" governing the exclusion from party membership of kulaks and people otherwise deprived of their voting rights, all party committees were to admit such people if their families counted among their number "Red partisans, Red Army and Navy men, and rural teachers who were loyal to the Soviet regime" on the condition that the latter vouched for the reliability of their relatives.[52]

Ultimately, the strains in the contract with military men and their families won the army a reprieve from any further large-scale involvement in the center's schemes for rural transformation. For 1931, instead of the 100,000 collective farm workers that the Commissariat of Agriculture wanted from the army, the Political Administration promised only 29,500 tractor drivers. The other area where veterans played an important role was as personnel in the machine-tractor stations. But never again would the army participate in a campaign that so threatened its stability.

For all the grumblings from military men, the army remained remarkably loyal during the collectivization drive.[53] The troops' loyalty was a product of the effective but relatively limited repressive measures employed against rebellious soldiers, and of the social contract that had long been in place between regime and soldiers and, importantly, of the increasing weight of urban blue- and white-collar workers in the recruit pool.[54] By using the army, the regime achieved a relative short-term success in breaking the initial resistance of the peasantry to its transformational plans, even though it virtually conceded defeat in attaining the longer-term goals of creating a productive and loyal peasantry.

Finally, the army did return veterans to the countryside, many of whom demanded greater roles in political life than they had been accustomed to prior to military service; thereby the regime found a considerable reserve to staff its rural administration among the collectivized peasantry as it built the political order that it called socialism. The state continued to single out peasant soldiers and ex-soldiers and their families as reliable allies in an otherwise indifferent or hostile countryside. Military service had become a constituent element in citizenship in the socialist state, and soldiers had won a firm place among the state's new constituencies in both towns and villages. For the soldiers, military service and values shaped their understanding of socialism; consequently, Soviet socialism bore a tragically heavy imprint of those military practices and attitudes that had worked so well for the soldiers during their army careers.

## NOTES

1. This essay was significantly rewritten from the version delivered at the National Seminar conference, and I thank the members of the seminar for stimulating me to think along some new lines. In addition to the seminar participants, I wish to thank Frank Wcislo, Stephen Kotkin, and Elizabeth Wood for their helpful comments. The arguments presented here are presented in a fuller and more nuanced version in my book *Soldiers in the Proletarian Dictatorship: The Red Army and the Soviet Socialist State, 1917–1930* (Ithaca, N.Y., 1990).

2. The Mensheviks were among the first Russian socialists to decry the militaristic tendencies of the new regime. For example, Menshevik historians have argued that the October Revolution in Petrograd was primarily a rebellion of the soldiers rather than a proletarian revolution. In part, this serves to vindicate the Mensheviks' own failure to lead the revolution, but in large measure it is an accurate description of events. See Raphael R. Abramowitch, *The Soviet Revolution* (New York, 1962), pp. 21, 83–84, 88.

3. I hesitate to introduce the term *militarism* because it frequently has been employed in bitterly ideological polemics and thereby has lost much of its analytic utility; however, I agree with Volker Berghahn that the concept retains its value for describing key aspects of states and societies at various stages of their histories. See Volker Berghahn, *Militarism: The History of an International Debate, 1861–1979* (New York, 1982). Especially because at least part of the Bolshevik leadership itself frequently and very consciously repeated the term *militarization (voenizatsiia)* by the mid-1920s, I argue that the Soviet polity, beyond the traits listed above, was geared for war and stressed the sacrifice of the individual for the common good even during peacetime in ways reminiscent of societies at war.

4. See William C. Fuller, Jr., *Civil-Military Conflict in Imperial Russia, 1881–1914* (Princeton, N.J., 1985).

5. See the article by Sheila Fitzpatrick, "The Civil War as a Formative Experience," in *Bolshevik Culture: Experiment and Order in the Russian Revolution,* ed. Abbott Gleason, Peter Kenez, and Richard Stites (Bloomington, Ind., 1985), pp. 57–76.

6. Leon Trotsky, *The Revolution Betrayed* (New York, 1965), p. 222.

7. I have borrowed the concept of "historical bloc" from Antonio Gramsci, *Selections from the Prison Notebooks of Antonio Gramsci,* trans. and ed. Quinton Hoare and Geoffrey Nowell Smith (New York, 1985), p. 323; for elaboration on Gramsci's concept, see Walter L. Adamson, *Hegemony and Revolution: A Study of Antonio Gramsci's Political and Cultural Theory* (Berkeley and Los Angeles, 1980), pp. 170–79.

8. This essay will focus on the relationship of the state to military men—active-duty soldiers and officers as well as veterans. Because of space limitations, I shall not devote attention to the important role in the rise of military values and interests in Soviet socialism that can be attributed to other factors, most notably the common Civil War experience of the Stalin leadership.

9. For a more comprehensive discussion of Bolshevik policies of discrimination and categories of citizenship, see Elise Kimerling, "Civil Rights and Social Policy in Soviet Russia, 1918–1936," *Russian Review,* vol. 41, no. 1 (1982), pp. 24–46.

10. See, for example, Mikhail Kedrov's proposals, quoted in Iu. I. Korablev, *V. I. Lenin i zashchita zavoevanii Velikogo Oktiabria* (Moscow, 1979), p. 183.

11. See comments by Tsar Nicholas and his army minister, Kuropatkin, in Petr A. Zaionchkovskii, *Samoderzhavie i russkaia armiia na rubezhe XIX–XX stoletii* (Moscow, 1973), pp. 118, 120. Despite military leaders' fears that their units would be subverted by these urban elements, the autocracy persisted in sentencing convicted revolutionaries to punitive army service.

12. The 1918 constitution fixed peasant representation at one deputy for every 125,000 inhabitants and urban representation at one deputy for every 25,000 electors.

13. The instruction that went out to local party committees on how to conduct the purge listed "deserters from the Red Army" as the second category to whom new party cards should be refused. In mid-1919, when the Bolshevik regime faced its greatest military threat, all Communists were declared eligible for mobilization to the army; thus, here too military service became a defining component of party membership in the now-dominant political organization in the country.

14. For more on these purges and membership drives, see T. H. Rigby, *Communist Party Membership in the U.S.S.R., 1917–1967* (Princeton, 1968), pp. 74–87; for the party recruitment week in the army, see Iu. P. Petrov, *Stroitel'stvo politorganov, partiinykh i komsomol'skikh organizatsii armii i flota (1918–1968)* (Moscow, 1968), pp. 91–93.

15. P. N. Dmitriev, "Organizatsionnye printsipy sovetskogo voennogo stroitel'-stva i ikh vliianie na sposoby vooruzhennoi bor'by," in *Iz istorii grazhdanskoi voiny i interventsii, 1917–1922* (Moscow, 1974), p. 196. The educational backgrounds of the new officers offer further evidence of the new discriminatory policies. Among the new officers, only 39 percent had middle and higher education, while 61 percent claimed they had completed only lower education.

16. For measures to aid Red Army families and some problems in delivering the promised aid, see E. G. Gimpel'son, *Sovety v gody interventsii i grazhdanskoi voiny* (Moscow, 1968), pp. 310–16. Sovnarkom decreed the first cash payments to Red Army families on December 24, 1918. A pamphlet from the Smolensk Party Committee summarized the welfare benefits promised in 1919: "The Red Army man's family is the highest priority of the Soviet republic; his family is exempted from all direct taxes; his family keeps its right to the land; his family can receive a subsidy to maintain his household; his family members who are no longer able to work are exempted from paying apartment rent; his family has the right to the ration card 'Red Star' and to receive bonus groceries; in case of death, [the Red Army man's family] receives his pension." S. Olikov, *Dezertirstvo v Krasnoi armii i bor'ba s nim* (Leningrad, 1926), pp. 57–58.

17. "Tezisy TsK RKP o mobilizatsii industrial'nogo proletariata, trudovoi povinnosti, militarizatsii khoziaistva i primenenii voinskikh chastei dlia khoziaistvennykh nuzhd," *Deviatyi s"ezd RKP(b), Mart–aprel' 1920 goda, Protokoly* (Moscow, 1960), pp. 556–57. For another, even more enthusiastic endorsement of these principles, see Trotsky's theses, pp. 533–38.

18. Trotsky confessed that even before the Civil War was over, he was relieved to rid himself of his combat responsibilities and shift his attention to economic matters and constructing the "Proletarian Sparta." For Trotsky's activities and writings on military and economic matters in this period, see Isaac Deutscher, *The Prophet Armed: Trotsky, 1879–1921* (New York and London, 1954), chapter XIII.

19. See the account by Anastas Mikoian, who was sent to Nizhnii Novgorod in November 1920 to combat mutinous soldiers and party oppositionists, *V nachale dvadtsatykh . . .* (Moscow, 1975), pp. 34–44.

20. See the Central Committee's desperate coded telegram sent to all provincial party committees in March 1921, cited in *V. I. Lenin i VChK* (Moscow, 1975), p. 435n.

21. See the debates over militarization at the 9th and immediately preceding the 10th party congresses, discussed by Robert V. Daniels in *The Conscience of the Revolution* (Cambridge, Mass., 1960), pp. 121–43.

22. Workers in the defense industry were first in priority.

23. Even Lenin during his final years expressed increasing concern with the security of the Soviet state in the hostile and unstable international environment of postwar Europe. The concern with national security was shared by nearly all the leaders, including Trotsky and his Left Opposition.

24. S. E. Rabinovich, "Delegaty 10-go s"ezda RKP(b) pod Kronshtadtom v 1921 godu," *Krasnaia letopis'*, vol. 2, no. 41 (1931), p. 32.

25. For labor legislation concerning demobilized and disabled former servicemen, see Margaret Dewar, *Labour Policy in the USSR, 1917–1928* (London and New York, 1956), pp. 114, 213, 219, 243, 246, 283, 387.

26. See the reminiscences in "M. V. Frunze na Ukraine," *Sputnik politrabotnika*, 27–28 (1925), p. 35. See also the negative reactions of soldiers to signs of urban prosperity that they clearly did not share in their garrisons in Emma Goldman, *My Disillusionment in Russia* (Gloucester, Mass., 1983), pp. 201–202. Goldman overheard a Red soldier say, "Is this what we made the Revolution for? For this our comrades had to die?"; also Evdokimov, "Soveshchanie," *Krasnaia prisiaga*, 15 (1923), p. 59.

27. See Stalin's speech to the Central Committee plenum on January 19, 1925, (Moscow, 1952), *Sochineniia* vol. 7, pp. 11–14.

28. A. Andreev, "Ob edinonachalii v Krasnoi armii," March 6, 1925, in *KPSS o vooruzhennykh silakh Sovetskogo Soiuza* (Moscow, 1981), p. 228.

29. *Piatnadtsatyi s"ezd VKP(b). Stenograficheskii otchet* (Moscow/Leningrad, 1928), p. 106, calculated by Oleg F. Suvenirov, *Kommunisticheskaia partiia—organizator politicheskogo vospitaniia Krasnoi Armii i Flota, 1921–1928* (Moscow, 1976), pp. 111–13. The 11th Party Congress adopted amendments to the party statute which formally recognized the informal practice that dated from the Civil War of granting Red Army men equal access to party membership with workers. See "Ob ukreplenii i novykh zadachakh partii," *Odinnadtsatyi s"ezd*, pp. 546, 549. The second category for membership access was peasants other than Red Army men and craftsmen who did not exploit others' labor; in third place were "others" (white-collar workers, etc.).

30. In fact, applications for admission to higher military schools far exceeded available places. In the Moscow Military District, applicants to army schools were running at between four and eight per available place in 1926. B. Bogdanov, "Itogi komplektovaniia voennykh shkol M.V.O. v 1926 g.," *Sputnik politrabotnika*, 51–52 (1926), p. 39.

31. See Il'ia Berkhin, *Voennaia reforma v SSSR, 1924–1925* (Moscow, 1958), for a discussion of the reforms in military service legislation after the Civil War, pp. 239–57. Under the terms of the 1925 law on obligatory service, women could volunteer for service during peacetime and were subject to call-up in the event of war. Disfranchised persons had to serve in the short-lived "service teams" *(komandy obsluzhivaniia)* or pay a special military tax. A series of deferments and exemptions regulated obligations for men with higher education, single breadwinners in families, and various national minority groups.

32. For details on the reforms in disciplinary policy, see Berkhin, *Voennaia reforma*, pp. 369–71. For reports on decreasing crime rates, see Frunze's report to the 3rd Congress of Soviets in May 1925, *Krasnaia zvezda* (May 22, 1925), p. 3; and

reports from the Ukrainian Military District for 1926–28, cited from archival materials in Dmitrii Pikha, "Bor'ba Kommunisticheskoi partii za ukreplenie Sovetskikh vooruzhennykh sil v 1924–1928 godakh (na materialakh Ukrainskogo voennogo okruga i partiinykh organizatsii Ukrainy" (candidate's dissertation, Kiev State University, 1964), pp. 186–87.

33. The volume of soldiers' mail grew so rapidly that in 1924 the Central Bureau of Red Army Letters began a regular supplement to the popular journal *Krasnoarmeets*, in which the bureau published hundreds of letters followed by answers from competent specialists. The supplement was entitled *Krasnoarmeiskii spravochnik*.

34. A. Maevich, "Po 19-i territorial'noi," *Krasnaia zvezda* (January 24, 1925), p. 3; for more on relations between army political departments and local agencies, see P. I. Sokolov, "Bol'she vnimaniia!" *Krasnaia zvezda* (February 1925); R. Shaposhnikov, *Krasnaia zvezda* (January 13, 1925), p. 3; *Krasnoarmeiskii spravochnik* (August 17, 1927), p. 2.

35. P. Kuz'min, "Itogi izucheniia politiko-moral'nogo sostoianiia krasnoarmeitsev," *Sputnik politrabotnika*, 3 (1924), pp. 56–57; I. Krupnik, "Nekotorye itogi raboty s 1902 godom," *Sputnik politrabotnika*, 52 (1926), pp. 18–19; see also E. Kosmin, *Politicheskaia rabota v territorial'nykh chastiakh* (Moscow/Leningrad, 1928), p. 54; *Voennyi vestnik*, 35 (1928).

36. S. Ivanovich (V. I. Talin), *Krasnaia armiia* (Paris, 1931), p. 92. For 1927–28 the army spent 5 rubles 80 kopecks per capita on political enlightenment, while the equivalent per capita expenditure of the Enlightenment Commissariat was 1 ruble 7 kopecks. During that year the army earmarked 3,260,000 rubles for political enlightenment. *X let Krasnoi Armii; al'bom diagramm* (Moscow, 1927), p. 76.

37. *Krasnaia rota*, 17 (1925), p. 79; *Krasnaia zvezda*, 1925 issues, especially January 8, 16, 25; February 17; October 16, 23; December 9. In Moscow, the labor exchange listed 100 enterprises that refused to hire former soldiers. Central Army newspapers warned that Moscow, Leningrad, Vladivostok, the Crimea, and Turkestan were "infected with unemployment" in September 1925.

38. For a particularly poignant statement of the dismal prospects facing peasant soldiers, see the suicide note left by one Comrade Parsh in late summer 1929. Parsh, a twenty-three-year-old peasant soldier, shot himself because, in his words, he was a *batrak*, he had been unable to find employment, and he saw "no point in wandering around the earth." Parsh thanked the Red Army for teaching him to read and write and left his meager belongings to his fellow poor soldiers. He had hoped to gain admission to a higher military school but was rejected, according to the political officer who filed the report on Parsh's suicide, because he was "badly prepared, learned poorly, and was insufficiently disciplined." But even the political officer concluded that Parsh had killed himself because he was disappointed with "his life as a *batrak* after demobilization." *Smolensk Archives* WKP 215, "Politdonesenie," September 25, 1929.

39. N. I. Kizilov, *NKVD RSFSR, 1917–1930 gg.* (Moscow, 1969), p. 114.

40. *Krasnoarmeets*, 59/60 (1924).

41. Iung, "O nastroeniiakh uvolennykh v zapas krasnoarmeitsev i o nekotorykh itogakh nashei raboty," *Krasnaia rota*, 43–44 (1924), pp. 98–100; A. Vyrvich, *Krasnaia armiia v bor'be s negramotnost'iu* (Moscow, 1925), p. 75; Ia. Iakovlev, *Derevnia, kak ona est'* (Moscow, 1923), pp. 70–71; see also PUR study summarized by Suvenirov, *Kommunisticheskaia partiia*, pp. 249–50.

42. Iakovlev, *Derevnia*, pp. 66–67.

43. S. Sorkin, "Ob aktivnosti terarmeitsev na sele," *Krasnaia rota*, 1–2 (1924), pp. 72–73; see also A. Kruglov-Landa, "Nashe popolnenie i nashi 'stariki,' " *Sputnik politrabotnika*, 6 (1924), p. 46; N. Kudrin, *Sovetskoe stroitel'stvo na sele i zadachi krasnoarmeitsa-otpusknika* (Moscow, 1925), p. 73.

44. "Kursy dlia demobilizovannykh krasnoarmeitsev," *Krasnaia zvezda* (July 4, 1925), p. 4; "O rabote v derevne," *Piatnadtsatyi s"ezd VKP(b)*, pp. 1420–21, 1467. See also Krupskaia's remarks on the Red Army as an increasingly important national cultural center, ibid., p. 1253. For figures on how many rural cadres were sent to the countryside, see V. F. Klochkov, "Rol' Krasnoi Armii v likvidatsii negramotnosti i podgotovke kadrov dlia sela v gody sotsialisticheskogo stroitel'stva," *Istoriia SSSR*, 3 (1980), p. 77. Klochkov estimates that the Red Army trained 65,501 men between 1925 and 1927, and 68,000 cadres in 1928.

45. "Pokazatel'nye s"ezdy sovetov," *Krasnaia zvezda* (August 14, 1925), p. 4.

46. *Perevybory v sovety R.S.F.S.R. v 1925–1926 gg.* (Moscow, 1926), p. 35; K. E. Voroshilov, *Stat'i i rechi* (Moscow, 1937), p. 171.

47. For a discussion of *Narkomzem* schemes, see "Kadry dlia kolkhozov," reprinted from *Sel'skaia gazeta*, 168 (1929), in *Voennyi vestnik*, 37 (1929), p. 53; and Dzyza, "Krasnaia Armiia i zadachi kolkhoznogo stroitel'stva," *Voennyi vestnik*, 4 (1930), pp. 36–37. For Voroshilov's announcement, see "Postanovlenie RVS SSSR ob uchastii Krasnoi Armii v kolkhoznom stroitel'stve," January 30, 1930, *Partiino-politicheskaia rabota v Krasnoi Armii. Dokumenty. 1921–1929 gg.* (Moscow, 1981), pp. 44–46.

48. See the discussion of procollectivization in Dzyza, "Krasnaia Armiia i zadachi kolkhoznogo stroitel'stva,' *Voennyi vestnik*, 4 (1930), pp. 36–37, and the anti-collectivization editorials in *Krasnaia zvezda* (February 9, 12, 22, March 13, 1930). See also R. Eikhe's address to a Siberian party conference in June 1930, cited in V. I. Varenov, *Pomoshch' Krasnoi Armii v razvitii kolkhoznogo stroitel'stva 1929–1933 gg. Po materialam Sibirskogo voennogo okruga* (Moscow, 1978), pp. 147–48.

49. See R. Davies, *The Socialist Offensive* (Cambridge, Mass., 1980), p. 280; Jonathan Haslam, *Soviet Foreign Policy, 1930–1933: The Impact of the Depression* (London, 1983), pp. 121–22. The earlier argument is found in Samuel Harper, *Making Bolsheviks* (1931), p. 137. Janos Decsy, who studied at the Frunze Military Academy in 1956, recalls that lecturers on military history told students that Bliukher, Uborevich, and Iakir—the first two were men of peasant origin and had served in the Great War—were particularly vocal in opposing collectivization (interview with author, April 16, 1988).

50. The troubles had begun during the winter requisitioning campaign of 1927–28, when "nests of kulak elements" were uncovered among the most belligerent soldiers. *Krasnaia zvezda* (March 29, 1928). See reports for 1929 from Ukrainian party archives cited in Pikha, dissertation, p. 237; for 1930 in Varenov, *Pomoshch' Krasnoi Armii*, pp. 41, 43–44.

51. For evidence of violence committed against veterans and Red Army families, see the memoirs of Lev Kopelev, *The Education of a True Believer*, translated by Gary Kern (New York, 1980), p. 270; also Merle Fainsod, *Smolensk under Soviet Rule* (New York, 1963), p. 244; for a fictional account, see Mikhail Sholokhov, *Seeds of Tomorrow*, translated by Stephen Garry (New York, 1935).

52. "Postanovlenie TsK VKP(b) o bor'be s iskrivleniiami partlinii v kolkhoznom dvizhenii," March 14, 1930, in *KPSS v rezoliutsiiakh*, vol. 5, p. 104.

53. John Erickson, the West's leading historian of the Red Army, wrote of the collectivization campaign, "In the face of considerable odds, the adhesion of the armed forces to the ruling group and its policies (which were to become increasingly identified with the name and person of Stalin) was achieved." See *The Soviet High Command* (Boulder and London, 1962, 1984), pp. 315–16.

54. Between 1927 and January 1930, the percentage of peasants in the army dropped from 63.4 to 57. Workers rose from 23.8 to 32.9 percent. Voroshilov, *Stat'i i rechi* (Moscow, 1936), p. 444.

# XI

# POLICING THE NEP COUNTRYSIDE

*Neil Weissman*

> Our militiaman must have a completely
> different goal, in truth a different psy-
> chology, from that of prerevolutionary
> Russia.
>
> —M. I. Kalinin, 1922

> When a Russian is armed by the govern-
> ment he is made into a brute.
>
> —Russian peasant, circa 1919

As part of the effort to create a new socialist order in Russia, the Soviet
government sought to alter drastically traditional forms of policing. In
their first months in power, the Bolsheviks hoped to eliminate formal
enforcement agencies altogether, relying instead upon the entire populace
essentially to police itself. After this vision evaporated in the heat of civil
war, the Soviet authorities sought instead to create a new and transformed
professional force, the militia. The militia was to differ from the hated
tsarist police not only in its subordination to the proletarian state but also in
its devotion to an ethos of civility and legality. Rather than serve as an
instrument of oppression over the people, the Soviet force would be a
vehicle for winning popular support, for legitimizing the regime in the eyes
of the masses.

This essay examines the effort at fundamental police reform during the
NEP era in the Russian countryside. A rural focus has much to recommend
it. Viewed from the standpoint of the history of the Soviet regime, the
stakes were highest in the villages. Here the resources available for law
enforcement were the least, yet the need was the greatest. In the cities the
government could count on some popular support among workers and
rely upon a series of reasonably effective administrative institutions ranging from soviets to unions. In the villages the central authorities faced a

neutral or even hostile peasantry, and few party or state agencies maintained a meaningful presence. These obstacles made it all the more vital for the government to develop an efficient rural police apparatus as an instrument for accomplishing the goal of fundamental social change.

The rural side of NEP law enforcement is also of special interest from the standpoint of comparative police studies. As David Bayley has noted in an article appropriately titled "The Limits of Police Reform," attempts to improve policing are often predicated upon the assumption that change can be made from within by focusing on the enforcement apparatus itself.[1] Yet, he argues, the broader social context in which the police operate may provide an intractable barrier to even the most determined reform efforts. The experience of the Russian countryside in the 1920s provides an extreme test case of this hypothesis. With the notable exception of the disappearance of the landed gentry, both the social setting of law enforcement and popular attitudes toward police remained much the same as in the prerevolutionary era. The impetus for police reform came not from the villagers but from a regime confident that change was very desirable and—through the construction of a renovated militia apparatus—possible as well.

The obstacles to the development of new patterns of law enforcement in the countryside were formidable. Certainly, the prerevolutionary legacy worked entirely in the opposite direction. Despite the general image of tsarist Russia as a police state, the actual law-enforcement apparatus of the ancien régime was small and inefficient.[2] In the countryside especially, the police force was thinly stretched over a widely dispersed populace. A government commission established in the wake of the 1905 Revolution, for example, called for the expansion of the rural force to a modest ratio of one patrolman to twenty-five hundred citizens, but the goal remained out of reach. Financial resources devoted to policing were equally skimpy. Low pay and miserly support services guaranteed that the quality of personnel in terms of education and training was very low.

The striking weakness of other local administrative agencies, especially in the countryside, meant that tsarist police were called upon to fulfill a wide range of tasks beyond maintaining order. Responsibilities such as tax collection, enforcement of sanitation regulations, and delivery of subpoenas and other official documents turned the force, as one imperial police chief contended with only modest exaggeration, into "the universal apparatus for fulfilling the tasks of every other branch of government."[3] Tsarist authorities took great care to see that in performing these duties the police were insulated from any popular control. Command over the force was completely centralized. Institutions of self-government had no power to direct the police, and the practice of "administrative guarantee" ensured that no policeman could be brought before a court without the approval of his superior. Only the rural gentry, through the office of land captain, exerted significant influence over the police.

The tension between the imposing duties and authority of the force and its meager capabilities and resources worked to create a highly arbitrary police style. The average policeman—overworked and miserably paid but also powerful and unsupervised—frequently resorted to violence and extortion in dealing with the citizenry. In the countryside especially, officers were wont to employ the "rule of the fist" (kulachnoe pravo) in dealing with villagers. The result was a wide gulf between the police and peasants, who viewed the officers as predators as much as protectors.

The tsarist legacy of alienation between state law-enforcement agencies and the rural populace was not overcome during the era of revolution and civil war. The Bolshevik government initially called for policing by the armed people, which in the countryside meant a force elected by the villagers from among themselves. Under the pressure of civil war, however, the government quickly abandoned this ultrademocratic approach to law enforcement. In the summer of 1918 the authorities created a new, professional police force—the militia.[4] What this meant for the countryside was the concentration of command over the police in provincial and district cities and, conversely, the rejection of village control. NKVD officials, in a 1919 review of the militia's formative period, clearly expressed the mistrust of the peasantry that underlay the new policy. "Earlier," they wrote, "militiamen elected from the local populace served in their own volosts among relatives and friends; they allowed all kinds of indulgences and sometimes even made deals with kulaks and village speculators. . . ."[5]

The regime's determination to insulate the militia from local influences heightened as the force was called upon to implement such unpopular policies as conscription, grain requisitioning, and labor service. A series of decrees militarized the police, placing the force (on paper at least) under firm central control and on the state payroll.[6] The rural populace responded by reasserting a desire for freedom from outside interference. Where possible, villagers elected their own peace officers, maintaining order without recourse to the militia, and even resisting the state police with force.[7]

The end of the Civil War and introduction of the New Economic Policy made it possible for the Soviet government to demilitarize the militia and take a fresh approach to law enforcement. Although the struggle against hostile partisans and bandits lingered in certain areas, by 1922 the authorities were elaborating a new police policy intended to break sharply with the tsarist—and, by implication, Civil War—past. "The militia," wrote official spokesman T. Khvesin, "is the antipode of the [tsarist] police. If the latter were the faithful servants of exploiters, then the militia has been called upon to be the defender of the laboring masses and the ardent local champion of all measures of Soviet power aimed at their well-being."[8]

In their attempt to build a new system of enforcement antithetical to past practice, Soviet authorities did not return to the initial concept of the populace policing itself, either directly or through elected patrolmen. For the rural police especially, the Civil War hostility even to recruitment from among the local citizenry continued throughout the decade. NKVD official B. Shavrov, in a 1925 article on rural enforcement, voiced the dominant sentiment in bemoaning the fact that low pay meant that volost personnel were often drawn from among residents. "Such a militiaman," he wrote, "is, of course, a bad and unreliable champion in the countryside of revolutionary legality, for as a local peasant with his own household he is naturally afraid of causing trouble and making enemies among the neighbors."[9]

If the rural militia was not in principle to be recruited from among the local peasantry, how was it to differ from the tsarist police? In part, Soviet leaders argued that the militia was unlike the old force simply by virtue of the nature of the government it served. As Leon Trotsky indicated in a welcoming address to the 1st All-Russian Congress of Militia Workers in 1922, in contrast to the situation in capitalist states, where the police were a "weapon for strengthening the commanding position of the ruling class," in the RSFSR the militia served as "the instrument of the worker-peasant authority which stands guard over the interests of the laboring masses."[10]

Yet there was another way, more closely related to the militia's own operations, in which Soviet law enforcement would be novel. As Trotsky also argued in his welcoming speech, the first task of the militia was "creation of a firm apparatus . . . through which the worker-peasant government can implement its plans to introduce revolutionary legality."[11] The new Soviet police would foreswear arbitrariness and caprice in favor of firm adherence to the law. By following legal norms precisely and treating the populace with tact and respect, militiamen would be not only enforcers but also legitimizers. In the countryside particularly, the police would use their interaction with the peasantry as an opportunity to teach the meaning of Soviet edicts and win over popular support. As Kalinin put it in emphasizing the need for an educated force, "the higher the intellectual development of our militiaman, the better champion he will be of the principles of the Soviet government."[12]

The first prerequisite for the transformation of rural law enforcement was the construction of what Trotsky called a "firm apparatus" in the countryside. From the start, this task proved difficult. The militia emerged from the violent struggles of the Civil War with swollen ranks. In order to reduce the force to peacetime size and remove "undesirable elements," the authorities initiated a purge. The transfer to local soviets in 1922 of responsibility for funding the militia caused the process of personnel reduction to snowball, in the resource-poor countryside threatening the basic stability of the apparatus. The traumatic impact of the purge was evident in the sharp contrast between officially mandated staff complements and the rural reality. In connection with a policy of consolidating volosts, for example, the NKVD established a police-to-populace norm of 1 : 5,000.[13] Although the figure was modest—half that set by tsarist authorities—few volosts achieved it. In White Russia, for example, a decision to consolidate the force in 1924 brought a 20 percent cut in staffs, leaving the average militiaman with between 8,000 and 10,000 citizens to patrol.[14] Elsewhere, the situation was far worse. Certain localities were completely without militia service. Overall, one NKVD official in mid-decade estimated that the militia was 38.8 percent smaller than the prewar force on paper. Actual complements were often two-thirds or half of that.[15]

The drastic reduction of militia ranks prompted central and local authorities to undertake steps to increase the size of the force. The effect of this effort is revealed by a study of the state apparatus published in 1929 by the Central Statistical Administration. The official data showed an overall increase of 33.1 percent in the staff of state institutions between May 1924 and January 1928. Although the "administrative-judicial" category expanded by only 8.6 percent, the police component of this group grew by 42.4 percent (from 109,426 to 155,859).[16] This is an impressive total for the militia, but the countryside was little affected. The number of police supported by local budgets, the key group for rural militiamen, expanded by only a modest 11.8 percent (from 110,512 to 123,527) between May 1925 and January 1928. Although the trend in virtually every other branch of the state apparatus was to increase the relative weight of officials serving in the countryside, the percentage of rural and small-town militiamen actually fell from 25.1 percent to 23.1 percent. The statisticians handled this embarrassing fact by simply omitting the police from the relevant chart in their study.[17]

Other factors worked to aggravate the difficulties caused by thin ranks. Poor communications and inadequate transportation across the sometimes formidable expanses of rural districts were obvious sources of trouble. Phone links were sometimes lacking at headquarters (a 1924 survey of 62 raion militia offices in rural Tambov found only 13 had phones, 21 had limited access to those of the volost executive committee, and 28 had none at all) and almost always absent in the field.[18] More serious was a shortage of horses. White Russian authorities reported a 62 percent shortfall at the start of 1925, with those available mainly nags "completely unfit for service."[19]

The lack of horses, taken in conjunction with reduced staffs and the substantial distances involved, made routine patrolling very difficult. In the absence of clear instructions from the NKVD, local chiefs often opted to keep militiamen at volost or raion headquarters, sending them out into the countryside only as needed. Those commanders who attempted to take the more radical approach of dispersing their staffs among the villages encountered serious obstacles, not the least of them the absence of appropriate lodging for militiamen and their families. Militiamen assigned to villages continued to reside elsewhere, found space in the local soviet's offices, or—worst of all—moved from one peasant home to another on a rotational basis.[20]

Under these circumstances, Soviet law-enforcement agencies in the countryside were limited to a reactive role. Rural police could not hope to emulate their colleagues in the cities—where patrolmen were stationed at street posts in an ideal ratio of 1 to 750 inhabitants—in exerting a constant influence on daily life. Responsible for a population of up to 20,000 in eighteen to twenty widely dispersed villages connected only by dirt roads that became impassable during spring flooding and winter snows, the militiaman was consigned to a career of limited and hectic intervention. Policeman K. Krukovskii of Kuntsevo in Moscow province described it this way:

> The *uchastkovyi* militiaman's work is most diverse: at one end of the *uchastok* it's necessary to take measures to liquidate hooliganism [and] liquor profiteering, at another to help peasants resolve some dispute, at a third to investigate a theft, etc. And all this work is accomplished by traveling on foot from hamlet to hamlet, village to village, with Criminal Code article 105 [setting a one-month statutory limit on completion of certain administrative tasks] in mind.[21]

As Krukovskii's comment suggests, the jurisdictional concerns of the rural militiaman were as expansive as the territorial. Under the emergency conditions of civil war, most local administrative functions were militarized. The militia, working in conjunction with the Cheka and Red Army, became deeply involved in such activities as conscription, organizing labor service, combating epidemics, and—especially crucial in the countryside—grain requisitioning. The restoration of peace made it possible for the authorities to circumscribe militia responsibility, particularly in offering "assistance" (*sodeistvie*) to other administrative agencies. In 1923, for example, the government issued instructions restricting the police role in agrarian taxation largely to carrying out legal measures against shirkers and, when necessary, protecting tax collectors.[22] Generally speaking, the militia were to assist other state organs only when the latter lacked local agencies or were unable to fulfill their basic functions alone. Even then, militia cooperation was to be considered "temporary" until the development of a more extensive administrative apparatus at the grassroots level.[23]

Impressive on paper, such restrictions lost much of their meaning under real conditions of the NEP countryside. The militia were among the few agencies of the central government capable of significant interaction with the peasantry. As a result, the provincial representatives of other administrative departments felt little compunction about piling duties on the volost police. Judicial officials, for instance, planned to assign delivery of sub-poenas and other court documents to "judicial executors" *(sudebnye ispol-niteli)*. When financial difficulties made it impossible to hire staff for the countryside, the courts turned to the militia.[24] Similarly, the failure to develop effective mechanisms for tax collection led the Council of People's Commissars in 1926 to declare a campaign against arrears with increased police activity.[25] Complaints from local militia chiefs prompted the NKVD in the spring of 1925 to protest against the exploitation of the police by other agencies on the grounds that most requests for assistance were illegal.[26] In fact, pressing need often forced the NKVD itself to cooperate in burdening the militia. Faced with a spread of hoof-and-mouth disease, for example, the commissariat in 1926 joined health and agricultural officials in requiring policemen to take preventive measures in cases of illness until veterinary officers could be summoned.[27]

The process by which weaknesses in the local administrative apparatus caused enlargement of police jurisdiction also extended to the militia's area of primary concern, crime fighting. In response to serious overburdening of the courts, the government in October 1924 "decriminalized" a series of petty infractions. The militia, along with local soviet executive committees, became responsible for processing certain forms of such violations as home brewing, timber poaching, and hooliganism.[28] Taken together with assign-ments from other agencies, these new duties overwhelmed the rural police. The cumulative effect was indicated by one assistant procurator who par-ticipated in a Rabkrin review of the Siberian militia. "If each *uchastkovyi* militiaman attended to his massive legal responsibilities carefully," he wrote, "he would have to become familiar with and follow changes in 124 legislative acts, many with supplemental explanatory circulars."[29]

A relatively small militia might have been able to cope with some of this burden had its personnel been of high caliber. Indeed, throughout the NEP era the Soviet authorities often described efforts to reduce adminis-trative staffs in terms of "rationalization," of replacing quantity with quali-ty. In reality, few resources were devoted to this end. The transfer of financial responsibility for the law-enforcement agencies from the central government to revenue-poor local soviets consigned the militia to low wages, which in the countryside sometimes fell below the subsistence level. Official data from late 1925 indicated that even after significant wage increases over the course of the year, volost militiamen still received only twenty-three rubles per month, or less than half the salary of an average textile worker.[30] This aggregate figure, of course, concealed wide regional variations and ignored the occasional failure of local soviets to pay. One NKVD specialist noted in 1925, for example, that while rural patrolmen in Moscow and Leningrad were relatively well off at monthly wages of up to thirty-five rubles, their counterparts in Smolensk, Voronezh, Viatka, and elsewhere received twelve rubles or less.[31]

Bad pay, coupled with the heavy burdens of service in the unpopular role of policeman, made it difficult both to recruit desirable candidates and to hold them. The authorities hoped to fill the militia with demobilized Red Army men, keeping them in the ranks long enough to acquire training and experience.[32] The militia oath specifically included a pledge to serve at least one year. In practice, volost militiamen often were local peasants who enlisted on a short-term basis. Annual turnover rates of patrolmen in excess of 100 percent were common in rural units.[33] Some peasants joined for several months until more suitable jobs could be found. Others entered the ranks on a seasonal basis, viewing militia service as a poor substitute for the prerevolutionary practice of seeking supplemental work in towns during agricultural slack periods. As one NKVD official protested, "the militia is not an 'almshouse.' "[34]

Given its parlous condition, the militia could hardly provide the kind of law enforcement envisioned by the central authorities. Lacking a routine police presence, many villages sought to provide their own protection. In some areas all male inhabitants acted as watchmen on a rotating basis. Elsewhere individual peasants served in return for meals and other benefits in kind.[35] Villagers turned to the state police only in cases of serious crime, and sometimes not even then. After all, the militia office might be a substantial distance away, and the trip did not always bring results. Among the criticisms frequently leveled against the force in this era was "*volokita*," or inaction that could last months or years.[36]

Of course, it could be fairly argued that the peasantry was happier without the militia near at hand, for police authority in the villages was often punitive and arbitrary. As one local officer explained, to the peasant the militiaman was "a person who by force of arms collected back taxes and halted home brewing, seizing kettles, casks and such. . . ."[37] Some of this was inherent in the police function. Yet the adversarial element was undoubtedly magnified by shortcomings in the militia apparatus.

Militia enforcement of local ordinances offers a good illustration of how deficiencies in the force could create hostility between police and populace. In order to entice the heavily burdened but woefully paid militiamen into upholding various local statutes, soviet executives adopted the practice of rewarding them with a percentage of fines levied on violators. The result was not only a sharp rise in the number of fines imposed but also a marked increase in the amounts exacted.[38] Worse yet, the militia frequently ignored the party's "class line," levying penalties that in some cases exceeded the grain tax on rich and poor peasant alike. Strenuous efforts by the NKVD, including a December 1925 edict outlawing the practice of awarding police premiums from local fines, helped curb abuse, but excessive levies remained an issue throughout the decade.[39] In a similar fashion, the commissariat forbade militia participation in the collection of "voluntary" charitable contributions when it became apparent that such activity was becoming a source of illegal revenue.[40]

In sum, when the militia did make their presence felt in the villages, it was often in ways antithetical to the regime's goal of constructing a positive relationship between police and peasantry. M. Boldyrev aptly evaluated the situation in a 1925 review of revolutionary legality in local administration. "Generally speaking," he wrote, "our apparatus, with all its defects, is crude [grubo], yet manages to carry out government assignments. But how does it fulfill its other task of serving the needs of the populace? Here it does incomparably less."[41]

One need not be a specialist in the history of Russian police to recognize the reemergence of prerevolutionary patterns of law enforcement in the postrevolutionary countryside. The militia, like the tsarist police, was caught in its own form of "scissors crisis." Demands on the force escalated while resources lagged sadly behind, giving rise to a punitive and arbitrary operational style. Under these circumstances, how did Soviet leaders expect to break with the past? In large part, they hoped to overcome militia shortcomings by turning to the populace for assistance. The NEP era was marked by a series of experiments aimed at enlisting mass support in the task of law enforcement. Three of these are particularly revealing in evaluating the success of the appeal to the citizenry in the countryside.

The tsarist police had been assisted in the countryside by a force of elected peasant patrolmen or, as they were called, desiatskie. These functionaries—illiterate, ill-trained, and often chosen from the dregs of the village—performed menial tasks such as guarding the police office or delivering messages.[42] As the militia's staff contracted in the early years of NEP, the Soviet authorities realized that the new police force would also require local assistance. A government decree of 27 March 1924 established the office of "village deputy" (sel'skii ispolnitel') for this purpose.[43]

From the start, Soviet leaders were emphatic in insisting that the deputy was completely unlike the desiatskii. As NKVD spokesman V. Vlasov later noted, the goal was "the broad involvement of the populace in [police] work and the development of popular initiative, not the creation of a new cadre of bureaucrats."[44] To this end, soviets were to elect village deputies from among all adult citizens (save the elderly), and the term of service was fixed at a brief two months to guarantee maximum participation. In a sharp break from past practice, the authorities encouraged the election of women. Like other executive agencies, the ispolniteli were to serve in "dual subordination"—in this case to village soviets and raion militia chiefs. Although the deputies' duties included such jobs as conveying prisoners and acting in emergencies, their chief function was to serve as the eyes of the militia in the village, reporting crimes and other unusual events.

Despite the government's best intentions, service by these rural agents quickly degenerated. Since the office carried no remuneration, many electees either arrived to take their post well into their two-month term or failed to appear at all. Some sent substitutes, including aged parents or children. Almost all were disinclined to take action on behalf of the militia against neighbors, even in cases of serious crime.[45] The militia, for their part, did little to help. The heavily burdened raion police chiefs found it impossible to offer any serious instruction, especially in view of deputies' two-month rotation.[46] Many *ispolniteli* served their terms without seeing the nearest militiaman, much less the raion chief. When militiamen did visit the village, they were inclined to treat the deputies rudely as lowly subordinates. Government efforts to invigorate the institution, such as a 20 December 1927 decree lowering age eligibility from twenty years for men and twenty-five for women to eighteen for all, had little effect.[47] By the end of the decade most police officials were prepared to agree with Ukrainian NKVD representative Slin'ko's judgment that notions of popular involvement through this institution were "a fiction." The deputies were merely a "survival" of the tsarist *desiatskie*.[48]

A second measure intended to move the militia closer to the populace represented a sharper break with the past. Among the results of concentration of control over the rural police in district cities during the Civil War was a substantial estrangement between patrolmen and volost soviets. A 1923 Rabkrin investigation revealed that in many areas militiamen operated with no contact with volost executives. In some cases relations were openly hostile.[49] As a corrective to this situation, the RSFSR government in October 1924 approved a new volost statute which expanded local responsibility for financing the militia but also gave volost executives (along with district police chiefs) control over the force.[50] The measure stood in stark contrast with tsarist practice, for prerevolutionary volost officials had never exerted authority over the state police. Soviet leaders hoped the step would expand the financial resources available to the militia and better relations with the peasant masses.[51]

The full effects of the 1924 statute are difficult to judge. Expectations of more ample funding were clearly disappointed. Although the statute broadened sources of revenue for the volosts, the units remained hard pressed throughout the NEP era.[52] Moreover, the militia did not stand high in local priorities. Militia officials frequently complained that volost executives were starving the force, often with the intention of reducing the police to menial dependency. One police chief in Ivanovo-Voznesensk province, for example, claimed that a warning to members of the volost executive about drunkenness prompted the officials to withhold funds for horses, uniforms, and supplies.[53] On the other side, reports continued that militia were failing to inform volost authorities and abusing local officials, especially in village *(sel'skie)* soviets.[54]

Whatever the actual balance of power between the militia and local executives, the extension of volost authority over the force seems to have done little to improve police relations with the average peasant. The chief reason for the failure of the measure in this regard was that volost executives could be as punitive in dealing with the citizenry as the militia. The 1924 statute, for example, granted volost authorities the right to issue local ordinances regulating such matters as sanitation and fire control. Seeing an opportunity to fill volost coffers, executives systematically abused their power by imposing all manner of interdictions on the peasantry (one ordinance forbade handshaking in the interests of controlling the spread of venereal disease; another sought to limit fires by forbidding illuminating huts at night) and then levying frequent and excessive fines for violations.[55] It was left to the militia to try to collect these fines, with predictably bad effect on popular attitudes toward the police.

A third method of mobilizing mass support in the effort to reform rural law enforcement, and undoubtedly the most direct, was a campaign to make peasants simply lodge complaints in cases of militia malfeasance. This effort must be understood within the context of the general issue of control over the militia. Throughout the NEP era, the shaky condition of the administrative apparatus made supervision of the police from the center a questionable proposition. Primary responsibility for oversight and direction fell to the NKVD, the agency charged with implementing government policy on policing as determined in broad outlines by the Council of People's Commissars and Central Executive Committee. The NKVD, however, had consistent difficulty communicating directives and instructions to district and volost police chiefs, much less ordinary militiamen. Inspections from above were usually cursory. A 1927 review of volost militia in Moscow's Bronnitsk district, for example, revealed that 79 percent of the deficiencies reported by visiting inspectors two years earlier were still uncorrected.[56] The shortcomings of NKVD supervision were not rectified by the Communist Party apparatus. As the official representative of the party and Central Control Commission at the 1928 2nd All-Russian Congress of Administrative Workers reported, "party influence [among the militia] is extremely insignificant."[57]

Aware of the problem of control from the center, the authorities in Moscow sought to compensate by opening avenues for the populace to participate in the supervisory function by complaining. In particular, the government in 1924 launched a campaign to encourage peasants to write to the press revealing abuses. Over the next two years the NKVD's new Bureau of Peasant Letters handled almost eleven thousand such communications from rural correspondents (sel'kory) or individual villagers.[58] The authorities investigated just under half of these complaints and confirmed one-quarter.

What was the impact of popular supervision on the rural militia? An official analysis by A. Voitchak of the peasant letter-writing campaign is instructive.[59] Militia personnel did figure in peasant complaints, but less frequently than private citizens and village soviet officials. A total of 238 policemen were disciplined in 1925–26 as a result of such letters. Ironically, this group included a not insignificant 2.5 percent of the more urban district chiefs, but only 1.6 percent of all volost chiefs and a mere .2 percent of the militia rank and file.

Voitchak suggested that the average militiaman was rarely the object of complaint because his limited authority gave him little opportunity for malfeasance.[60] A much more persuasive case can be made for the opposite proposition that militia power prevented popular supervision. The central authorities frequently criticized local police for failing to encourage complaint, impeding investigation, and intimidating *sel'kory* and other protesters.[61] Peasants responded with fear and suspicion. M. Boldyrev encountered one example of the dominant attitude at a conference of peasant representatives. Asked by a village woman if complaint against militiamen would lead to arrest, the official patiently explained three times that honest criticism was welcome. At the session's close the woman surprised Boldyrev by asking for his address. When asked why, she responded, "Just in case."[62]

Much of the responsibility for the failure to reach out more effectively to the populace and, indeed, for the overall inadequacy of efforts to transform rural law enforcement must be assigned to the Soviet government. The consistent shortages of men and matériel which undermined the militia apparatus throughout NEP reflected the relatively low priority the central authorities gave to police reform. Moreover, in seeking popular assistance, the Soviet leadership never really divorced itself from the Civil War suspicion of the peasantry. Police officials knew, for example, that one cause of the passivity of village deputies was a lack of legal authority for autonomous action. Yet as V. Pomerantsev explained in connection with the specific issue of the subordinate status of the deputies, it would be impossible to allow the peasant patrolmen to operate independently of militia command as a result of their low cultural level and "specifically local [*obyvatel'skii*] outlook."[63]

At the same time, however, the social context of rural law enforcement severely constrained the Soviet rulers in their options. The relative poverty of the countryside—evident, for example, in the struggle of volost executives for resources—blocked efforts to improve the militia apparatus through decentralization. The retention of traditional attitudes among the peasantry undermined plans to enlist the populace in the police function. The appointment of women as village deputies, for instance, was greeted by what one official called "wisecracks and jokes in the old-regime spirit."[64]

In general, peasants remained reluctant to serve in a position which made them agents of outsiders, whether tsarist police or Soviet militia.

It is important to recognize that the shortcomings of the rural militia—simultaneously a cause and an effect of the reemergence of prerevolutionary patterns of law enforcement—did not prevent the Soviet regime from taking a far more activist approach to deviance in the countryside than its tsarist predecessor. The willingness of the Communists to employ the rural militia in this way was evident in two major anticrime campaigns of the NEP era, one directed against home brewing of illicit alcoholic beverages and the other against hooliganism.

Tsarist authorities introduced prohibition in Russia in connection with the outbreak of war in 1914. The new Bolshevik government confirmed the policy, though during the Civil War, enforcement was sporadic.[65] With the restoration of peace and the introduction of NEP, the regime faced an increase in illegal home brewing on a scale that some claimed threatened the nation's food supply. Soviet rulers responded by launching a vigorous campaign of repression. Police action initially concentrated in the cities but soon spilled over into the countryside. Militia detachments conducted thousands of raids in the villages (Gosplan reported 300,000 cases in the RSFSR in the first half of 1923 alone), arresting or fining violators and confiscating stills and other peasant property.[66] Although repression slackened in mid-decade, the government in late 1927 renewed the assault on home brewing with intensity and a specifically rural emphasis.[67]

The campaign against hooliganism was less focused. In the middle of the decade, the Soviet authorities became alarmed over a perceived wave of antisocial, often motiveless crimes loosely categorized under this rubric.[68] Although the highest incidence of this type of deviance was held to be in the cities, hooliganism also had a distinctive rural dimension. Given the parlous state of recordkeeping, the thinness of the rural militia apparatus, and the fluctuations in police activity caused by various campaigns, it is difficult to determine the real magnitude of deviance in the NEP countryside.[69] There was consensus among police, judicial workers, and criminologists, however, that rural crime—including hooliganism—was particularly violent.[70] Commentators attributed this, in part, to traditional practices such as brawling, often in a drunken state while armed with knives. Yet they also pointed to the disruptive impact of change, including the extension of administrative activity in the countryside, as a stimulus to violence. The militia seem to have been frequent targets of assault.[71] As one hooligan song declared,

> There was a revolution—it didn't give us freedom;
> There were police—the militia are twice as bad.
> I walk the streets and do what I please,
> If the militia say anything, I show them the knife.[72]

In order to control the "wave" of antisocial acts believed to be sweeping the USSR, the central authorities in 1926 launched a campaign against hooliganism. Repressive measures in the countryside included broader power for militiamen to impose fines for petty deviance and expanded authority for volost executives in introducing and enforcing local ordinances.[73] Taken together with the renewed effort against home brewing, the antihooligan campaign brought a sharp increase in militia operations. During 1926 alone, the number of criminals sentenced by the courts for hooligan crimes in towns and the country rose over seven times.[74] By one NKVD estimate, the number of rural inhabitants punished administratively (i.e., exclusive of judicial action) jumped from 708,000 in 1927 to 1,231,449 in 1928, largely because of increases in fines for home brewing (up from 20,625 to 234,927), hooliganism (131,930 to 191,950), and forest violations (372,311 to 558,813).[75]

The actual impact of the two campaigns on rural criminality is hard to measure. Most commentators of the era seemed confident that home brewing had been defeated in the cities—where the authorities not only commanded a stronger militia apparatus but also benefited more directly from the reintroduction of state sale of full-strength vodka in 1925—but still flourished in the villages. Government studies late in the decade uncovered staggering levels of rural home brewing, and prohibitionists warned of the "alcoholization" of an entire generation of peasant youth.[76] There was less agreement in regard to the admittedly more elusive category of hooliganism. Responding to an official inquiry in 1927, for example, provincial authorities divided almost equally on the likelihood of continued waves of such deviance, though all favored continued vigilance on the basis of "heightened popular initiative in the struggle for social discipline."[77]

The effect of the campaigns on the rural police apparatus itself is clearer. In both cases, the Soviet government was sending a charge that the wires of law enforcement could not bear. In some places the impulse from the center simply died as local officials proved either unable or unwilling to act. Drunkenness was the most common vice of militiamen in this era. Many of the peace officers apparently succumbed to the temptation to overlook home brewing in return for a share of the product; some used their authority to extort a supply of drink. One commentator in 1925 estimated that 90 percent of the critical notes in the press about rural militiamen involved home brew.[78] As a Tver peasant "poet" put it, "Those who are against this fight, also drink with appetite."[79] Village officials were even more likely to be complicit.

Similar forces undermined the antihooligan campaign. A majority of the provincial officials reporting on the subject to the NKVD in 1927 identified the shortage of militiamen in the countryside and the passivity of peasant functionaries, including especially the village deputies, as fundamental obstacles to proper enforcement.[80] "In certain places," reported administrative expert N. O. Lagovier, "volost executive committees and village militia stand aside from the struggle and ignore shocking cases of outrageous hooliganism occurring before their very eyes."[81]

From the standpoint of the effort to develop a new, positive ethos of law enforcement, even more destructive than inactivity was the tendency for campaigns to overheat. Pressed by superiors to produce results, militiamen often overreacted, indiscriminately arresting or fining rich and poor, guilty and innocent alike.[82] Home-brew raids became occasions to loot peasant homes not only of spirits but also of household goods.[83] Volost officials were similarly inclined. The antihooligan campaign in particular produced a spate of restrictive local ordinances, often arbitrarily enforced. Individual volost executive committees, for example, forbade all singing, accordion playing, dancing, and parties.[84] The average magnitude of rural fines, perhaps the best barometer of the intensity of administrative activity, rose from 4 rubles 79 kopecks in 1927 to 8 rubles 62 kopecks the following year. Indeed, the imposition of fines in the villages was so vigorous that only 62 percent could actually be collected.[85]

The tendency of the campaigns to degenerate into arbitrariness and administrative overreach indicates the dilemma in which the authorities found themselves in the NEP countryside. Moshe Lewin has described Soviet policy toward the peasantry in this era as characterized by an "inherent 'schizophrenia,' " reflected in official infringement of laws established by the government itself.[86] The Soviet leadership was, in fact, of two minds in approaching rural law enforcement. On the one hand, the authorities wanted to reform—to build an efficient, law-abiding, responsive militia apparatus, capable of legitimizing the new order and winning popular assent through patient work over time. On the other hand, the government remained distrustful of the peasantry and anxious to transform the countryside quickly. The social context of policing in the villages—particularly in its resistance to change—proved decisive in resolving this dilemma. The regime was unwilling and unable to devote either the resources or the time needed to overcome the formidable external obstacles to the gradual reform of law enforcement. The result, foreshadowed by the punitive nature of the campaigns against home brewing and hooliganism, was the Stalinist resort to coercion.

NOTES

1. David H. Bayley, "The Limits of Police Reform," in Bayley, ed., *Police and Society* (Beverly Hills, 1977), pp. 219–36.

2. On prerevolutionary law enforcement agencies see Neil Weissman, "Regular Police in Tsarist Russia, 1900–1914," *Russian Review*, 44 (1985), pp. 45–68.

3. *Tsentral'nyi gosudarstvennyi istoricheskii arkhiv SSSR*, f. 1217, op. 171 (1909 g.), d. 1, t. I, pp. 29–30.

4. On the early months of the militia see E. N. Gorodetskii, *Rozhdenie Sovetskogo gosudarstva, 1917–1918 gg.* (Moscow, 1965), pp. 306–17. The author wishes to note that in this essay NKVD will refer to the interior commissariat of the RSFSR unless otherwise indicated.

5. *Vlast' sovetov (VS)*, 11 (1919), p. 31.

6. Ibid., pp. 6–7 and 30–32.

7. See, for example, John Rickman, "Russian Camera Obscura: Ten Sketches of Russian Peasant Life (1916–1918)," in Geoffrey Gorer and Rickman, *The People of Great Russia: A Psychological Study* (New York, 1962), pp. 72–74.

8. *Raboche-krest'ianskaia militsiia (RKM)*, 1 (1922), p. 6.

9. *Administrativnyi vestnik (AV)*, 5 (1925), p. 39.

10. *RKM*, 1 (1922), p. 4.

11. Ibid.

12. Ibid., p. 3.

13. *AV*, 5 (1925), pp. 37–38.

14. *AV*, 4 (1925), pp. 65–66, and 2 (1926), pp. 82–83.

15. *AV*, 5 (1925), p. 6, and 9–10 (1925), p. 11.

16. *Tsentral'noe statisticheskoe upravlenie, Gosudarstvennyi apparat SSSR* (Moscow, 1929), pp. 11–12.

17. Ibid., pp. 25–26 and 29–30.

18. *RKM*, 1 (1924), p. 38.

19. *AV*, 4 (1925), p. 66.

20. *AV*, 12 (1925), p. 51; 3 (1926), p. 39; and 5 (1928), pp. 39–41.

21. *AV*, 11 (1928), p. 49.

22. *RKM, Iubileinyi nomer* (1924), p. 21.

23. Ibid., p. 23.

24. *Narodnyi komissariat vnutrennikh del, Biulleten'*, 11 (1925), pp. 78–79; and *Ezhenedel'nik sovetskoi iustitsii (ESIu)*, 19–20 (1924), p. 475.

25. *NKVD, Biulleten'*, 23 (1926), pp. 244–45.

26. Ibid., 10 (1925), pp. 71–72; and *AV*, 4 (1925), pp. 76–77.

27. *NKVD, Biulleten'*, 18 (1926), p. 204.

28. See Peter H. Solomon, Jr., "Criminalization and Decriminalization in Soviet Criminal Policy, 1917–1941," *Law and Society Review*, 16, no. 1 (1981–82), pp. 9–43.

29. *ESIu*, 36–37 (1928).

30. *AV*, 9–10 (1925), p. 9. On worker and administrative salaries see Stephen Sternheimer, "Administration for Development," in Walter M. Pintner and Don K. Rowney, *Russian Officialdom* (Chapel Hill, 1980), p. 333.

31. *AV*, 5 (1925), p. 39.

32. *NKVD, Biulleten'*, 25 (1923), p. 176, and 4 (1924).

33. *AV*, 5 (1925), p. 39, and 6 (1928), pp. 49–50.

34. *AV*, 11 (1925), p. 59.

35. *VS*, 5 (1923), p. 48; and L. F. Morozov, *Organy TsKK-RKI v bor'be za sovershenstvovanie sovetskogo gosudarstvennogo apparata (1923–1934 gg.)* (Moscow, 1964), p. 188.

36. *NKVD, Vtoroi vserossiiskii s"ezd administrativnykh rabotnikov* (Moscow, 1929), p. 77.

37. *AV*, 3 (1925), pp. 52–53.

38. *AV*, 7 (1925), pp. 61–63; and Solomon, pp. 22–27.

39. *AV*, 3 (1926), p. 66, and 5 (1928), p. 17. The central authorities rather hypocritically resorted to premiums themselves at several points during the decade,

though they described this as a temporary expedient. See *ESIu*, 12 (1923), p. 273; and *NKVD, Biulleten'*, 21 (1927), pp. 364–66.
    40. *NKVD, Biulleten'*, 24 (1925), p. 207.
    41. *AV*, 5 (1925), p. 9.
    42. See Neil Weissman, *Reform in Tsarist Russia* (New Brunswick, 1981), pp. 29–30 and 62–64.
    43. *NKVD, Biulleten'*, 12 (1924), p. 52, and 17 (1924), pp. 75–76.
    44. *AV*, 8 (1929), p. 16.
    45. *NKVD, Vtoroi s"ezd*, p. 35; and *AV*, 2 (1926), pp. 17–20, and 8 (1928), pp. 15–16.
    46. *AV*, 2 (1929), pp. 16–17.
    47. *NKVD, Biulleten'*, 2 (1928), p. 36.
    48. *NKVD, Vtoroi s"ezd*, p. 38.
    49 *VS*, 3–4 (1924), pp. 80–85.
    50. *VS*, 7 (1924), pp. 70–77.
    51. *AV*, 3 (1926), p. 38.
    52. See E. H. Carr, *Socialism in One Country* (Baltimore, 1970), vol. II, pp. 482–94.
    53. *AV*, 3 (1926), pp. 38–39; and *NKVD, Vtoroi s"ezd*, p. 38.
    54. *AV*, 8 (1929), pp. 13–14.
    55. N. O. Lagovier, *Administrativnye vzyskaniia v volosti* (Moscow, 1928), pp. 16–19. On futile efforts of the central authorities to curb abuse see *NKVD, Biulleten'*, 7 (1925), p. 46, and 34 (1927), pp. 635–37; and *ESIu*, 42–43 (1928), p. 1121. The arbitrary nature of rural administration is discussed in Moshe Lewin, *Russian Peasants and Soviet Power* (New York, 1968), pp. 32–37; Olga Narkiewicz, *The Making of the Soviet State Apparatus* (Manchester, 1970), pp. 90–91; and Yuzuru Taniuchi, *The Village Gathering in Russia in the Mid-1920's* (Birmingham, 1968), pp. 33–36.
    56. *AV*, 1 (1926), pp. 8–9; 2 (1926), p. 72; and 7 (1928), p. 49; and *NKVD, Biulleten'*, 11 (1926), pp. 144–45.
    57. *NKVD, Vtoroi s"ezd*, p. 60.
    58. *AV*, 10–11 (1927), p. 11, and 3 (1928), pp. 50–51.
    59. *AV*, 3 (1928), pp. 50–52.
    60. Ibid., p. 52.
    61. *AV*, 12 (1927), pp. 16–17; *ESIu*, 52 (1925), p. 1174; N. O. Lagovier, *Sovetskaia obshchestvennost' v bor'be s prestupnost'iu* (Moscow, 1929), pp. 12–15; and *NKVD, Biulleten'*, 24 (1925), pp. 206–207. One NKVD circular criticized efforts by militia to use their office to avoid punishment for crimes in terms of illegal reestablishment of the prerevolutionary practice of administrative guarantee. Ibid., 18 (1925), p. 157. G. Manns went so far as to suggest that officials were in part responsible for a wave of murders of *sel'kory* which was reaching "very threatening proportions." Manns, "Derevenskie ubiistva i ubiitsy," in E. Shirvindt et al., eds., *Problemy prestupnosti* (Moscow-Leningrad, 1927), vol. II, p. 33.
    62. *AV*, 5 (1925), p. 10.
    63. *RKM*, 1 (1924), p. 6.
    64. *AV*, 2 (1926), p. 19.
    65. On the Soviet campaign against illicit alcohol see Neil Weissman, "Prohibition and Alcohol Control in the USSR: The 1920's Campaign against Illegal Spirits," *Soviet Studies*, 3 (1986), pp. 349–68.
    66. V. M. Chetyrkin, "Tainoe vinokurenie v derevne," *Planovoe khoziaistvo*, 4–5 (1924), p. 89.
    67. Weissman, "Prohibition," pp. 359–60.
    68. See, in particular, V. N. Tolmachev, ed., *Khuliganstvo i khuligany: Sbornik*

(Moscow, 1929); and V. Vlasov, "Khuliganstvo v gorode i derevne," in Shirvindt, vol. II, pp. 51–75.

69. A good introduction to the issue is A. A. Gertsenzon, *Bor'ba s prestupnost'iu v RSFSR* (Moscow, 1928).

70. Ibid., pp. 54–55; Vlasov, "Khuliganstvo," pp. 60–61; Manns, "Derevenskie ubiistva," pp. 25–28; Moshe Lewin, *The Making of the Soviet System* (New York, 1985), pp. 55–56; and Helmut Altrichter, *Die Bauern von Tver* (Munich, 1984), pp. 123–34.

71. Vlasov, "Khuliganstvo," p. 58; and *AV*, 9 (1927), pp. 19–20.

72. Vlasov, "Khuliganstvo," p. 66.

73. *NKVD, Biulleten'*, 18 (1926), p. 208; 28 (1926), p. 279; and 5 (1927), pp. 72–75; and Lagovier, *Administrativnye vzyskaniia*, pp. 50–52.

74. Gertsenzon, *Bor'ba s prestupnost'iu*, p. 30n.

75. *AV*, 9 (1929), pp. 10–11.

76. See, for example, *Statisticheskoe obozrenie*, 1 (1929), pp. 106–107, and 2 (1929), pp. 101–103.

77. *AV*, 9 (1927), pp. 22–23.

78. *AV*, 8 (1925), p. 75. See also *ESIu*, 26–27 (1922), pp. 21–22; *Pravda*, 14 April 1923, p. 4, and 26 September 1922, p. 5, and *Izvestiia*, 9 February 1928, p. 3.

79. A. M. Bol'shakov, *Sovetskaia derevnia* (Leningrad, 1924), p. 90.

80. *AV*, 9 (1927), p. 20.

81. Lagovier, *Administrativnye vzyskaniia*, p. 52.

82. *ESIu*, 38 (1923), p. 875, for example.

83. Weissman, "Prohibition," p. 365.

84. Lagovier, *Administrativnye vzyskaniia*, pp. 18 and 52; and *AV*, 9 (1927), pp. 19–20.

85. *AV*, 9 (1929), p. 12.

86. Lewin, *Russian Peasants*, p. 34.

# XII

## INSOLUBLE CONFLICTS
### VILLAGE LIFE BETWEEN REVOLUTION
### AND COLLECTIVIZATION

*Helmut Altrichter*

In the eyes of the Bolsheviks, rural Russia was a stronghold of conservatism. They regarded the peasant economy as primitive and underdeveloped, the peasant as retarded and uneducated, and peasant behavior as rough, stupid, and slow. During the 1920s, the Soviet government and party leadership sought to modernize rural society and maximize agricultural output; every effort was made to "uplift" the peasants and to eliminate their "backward" ways.

Bolshevik efforts were only marginally successful in this regard, not just because of peasant "stubbornness" but also because many peasant actions and practices, institutions and customs, had their own internal, compelling logic and functionality. It was the logic and functionality of a precapitalist peasant society, subsistence-oriented and averse to running risks, with the family as the basic unit of production and consumption, and with the village, the *mir*, a world in itself, both a microcosm and a network of relatives and neighbors to help in times of crises.[1] Focusing on these areas of conflict, my essay describes the "toughness of tradition" in Russian rural life during the 1920s.[2]

The setting for the following observations is the province of Tver.[3] Located northwest of Moscow, in the center of European Russia, Tver covered some 24,400 square miles, about the size of West Virginia. In the mid-1920s, the province had a population of 2.2 million, which for Russia was relatively dense. The center of provincial activity was the city of Tver, now Kalinin, with a population of 100,000. The province also included two dozen small towns. But the majority of the population, about 90 percent, lived in Tver's 11–12,000 rural communities *(obshchiny)* and on its 350–

400,000 farmsteads *(dvory)*. My observations will focus on these rural settlements.

Geographically, the province of Tver consisted of two parts. In the northwest were the Valdai Heights, a terrain formed by terminal moraines with numerous lakes, rivers, and marshes. Toward the east the terrain flattened out until it merged smoothly with the surrounding flatlands of Yaroslavl. The two geographical regions were connected by the Volga River, the lifeline of the province. Settlement followed the natural resources and lines of geographic communication, the rivers, lakes, and arable land. In the inhospitable northwest there were only a few villages, and these usually consisted of no more than a few cottages. Farther east and south, however, where the valleys became wider and flatter, the number and the size of the villages increased. These villages contained twenty to thirty and often as many as fifty homesteads with wooden, planked, shingled, or thatch-roofed houses.

Natural conditions severely restricted the amount of arable land. In some places, the soil was too sandy and dry, in others too loamy and acidic. Some of the ground was covered with gravel and rocks, indicative of its ice age origins. Agriculture was possible only in places where the soil was moist enough but not too heavy. Severe climatic conditions—harsh, cold winters and humid summers—also restricted farming in the region.

At the turn of the twentieth century the land was roughly divided into one-quarter woods, one-quarter meadow, one-quarter arable land, and one-quarter pasture and wasteland. Even at the end of the 1920s land utilization was hardly intensified. Agriculture was dominated by smallholding. Most farm homesteads consisted of three, six, or nine but certainly not more than twelve acres, divided into thirty, forty, or more parcels of land. The three-field system continued to dominate farming practice even into the twenties, and farmers continued to produce the traditional crops—winter rye, oats, flax, potatoes, barley, and clover. With the exception of oats and flax, these crops did not yield enough to satisfy even the local Tver market. Because the grain harvest in Tver was not self-sustaining, most of its inhabitants were forced, over the years, to supplement their farming by working as artisans or labor migrants.

Before World War I, 75 percent of all Tver farmers preserved the existence of their farms in this way. Although the revolution and the Civil War decreased the number of migrant workers, the main problem persisted. Indeed, the land question was not resolved by the expropriation of noble, church, and monastic properties. While it is true that another 840,000 acres of arable land were made available to the farmers of Tver, the size of homesteads increased by only 0.5 acre per capita, or less than 2.5 acres per homestead.

More important than these shifts were the social consequences of the revolution within the farming communities: The large landowners and farms disappeared, and for the first time households that had been propertyless before the revolution now acquired arable land of their own. Thus, in this, as well as in other, areas of reform, the developments of the Stolypin era were reversed.

Whether or not this was a result of leveling, after a transition period during the era of War Communism, overall developments tended to strengthen the institution of the *obshchina*. (From 1922 on the communes were also supported in their rights and duties by agricultural legislation.)

Regional studies enable us to study in depth a complex contextual framework through a focused set of variables: geography and climate, forms of settlement and economy, social and family structure, cultural and religious traditions, everyday behavior, and mentality. Only within a regional context can these variables be described and related to each other with the necessary precision. If, as in this case, the selected region forms a unit, it is possible to discover and describe its peculiarities and specific problems.

In the course of such a description, not only the region itself but its social groupings, organizations, and institutions are revealed in their specificity. Their particular interests, goals, and plans take shape and become the focus of investigation. Their emergence as the center of interest proportionately diminishes the perception of the region as a mere object of state policy.

The extent to which one can reconstruct the relationship between the region and the state as a whole and describe their common interests as well as their conflicts depends on the sources available. Sources for a regional study of Tver are rich and ample.[4] A relatively large number of relevant publications allow us to develop a picture of life in Tver during the NEP period. Party committees and Soviet organizations published their programs, reports, and announcements, as well as minutes of their meetings in the rural districts and the regional center. In the tradition of the old *zemstvo* organizations, regional offices and sections for compiling statistics published statistical yearbooks based on their own investigations. There were tracts and memoranda which explained particular regional problems to party functionaries and agronomists. There were also regional journals and newspapers aimed at a wider, but nevertheless small, readership. Only toward the end of the twenties did these sources begin to become murky or to dry up. By the end of the twenties these publications were no longer used to explain and debate policies but rather to justify and execute them.

Despite the fact that the Bolshevik point of view dominates these sources, the sources themselves reveal the nature of contemporary problems, especially when they document the difference between targets and reality, when peasant behavior comes into conflict with the values of the Soviet government, and when local peasants comment on the course of events. Documents such as compilations of economic and social statistics, reports and discussions of the local soviets, critiques of rural customs, criminal statistics, legal reports, letters to the editor, and glossaries enable us to develop a picture of everyday life in the villages and to understand the nature of the villagers' own interests.

On the basis of my study of these sources, I will examine a number of problems concerning daily life and holidays, the official church and popular religion, folk medicine and magic.[5] Although intrinsically of minor interest to the Bolsheviks, these issues were extremely important to the village. In the course of my discussion it should become clear just how difficult it was for the Bolsheviks to solve problems even in areas such as these which were not political in the narrow sense of the word.

One of the peculiarities of the industrial age is that work is measured in terms of time and time in terms of hours, minutes, and seconds. The beginning and end of a workday are fixed, followed by free time for leisure. Such concepts were unknown in agricultural societies, where life was not structured according to the division of labor. In such societies, to the degree to which time was not also associated with transitoriness, otherworldliness, and eternity, it was measured in terms of factors arising out of the natural rhythm of the earth—the years and seasons, night and day, and the position of the sun—and of things which everyone knew, such as the duration of the Lord's Prayer. It was not the clock which regulated work but rather needs and tasks: sometimes people worked from sunrise to sunset, sometimes for only a few hours.[6] Work and leisure time were not separate, and indeed there is no evidence to indicate that peasants thought in these categories.[7] It was not so much contrast between work time and free time which constituted a point of orientation for village life but rather the sequence of holy days and feast days that interrupted the rural routine and broke the year up into smaller, more comprehensible parts. The cycle of holy days and holidays which ran parallel to the production cycle served to strengthen and to condition the rhythm of work and production.

Life in Tver during the 1920s followed such a pattern. The peasants lived from holiday to holiday—and there were lots of them. Almost without exception, these holidays coincided with the traditional Orthodox holidays, the more significant of which corresponded to the same holidays in the West: Christmas, Easter, Whitsun, New Year's, Epiphany, the various feasts of the Virgin Mary. Then there were the feasts of the saints: Elias, Michael, John the Baptist, and Nicholas, the last three of which enjoyed several feast days. Finally, every year people celebrated the miraculous wonders of the Icon of the Holy Mother of Kazan (July 8), and on October

22 thanks were given to the Holy Mother for saving Moscow from the Poles in 1612.

In addition to these general feast days there were local events which varied from place to place, from region to region. Going back to specific traditions (a vow, for example), these local occasions were celebrated as intensely as the general feast days. Not all feasts were observed with the same extravagance. Only four or five per year were celebrated in the "grand" manner, that is, for more than one day. In addition to Christmas, Easter, and Whitsunday, the period just before Lent (Mardi Gras) and the feast days of George, Kazan, Elias, and Michael were also "grand" festival occasions. Added together, these free days totaled 50. As a rule, Sundays were also free of work, but in the hierarchy of holidays they ranked below feast days. If these were to be added to the total of feasts and holidays, the number of free days amounted to more than 100, and in many areas there were even more.[8]

Most feast days, including the feast of the Blessed Virgin Mary, fit conveniently into the agricultural cycle, in spring (without disturbing planting) or in fall (after the harvest). Other feasts came at less opportune times: thus, the Kazan feast sometimes conflicted with haymaking, the feast of Elias interfered with preparations for the grain harvest, and the feasts in August always took place during the hectic days of high season. For this reason, the state-directed agitation against feast days was especially great, since celebrations were not confined to one day but often lasted a week, including preparations and aftermath. The admonition that economic necessities should take precedence over religious custom was repeated each year, obviously without much result. Even if, under pressure of the authorities, the villagers decided to cancel the feast for the following year, once the holiday arrived, good intentions were altogether forgotten.[9]

Feast days differed completely from ordinary weekdays. During a feast, according to Fenomenov's monograph on the village of Gadyshi published in 1925, a farmer hitched up his two-wheeled cart very early in the morning and went with his family to the service in the nearest village church. There, he had long talks with the peasants of the area about issues of the day. On special local feast days, the priest was invited to Gadyshi. He celebrated vespers and mass, after which he visited every house.

Other religious customs could also be observed at local feasts. In Gradobit, a village near Gadyshi, the peasants had vowed on a special day to "cleanse" themselves. In a procession, the villagers went down to the river. There men and women of every age took off their outer clothing, went into the water, and removed even their undershirts. Often, the poor of the area made off with the shirts. According to Fenomenov, old and poor people were particularly drawn to local feast days. Even if we do not know a great deal about the religious customs of the 1920s, there can be no doubt that they continued. Gadyshi may be taken as representative of the situation in the area of Tver province.[10]

According to Orthodox church doctrine, one must fast before taking communion, and at least in Gadyshi this requirement was followed. Until churchgoers returned home, nobody ate or drank. Even families that did not attend church observed this custom. Afterward, the secular part of the feast commenced, with its own forms and rules. For "high" feasts, preparations began days before. Houses were thoroughly cleaned. Beer was brewed and brandy distilled.

The beer brewing during the day and night before the feast was a specific and solemn process reserved for the men. They built a fire outside the house, fetched the water themselves (which they otherwise never did), and, before the eyes of a critical public, began to brew a bittersweet concoction of malt, rye, and barley flour, water, and hops. Bystanders were invited to taste the brew, and neighbors gave expert opinions on each other's attempts.[11] In practice every peasant brewed, the poor as well as the rich, the head of the village soviet as well as the party member. Alcohol was part and parcel of this ritual; common brewing had long since become an indispensable part of the celebration. In addition to beer, in many places a liquid concoction of corn and potatoes was produced. This product of home distillation, or *samogon,* enjoyed a growing popularity. With the help of a simple distillery, one could produce from 1 pood of flour (about 16.4 kgs) 4 to 5 liters of liquid with an alcohol content of 25–30 percent; after another stage of distillation the yield was 70 percent.[12] The fact that the state banned this practice meant merely that in some places, the action was removed to a place outside the village. But this did not really eliminate general brewing and distilling. The militia drank along with everyone else, and higher authorities had to acknowledge that bans and punishments could not stop illegal distilling.[13]

Friends and relatives from the village were invited to the feast itself. They arrived after church. Upon entering the hut *(izba),* the guests blessed themselves before the icon, toasted the host, and were served appetizers. During the dinner which followed, everyone ate from a common bowl. Between eight and nine courses were served. Especially when guests were present, the host sought to show off his possessions. Scarcely had this hours-long opulent lunch concluded when the guests would be invited to eat again, in the afternoon and in the evening. Young people met in the main street of the village; people strolled along the streets and enjoyed themselves. The day ended with singing and dancing and a general air of drunkenness. The next day, the men had hangovers and, according to reports, tried to revive their inebriation. The celebration continued. In addition to relatives, guests from other villages were invited to take part in the special local feasts. Thus during the general feasts, relationships within the village were cemented, and local feasts served to strengthen bonds between villages. In both cases these bonds were based on kinship.[14]

The festival meal reinforced the ties between families within the village, while the alcohol, imbibed in abundance, served to heighten emotions and to break down existing standards and barriers. In the intoxicated atmosphere of these celebrations, conflicts were settled violently, often according to the rural aphorism "What a sober man has in his head, a drunk man has in his fist." A long police report followed every festival. According to the Tver newspaper, during the four Easter holidays in 1926, the provincial militia of Tver registered 286 instances of hooliganism, 207 minor brawls (without weapons), 31 severe and 769 minor injuries, 46 cases of slander, 111 thefts, instances of illegal distilling, and rapes, 46 cases of alcohol-related manslaughter, and 419 cases of public nuisance. In addition, 355 drunken hooligans and other criminals were arrested.[15]

During a festival the same year, two young men raped a girl in the village of Marfino in the district *(uezd)* of Kimry. The deed occurred on the village road in the presence of a number of youths and adults, none of whom tried to help the girl. Many of these witnesses refused to appear in court, or they used their testimony to protect the rapists, who continued to deny any guilt for the crime. No local *(volost)* party cell, Komsomol, or education functionary intervened on behalf of the girl.[16]

Also in 1926, Egor Andreevich Sokolov, the local correspondent for the peasant newspaper, was beaten to death in the Tver village of Ill'inskoe on New Year's night. He was on his way home with his brother when they met two men from the Volkov clan, Ivan Filippovich and his uncle Ivan Egorovich. Hostilities between the two families were long-standing. One of the Volkovs had already been sentenced to six months in jail for smashing the correspondent's windows. And it was never clarified who had twice set fire to the barn and warehouse of the Sokolov family, or how their horse came to break its neck in the pasture, or who had spilled tar in the family's well. When the inebriated Volkovs met their "enemies," a violent fracas broke out. One of the Sokolovs was able to flee, but the other, the correspondent, was left at the scene of the crime with his skull bashed in. After their arrest, the Volkovs' relatives tried to get them a good-conduct affidavit and obtained thirty signatures in Ill'inskoe.[17]

In Gadyshi, according to Fenomenov, the Bol'shakov family took advantage of a local celebration to settle an old score with the leader of the village soviet, Vasilii Sergeevich Pavlov. Vasilii, who was by no means a poor peasant *(bedniak)* but an ambitious owner of a medium-sized farm, had violated the traditional practice of declaring only a part of his cropland to the government tax officials. In August, on the second day of the Feast of the Holy Savior, while everyone was drunk, the Bol'shakovs lured Vasilii into their house on the pretext that the volost militia officer wanted to speak with him. Although the officer was present and obviously knew about the plot, he did not intervene when the clan attacked the leader of the soviet to "teach him a lesson." The peasants saw how the village soviet leader was beaten up, but none came to his defense. In fact, only his family deplored the act. The volost officer refused to record the incident, claiming that Vasilii himself had been drunk. In court, the affair came to naught, based on the principle that "it takes at least two people to make a fight."[18]

In all three instances cited here—and it would not be difficult to add to them—the villagers' attitudes were no less characteristic than those of the culprit. Except for the victim's relatives, they remained passive. And as the peasant newspaper argued, the villagers were all too ready to aid the culprit in his attempt to evade the state's legal authority. The extent to which the village stood behind the crime, or the degree to which it considered the crime an internal village affair in which the state should not intervene, is an open question. In any case, the culprit was conceded mitigating circumstances. Indeed, behavior during festivals and celebrations was judged according to special laws. Whereas people otherwise lived a Spartan life, during holidays and feast days they celebrated. For a while they could drown the sorrows of daily life in alcohol, release their emotions, and give vent to aggressions and social conflicts.

In the same spirit, in the Rzhev district there was a special feast day during which the patriarchal order was suspended and women assumed command for one day. (Similar events have been noted in central and western Europe.)[19] In Rzhev, the women began their feast on a Sunday in May in exactly the same manner as the men. During the preceding week they went from house to house gathering flour, eggs, and money and brewed *samogon*. On the appropriate Sunday they gathered to feast and drink homemade brandy. When the mood was finally right, according to the reports of the village newspaper, they sang lewd songs. The women abused each other as coarsely as did the men, and occasionally fights broke out in which they hit each other like the roughest village hooligans. In the evening, according to a stern report in the village paper, the husbands (at least those who had not taken part in the festivities) came to "pluck their stray wives out of the gutter." The patriarchal order was then restored.[20]

Both the government and the party opposed the religious holidays and condemned the manner in which they were celebrated. For the authorities, all of these events were orgies of gorging, boozing, and brawling. According to the calculations of the Tver newspaper, each farm spent twenty, thirty, or forty rubles for each of the four or five annual festival celebrations, which amounted to at least eighty rubles a year and, with fifty farms in the village, came to about four thousand rubles or the price of forty cows.[21]

The government decided to substitute new holidays for the old ones: International Labor Day on May 1; Journalism Day and Harvest Preparation Day, also in May; International Cooperation Day at the beginning of July; Harvest Day in mid-October; and the anniversary of the October Revolution on November 7. In addition to these holidays, March 8 was designated International Women's Day. These new holidays differed fundamentally from the old ones in style and content. According to the new instructions, streets were to be decorated and parades organized. Schools were to arrange festive activities for the students; progressive agricultural methods were to be demonstrated in exhibits; and functionaries and agronomists were to give introductory lectures on the most pressing economic and political problems of the day. The festivities were to close with theater and cinema performances.[22]

It is doubtful that these new holidays were widely accepted in the villages. In any case, they failed to replace the traditional ones. Those who placed great hopes in such a transformation ignored the fact that the old holidays were deeply anchored in rural customs and that they had served a social function even if their religious origins were disappearing. Moreover, those who sought to alter these traditions forgot that they served the social function of developing and ritually reinforcing a village collectivity based on family relationships. The socialist holidays were both new and different. They invoked collective interests of the state and the relationship between the city and the countryside. They appealed to reason and economic rationality. The authorities wanted the festivities to be organized by party cells, soviets, the Komsomol, teachers, and agronomists, with the peasants in the role of an anonymous civic public. At bottom, they presupposed a society that still had to be created. The existing Tver village had very little in common with it.

Following the revolution the Orthodox church lost its status as a state church. It was stripped of all its rights and privileges. Its land was expropriated, and its property was declared the property of the people. It lost any claim to fiscal support from government or semigovernmental sources. Church and state were to be separated, religion was to become a private matter, and the church, if it continued to exist all, would exist as a loose, anonymous community of believers and not as an institution or organization.

The dissolution of the state church in Tver province seems to have been carried out quickly and quietly. Obviously, it had already ceased to be a political factor by the early 1920s, at which time the villagers began electing their priest themselves to avoid having one imposed on them by the official church hierarchy. Before an election, the village gathering, or *skhod*, determined that the priest's family was not too large and that it would not be too expensive for the village to support. The priest received a plot of land in the village, the size of which was calculated according to the customary land distribution regulations, taking into account the number of people who would be fed by the produce from the plot and the number of workers. Church buildings and liturgical objects—robes and instruments— could be borrowed from the state without charge. To do so, according to the law, a request with at least twenty signatures had to be submitted in which the undersigned assumed liability for the borrowed objects. The sources do not reveal the extent to which this formal procedure was followed in rural districts, but even when it was followed, it did not succeed in altering the peasants' view that the village church was theirs, and only theirs, and that the state had no claim on it.[23]

Bolshevik policy was directed not only against the state church but against religion as such. The Tver village newspaper did its utmost to support this campaign. The paper informed the peasants that the Christmas holiday originated in pagan midwinter celebrations and that the story of Christ's birth arose from myths about the birth of the sun. According to the paper, the story of Mary and Joseph was just a legendary embellishment of views widely held by natural religions. The significance of the sun in agricultural societies—according to the paper—was expressed in the latter's ritual worship and in the attempt to influence nature's capriciousness with sacrifices. The paper concluded that this pagan/Christian midwinter celebration did not make sense now that people had come to understand the scientific laws of nature and could profit from this knowledge.[24] The holiday following Christmas, "the Feast of the Circumcision of Jesus," was presented as a relic of human sacrifice. The feast of Jesus' baptism as well as the celebration of the Twelfth Night and the consecration of the water on January 6 were compared to the Egyptian Feast of Osiris.[25] On another occasion the newspaper pointed out that the Feast of St. Elias, the bearer of thunder, originated in the old Slavic celebration of Perun, who was worshipped as the god of lightning and thunder. As part of the government campaign against the traditional holidays, explanations of their pagan origins were supposed to be supplemented with lectures on electricity and its practical applicability.[26]

The peasant paper also reduced the popular worship of Mary (very widespread in Russia) to a relic of pre-Christian times. The legend of a female bearer of god is common to many societies. Had the Mary of the New Testament really lived, argued the paper, her bones would have long since been discovered. But to cover up this discrepancy, the Church had invented the story of the bodily "Assumption of the Blessed Virgin."[27] The Tver paper argued further that the biblical story of the Annunciation as well as the pregnancy allegedly caused by the "Holy Ghost" was also patterned on an Egyptian tradition dating from 2000 B.C. These legends derived from the practice of communal marriages in primitive communities, in which the mother did not know the father of her child, and in the context of which the "uneducated savage" believed the supernatural forces were at work.[28] The feast of the "Presentation of Mary in the Temple," celebrated by the Orthodox church on November 21, did not—according to the newspaper's own research—originate in the Bible but rather in the apocryphal Gospel of Jacob, the authenticity of which was not even recognized by the Church. If the Church used these legends to encourage the faithful through Mary's model to do penance and attend church, it was doing so as an agent of landowners and merchants; the "opium of religion" confined working people to intellectual immaturity. In the paper's view, it was all the more important finally to abolish religious holidays and to put church buildings to good use.[29]

The Tver newspaper also had a special interpretation of the wedding feast at Cana. In the paper's depiction, the transformation of the water into wine was not a miracle. Instead, a close reading of the Gospel of John reveals that it was an example of *samogon*. Moreover, there is no mention in the Gospel of John that Christ administered the sacrament of matrimony. In actual fact, Christian marriage was simply the continuation of ancient customs. Both the festive drink and prayers for divine assistance were common to many ancient societies. In the same way that civil marriage was intended to replace marriage in the church, other religious rites of passage such as christening and religious funerals should be replaced. Christening was to be replaced by a ceremony of commitment to the revolution *(oktiabrina)* and funerals with intercessions; holy water and ecclesiastical blessing were to be replaced by civil commemoration.[30]

The village paper also sharply criticized the village priests *(popy)*. They were depicted as greedy hucksters who supplemented their wealth in land by charging the poor parishes high fees for the performance of their ecclesiastical duties. The paper alleged that they would celebrate Christmas and Easter several times a year if they could. As a result of their greedy disposition and practice, they manipulated rustic superstition for dishonest ends.[31] The paper reported a number of lawsuits against priests for using the restoration of icons as a source of profitable income. Allegedly, they rubbed the icons entrusted to them with a mixture of alcohol, turpentine, and ammonia and passed off the ensuing restoration of the varnish as a miracle![32] The paper also told of priests who manipulated the peasants' dependence on rain to swindle them out of eggs. It insinuated that such priests prayed successfully with the peasants for rain, after having looked at a barometer to determine their chances. On Christmas Day 1926, the Tver newspaper calculated that if each farm gave the village priest only 20 kopeks in connection with holy days and each church received only 10 rubles, this sum would amount to about 153,136 poods of oats, or enough to fill 153 railroad cars. In the town of Tver alone, priests were said to have received 48,000 rubles just on the marriages contracted in 1926. In 1925, all told, people spent 863,722 rubles on church weddings, or the price of 14,395 cows at 60 rubles each (or 107,971 plows at 8 rubles each).[33]

The Tver paper's broadsides against saints and their feast days, ecclesiastical rites and their justification, and priests and their shady dealings appear to have had little or no effect on village life. Indeed, it is doubtful, given the relatively small circulation of the paper, that the peasants took note of them all. But lack of information was certainly not the only reason for the fact that old customs and traditions remained relatively unaltered. Criticism of Christ's circumcision, Mary's presentation in the Temple, or the story of the wedding feast at Cana presupposed a certain level of knowledge about theology that most peasants probably did not possess. It is equally doubtful that readers understood the references to sun worship and natural religion, to the ancient Slavic god Perun and the ancient Egyptian god Osiris, to biblical tradition, and to the demythologizing of the Gospel of Jacob, not to mention the extreme capacity for abstraction required to understand the transition from history to the criticism of religion.

Similarly, official criticism did not alter traditional christenings, weddings, or funerals. Although the paper continued to report on civil marriages, civil funerals, and ceremonies of dedication to the revolution, these were isolated occasions. According to the paper's 1927 estimates, 80 percent of all marriages were still performed according to ecclesiastical rites, and only 10 percent of farms in the village refused to receive the priest on a high feast day. These figures are confirmed by other evidence: comparing the number of christenings, weddings, and requiem masses with the number of recorded births, marriages, and deaths in the southeast of the province, one scarcely finds any difference.[34]

It is possible that for some peasants the prices demanded by the priests were too high, even on a sliding scale. In the village of Mednoe in Rzhev district, for example, the priest required fifty kopeks for intercessions, three rubles for christenings, seven for funerals, and as much as twelve for weddings. Although the peasants tried to haggle, the fact that the priests took money for their services did not yet discredit them in their eyes: "Everything costs money; it's that simple." And even if the prices were too high and the priest himself led the opposite of a Christian life, nothing seemed to undermine the peasants' belief that these services were needed and that they had to be paid for.[35]

As always, the priest was summoned to baptize each newborn child in order to protect it from evil. At the end of 1924 two peasants from Goritsy volost (in Kimry district) had their child dedicated to the revolution instead of being baptized. One of these infants died—reason enough for the peasants to think carefully about the effectiveness of the ceremony of dedication to the revolution.[36] If a peasant was married by a priest, he hoped for happiness and fruitful marriage—with God's help. In the same volost of Kimry district, brides wore a fur with a cross of needles for protection from witchcraft and evil spirits. When a priest was called to a funeral, he was supposed to help the dead person acquire a better place in the next world. When a priest was received during the high feast days, he gave his blessing to the house and the farm. According to Bol'shakov, the chronicler of Goritsy volost, no house in the area dared break with these customs. Even a person who had declared himself a Communist did not intend to run any unnecessary risks. At best he left the room during the prayers.[37]

It was customary throughout the province for a priest to bless the cattle before they were driven to pasture. This occurred in the northern districts on the Feast of St. George, April 23, in the course of a festival procession. For this occasion peasant women baked two round *pirogi*, or pies, each containing an egg complete with shell baked in. The peasants would take one of the *pirogi*, a candle, an icon of St. George the dragon-slayer, and a Holy Thursday willow branch and go to the stable to feed each animal. The baked-in egg would be thrown into the river. Then the cows were let out of the barn and made to march across the Holy Thursday willow branch. In the pasture, the cows were herded together, and an icon of St. George was brought out. Praying, the priest circled the cattle three times, sprinkling them with holy water. The peasant's wife, who had brought along the second *pirog*, broke and salted it with "Holy Thursday salt," after which it was eaten.[38]

"Holy Thursday salt" had been placed in the oven on Holy Thursday and left for three days. Removed on Easter Sunday, it was stored and used throughout the year as a cure-all for both people and animals. Reports from the northern districts indicate that peasants also used other methods to protect their cattle during the winter season. On the Feast of the Protection of Mary, October 1, peasants sought to appease the "ghost of the house" by harvesting a last corn stalk, which had been left for the occasion. In the evening when the cattle returned from pasture, the peasants would cover the floor of the stable to protect the cattle from witchcraft. Preventive measures against witchcraft marked both the beginning and the end of the harvest season. Before beginning the harvest, farmers burned two sheaves from every parcel of land to protect the rye from evil powers. This practice stemmed from the belief that a witch, naked or clad only in a shirt, cut along the fields or across them. The burning of two sheaves was believed to prevent this.[39]

These examples illustrate how Christian and pagan customs merged in popular religiosity and how one was unconsciously transformed into the other. Harvesting of grain during the Feast of the Protection of Mary served to exorcise witches just as did the cross of needles on the bride's fur. Holy Thursday salt was used for healing. The icon of St. George, holy water, and *pirogi* protected cattle. Sometimes there was a close connection between Christian and pagan practices—in the cases of the holy water and the Holy Thursday salt, for example—sometimes there was a loose connection—such as the practice of exorcising witches from the grain harvest during the Feast of the Protection of Mary. Sometimes there was no connection at all, as in the case of the egg *pirogi* and the preventive burning of corn at the beginning of the harvest season. These rites and customs had a common basis in magic. Peasants also regarded the Christian sacraments of marriage and baptism, as well as the blessing of houses and cattle, as forms of magic. They did not interpret these as symbolic, ritual acts referring to the next world. Instead they expected practical results and sought material gain from participation in these rituals.

The Bolshevik attack on religion, which emphasized Christian dogma, biblical tradition, and catechism, totally missed the central point of popular faith. Pointing out that popular religiosity was "only of a formal nature," the Tver Bolshevik newspaper ignored the deep embeddedness of the beliefs upon which these "forms," rites, and customs were based. In providing a scientific explanation of the origin of natural religion, it ignored the fact that these same fears and hopes still determined the religiosity of the village. And even if this attack on religion was heeded—which was a rare occurrence—and led to an intense preoccupation with the "genuine" meaning of religion, this did not turn the peasants into agnostics. There is much evidence that they turned to Protestant sects, to the evangelists, the Baptists, the Knights of St. John, and the Adventists, sects which experienced a new blossoming in the 1920s.

In January 1925 the Tver village newspaper reported the following incident: When a child fell seriously ill in the village of Arkatovo, a *babka* or old woman was summoned. On arrival she demanded a sieve, small spoons, scissors, and spindles. She placed the various articles in the sieve, sprinkled them with (holy?) water, recited prayers before the icons, then sprinkled the water from the sieve over the child's face. The nature of the illness was not disclosed, but the child's health was said to have deteriorated. Only when taken to a hospital did the child recover.[40]

In the same issue, the paper reported on the activities of Grunia Smirnova, a *znakharka,* or healer, who lived in the village of Laptevo in Rzhev district. People suffering from toothaches and the like would come to her, as she had healing potions for just about anything. Murmuring secret formulas over these potions and cursing from time to time, she would pray and sprinkle the potion on the sick person. She claimed that the cause of the illness was the "evil eye." For stomachaches she had a peculiar remedy. She put the patient to bed—a woman in this case—rubbed the patient's stomach, and sprinkled water on it. She then placed on the patient's abdomen a large pot, containing some burning chips. The ensuing vacuum sucked the woman's abdomen into the pot. To the patient, now screaming in pain, she murmured soothingly: "Now, now, little Mama, you can stand a little pain. It will soon be all right."[41]

The same issue reported the following story: In the village of Briuchevo in the Torzhok district lived Anisia Ivanovna, a woman involved in healing practices *(znakharstvo)*, witchcraft *(koldovstvo)*, and exorcism *(izgnanie besov)*. If a husband quarreled with his wife, if a cow failed to conceive, if a person or an animal fell ill, or if a young man broke up with his girlfriend, people would turn to "Mother Anisiushka" for help. Before they even entered her house, she would greet them with: "You are possessed of the devil! Quickly say a prayer!" She would raise her skirt over her head, climb up on the oven, or crawl under a table, emerging once the visitor had recited a litany of prayers. Only then did she inquire about the reason for the visit. She would make the visitor drink a cloudy brew that was supposed to exorcise the devil, or she would give him a potion to mix in his tea or feed to his infertile cow. The villagers persisted stubbornly in the belief that there was something "holy" about Anisia, and they would travel fifteen to twenty kilometers to seek out her assistance.[42]

There were many villages with such women as Anisia Ivanovna and Grunia Smirnova, and many villagers trusted their skills. The women knew the arts of incantation, conjuring of spirits, and exorcism; they professed to see what others could not see, and they could assist in cases of the "evil eye" or bewitchment. They seemed to be able to explain the inexplicable and knew what to do even when all other remedies had failed. They were called in especially in cases of illness and afflictions. Village observers described them variously as "old women," "midwives," "witches," "wizards," "soothsayers," or "female soothsayers." These concepts were often used interchangeably, and the meanings merged and became blurred.[43]

Surviving descriptions of village life are insufficient to analyze the positions and functions of the *babki, znakharki,* and *kolduny* in any detail. The accounts are confined mainly to reports of odd cures and procedures in which observation and interpretation are merged and tangled. What we do have, however, makes it clear that to dismiss these practices as merely quack medicine is to miss the point. For the villagers, women such as Grunia Smirnova and Anisia Ivanovna operated as interpreters of an inexplicable and hostile natural world; their interpretations of the world, combining empiricism and Christian and pagan-animistic ideas into a meaningful whole, were of practical assistance to the villagers. These beliefs enabled peasants to cope with uncomplicated medical problems and to decipher nature's secrets: Villagers knew that to come upon a grey or a black cat foretold bad luck, that if a bird flew into the living room or an owl hooted near the house, it foretold death. They could treat minor illnesses with the simple application of holy water, Holy Thursday salt, or other home remedies.[44] In difficult cases, however, where the victim was completely baffled, one had to rely on the skill and advice of the "specialist." In such cases, one turned with confidence to *babki, znakharki,* and *kolduny,* whose skills ranged from marriage counseling to veterinary practice, from exorcism to finding stolen horses. .

The government, on the other hand, countered the *babki, znakharki,* and *kolduny,* with a network of medical health and information centers. By the mid-1920s, Tver province had 116 such clinics and hospitals, with 376 doctors in service. On the whole, the medical equipment in these installations was approximately the same as before the revolution, and they were concentrated mainly in the towns and larger villages. The countryside, however, lagged considerably behind. Frequently, the nearest medical center was a full day's journey away, and transportation was generally lacking. Rural clinics were poorly equipped. There were shortages of medicine, instruments, linen, and heating materials.[45]

Even so, it would be wrong to conclude that the continued existence of *babki* and *znakharki* was due solely to the inadequacy of rural medical facilities. For in villages with a clinic or hospital, peasants, even in difficult cases, often turned to the *babka* instead. Not only poor and simple peasants did so but also the educated classes. In general, the village doctor was held in low regard. All indicators point to a deeply and firmly rooted tradition of popular medicine in the village.

Although the preceding observations represent some fleeting impressions, some stones in the mosaic of village life in the 1920s, they do demonstrate how deeply embedded were traditional peasant conceptions and beliefs, procedures and institutions. They possessed their own sense and inner logic. The peasants defended them stubbornly against the interventions of the Bolsheviks. Only by understanding the prehistory of collectivization can one appreciate what a tremendous turning point was this second revolution which dissolved the farm and the peasant family as the basic units of Russian rural society and culture. Only in the late 1920s and early 1930s were the conditions created upon which the culture, society, and economy of the Soviet Union are based to the present day. From the perspective of the Russian villagers, these interventions in the life and work of the village were much more far-reaching than anything that had occurred in 1917.

## NOTES

1. For a more detailed presentation of this pattern, see the works of A. V. Chaianov, who, as far as I can determine, was the first to approach peasant economy as an economic system sui generis. See also the works about household

and family, popular culture and society, the problems of class and class consciousness, work time and leisure, religion and magical practices, peasant behavior, and peasant rebellions in early modern times and in present agrarian societies by Hamza Alavi, Natalie Z. Davis, Eric J. Hobsbawm, Peter Laslett, Alan Macfarlane, Robert W. Malcolmson, Robert Redfield, James C. Scott, Keith Thomas, Eric R. Wolf, Aristide Zolberg, and others. See also the regional studies of the Ecole des Annales, which demonstrated the interdependent relationship between geography and climate, forms of settlement and economy, social and family structure, cultural and religious traditions, everyday behavior, and mentality. This essay is deeply indebted to the work of these scholars.

2. I summarize here some of the findings of my book *Die Bauern von Tver. Vom Leben auf dem russischen Dorfe zwischen Revolution und Kollektivierung* (Munich, 1984). The notes in this essay give references only. For fuller discussion of sources, see *Die Bauern von Tver.* I am grateful to Oldenbourg Verlag, Munich, for kindly allowing these materials to be reproduced here in a slightly altered version. I thank Rose Gatens, Walter Renn, and Eva Sturm for rendering my ideas and reflections into readable English. I also express my thanks to Bill Chase and Larry Glasco for friendly help and advice during my stay as a visiting professor at the University of Pittsburgh in 1987.

3. See Altrichter, *Die Bauern von Tver*, pp. 10–41.

4. For complete bibliography, see ibid., pp. 351–61.

5. For further information about the structure and dynamics of the peasant economy (household and family, livestock and equipment, agriculture and trade, lease of land and labor), state and conditions of local society (land commune and village gathering, formation of classes and groups, conflicts and crime), presence of government and state (the institutions of village soviet and party cell, Komsomol and smallholder groups, trade unions and cooperatives, militia and school), see ibid. pp. 50–100, 123–74.

6. For conceptions of time in preindustrial societies see A. Borst, *Lebensformen im Mittelalter* (Frankfurt/Berlin/Wien 1979); E. P. Thompson, "Time, Work-Discipline and Industrial Capitalism," *Past and Present*, 38 (1967), pp. 57–97.

7. K. Thomas "Work and Leisure in Pre-industrial Society," *Past and Present*, 29 (1964); and "Work and Leisure in Industrial Society," ibid., 30 (1965).

8. M. Fenomenov, *Sovremennaia derevnia. Opyt kraevedcheskogo obsledovaniia odnoi derevni*, 2 volumes (Leningrad/Moscow 1925), vol. 1, pp. 256–57; reports in the village newspaper *Tverskaia Derevnia* (TD), passim.

9. See, for example, TD, 1927, no. 57, July 28; 1925, no. 50, June 24; 1929, no. 1, January 3.

10. Fenomenov, *Sovremennaia derevnia*, vol. 2, pp. 98–111; A. N. Vershinskii and A. Il'inskii, *Verkhne-Molzhskaia ekspeditsiia 1925–26*, vyp. 1: *Lesnaia derevnia* (Tver, 1927).

11. Fenomenov, *Sovremennaia derevnia*, vol. 2, pp. 99–103.

12. A. M. Bol'shakov, *Derevnia 1917–1927* (Moscow, 1927), pp. 387–89.

13. See, for instance, TD, 1925, no. 1, January 8; no. 41, October 16; 1926, no. 49, June 28; no. 53, July 12; 1927, no. 4, January 13; no. 31, April 24; no. 26, May 15; no. 42, June 6; no. 60, August 7; no. 100, December 28; 1928, no. 5, January 15.

14. Bol'shakov, *Derevnia*, pp. 338–39; Fenomenov, *Sovremennaia derevnia*, vol. 2, pp. 103–107.

15. TD, 1926, no. 49, June 28; 1927, no. 31, May 12.

16. TD, 1926, no. 101, December 30.

17. TD, 1926, no. 13, February 15; no. 37, May 17.

18. Fenomenov, *Sovremennaia derevnia*, vol. 2, pp. 29–30.

19. For instance, the German custom or "Weiberfastnacht." See also N. Z. Davis, "Women on Top," *Society and Culture in Early Modern France* (Stanford, 1975), chap. 5.

20. TD, 1927, no. 37, May 19; no. 38, May 22; also 1925, no. 30, July 31; 1926, no. 42, June 4.

21. TD, 1926, no. 49, June 28; no. 26, April 7; no. 60, August 7.

22. TD, 1925, no. 29, July 24; no. 40, October 9; no. 43, October 31; 1926, no. 31, April 19; no. 49, June 28; 1927, no. 70, September 11; no. 72, September 18; no. 76, October 2; no. 87, November 13.

23. Bol'shakov, *Derevnia,* pp. 402–20.

24. TD, 1925, no. 1, January 8.

25. TD, 1927, no. 4, January 13.

26. TD, 1926, no. 57, July 26.

27. TD, 1926, no. 64, August 20.

28. TD, 1927, no. 25, April 3.

29. TD, 1926, no. 93, December 2.

30. TD, 1927, no. 10, February 8.

31. TD, 1926, no. 27, April 5; 1927, no. 2, January 6; no. 76, September 30; no. 79, October 10; no. 81, October 17.

32. TD, 1925, no. 11, March 19; no. 42, October 25; no. 54, July 16.

33. TD, 1926, no. 61, August 9; 1927, no. 5, January 13; no. 10, February 8; no. 12, February 13.

34. TD, 1927, no. 4, January 13; no. 10, February 8; no. 12, February 13; Bol'shakov, *Derevnia,* pp. 412–13.

35. TD, 1926, no. 10, February 4; no. 36, May 14.

36. Bol'shakov, *Derevnia,* p. 412.

37. Ibid., pp. 398, 410, 412; see also TD, 1926, no. 94, December 5.

38. TD, 1926, no. 40, May 28; no. 46, June 18; Fenomenov, *Sovremennaia derevnia,* vol. 1, pp. 104–105; Vershinskii/Il'inskii, *Verkhne-Molozhskaia ekspeditsiia,* p. 125.

39. Ibid.

40. TD, 1925, no. 1, January 8.

41. Ibid.

42. Ibid.

43. For details see Altrichter, *Die Bauern von Tver,* pp. 119–20.

44. Fenomenov, *Sovremennaia derevnia,* pp. 87–91.

45. TD, 1925, no. 50, December 13; Tverskoi gubispolkom, *Tverskaia guberniia v 1925–1926 g., otchet gubispolkoma XV-mu s"ezdu sovetov* (Tver, 1927), pp. 220–23; Bol'shakov, *Derevnia,* pp. 288–98.

# XIII

# THE "QUIET REVOLUTION" IN SOVIET INTELLECTUAL LIFE

## Katerina Clark

NEP, as a time when limited private enterprise was permitted, has often been seen in the West as ushering in a period of relative intellectual pluralism, something closer to "normal" Western intellectual life. Private publishing houses were allowed to operate, and writers were able to publish their works in Berlin; with the blockade of the Soviet Union lifted, scholars and creative people were permitted to receive any materials published abroad they wished; and Western and Soviet films, theatrical troupes, star performers, scholars, and writers passed back and forth across the border with greater ease than at any other time. The scholarly intelligentsia was left largely at its posts; indeed, this was a productive period for Soviet science and scholarship.[1]

NEP is remembered as the heyday of the *poputchik*, the fellow traveler, the intellectual who, though generally sympathetic to the revolution, was not committed to any party. The confidence such people felt is reflected in such pronouncements as the (best-known but by no means untypical of the time) statements by the Serapion Brothers, a group of young Leningrad writers,[2] who declared that they wanted to be independent of all political affiliation, and above all to avoid being identified as a writers' society "under the auspices of Narkompros" *(pri Narkomprose)*.[3] Not surprisingly, many left-wing intellectuals detested NEP as a slide into embourgeoise-ment (several proletarian writers resigned from the party in protest).[4]

There were, indeed, elements of "pluralism" to be found in intellectual life during NEP, but they were not defining of the times. NEP should not be defined, as it so often is, as a period of relative intellectual freedom before the "great breakthrough" *(velikii perelom)* of the Cultural Revolution implemented during the First Five-Year Plan. For a start, the majority of the private publishing houses existed in little more than name, and costs and increasingly heavy taxation ensured that they progressively dwindled in numbers and were effectively eliminated well before the plan years.[5]

Above all, however, the issue of freedom, or the degree thereof available to intellectuals, is, while significant, not the crucial one for any characterization of the essentials of cultural life during NEP. The real question was who was to dominate in Soviet culture. And it was during NEP that that question was largely answered.

In intellectual life NEP essentially witnessed a revolution, a partial revolution to be sure, and a quiet one as compared with the more dramatically "revolutionary" periods which framed it. NEP's revolution was "quieter," but less superficial in the sense that during NEP the people in power in intellectual life changed as had not been the case to any marked degree under War Communism; during NEP a series of changes occurred at a fundamental structural and institutional level, and those changes established many of the prevailing, enduring patterns of Soviet intellectual life. Russian intellectual life was sovietized.

NEP was the time when Russian intellectuals first confronted a reality that was in Soviet terms *normal,* as distinct from the abnormal conditions of the revolution itself and War Communism. By "normal," I do not mean just the fact that during NEP there was less chaos and confusion, or that there were fewer breakdowns and shortages than there were during the revolution and Civil War. Rather, I am making a distinction between "revolutionary," that is, a time of extremism and upheaval, and "Soviet," meaning a time of greater normalcy, when the distinctively Soviet institutions and sociopolitical conditions functioned without battering from extremists. Of course, these are relative terms. NEP was not a "revolutionary" time, even though some sort of revolution took place then, because it was not a time of great upheaval dictated by extremist views.

One can look at Soviet intellectual history in terms of a diastole and systole of revolutionary upheaval and Soviet normalcy. Thus after NEP there occurred intermittent periods of political and cultural extremism, such as the cultural revolution, the Great Purge, and Zhdanovism, but in between these, and since Stalin's time, one finds distinctively Soviet but more "normal" times. The general structure of Soviet intellectual life in such relatively tranquil times has continued to be similar in many respects to that which formed under NEP. It was during NEP, rather than before or after, that Russian intellectual life was sovietized in the sense that a broad-based *smena* or changeover occurred, a reshuffle of such a fundamental order that the intellectual scene was never the same again; it did not—as it did, for instance, after the extremes of the "Cultural Revolution"—revert at the end to a situation rather like what had obtained before the changes. Even such momentous events as the abolition of all independent writers' bodies in 1932 and the formation of a single association for each professional group can be seen not just as a case of state intervention but also as a continuation of the trend during NEP for intellectuals to band together in ever-larger organizations representing a cross-section of ideological or aesthetic positions. From this perspective, the First Five-Year Plan emerges as an interregnum when revolutionary extremism distorted the emerging patterns of Soviet intellectual life, but they were largely resumed, *pace* socialist realism and all that, in 1932.

The "changeover" of NEP involved intellectual movements, personnel, patterns of publishing and patronage, the relationship of "the center" to "the periphery," and even the genres which predominated. Its beneficiaries came to dominate Soviet intellectual life as a new guard, and those who survived (the purges, the war, and natural attrition) remained prominent until very recently (when they finally began to die off).[6] Indeed, given that in times of revolutionary upheaval there is an element of contingency in the fates of individuals which is less present in times of normalcy, one could argue that had, for instance, Babel not been purged in the thirties, he might have continued his literary career to refresh Soviet literature with his works, as did his Odessa compatriot Kataev who, like him, rose to literary prominence under NEP.

This account raises the issue of whether the "sovietization" of Russian intellectual life in the twenties had much to do with NEP at all. If the economic concessions which came as part of NEP and which made possible greater "pluralism" did not have a decisive impact on the patterns characteristic of intellectual life in these years, in what real sense could they be called NEP patterns? Indeed, some of the changes in cultural life which occurred at the onset of NEP and which were to establish patterns which remained generally true for the rest of the Soviet period have only a tenuous connection with the onset of NEP. These include a series of events of crucial political importance, such as Lenin's death in 1924 and the defeat of both the "left" and "right" factions in the ensuing power struggle. They also include changes with no ostensible connection to politics, let alone economics, such as the change in the reigning forms of artistic expression; during War Communism, poetry, art, and a variety of forms of theater dominated cultural life, but under NEP they were eclipsed by the dominant Soviet cultural forms—prose fiction, film, and architecture (the last of these, it will be noted, is an exception to the general pattern in that it has not remained a dominant Soviet artistic form to the present day). Such qualifications notwithstanding, it might be said that Russia was sovietized under NEP not so much because of anything intrinsic to NEP but more because, given an inevitable time lag before those in power in the party began to worry much about intellectual life (a lag which was exacerbated by the crisis of civil war), it was not until sometime between 1920 and 1922 that the Bolshevik Revolution's true impact began to be felt in Soviet intellectual life. At that time more figures in the party and Komsomol (as distinct from Narkompros, the commissariat responsible for education and culture, or PUR, the Political Department of the army) became involved in the fate of Soviet culture and scholarship.

According to such an account, this period in Soviet intellectual history has been called the NEP period because, almost coincidentally, the beginning of NEP in 1921 falls between these two dates, while the Cultural Revolution which was launched during the next economic period of the First Five-Year Plan ushered in a new phase in cultural life and brought the "NEP" period to an end. Moreover, one can question whether there was a *single* homogeneous and intrinsically NEP period; in looking at most areas of intellectual life, one is inclined to talk at least of two subperiods, with the dividing line coming around 1924/1925 (after which the power struggle in intellectual life intensified, as did the efforts of the lobby for some sort of affirmative-action program to promote the lower classes in the intellectual sphere).

It is not, however, entirely true that NEP qua NEP had only a marginal impact on Soviet intellectual life, though its impact must not be sought merely in the area of permitting a greater "pluralism." It would be more accurate to say that in 1921 a series of events occurred, including, among others, the introduction of NEP, which ushered in a new phase, the defining patterns of which were in many ways antithetical to those of the preceding Civil War years. These events which in their combined effect heralded the end of an era include the Kronstadt uprising in March 1921; the death of the poet Aleksandr Blok and the execution of Nikolai Gumilev in August of that year; a series of emigrations, including those of Shaliapin and Remizov and, most crucially, Gorky in 1921; and the expulsion of around 150 intellectuals from the Soviet Union in 1922. Such individual events, together with certain general trends to be discussed below, precipitated a changeover of the figures and movements which dominated Soviet intellectual life, and shifted its center of gravity so that (except among the scholarly intelligentsia, scientists, and engineers for whom this sort of shift occurred later) it came to be dominated by fellow travelers and self-styled "proletarian" groups.

NEP played no small part in precipitating this shift. In particular, when the government withdrew its subsidies from many intellectual endeavors (theaters and publishing houses especially) and required that thenceforth patrons pay to see plays, buy books and newspapers, etc., many theaters and periodicals closed down virtually overnight; this "new economic policy" killed a large number of avant-garde, experimental efforts which could not, without subsidization of some sort, capture sufficient audiences or readership to be economically viable, but which had flourished in the preceding era of free or cheap theater tickets and free newspapers (this new policy also cut drastically the readership of *Pravda* et al., but they were less vulnerable economically).

In this essay I will present briefly some of the most important patterns which highlight how the situation of the intellectual during NEP differed radically from that which obtained under War Communism, such that it is

generally possible to talk of relative continuity between pre- and postrevolutionary Russian culture, with the distinctive rupture occurring only during NEP (at the earliest). Then I will describe in greater detail the sociological dynamic of this rupture. In this account, I will draw most of my
examples from the two areas I know best, literary and scholarly life.

Intellectual life under War Communism was more dramatically "revolutionary" than it was to be ever again, and yet the real revolution, the great
upheaval in intellectual life, was yet to come. Many might object to this
statement and claim that the preceding years of War Communism saw a
true revolutionary culture; *that* was the time when the intellectuals really
responded to the revolution, and what happened during NEP and beyond
represents a devolution. But I maintain that the response to the revolution
in the first years—and I say this in the face of all the revolutionary mass
festivals, the ROSTA posters, the agittrains, the destroying of the old
symbols and ceremonial (statues, calendar, and even alphabet) and replacing them with new revolutionary ones—was in many respects only superficially "Soviet." *The* fundamental break with the past came only during
NEP.

Most of the apparently distinctive trends and changes in Soviet intellectual life which marked the period from October 1917 to around 1921
represent the continuation or implementation of policies and movements
which originated (usually within the intelligentsia) in the prerevolutionary
period. Thus they cannot be described as being in some way either radically
new or intrinsically Soviet. In some instances, the phenomenon in question
was already being planned or even in force in the tsarist period; in others it
was initiated or at least planned after the February Revolution. Examples
here include the calendar and alphabet reforms (both of which had active
intelligentsia lobbies under Nicholas which were not associated with the
Bolsheviks)[7] and even such seemingly distinctively Bolshevik aspects of
early Soviet culture as the mass spectacles, the agittrains, and the Free Art
Studios or SVOMAS. Many of the figures who initially administered Soviet
cultural life, such as Lunacharskii himself, Gorky, and Blok, had also been
active in running the cultural life of the February Revolution.

For all the revolutionary content of cultural endeavor under War Communism, if one looks at it in terms of the informing aesthetic theories or
personnel involved, it is possible to categorize most of it in terms of a
continuation of the old prerevolutionary struggle between the symbolists
and the futurists, between the retrospectivists or preservationists and the
cultural iconoclasts. The symbolists, their epigones, and representatives of
allied movements from that particular branch of prerevolutionary Modernism, such as Nietzscheanism, Wagnerism, and ornamentalism, dominated much of the early Soviet theater (such as the Proletkult theater),

prose fiction, and music, while initial futurist successes in the art world, in some sections of the theater, and in mass ceremonial were in many instances later reversed in favor of the symbolists. Under NEP, however, symbolism and allied movements quickly ceased to be important factors in Soviet cultural life.[8] With futurism, which largely regrouped and reoriented itself as the constructivist movement, the situation was more complicated, and constructivism's influence in architecture, theater, the applied arts, and film was of course strongly felt during NEP. Nevertheless, a palpable "changeover" occurred here, too, such that those futurist figures who under War Communism had been leading administrators of Soviet cultural life, such as Punin, Shterenberg, and Malevich, were no longer in commanding positions and tended rather to cluster in pockets of avant-garde endeavor such as the Institute for Artistic Culture (INKHUK) in Dom Miatlevykh in Leningrad.[9]

This shift was in large measure a function of patronage. In prerevolutionary Russia, it will be recalled, a crucial factor in the flowering of Russian modernism was funding of avant-garde projects by patrons from wealthy merchant families, the nobility, or the imperial family; in addition, the ballet and several of the major theaters were imperial institutions. Under War Communism, the principal purser for culture was the state rather than the party, and principally Narkompros and PUR.

These state bodies tended to channel their funds through organizations and committees headed and peopled by such members of the intellectual community as could be coopted for the purpose. These intermediaries tended to be either young Turks from the futurist camp (who ran much of the art world) or respected elder statesmen such as Blok and particularly Gorky, who after his reconciliation with Lenin in 1918 became a veritable Lorenzo the Magnificent or patron extraordinaire of Soviet cultural life. The purposes for which such funds were intended were often decided by people occupying higher positions and who were party members (such as Krupskaia, Kameneva, and Lunacharskii himself), and their tastes and prejudices influenced to some degree the choice of intermediary personnel to staff these committees. Nevertheless, at this crisis time these intermediaries enjoyed wide discretionary powers.

Thanks to the de facto patronage system, intellectuals under War Communism not actively hostile to the new regime were able to run their own show to a remarkable extent, the main obstacles to this being less the political order than the considerable hardships, and the need to be thought worthwhile by the mandarins and Young Turks who had access to money and commissions. A striking example of intelligentsia home rule would be the major conference on extramural education held in Moscow in 1919, which was intended to give guidance to those working in the Soviet mass theater. A mark of the conference's importance in the eyes of the leader-

٬ ship, it was addressed by Lenin. However, its keynote speaker was the symbolist poet Viacheslav Ivanov, then head of the Historico-Theatrical Section of the Theater Department of Narkompros. Ivanov could find no better example for the "theater of the future" than Wagner's *Walkyrie*, and he took the conference delegates to see a performance of it, introducing the performance with a speech in which he quoted liberally from Nietzsche's treatise on tragedy.[10]

With the advent of NEP, when so many of the subsidies were withdrawn, the house of cards which such powerful patrons as Gorky had set up for the intellectual community began to fall. In addition, as Narkompros's budget was cut drastically, and as most of the soldiers were demobilized and the need for a mass cultural effort among them diminished, many of the committees on which the intellectual mandarins had sat were closed or in some way superseded by new committees. Even before these changes occurred, both "left art" (that is, more or less, the former futurist camp) and the Proletkult fell into disfavor with the party and Narkompros, with resulting drastic cuts in the subsidies for their activities. Many of the mandarins, such as Gorky, in fact emigrated—or died—at precisely this point. All these events combined effected a reshuffle in the power structure within culture.

In many areas of Soviet cultural life, the party and Komsomol now effectively superseded Narkompros or the military as the main funders (except in the area of scholarship). When the party and Komsomol sought out "intermediaries" to run the intellectual ventures they funded, they tended to choose people from their own ranks rather than from the sympathetic but uncommitted intelligentsia. Indeed, the Serapion Brothers' defiant gesture in proclaiming that they did not want to be known as a writers' society "under the auspices of Narkompros" takes on new meaning in the light of this major reorientation of Soviet cultural life which began more or less at the precise time they made it.

The reorientation I have in mind did not mean that the party began to direct Soviet cultural life. The consensus of Western scholars on this issue is that it was reluctant to do so in any direct way. But during NEP the party emerged increasingly as the body which intellectuals petitioned and to which they turned for arbiters in their disputes.[11] At the same time, various party leaders began to take a greater interest in cultural matters, as can be seen in, for instance, Trotsky's *Literature and Revolution*, published in 1923 but comprising largely articles on literature he had published over the preceding two years.

One of the main ways that both the party and the Komsomol emerged as a significant factor in the cultural scene was in funding many of the principal journals of NEP. Prior to NEP, most of the Soviet journals published had been associated with a particular intellectual coterie or organization and had had relatively small circulations, primarily among that particular coterie's clientele. Between 1921 and 1924 the majority of these journals closed down, but their place had to some extent already been taken by others. In 1921 the party leadership recalled A. K. Voronskii from Ivanovo-Voznesensk to edit the new journal *Krasnaia nov'*, the first major nonparty cultural journal it was to sponsor. At the time, *Krasnaia nov'* was intended to counteract the drift of good Soviet writers to publishing in the West or emigrating; it was to publish a spectrum of Russian *poputchik* and leftist writers, in the interests of unifying the factions and achieving a quality Soviet literature.

*Krasnaia nov'* was followed by other thick journals such as *Molodaia gvardiia* (1922–   ), organ of the Komsomol; *Oktiabr'* (1924–   ), organ of a literary faction with roots in the Komsomol; *Novyi mir* (1925–   ), a subsidiary of *Izvestiia;* and in Leningrad, *Zvezda* (1924–   ). There were, to be sure, other journals also founded in this period which were the mouthpieces of specific factions. Since, however, such journals did not enjoy party patronage, they chronically suffered from budgetary and other problems, which meant that they appeared neither as frequently as nor with anything like the circulation of the more official "thick journals." The contrast can be seen in the fact that *Krasnaia nov'* came out monthly, while the journal of the VAPP leadership, *Na postu*, was able to secure publication for only five of all its projected monthly issues during the period it was published, 1923–25.[12] Its successor, *Na literaturnom postu* (1926–32), founded after accommodations had been made to the party position in its 1925 resolution on literature, enjoyed greater financial security and had an initial circulation four times that of its predecessor, increasing gradually over the next four years. But even then the journal was only modest in size and circulation if compared with *Krasnaia nov'* or *Novyi mir* (edited by the Bolshevik Viacheslav Polonskii).

During the First Five-Year Plan when "proletarianization" became an official policy, *Na literaturnom postu* enjoyed official favor; in 1931 its circulation doubled as compared with 1930, and it came out twice monthly. But, as was true of all factional mouthpieces, it was vulnerable politically, and it closed only the next year, after the party's 1932 resolution on literature.

The case of the journals provides a good example of the way patterns and configurations which emerged during NEP were to prove enduring, and consequently defining of specifically *Soviet* intellectual life. All the major literary thick journals which were founded during NEP under party or Komsomol patronage have survived to play important roles in Soviet literary politics to the present day (the only major exception is *Krasnaia nov'*, originally the most popular and privileged journal, which later proved doomed because its original editor, Voronskii, was marked as a Trotskyite).

The fate of the literary journal during NEP also highlights another characteristic trend which could be seen as part of "sovietization," and that is the trend to centralization. The years of War Communism had seen what was, for Russia, a marked degree of decentralization in intellectual life. This was a consequence in part of the chaos and confusion of revolution and civil war, in part of deliberate policy shared by both the February and October revolutions, the expression of a reaction against tsarist centripetal tendencies and of a desire to redress cultural deprivation in the provinces. Signs of this decentralization include the minirenaissances which occurred in such previously unremarkable provincial places as Vitebsk, Baku, and Koktebel' in the Crimea, as well as Kiev, Kharkov, and Tiflis, and the profusion of new universities founded in provincial towns between 1918 and 1920.[13] Under NEP this trend was reversed. Lack of funding brought a closure of many of the new provincial universities, and those intellectuals who had participated in the cultural flowerings in the provinces tended to drift back to the capitals or emigrate. In publishing, the problem of reduced funding for the provinces was compounded by chronic shortages of paper and operable printing presses, problems of distribution, and the high cost of publications. In consequence, official (and even private) publishing organs were largely servicing only the two capitals, Moscow and Leningrad.[14] When, later in NEP, this situation improved, the domination of "the center" was already entrenched and not reversed.

The founding of major literary journals in Moscow and Leningrad contributed to this trend for centralization.[15] Lesser journals, whose existence was in any case much more precarious financially, could not compete with them in the royalties or circulation they offered.[16] Intellectuals who aspired to a place in the mainstream flocked to the new journals, while those who were disaffected, were scornful, or represented ideological or aesthetic positions which were not favored, tended to publish in short-lived almanacs or factional periodicals.

Effectively, and as was intended, the new journals *created* a new, mainstream Soviet culture (not, of course, single-handedly). Those writers who achieved prominence on their pages, such as Babel, Vsevolod Ivanov, and even the returned émigré nobleman Aleksei Tolstoy, became thereby the leading, mainstream Soviet writers. But this new culture also became progressively more *Moscow-centric* (as is suggested in the fact that Aleksei Tolstoy from Leningrad generally published in Moscow thick journals).[17] Leningrad, formerly more or less Moscow's equal as a cultural center, and the leader in academic and scholarly life, declined markedly in cultural importance under NEP. In literature, a sign of the times, not only was Leningrad given only one "thick" journal *(Zvezda)*, while Moscow had several, but its journal was less important and had a smaller circulation than the Moscow counterparts (which were thus able to lure away the more successful or acceptable Leningrad writers).[18]

The pattern with the Moscow and Leningrad journals also points to a change in the respective roles the two cities were to play in Soviet culture, Moscow now being the "center," the home of mainstream culture, with Leningrad as a center for peripheral, or out-of-favor—"other"—culture. During NEP, Leningrad's *Zvezda* functioned as a place where fringe figures on the "left" (such as G. Gorbachev after he was ousted from the VAPP leadership) and "right" (such as B. Pilniak, B. Pasternak, and O. Mandel'shtam) could publish.[19]

Another, parallel development which likewise tended to centralize literary life was the founding of larger creative organizations amalgamating a variety of lesser groups. In literature, this process can be seen in the setting up in 1922, with Politburo blessing, of the Union of Writers, or VSP, an organization which banded together primarily the nonproletarian writers. Later, after the party's 1925 resolution on literature, a rival writers' organization which was farther to the left,[20] the Federation of Organizations of Soviet Writers, or FOSP, was set up; for the rest of NEP one can observe a pattern whereby, successively, most of the writers' organizations which claimed to be enthusiastic about the revolution joined the federation. When the Writers' Union was formed in 1932, it effectively entailed amalgamating VSP with FOSP, the two organizations having been purged of their extreme right and extreme left respectively.

Together with this increased centralization of intellectual life under NEP came a radical intensification of *razmezhevanie*, the sorting-out process, the drawing up and hardening of lines between the intellectual factions. Under War Communism, there were factions, to be sure, and some of them, such as those advocating "left art," went in for some rather aggressive posturing and extreme intolerance of rival positions. Relatively speaking, however, factions coexisted and accommodated each other. For instance, some individuals managed to be members of both proletarian and nonproletarian groups (e.g., Vsevolod Ivanov, I. Oksenov), and the Proletkult bards of the urbanist ideal generously accorded space in their journals to representatives of the opposite, Scythian point of view.[21] Also, those representing a distinctly non-Soviet position could, if not actively hostile, continue to publish in legal journals. A vivid example of this sort of coexistence would be the journal *Krasnyi militsioner*, organ of the Leningrad police, where their own fictional and nonfictional accounts of police raids and the like shared space with works by members of the highbrow intelligentsia; the incongruity is most vividly demonstrated in the 1921 issue dedicated to the suppression of the recent uprising at Kronstadt and the lessons which must be learned therefrom, but which also includes Mandel'shtam's poem "The Twilight of Freedom" *(Sumerki svobody)*.[22]

During NEP, much of the effort among intellectuals went into first working out where the lines of demarcation lay, and then securing them. During the period through 1924 there was a certain amount of trial and error so that, for instance, even the militant *Na postu* group attempted an alliance with first Lef, in 1923, and then the rival proletarian group Kuznitsa in 1924. Intellectuals from the party press, no longer preoccupied with the Civil War and justifying the revolutionary terror, turned their attention to eradicating undesirable elements from Soviet intellectual institutions. Thus, for instance, they launched a concerted press campaign in 1922 and 1923 against those who in the universities and Soviet publications were still proselytizing for an idealist (that is, primarily Kantian or neo-Kantian) or religious position (a campaign which is also reflected in the choice of intellectuals expelled from the Soviet Union in 1922). By 1925, however, the main lines of demarcation had been drawn, and a naked power struggle ensued. While the neo-Kantians and so on had not been wiped out, they had ceased to be a significant force. In most areas of intellectual life, the issue of "proletarian culture" now overshadowed almost all other considerations.

During War Communism, the issue of "proletarian" culture had not had the edge to it which it acquired during NEP. For a start, few organizations were committed to it, other than the Proletkult, and although in theory that organization sought to develop a proletarian culture which was to be independent of and ultimately to supersede the bourgeois, in practice it relied heavily on bourgeois culture and intellectuals. In addition, most of the (very extensive) cultural work with the lower classes undertaken during War Communism was done in a somewhat paternalistic spirit, conducted largely under the banner of the *"narod,"* traditional cause of the intelligentsia, rather than that of the proletariat. But this was to change.

In 1918, as part of the celebrations for the anniversary of the revolution, the artist Natan Al'tman made a huge panneau for the Winter Palace which used twenty thousand arshins of canvas. On it, a worker held a placard with the lines from "The Internationale": "He who has naught / He shall be all! "[23] Al'tman and his fellow members of "left art" endorsed such sentiments in the belief that they heralded the inevitable triumph of the avantgarde (which the proletarian was bound to appreciate as more "his" than any other movement in art because it most nearly anticipated the art of the future). Many other high-minded intellectuals looked forward, as did Lenin himself, to the day when "every [female] cook would rule the state." But little did they realize the implications for intellectuals of giving power in their field to representatives of another class or caste. During NEP they lost some of their innocence and became more aware of these implications, for it was then that a militant lobby for "proletarian culture" emerged.

In literature, the change from the relative gentility of the days when the Proletkult was the main body actively concerned with the cause of "proletarian culture" was particularly marked after the literary organization October was founded in 1922. Thereafter, the issue of "proletarian culture" became much less a theoretical one and more immediately politicized.

October sought to define "proletarian" as meaning of and about the party. This group of "implacable zealots," to use the title of a Soviet book about them, came to run VAPP[24] and a series of journals (*Na postu, Oktiabr', Molodaia gvardiia,* and later *Na literaturnom postu*). In their relentless zeal to purge Soviet intellectual life of the hated *poputchik,* they so polarized it that by 1924/25 it was possible to talk of the total dominance in the literary scene of two antagonistic factions, the *Na postu/Oktiabr'/Molodaia gvardiia* camp, on the one hand, and, on the other, that of the *poputchiki,* led by Voronskii.

It was not that under NEP intellectual life was "proletarianized." Proletarianization did not, generally speaking, begin until the cultural revolution of the First Five-Year Plan, except in some isolated areas, such as, after 1924, an affirmative-action program for student admissions to institutions of higher education. At this time, proletarian factions were generally left grinding their teeth while their opponents prospered. Voronskii, for instance, not only was the founding editor of *Krasnaia nov',* on which he worked from 1921 until 1927, but also was editorially involved with such journals as *Prozhektor,* the almanacs *Nashi dni* and *Krasnaia nov',* and the publishing houses Krug and Krasnaia nov'. In addition, he had considerable, and perhaps inevitable, influence in such writers' organizations as Pereval. Undoubtedly, for most of NEP, no one in Soviet literature was as powerful as he.

The very presence of the "proletarian" militants, however, with their demands that Soviet culture be purged of the *poputchik,* made more urgent the existential dilemmas of the intellectual in a revolution and the issue of what role the proletariat should take in Soviet cultural life. In literature, their prominence is obvious in all criticism of the time, but it can also be sensed at the level of thematics. During the Civil War, Soviet literature had been obsessed with the question of what urbanization and modernization might do to traditional Russia. But during NEP, the time when ostensibly the country was concerned with the restoration of the economy and the "union" *(smychka)* of city and countryside, such themes were relegated to the attention of lesser writers (Doronin, Dorogoichenko, etc.) while the major writers tackled primarily the question of the intellectual's role in the new society (albeit commonly using a theme that was ostensibly about the Civil War or from science fiction).[25] From 1926 and continuing through the years of the First Five-Year Plan, one finds in Soviet literature the curious phenomenon of the anti-intellectual *roman à clef* written by *poputchik* writers about their own milieu.[26] These novels are fraught with ambiguity and require careful decoding; even after that, they elude final interpretation, but what does emerge clearly from all of them is existential anguish.

Of course, as we know, the "cook" never did achieve much meaningful power in intellectual matters. But under NEP a major reshuffle did occur which brought into power and prominence in culture groups representing a different generation from the one which had dominated during War Communism, and also a different, *lower* and generally less-well-educated, stratum within the bourgeoisie; this *smena* brought with it a different ethos and a different sense of the Soviet intelligentsia's mission.

At the time of the revolution, the make-up of the Russian intelligentsia could be characterized in terms of two distinct, *but not mutually exclusive,* categories which I shall refer to as intellectuals and intelligentsia. The category "intellectual" includes what Sheila Fitzpatrick refers to as the "professoriate"[27] (that is, academics, researchers, museum curators, and the like), and also all those intellectual workers who in their activity sought to advance the cause of highbrow culture, or to spread it among the masses. To a large extent they were the sort of intellectuals whom Gramsci identified as "a traditional 'caste' that absorbs new members and is not created by the class rising to power"[28]—although of course not unaffected by it, either. Such a "caste" was fairly universally to be found, but the category "intelligentsia" was more specifically Russian and involved those people who traditionally defined themselves more by their social conscience than by serving the cause of *kul'tura* or scientific truth. The party leadership and intelligentsia must be regarded as forming a special subset within this category "intelligentsia."

The "intellectuals" were largely middle-class and on the whole fairly conservative politically (many of them were of Kadet persuasion); there was considerable resistance to the revolution from this quarter. To put this in perspective, however, their counterparts in most of the other advanced nations, such as (very comparably) Weimar Germany, were also largely conservative at this time.[29] During these years the "professoriate" continued, as during NEP and before,[30] to be largely middle-class in origins, privileged in status, and with a strong sense of their intrinsic worth and pride in their lineage.[31] Consequently, they suffered a somewhat rude jolt in the period of "cultural revolution" immediately thereafter.

The cultural intermediaries of War Communism were closely connected with the "professoriate." It has often been remarked that in the period prior to the revolution, many of the elite among the creative intelligentsia (writers particularly) were the sons or daughters of leading academics or took an academic approach to their intellectual work.[32] But it was also the case that under War Communism, much officially sponsored cultural activity was organized or led either by the sons and daughters of the academic elite, or by people of a distinctly academic or highbrow orientation. Thus the culture of revolutionary Russia was, like the parliament of Weimar Germany, to a significant degree run by "zweiundzwanzig Professoren." To cite just one example: prominent among the organizers of the famous mass revolutionary festivals of 1920 Leningrad were A. Piotrovskii and S. Radlov, both active, professional classicists and sons of distinguished scholars, and N. Evreinov, who was at the time working on scholarly treatises about, inter alia, Greek drama and the origins of the satyr play.[33]

A second major group which emerged during the decade prior to the revolution, and who during War Communism were the principal other source of cultural bureaucrats from within the intelligentsia, might be called the antiacademicists. This group, which includes principally the futurists and formalists, many of whom in the twenties joined together as the "Left Front in Art," defined themselves principally as in opposition to the academy (a second *bête noire* for most of them was the symbolists). I classify this group as part of the category "intellectual" because of their intensely Oedipal relationship to the elders of the academic tradition, and because they were essentially more interested in high culture than in social justice (albeit most of them sided with the revolution, which is certainly not true of the intellectuals as a group). Most of the "antiacademicists" emerged from the academy, sometimes as dropouts, other times as challengers from within it who took their courses through to graduation. They were generally of a similar class and educational background to the professoriate, although there was a greater tendency among them to an ethnic diversity.

During NEP, the decline in the influence of the antiacademicist faction, already marked since 1920, increased (except in such areas as stage design and architecture) as they split into factions. Ironically, the avant-garde's Young Turks who had enjoyed power during the years of War Communism retreated back into the academy (against which they had originally rebelled), finding pockets in institutes and museums where they could take up their work in increasingly academic conditions, while the formalists were "reabsorbed" as literary scholars, immersing themselves in literary biography and historiography, the very scholarly approaches against which they had originally rebelled. Their academicist rivals in the cultural sphere, however, suffered a worse fate, for they were the principal group which lost out in the great reshuffle of NEP.

During the "quiet revolution" of NEP, a new generation of nonparty sympathizers emerged to take the places of the cultural leaders of War Communism. This was a younger generation, one which was educated, but generally from a background lower on the social and educational scale than their predecessors; certainly they did not have an academicist background. In literature, this new generation has a fairly common sociological profile: most were born in the late 1890s and some as late as the early 1900s (in contrast to Blok's cohort, born in the 1880s); most came from a petty intelligentsia or merchant background in the provinces, and the few who came from one of the capitals had no childhood connection to the academic elite;[34] many of this new generation were Jewish, but they were not, like Pasternak and Mandel'shtam of the preceding generation, ethnic Jews of

Christian persuasion; most attended university; most fought for the Bolsheviks in the Civil War or in some other way supported its cause during
War Communism; most began their literary careers in the first years of the
revolution. Thus their entry into adult life coincided with the revolution,
and they defined themselves in large measure in terms of it. They wanted
to create a new, Soviet literature. Some were more interested in experimental literature than others, but few were particularly interested in
furthering the cause of highbrow culture.

A comparable sociological shift may be observed among the party and
Komsomol intelligentsia. It will be noted that around the beginning of NEP
(or before), the party elite selected several party members of its own
generation and, usually, milieu who had intellectual credentials to run such
things as the new "thick" journals and Gosizdat—and for that matter
Narkompros itself. But around the end of NEP, many of these figures were
replaced. Admittedly, some were considered Trotskyite, but not all. The
phenomenon must be regarded, rather, as part of a general generational
changeover. But with the new generation came very different attitudes.

A marked feature of early Soviet intellectual life was that so many from
among the party leadership and its intelligentsia were, despite their acces-
sion to power, frequently able when not clearly pronouncing *ex cathedra* to
function as members of the old intelligentsia from which they came, participating with other nonparty but socially concerned intellectuals in certain
periodicals where they all published under conditions of relative equality.[35]
To be sure, when, for instance, Lunacharskii wrote a play, it was more
likely to be praised and to be performed (especially for a revolutionary
anniversary) than might have been the case if he had not had such substantial purse strings, but the many articles he wrote and published in an
unofficial capacity (reviewing recent trends in the West and the like) were
given no special billing and blended in with other such articles in the
periodical in question. No matter how senior a party author might have
been in its hierarchy (other than Lenin), there was rarely any sense that his
articles had to come first in a periodical, or be marked off in any way. To be
sure, party intellectuals showed extreme intolerance of their counterparts
from rival leftist groups, such as the Mensheviks and Socialist Revolutionaries, and also generally of idealists and religious thinkers. But as representatives of these positions began to disappear from the Soviet press, a
relatively cordial and mutually respectful atmosphere prevailed among the
remaining members of the old intelligentsia still publishing.

At about the end of NEP, however, there was a general trend for the old
party intellectuals to be replaced in their positions by representatives of a
younger and very different generation. This generation did not suddenly
appear on the horizon but had progressively been coming into power over
the course of NEP. In literature, they were often from a background with

more experience in Komsomol than in party work. Their general sociological profile is, however, strikingly similar to that of the new wave of nonparty writers. This similarity is most striking in the case of the leadership of
VAPP. Most of its leaders came from the provinces and were born in the
late 1890s or, above all, the early 1900s. Their parents came from the petty
intelligentsia (such as schoolteachers) or were known to support radical
causes. Since they were all young at the time of the revolution, they both
joined the party and started writing *after* it. Indeed, the timing of the
revolution in their lives meant that most of them joined the revolution
rather than go on to higher education, in contrast to the nonparty group
who, being generally those crucial couple of years older, generally did
attend university.[36] Nearly all of them began their literary activity only *after*
working full-time in some party or Komsomol administrative position, or
on one of their periodicals, usually as editors.

The VAPP leaders, then, were generally very slightly younger, from very
slightly lower on the social scale, and less well educated than their *bêtes
noires,* the leaders of the new, young generation of *poputchik* writers.
However, they could not claim to be radically different in class terms from
their opponents, only in terms of party membership and service. *Not one of
them came from the working classes,* and yet they demanded exclusive hegemony as "proletarians." The element of illusion or deception here can be
seen in the fact that one of their number, V. Ermilov, wrote a scurrilous
attack on the Formalist V. Shklovskii in 1929 under the title "Gymnasium
Student Viktor Shklovskii," disregarding the fact that he, Ermilov, had also
attended a gymnasium.[37]

There were, of course, genuine proletarians—the "cooks" of the proletarian literary movement (albeit male and not female). In fact, an entire
generation of them had emerged during the years prior to the revolution;
most of them had contributed to the party journals *Pravda* and *Zvezda.*[38]
Their social origins and biographies were often similar to Gorky's, and yet
he went on to earn an international reputation and to be absorbed into the
intellectual "caste," while they remained lowly (one of the many cases which
cause one to call into question the wisdom of relying too much on sociological analysis). In this period the veterans of proletarian literature, although
considerably older, found themselves subordinated to and to some extent
bullied by this younger generation of literary politicians from the party and
Komsomol.

The new group of militants which took over proletarian literature were
then, although in origins from within the middle classes and to some extent
even from within the intelligentsia, somewhat upstart and nouveau in
comparison with the less superficially educated representatives of the prerevolutionary party intelligentsia whom they replaced. When, for instance,
the VAPP leaders felt constrained to produce a literary theory to add

respectability to their position, few of their number could elaborate one; the task was delegated to Iurii Libedinskii, but the theoretical writings he produced after long delays bore uncanny resemblance to those of Voronskii, whom his group had ostensibly discredited.[39] Yet the VAPP leadership demanded for themselves exclusive hegemony within Soviet letters, something which the old party intelligentsia never presumed to claim.

One of the most consequential aspects for subsequent Soviet intellectual history of this "changeover" in literature was the new generation's reduced intellectual horizons. While their predecessors had generally brought to bear in their thinking on the future of Soviet culture a distinctly pan-European or internationalist perspective, this new generation had much narrower, more parochial horizons. A Lunacharskii might in the general course of things contribute to the journal *Sovremennyi zapad* an article on then-current German poetry,[40] but in the new generation's writings, the horizons had shrunk to Tolstoy, Belinskii and a few others who can be associated with the native radical tradition. To be fair, this new generation was, as it were, snatched from the schoolroom to take part in the revolution and never got a chance to further their education or travel in Europe, as so many of the old party intelligentsia, and even many of the old guard of proletarian writers, had done in voluntary and involuntary exile.

This parochialism was generally not shared by this new generation's counterparts among the nonparty writers. Indeed, many of them advocated revitalizing Russian literature with a healthy dose of such Western vogues as the detective and adventure novel, and others whose fiction was highly influenced by the Western (and especially the recent German) science fiction.[41] But ever since NEP, Eurocentrism or a cosmopolitan perspective has been a difficult position to maintain within Soviet culture. Socialist realism represents, if nothing else, a parochial, highly conventionalized, and antimodernist tradition. Even as recently as the sixties and seventies, when socialist realism was watered down—some have claimed that then Soviet culture went "beyond" socialist realism altogether[42]—much more favor was shown the parochial "village prose" writers, most of whose work was informed by a Russian Orthodox point of view, than was shown writers such as Andrei Bitov and Vasilii Aksenov, whose orientation was more toward Western literature.

The parochialism of Soviet culture cannot be single-handedly laid at the door of the new generation of party-oriented writers who came to power during NEP. Obviously, the general reorientation of the party away from internationalism and the new doctrine of "Socialism in one Country" were significant factors in this development. But at the beginning of the twenties, when this new generation made its entry into Soviet culture, their militant parochialism went against the general tenor of intellectual life. The consequences of their triumph are with us still.

Most who study the end of the Cultural Revolution in 1931–32 maintain that the Writers' Union was founded to curb the power of VAPP (by then generally known as RAPP): not only was RAPP the *only* writers' organization to be disbanded involuntarily then, but most of its leaders were purged later in the thirties. Such an account, however, overlooks the fact that the careers of two of their number, Fadeev and Ermilov, by no means ended in 1932. On the contrary, they went on to enjoy great power in Soviet literature and scholarship (Fadeev, for instance, was to head the Writers' Union for many years). In addition, socialist realism itself draws primarily on "proletarian culture" of the NEP period for its models, while nonproletarian culture continues to provide *officially acknowledged* classics of Soviet, as distinct from socialist realist, culture.

The issue of class origins, so important during the Cultural Revolution, was never again to be as central in intellectual life as it had been then. But the great debates of NEP were at base less about class origins than they were about the desirable degree of party and Komsomol commitment and power in cultural life. In Soviet culture a recurrent feature has been a tension analogous to the one which prevailed during NEP, but now largely rid of its rhetoric of class; this is the tension between, on the one hand, those intellectuals who might be described as *"poputchiki"* in the sense that they are definitely "Soviet," that they define their mission first of all in terms of professionalism within their field, and, on the other, those who are more "proletarian" in the sense of self-appointed guardians of ideological purity.

Rather than "killing" the RAPP faction or proletarian culture, 1932 had the effect of creating a greater equilibrium within the world of Soviet writers: the main parties who had been in contention during NEP remained powerful, but now with the reduced possibility that either would achieve complete domination.[43] Normalcy was restored.

## NOTES

1. E.g., Ukhtomskii did his famous work on the dominanta in 1923, Propp's work on the morphology of the folktale was published in 1929, etc.

2. I will consistently refer to Leningrad as Leningrad, even though it was of course known as Petrograd in the immediately prerevolutionary period, during War Communism, and for the early years of NEP (through January 1924).

3. "Serapionovy brat'ia o sebe," *Literaturnye zapiski*, 1922, p. 25.

4. Notably Kirillov and Gerasimov, leading poets of the group Kuznitsa.

5. See, e.g., L. Meshcheriakov, "O chastnykh izdatel'stvakh," *Pechat' i revoliutsiia*, 1922, no. 2, pp. 129–31; Jeffrey Brooks, *When Russia Learned to Read* (Princeton, 1985), p. 156.

6. In literature, writers in this category include Fedin, Leonov, Kataev, and Kaverin, in film Kozintsev and Trauberg, and in music Shostakovich. Jay Leyda has remarked that everyone who was anyone in Soviet silent film (and this is to a marked degree true of Soviet film in general) entered film during the period from February 1924 through February 1925 (Jay Leyda, *Kino: A History of Soviet Film* [London, 1960], p. 170).

7. On the alphabet reform, see P. Sakulin, "Nasushchnaia reforma," *Delo naroda*, 1917, no. 57 (May 25), p. 1.

8. There was some time lag such that, for instance, Pilniak's "ornamental" fiction remained the most popular literature in the Soviet Union in 1922, but his popularity and above all his political position declined rapidly thereafter.

9. Even that institute was closed down in 1926, obliging such figures to seek a niche in the neighboring "Noah's Ark" of avant-garde intellectual endeavor (in this case primarily scholarly) of NEP Leningrad, the State Institute for the History of the Arts (GIII), which was in turn itself heavily purged of such non-Marxist elements, although not closed down, during the First Five-Year Plan.

10. The speeches by Ivanov were published in *Vestnik teatra*, 1919, no. 26, p. 4, and no. 30–31, pp. 8–9.

11. It was particularly common for *poputchiki* to petition the party for help in the face of virulent attacks from "proletarian" militants. Thus in 1924, for instance, thirty-six *poputchiki* appealed to the Party Central Committee for protection against attacks leveled against them in *Na postu (Voprosy kul'tury pri diktature proletariata* [Moscow-Leningrad, 1925], p. 137). Such petitions led to the Central Committee meeting on literature in May 1924 at which Voronskii and Vardin were the main spokesmen for the *poputchik* and "proletarian" viewpoints, respectively, the outcome of which was the party resolution "On the Press" of June 1, 1924 (*Voprosy kul'tury pri diktature proletariata*, pp. 57–60), and in 1925 the party resolution on literature.

12. It should perhaps be added here that the faction which ran *Na postu* also had editorial control in these years over the journals *Molodaia gvardiia* and *Oktiabr'* from the time they were founded (1922 and 1924 respectively) until the *Na postu* faction suffered a political defeat after the party resolution on literature of 1925.

13. For material on the new universities, see Akademiia obshchestvennykh nauk pri TsK KPSS, *Sovetskaia intelligentsiia (istoriia formirovaniia i rosta 1917–1965 gg.)* (Moscow, 1968), p. 104; and D. P. Konchalovskii, *Vospominaniia i pis'ma (ot gumanizma k Khristu)* (Paris, 1971), pp. 158–61.

14. This is quite clear in the many articles on the situation of Soviet publishing, the paper shortage, distribution, printing presses, etc., published in *Pechat' i revoliutsiia* in the early twenties. See, e.g., 1921, no. 1, pp. 9–42.

15. An exception would be *Sibirskie ogni*, founded in 1922, which helped launch the careers of several young writers.

16. *Krasnaia nov'*, for instance, had a theretofore unprecedented circulation of 15–20,000 in its first year, although this declined to 8,000 during 1922, before settling down to 10–12,000 for some years.

17. In book publishing, this trend toward Moscow-centrism was somewhat mitigated early in NEP because it was cheaper and easier to publish in Leningrad than in Moscow, and many books awaiting publication were sent there. Also, Leningrad was still the capital for scholarship and research, particularly in the natural sciences, and an overwhelming proportion of works and scholarly journals in the natural sciences came out of Leningrad, as can be sensed by, for instance, looking at the sections reviewing scientific literature in *Pechat' i revoliutsiia*.

18. *Zvezda*'s circulation was around 3,000, increasing by the end of 1926 to 5,000, but that could not compete with a circulation of 15,000 offered by *Novyi mir*.

19. It was during NEP that Leningrad first assumed its role as symbolic center of an "other" culture, other than the mainstream, which offended the would-be guardians of Soviet cultural purity. It is no accident that most of the intellectuals who have been singled out for "show" campaigns have been associated with Leningrad, starting with Pilniak (ostensibly a Moscow writer but closely associated with Leningrad in his publishing career) and Zamiatin in 1929, and then Shostakovich and the formalists in the thirties, Akhmatova and Zoshchenko in 1946, and Brodskii in the sixties. Under NEP the majority of the writers consistently singled out for attack in *Na postu* and later *Na literaturnom postu* were from Leningrad (such as the Serapion Brothers, Marietta Shaginian, A. Grin, A. Akhmatova, and A. Tolstoy).

20. In fact it was dominated by the new, more moderate VAPP leadership, which had, unlike its predecessors, accepted the party resolution on literature.

21. See, e.g., N. Kliuev, "Krasnyi kon'," *Griadushchee*, 1919, no. 5–6, pp. 14–15, and "Ognennaia gramota," *Griadushchee*, 1919, no. 7–8, pp. 17–18. Kliuev also published in *Plamia*, an organ of the Petrograd Soviet which published mostly proletarian writers; see, e.g., his "Respublika," *Plamia*, 1918, no. 29, p. 475.

22. In *Krasnyi militsioner*, 1921, no. 2–3, compare O. Mandel'shtam, "Proslavim, brat'ia sumerki svobody" (p. 31), with, on the facing page, "Petrogradskie razmyshleniia na Kronshtadskom fronte (beseda s tovarishchem Kishkinym)" (p. 32).

23. Z. V. Stepanov, *U istokov kul'turnoi revoliutsii* (Leningrad, 1972), p. 79.

24. See S. I. Sheshukhov, *Neistovye revniteli* (Moscow, 1970).

25. See, for instance, the fiction about the party and the intelligentsia by the leading VAPP/RAPP writer and chief literary theoretician Iurii Libedinskii: *Nedelia* (1922), *Zavtra* (1923), *Komissary* (1925), *Povorot* (1927), and *Rozhdenie geroia* (1931).

26. E.g., M. Slonimskii, *Lavrovy* (1926) and *Foma Kleshnev* (1929); K. Vaginov, *Kozlinaia pesn'* (1927); and V. Kaverin, *Skandalist, ili vechera na Vasil'evskom ostrove* (1929) and *Khudozhnik neizvesten* (1931).

27. I.e., in her book *Education and Social Mobility in the Soviet Union, 1921–1934* (Cambridge, England, 1979).

28. Antonio Gramsci, *Selections from Cultural Writings*, translated by William Boellhower and edited by David Forgacs and Geoffrey Nowell-Smith (Cambridge, Mass., 1985), pp. 168–69.

29. See, e.g., Peter Gay, *Weimar Culture: The Outsider as Insider* (London, 1958), pp. 3, 119–20, 139–40.

30. Iu. A. Filipchenko, "Statisticheskie rezul'taty ankety po nasledstvennosti sredi uchenykh Peterburga" and "Nashi vydaiushchiesia uchenye," *Izvestiia. Biuro po evgenike*, 1922, no. 1, pp. 12–13 and 27–28, respectively.

31. See especially *Education and Social Mobility*, pp. 78–81, 85–86. I am in general agreement with the findings of Sheila Fitzpatrick, although I believe she has overstated the extent to which the professoriate was able to conduct business as usual during NEP. Greater distinction must be made here between those working in the sciences and those in the humanities and social sciences. In the humanities, especially, scholars encountered more problems in such areas as being able to have graduate students than her account (e.g., on p. 82) would suggest.

32. The list here includes Bely, Blok, Bulgakov, Pasternak, and Tsvetaeva. However, in other cultural fields there were strong links between art and the academy (for instance, in the Benois dynasty, and in a figure such as the artist A. P. Ostroumova-Lebedeva, who was married to the famous chemist Lebedev).

33. Piotrovskii was the illegitimate son of F. F. Zelinskii, the most distinguished classical scholar of the time (who emigrated in 1921); Radlov was the son of E. Radlov, an eminent idealist philosopher and classical scholar; see N. Evreinov,

*Proiskhozhdenie dramy. Pervobytnaia tragediia i rol' kozla v istorii ee vozniknoveniia* (Petersburg, 1921).

34. L. Leonov, for instance, came from Moscow, but his family were minor merchants of the Zariad'e district. An exception to this general rule would be Mikhail Slonimskii, whose family included several prominent scholars (his uncle was S. Vengerov and his brother A. Slonimskii) and musicians (an aunt) in Petersburg/Leningrad.

35. The career in the 1920s of V. Bystrianskii, originally an editor of *Pravda* and then of *Leningrad Pravda,* provides a particularly good example of this.

36. It is interesting to note that the one major exception in this, D. Furmanov, who attended Moscow University, was also less intolerant of the *poputchiki* than were his peers in VAPP.

37. "Uchenik gimnazii Viktor Shklovskii," *Na literaturnom postu,* 1929, no. 7. Admittedly, Ermilov had dropped out of the gymnasium after five grades, but then Viktor Shklovskii as a rebel of long standing and associate of the SRs was hardly your typical gymnasium student, either.

38. My account of the proletarian writers is taken largely from the biographies provided in S. A. Rodov, comp., *Proletarskie pisateli. Antologiia proletarskoi literatury* (Moscow, [1924]), but is supplemented with biographies obtained from *Kratkaia literaturnaia entsiklopediia* and elsewhere for writers who for ideological reasons were excluded by Rodov.

39. Cf. Iu. Libedinskii, "Khudozhestvennaia platforma RAPPa," *Na literaturnom postu,* 1928, no. 19, p. 16; "Iskusstvo kak poznanie zhizni i sovremennosti," in I. Oksenov, ed., *Sovremennaia russkaia kritika, 1918–1924* (Leningrad, 1925), pp. 36–50. Libedinskii's theories were also influenced by Belinskii's unpublished essay "Idei iskusstva" of 1841.

40. *Sovremennyi zapad,* 1923, no. 2.

41. See the many examples of German science fiction described in *Sovremennyi zapad,* 1923, no. 4, pp. 204–205, and which closely resemble much of the kind of science-fiction writing which appeared in the Soviet Union during NEP.

42. E.g., Geoffrey Hosking, *Beyond Socialist Realism: Soviet Fiction since Ivan Denisovich* (New York, 1980).

43. Gorky's role in all this is too complicated to be discussed here.

# XIV

# THE PRESS AND ITS MESSAGE
## IMAGES OF AMERICA IN THE 1920s AND 1930s

## Jeffrey Brooks

Soviet newspapers differed from those in market economies because of the nature of Soviet society and of the journalists' role.[1] The Western democratic press arose within what Jürgen Habermas aptly described as the "public sphere," the arena of social life situated between the realm of the state and the circle of private family and individual activity.[2] The constitution of Soviet society left little room for such public or civic space outside official structures, and party and state bureaucracies were intolerant of the expression of dissident opinions in newspapers or elsewhere. During the first years of the revolutionary era, unofficial organizations vanished, and all organized group activity was brought under government control. This contraction of "civil society" was a characteristic of all Soviet-type systems, and the recent rebirth of independent public activity and opinion in the Soviet Union signifies a fundamental change.[3]

The development of journalism as a Western profession depended, as did other professions, on a measure of independence from the state. The Soviet system doubly limited the scope of the professions, since service within the bureaucracies remained the main criterion for advancement, and neither prestige among colleagues nor money was sufficient to secure social status and material reward. Journalists therefore had little cause to enlarge the public sphere and their own importance by criticizing the government. They had no reason to stress "objectivity," as did American reporters in the early twentieth century.[4] The integration of journalism into the state administration in this sense initially precluded the development of a Soviet fourth estate.

The Soviet press had room for social criticism, but not from professional journalists, whose primary task was the presentation of an official viewpoint. Critical commentary was reserved for unofficial local reporters, such as the worker and peasant correspondents, who were paid a few rubles for each accepted contribution. These occasional commentators lacked the autonomy, education, and economic security to become an independent voice in Soviet society. They addressed local issues, and when they challenged local authorities, they appealed to the central government as arbiter. As a result, their role in bringing a critical perspective to governmental affairs was limited. Nor did the disputes among the party elite that were sometimes aired in the press during the 1920s serve a function similar to that of the Western democratic press, which, despite its limitations, provided a running commentary on affairs of state.[5] Party leaders permitted themselves to disagree openly in the early years of the Soviet government, but such disputes were never allowed to overflow the limits of an internal party discussion.

Newspapers, like other commodities, also reflected the reality of an economic system in which consumers counted for little, and producers dictated the nature of the product. As a result, professional journalists' links with readers suffered.[6] Claims to independence and personal prestige based on popularity had little weight once institutional arrangements replaced commercial calculation as the primary bond among producers, distributors, and consumers. Under these conditions, the notion of the newspaper as a source of public opinion became problematic and liberal ideals of a critical press irrelevant.[7]

Soviet newspapers also diverged from an authoritarian model of the press in which newspapers that were subservient to state interests were directed through censorship and state intervention.[8] German newspapers were coopted by the Nazis, and they were supposed to serve the state, but the German press continued to operate within a market economy. Nazi control of the press was effected through ownership, but private nonparty newspapers continued to exist.[9] In the Soviet Union, on the contrary, the newspapers were created anew in complete dependence on the state, and they were often distributed free until the New Economic Policy of 1921. Even then, private individual sales remained secondary and subsidies were common.[10]

The internal logic of the Soviet media system was reflected in the variety and hierarchy of newspapers. There was an early division between the "leading" institutional publications, such as *Pravda* and *Izvestiia*, where the most influential journalists worked, and "mass" newspapers produced for specific groups of common readers by journalists who specialized in simplifying the message of the elite press.[11] Among the mass newspapers, the most important included *Rabochaia gazeta* (The Workers' Newspaper, 1922–39), *Rabochaia Moskva* (Working Moscow, 1922–39), and *Krest'ianskaia gazeta* (The Peasant Newspaper, 1923–39), which the Bolsheviks founded once they realized that ordinary peasants and workers would not read *Pravda* or *Izvestiia*. *Bednota* (The Poor, 1918–31) was an unsuccessful precursor of these publications. Newspapers tied to lesser institutions, such as the labor union organ, *Trud* (Labor), and the youth paper *Komsomol'skaia pravda* (Komsomol Truth), as well as provincial papers, also tended to follow the lead of the two elite institutional publications (P/4/11/28).[12]

The system proved unwieldy in its first decade, simultaneously creating shortages and surpluses of unwanted materials, but newspaper production surged and newspapers came to exemplify a new official public culture.[13] The Bolsheviks had no single model for the ideal newspaper. They wanted to communicate their ideals, mold opinion, and organize support for their policies, but also to generate discussion, collect information, stimulate public criticism of malfeasance, and, to a limited extent, address readers' demand for information.[14] As a result, journalists prepared different types of articles for different purposes, and some issues were treated differently simultaneously in the same newspaper. In this respect, newspapers contained three spheres of discourse—an explanatory or inspirational sphere, an active one for the exchange of opinions among readers, and one that was largely informational.[15]

The Soviet press took its distinctive look from its explanatory content. The party was the driving force in the new public culture, and the job of those who wrote the lead editorials, signed columns, and other commentaries with a byline was to provide the big interpretations of ongoing stories that brought an official meaning to the newspapers' diverse content.[16] In Western studies of the media this function is often described as agenda setting; this was the part of the newspaper in which authors told readers what to think about as well as what to think.[17] Cartoons, illustrations, and photos reinforced this message.

The speeches of the Bolshevik leaders, which were often printed in full even in the early years of the press, also served this purpose, although less effectively. The explanatory perspective was particularly intrusive during moments of official culture such as May Day or Lenin's birthday, which the editors of different papers commemorated with nearly identical articles and illustrations. Despite the key function of this sphere, its general intelligibility was limited by the employment of difficult political terminology, and as a result other parts of the newspaper were open to counter-readings.[18]

The informational sphere, consisting mostly of wire service reports on events in the news, was more intelligible and accessible. Jargon and political concepts counted for less, and there was a tendency to present events as evidence rather than argue a case for interpreting them. This did not mean that the news was not slanted, but only that the why and how were often excluded. Nevertheless, this sphere was also restrictive, since the subjects and events presented were not open for discussion, except to the party elite. When a subject was opened for public comment, as, for example, the sale of the church's valuables to pay for food imports during the famine of 1921–22, the discussion began in the interactive sphere.

The interactive or participatory sphere was the most innovative aspect of the Soviet press. It embraced topics on which local comments were solicited and included regular features about "Party Life" and "Workers' Life," topical sections such as "On the Cultural Front" and "Soviet Construction," as well as occasional columns, such as "On the Themes of the Day," and public discussions initiated by the professional journalists.[19] Issues discussed usually concerned local affairs, and the likely readers were interested people, often referred to as the *aktiv*.[20] Contributions usually came from regular worker and peasant correspondents, who numbered 150,000 by 1925 (P4/18/25) and 500,000 in 1928, as well as other concerned readers.[21] Letters from readers and contributions from correspondents represented "Soviet civic consciousness" or simply "the Soviet public" *(Sovetskaia obshchestvennost')* (P2/3/24) and were channeled to appropriate authorities for action, whether published or not (P4/5/28). The opinions expressed in this sphere were managed by the editors for specific purposes, and the comments of the "politically literate" minority of ordinary people served to enhance the authority of the party and the state.

The effect of this tripartite division was to create a new kind of public sphere. The party elite could express some differences of opinion in the press, at least for much of the 1920s, and there was also room for criticism from the *aktiv*, largely in the form of comments by workers and peasants on local issues. The rest of the population, however, was largely excluded. This was not remarkable in the case of the common readers, who were largely excluded in other systems, except insofar as they manifested their taste and interest as consumers. It was unique with respect to the educated minority, however. Such readers saw their access to the media severely restricted, and their comments were limited to subjects of professional specialization.

The interplay of the three spheres lent diversity, although not independence, to the Soviet press. So did the ineffectiveness of central control by the party, despite the frequent description of the newspaper as "a powerful weapon of propaganda" (P11/22/21).[22] Current research on the reading of newspapers suggests the importance of the readers' own schemata or conceptualization for the organization and retention of information from the daily press.[23] Soviet editors provided encompassing ideological interpretations from above, largely in the explanatory sphere, but what did these official schemata have to do with the readers' readings? The question is not entirely unanswerable, since journalists openly addressed what they believed to be the alternative attitudes and conceptions of their readers. They also relied on preexisting attitudes to transmit their own message.

The metaphorical use of America is an example. America loomed large in Russian popular fiction on the eve of World War I, and it was also an important symbol among intellectuals.[24] Soviet journalists pointed to American technology and industry in the 1920s when they wrote of the promise of a socialist society; they stressed American poverty and racism when they damned capitalism; and they looked to America when they thought of possible capitalist partners for the economic development of their country. Articles specifically about America featured two ongoing stories articulated in the explanatory and informational spheres: negative descriptions of life "over there," "on the other side of the barricades," and positive or neutral commentaries on friendly relations between the two countries or favorable aspects of life in America, particularly science and technology.[25] The first big story was central to the Bolsheviks' overall message; the second was less so, but it was nevertheless important as a way of legitimizing the place of the Soviet system in the modern industrial world. In addition to articles specifically about America, the United States was often used as a metaphor for excellence in articles about Soviet domestic life.

Coverage of America differed from that of Western Europe, largely because the United States was not good copy for the two other big ongoing foreign stories of the 1920s, the progress of revolution abroad and the threat of foreign invasion. Although the American Communist Party figured in reports of Comintern meetings out of proportion to its actual importance, comments on the progress of revolution in America were scarce. Similarly, attempts to fit America into a xenophobic story of the Soviet Union surrounded by hostile enemies were sporadic and half-hearted. *Pravda,* for example, depicted America as an imperialist world power from Latin America to China.[26] America was also sometimes portrayed as the "boss of Europe" (P12/4/21), eager to extend its "predatory grip" to Soviet Russia (P5/3/22). Soviet journalists even made much of the potential rivalry between the two nations for domination of the world grain market (P3/11/23), but when recognition seemed near or industrialists likely to invest in Soviet projects, the press became almost friendly (P1/15/25). Even American intervention in the Russian Civil War, which became an important reference in the cold war era, was forgotten during the 1920s. By the end of the decade the changing world situation precluded concern with American imperialism, and in the face of the expansion of Japan in North China, Soviet comments on American military preparedness became neutral and even friendly.

The presentation of America as the exemplar of capitalism was the big American story. When they wrote of "life over there," however, the journalists not only organized news events around their own story, but they also paid homage to an alternative view in which America figured as the land of opportunity and progress. Both notions predated the revolution and were changed by it. Nineteenth-century Russian thinkers denounced America according to their politics, but they were in no position to realize an alternative vision of society.[27] To Slavophile critics such as Dostoevsky, and populists such as V. G. Korolenko, America signified an unacceptable modernity, and late-nineteenth-century liberals also picked out unpleasant aspects of American life despite their general approval.[28]

Popular journalists echoed these complaints on the eve of World War I, and Soviet commentators repeated them in the 1920s. The prerevolutionary journalists who condemned American racism and exploitation in such popular newspapers as *Russkoe slovo* (Russian Word) and *Gazeta kopeika* (The Kopeck Newspaper), however, often shared their readers' assumptions of America's promise. They warned against emigration but usually granted America its own future, championing the progressives against business and the trusts, and hoping for a victory of "the people."[29] Soviet journalists were more sanguine about America's prospects.

The popular mythology Soviet journalists opposed also predated 1917. Prerevolutionary intellectuals and publicists had looked to America as an economic model for Russia and an inspiration for future development.[30] This kind of "Americanism" was a strategy for development that appealed to a predominantly liberal educated minority. When popular journalists and the authors of cheap fiction wrote of America for newly literate readers, they had different issues in mind. Popular fiction is moral fantasy, and America's was identified with notions of success and self-improvement that gained wide currency in this period.[31] The intellectuals' dream of America was more national and political; the popular writers' concerns were more commonly psychological. They praised Americans for their "energy, staunchness, and efficiency" (GK8/16/08), and ragtag writers peddled detective stories with heroes such as Nat Pinkerton and Nick Carter who exemplified these qualities.[32] Neither the dream of individual mobility nor the idea of self-help ended in 1917. Both the popular and elite ideas of America came into play in the Soviet period.

Prerevolutionary popular culture had a long half-life in the 1920s in popular literature and film. Old booklets were read by readers hungry for light fiction until they disintegrated. Soviet theaters showed prerevolutionary films based on the popular fiction, as well as prerevolutionary imports, often of American films, until 1924, when new, also largely American films replaced the old. Soviet films gained slowly, and the income from home productions did not exceed receipts from the largely American imports until 1927.[33] As late as 1925, 87 percent of the films shown were foreign (P2/15/28). Soviet audiences chortled at the antics of Charlie Chaplin and Buster Keaton and thrilled to the adventures of Mary Pickford and Douglas Fairbanks.[34]

So popular were the American stars that *Pravda* quoted Fairbanks and Pickford to promote *Potemkin*.[35] When asked in 1928 what they liked about foreign films, children invariably mentioned Fairbanks (P1/6/28). "That Doug, he is so brave and bold," they replied. "He jumps about so cleverly all the time." "I want to be as brave as Doug," remarked another. "Almost all the children regarded foreign films more favorably than Soviet films," the authors of the study concluded, because "another life is shown there," and because "what they show in our land is boring and *poor*." As a result, in workers' clubs and elsewhere, ordinary people were more likely to see *The Thief of Baghdad* than Soviet life (P2/15/28). There were intrinsic reasons for the popularity of the American films, but their success was most of all a result of the Bolsheviks' failure to create a viable alternative. On one level, this was a failure to entertain an audience, but on another, more serious level, it signified the larger tragedy of the revolutionaries' inability to translate their goals into popular imagery and popular language. The American myth was important because the Bolsheviks had so little to counter it when they addressed the common reader.

Fairbanks and Pickford represented the myth of success, which had gained such a hold on the popular imagination in prerevolutionary Russia. Fairbanks succeeded in business as well as in physical contests and perhaps found an audience among Soviet achievers as well as dreamers.[36] "Preaching the Horatio Alger code of success, he triumphed over lusty villains and moved up the class order," as Lary May explains in his study of early American cinema.[37] Above all, however, the magic couple of the American movies were physical, optimistic, and democratic. Like Pinkerton and Carter before them, they mixed freely with all classes and snubbed snobs and villains who had not personally achieved the status they held. Mary Pickford had her own special appeal, as a woman who enjoyed moral autonomy and economic independence, without giving up the pleasures of luxury.

The American stars also spoke to new interests in sports and leisure. While Fairbanks jumped about on the screen and Pickford showed off a perpetually youthful figure, Soviet newspapers promoted athletes with similar qualities. The cultural revolution cut short the influence of American films, but the advent of sound in the West was also important in this long hiatus in foreign influence in the media. Soviet sound production was slow in coming, and the showing of foreign sound films required new equipment and new techniques of translation.[38] The ban on film imports in the late 1920s may have frozen this movie-made America in the Soviet imagination simply because the subsequent films that would have dispelled it were so delayed in their arrival.

Soviet journalists ridiculed the image of America as a land in which ordinary people with talent and energy could get rich, but they acknowledged the power this image had over their readers. Even peasants were enthralled with "America's heavenly wonders," complained a journalist in *Pravda* in 1926 (P4/3/26). As he explained bitterly, they believed that American peasants lived on farms "nicer than any sovkhoz" ("but what a farm is, is not exactly known"), and they all had cars. Moreover, "to buy it [a farm] is altogether simple and easy; only work two years at a factory and save a little American money." This was the view the journalists set about to refute. They sought to dismantle the popular mythology of America and sweep away the materialistic and market-oriented hopes and expectations that went with it.

The conflict between official and unofficial views of America affected the Bolsheviks themselves. The Old Bolshevik V. Nogin, for example, who went to America to buy cotton for the Textile Syndicate in 1924, wrote on returning from his trip about the evil of racism, but he also expressed surprise at the quality of American food and living standards. The writings of Upton Sinclair were widely promoted in the Soviet Union, and Nogin confessed his fear of eating anything. "But to my great surprise," he wrote, "most shops and restaurants always provide quality products; for example, they offer meat of wonderful quality, and the milk and other products are fresh and tasty" (P3/16/24).

To the image of America as the land of opportunity and wealth, the Bolsheviks replied with America as the capitalist behemoth, the land of Morgan and Rockefeller, of the "kings" of industry (RG7/10/23), of the Klan and the American Legion (RG8/9/22). In cartoons, a thin and menacing Uncle Sam drove the capitalists of the world on a grim march for profits and booty (RM5/16/22). Journalists described workers "Sold into Slavery at Auction in Boston" (P10/27/21), and commentaries on American politics and race relations, as well as events such as the Sacco and Vanzetti case and the Teapot Dome scandal, pointed up class struggle and oppression.

Yet whether they wrote of exploitation or heroes of the American left, such as Sinclair ("who showed the real capitalist essence of 'free' America"), they kept the other America before their readers (RM5/9/23). Typical captions in *Rabochaia Moskva* included "Life in Rich America" (RM8/16/22), "In the Democratic Heaven" (RM8/25/22), and "In the Country of Freedom" (RM12/28/27). "The great democracy is a hell for Negroes," observed one correspondent in *Rabochaia gazeta* (RG8/9/22). Testimony by American Communists and unhappy émigrés who returned to Russia with tales of woe amplified such reports. In *Bednota*, an article captioned "The Slavery of Peasants in America" was subtitled "From the Notebook of a Russian-American Farmer" (B7/19/22). "How They Wanted to Make Us Slaves," reads another émigré's account in the same paper, about a worker who found life worse "in the country of freedom" (B8/21/23). These accounts became less frequent in both *Pravda* and the mass newspapers in the later 1920s, when Soviet publicists became preoccupied with a domestic agenda.

What was most novel in such commentary was linking America with the larger effort to dispel the illusion of personal success and mobility in a market economy. Although the First Five-Year Plan and collectivization made such concerns less pressing, the depression inspired portrayals of the miseries of capitalism throughout the 1930s. The second big official story that involved America was the presentation of the Soviet future and Soviet modernity. Although America was "the country of the machine" to pre-revolutionary journalists (GK4/8/10), the Soviet discovery of American technological preeminence was something of a novelty, as Kendall Bailes has suggested.[39] The automobiles and airplanes described in the prerevolutionary press were likely to be German or French and not American. As a columnist explained in *Russkoe slovo*, the statement "science gives a fully clear and definite answer" usually meant "German science" (RS7/14/10). For Soviet journalists, however, America displaced the great European powers in science and technology from the start.

"In America they have invented a machine" was a formula for promoting new technology (RM4/4/23), and equal to "American machines" meant quality (KG6/21/27). Anything new or useful could be linked with America. When a journalist promoted corn, America was its "homeland" (P1/26/22). When another told of radio, America was "where millions listen" (P2/18/23). America was also the land where airplanes did the sowing and a single flyer replaced a hundred men and a hundred horses (RG6/22/22). During collectivization, America became the land of the combine (B1/19/29; B2/27/29).

The use of America as a metaphor of modernity facilitated the promotion of American techniques of industrial organization, largely but not exclusively in the third sphere of the newspaper, which was directed primarily at the activists. Soviet journalists advocated Taylorism and "Fordism," as well as vague notions of "American" efficiency, practicality, and organizational skills, in the hope of solving specific economic problems. When they promoted American techniques and qualities among activists, who shared their dream of a Soviet future, they did not have to condemn America. Among this audience, the rejection of capitalism was a given. Soviet Taylorists flourished in the early 1920s, but their influence, as well as importance in disseminating images of America, is questionable. They were active in peripheral institutions, such as the Scientific Organization of Labor (NOT), the Central Institute of Labor, and the League of Time. Taylorism was only loosely associated with America in the press, and Soviet Taylorists were eager to distinguish their "science" of work from capitalism.[40] Lenin had done the same when he adopted Taylorism after the October Revolution, and Soviet promoters liked to quote him to the effect that Taylor combined "the refined bestiality of the bourgeois exploitation with a series of the richest scientific achievements" (P2/24/24).[41]

"Fordism" was more popular than Taylorism and more "American" in Soviet eyes, but it took hold more slowly.[42] Ford was initially part of the story of capitalist depravity, and he was described in the informational and explanatory spheres during the early 1920s as "the automobile king" (RG7/8/24) and a brutal industrial despot (P2/15/21). So hostile were reporters to Ford in the early 1920s that the Ford tractor, later to become so famous throughout Russia that children were named after it, was ridiculed in a series of signed articles in *Pravda* as unsuitable for Russian conditions (P1/12/23). One journalist even suggested in the same newspaper that Russians were better off with horses (P4/12/23). There was an immediate rejoinder, however, in favor of tractors (P6/2/23). Soviet Fordism began when the recovery of existing factories was largely complete in the mid-1920s and the Bolsheviks could think of new investments. It was used to promote "socialism in one country" and the idea that Russia could become an advanced industrial power without outside assistance from other socialist states (P6/28/25). At the outset, Fordism meant the assembly line and the conveyer belt, whose use in Russia publicists were eager to contrast with the exploitative practices of capitalism. "There is nothing frightening about Fordism in a Soviet country" (RG5/3/26), wrote one publicist, who added that one could adopt Ford's conveyer without "his system of slavery." There was a flood of articles with captions such as "Well, How Are Things at Ford," to remind readers that praise for Fordism was not praise for Ford or America.[43]

Fordism seemed to promise quick results. Ford built a thousand tractors a day, compared with yearly Soviet production of two thousand (P11/15/24; P12/31/25). "Why Is It Possible for America and Impossible for Us," a journalist asked in a front-page article in *Pravda* (7/2/25). The answer, as far as the author could see, was unclear. The Soviet Union, "with all its natural gifts and economic possibilities," should be "a second America," since the state organization of the economy was better than the American. Yet the tractors were not forthcoming. Borrowing from Ford was an answer. "Ford knows what the organization of production is," wrote one journalist (P9/23/28).

Ford's system may have appealed to Soviet managers as a means of achieving industrial harmony, as it did to their Western European counterparts.[44] Fordism meant order, as Antonio Gramsci pointed out at the time; its promoters preached rationality, sobriety, and puritanism for workers as a means of internalizing and perfecting labor discipline.[45] Such ideas gained currency in Russia during the late 1920s. Gastev, the inspirer of the Central Institute of Labor, claimed to see a potential "Ford" within every worker who "gave his strength" to the "fatherland" (P11/27/25). It was tempting, in this way, to link Fordism and industrial efficiency with cultural revolution. As one commentator observed, Russia could achieve an "American tempo" of development, thanks to its "enormous cultural upsurge, its powerful supply of psychic energy" (P7/30/25).

So attractive was Fordism to those who wrote the lead articles in the columns captioned "Workers' Life" that the notion of Fordism was sometimes confused with that of "Soviet Americans," and the phrase "Russian Fords" was used to refer to active groups of workers and managers.[46] The idea of American qualities was different from Fordism, however, and it had a wider circulation. The one was usually linked with social control, the other with individual motivation and energy. The first was likely to appeal to managers, the other to all who actively shared the dream of a new society.

When they wrote for worker-activists in agriculture and industry, the journalists were able to use phrases such as "the practical Americans have understood" to promote any innovation, from tractors to horse manure (B2/23/22). Telling readers that they could follow the American lead was also a way of showing what was possible and desirable. "The Mechanization of Agriculture is not a Utopia," wrote one author; work can be organized as on "a great American farm" (RG11/28/22). "We know the organization of a new type [of farm] in America, where only 250 people work constantly on 35,000 *desiatiny*," wrote another proponent of collectivization (P5/29/28).

It was a simple step to shift American qualities from America to Soviet Russia. Some of the émigrés who returned from America in the early 1920s to help the new socialist society were praised for their "American" energy and initiative, as were American businessmen who seemed likely to invest.[47] As Trotsky explained to a visiting American senator in 1923, "there is also a very important moral and by no means sentimental factor easing our cooperation with the United States of America. The words *Americanism* and *Americanization* are used in our newspapers and technical journals in an altogether sympathetic way, and by no means in the sense of reproach" (P9/30/23). Trotsky's stress on the moral aspect is revealing, since America figured here not as an economic model but as a human one, for a new type of person. Reference to American ways and qualities became a form of praise for energetic and successful groups of workers or managers.

This was the sense of a whole range of articles about "Russian Americans" that peppered the Soviet press throughout the 1920s. As in the first article of this sort in *Pravda*, captioned "A Little Corner of America," the subject was people, not machines or industry. Describing the prosperous and energetic peasants, he writes, "The Russian American points his finger to the left, across the lake," to show proudly the first separate farmstead, with stone buildings (P8/30/23). This was a way of saying to the activists, "You can reap the benefits if you expend the effort."

"What are 'the Americans,' " asked a reporter in a 1924 article captioned "Russian Americans." "They are people who know how to work at such a speed and with such vigor, and pressure, as was unknown in Old Rus' " (RG1/24/23). "The Americans," he continued, "are those who most of all know how to take things in hand." These moral lessons were part of a broader effort to create new ways of thinking and new attitudes toward the self and society in the early 1920s. They were implicitly paired with the contrary image of traditional Russian sloth and backwardness. "At our Il'ich Oil Fields," wrote a correspondent, "there is 100 percent Soviet Americanism," and "each worker fully consciously lays the foundation for prosperity" (RG3/3/23). Similarly, another correspondent dubbed a new paper mill "America on the Volga" and praised workers for "turning the old Volga into our young Soviet America" (RG11/10/26).

Even the idea of borrowing American economic organization and technology had a particularly Soviet slant. America possessed technology, science, industrial organization, and even human qualities the Bolsheviks should borrow to transform their society, but America itself was not the issue. As Trotsky explained in 1926, "The technology of America, joined with the Soviet organization of society, would produce communism, or in any case, conditions of life approaching it" (P11/29/26). There was nothing un-Marxian about the idea of borrowing, and nothing American about Soviet plans for the future.

By the late 1920s, "Soviet America" referred to the fulfillment of the dream, not the process of advancing it. The promotion of Ford tractors in the mid-1920s meant investment in agriculture. In 1928, tractors spelled collectivization. As one journalist explained in an article on state farms, "a tractor demands a farm with an expanse of 150 to 200 *desiatiny*," and an electric station, he added, required a much greater expanse (P1/15/28). A Soviet vision displaced America in such accounts. "The victorious song of the machine sounds in the motors of a hundred tractors, glorifying the proletarian state in the peasant fields," wrote another journalist (P4/19/28).

The same was true for the great industrial projects. When journalists called a mine "The American" *("Amerikanka")* or a strip of Kazakh steppe "Colorado" (P11/24/28), they were less concerned with America than with giving the Five-Year Plan a patina of plausibility in the eyes of the activists. "Here at the *Amerikanka*, the past does not prevail. . . . Here in the wide steppe, planners have gained the possibility of creating something really new" (P11/7/28).

The "romance" with America, which reached a crescendo during the First Five-Year Plan and collectivization, was part of an increasingly nationalistic public culture and extended no further than the borrowing Lenin suggested with respect to Taylorism. Acclaim for "Russian Americans" as well as for "American" qualities appeared amid condemnations of foreigners, and the most enthusiastic praise of America was directed at the *aktiv*, who could be expected to know its limits. "Russian Americans" were, after all, Russians, not foreigners, and they were the equivalent of native inventors and other innovators who were promoted in columns sometimes captioned "We Will Get Along without the Foreigners" (P3/24/25) or "We Will Get Along without Foreign Specialists" (P1/18/23). American machines were similarly praised with the proviso that "this new machine will free Soviet industry from foreign dependence" (P11/20/28). Such comments signified a realism born in experience with new projects. "In a Bolshevik way" (*po-Bolshevistski*) often supplanted *po-Amerikanski*, and the Russian word *lent* replaced *conveyer*, first in parentheses and then standing alone (P11/6/28). Soviet plants and projects were often praised in their own terms.

The depression in America, the seemingly successful Soviet drive for industrialization, and the victory of Stalin and his supporters also changed the terms of this discussion. Soviet "Fordism" and articles in praise of American technology continued to appear during the early 1930s, although they occupied somewhat less space. These articles about positive aspects of American life account for roughly 5.2 percent of the space in the sampled articles about America in the 1920s, and 3.5 percent in the 1930s. The tone of the articles had changed, however. Typical of the new isolationist perspective was a report from early 1935 captioned "At an American Railroad Roundhouse," by a Soviet engineer who had visited America (P2/9/35). Although he praised the American depot for its cleanliness and the speed with which the engines were outfitted for new trips, the observations were largely practical.

The admiration was gone. What was left was apparent from an article in the spring of 1935, captioned "Comments on American Efficiency" (P5/17/35). "Comrade Stalin teaches us to combine the broad scope of the Russian Revolution with American efficiency," the author began (P4/19/35).[48] He quickly added, however, that America should not be copied; "we have already sufficiently developed our own creative work." "For us," he wrote, "America ought to be that standard according to which we can constantly test our technical attainments."

American heroes and the notion of American national character also faded in the new discourse. Under the heading "USA: We Hate Our Work" appeared a selection of letters from Americans (P12/7/35). "Among us, everything is done under the lash," observed an electrical worker; an Afro-American laborer complained of mechanization; and a labor leader noted that "an engineer at our plants is a hireling, working for the most part without any love or enthusiasm." American heroes also fell from grace, and when Edison died in the fall of 1931, the author of his obituary in *Pravda* wrote, "The 84-year-old Thomas Alva Edison has died; with him into the grave goes a whole epoch of the technological development of capitalism" (P10/20/31). He concluded, "Only in our proletarian state, which has written on its flag—Soviet power plus the electrification of the whole country—will the invention of Edison receive its full and clear illumination."

The journalists' double image of America had little effect on politics, and its partial eclipse went unnoticed. Relations were strained throughout the 1920s, and the United States did not recognize the Soviet Union until 1933, long after other industrial nations had done so. As George F. Kennan observed, "Never were American relations with Russia at a lower ebb than in the first 16 years after the Bolshevik seizure of power in 1917."[49] Yet despite a lack of formal relations, the United States had a unique place in Soviet thinking about the Western world during the 1920s, and, paradoxically, America represented the greatest projection of hopes for Soviet cooperation with the West.

Representation of actual Soviet-American relations in the press involved various issues and events, as well as divisions among party leaders and differences in the functions of the three spheres. America featured obliquely but importantly in the dispute over "socialism in one country" between Trotsky and the opposition, on one hand, and Stalin and Bukharin, on the other. America was Soviet Russia's most plausible and least threatening potential economic partner, and in this sense more interesting to the opposition, who advocated Soviet participation in world markets as well as world revolution, than to Stalin and Bukharin, whose visions of Soviet development were autarchic and isolationist.[50]

The presentation of actual relations became important with the scanty, but nevertheless real, commentary on famine aid to the Soviet Union organized by the American Relief Administration (ARA) in 1921–23. During the period, occasionally hostile articles in the explanatory sphere were interspersed with brief matter-of-fact reports captioned "Help from America" (P4/27/22). *Pravda*'s coverage showed the difference between the informational and explanatory spheres, as well as the party newspaper's leading role.

Hoover's ARA spent roughly $60 million, including a $12 million Soviet contribution from August 1921 through June 1923, and during the summer of 1922, 200 ARA employees worked with 120,000 Soviet citizens to feed roughly 11 million Soviet citizens daily.[51] *Pravda* led in a critique of American aid, expressing the Bolsheviks' ambivalence and anger at accepting American help, as well as their distress at the country's predicament. The tone was set at the outset by Karl Radek, who explained in August 1921 that although the Soviet government had decided to "permit" the bourgeoisie to help the hungry, it had no illusions about the motives of "Mr. Harding" and other bourgeois leaders (P8/2/21).

The regular journalists of *Pravda* largely ignored the ARA operation as it took shape, and they used the famine to criticize the Orthodox church for not selling its valuables to purchase grain.[52] When the *Pravda* journalists took up the relief issue in earnest, they attacked the myth of American qualities that was soon to figure importantly in the active sphere of Soviet newspapers. Aleksandr Zuev, in an article captioned "John and Vanka," portrayed the *Arovtsy*, as the American ARA administrators were called, as greedy, pitiless, and insensitive to the needs of their Russian wards (P4/13/22). John, fat and dressed entirely in yellow leather, sticks to ARA rules and prevents hungry women from sharing the food intended for their children, since "America did not order him to feed big people, only little ones."[53] When young Vanka steals food for his grandmother, he is branded a criminal. The message was echoed in other articles.[54]

Other newspapers were more moderate. *Bednota* published an account in January 1922 captioned "American Aid," with figures on American grain purchases. "The Americans act quickly," the author exclaimed enthusiastically, "in a really American way" (B1/17/22). Two weeks earlier, however, another journalist had explained in the same paper that foreign capitalists were concerned about Russia only because "they cannot get by without Russian raw materials and Russian grain in the future" (B1/6/22). Several months later *Bednota* featured an interview about U.S. aid with Krasin, who announced the aid as a gift which would increase American "popularity" in Russia and give Americans a chance to see the Soviet Union as it was (B3/11/22). Trotsky praised America in the same paper for "unforgettable aid to the hungry masses of Russia." "America," he explained, "saw us as we are" (B8/25/22).

The divergence between the comments in the two types of newspapers is perhaps best explicable in terms of a lack of control or divided purpose. Some Bolsheviks were enthusiastic about the aid, others were not. Both views found their way into the press, although the hostile commentary predominated.[55] The subsequent treatment of practical issues of economic cooperation and recognition was similar. America figured as a hope that was never realized for some; for others the idea of cooperation with the West was illusory. Both views appeared in the press. The author of a short article captioned "Trade with America (The Oil Question)" explained that Soviet Russia did not need Western Europe, only America (P6/18/22). "We can give her oil, which she needs, and receive from her the technological equipment for industry and agriculture," the author wrote. "Tractors from America" was the caption of an article in the peasant paper in 1926; "the dock warehouses of New York are overflowing with tractors, plows, threshers, harvesters, and other agricultural machines purchased for the USSR."

Soviet reporters sometimes wrote as if diplomatic relations would spark an expansive economic partnership. Since Hoover was a man "with a practical mind," a reporter observed in the peasant newspaper, he would understand that without diplomatic relations, there could be no "close economic relations between our proletarian country and America" (KG11/13/28). Yet even under Hoover, the establishment of normal relations proved impossible. The pursuit of the recognition which proved so elusive, however, explains a significant group of articles with references to American opinions and titles such as "American Capitalists about the USSR" (P5/29/24) and "In America They Demand Recognition of the Soviet Union" (KG4/9/26).

Sympathetic Americans were used by Soviet reporters to legitimize policy, as were Westerners generally. Sometimes such articles were so improbable that it is hard to imagine any effect but guffaws, such as one in which a delegation of American workers was quoted as stating that "in the USSR the workers actively participate in the life of the country; the level of production and real wages are higher than they were before the war; private trade is dwindling, and cooperative trade, on the contrary, is growing; the trade unions in the USSR are a powerful force, and they are by no means under the control of the government" (P9/28/27).

The tragedy of American recognition was that when it finally came, in 1933, it was too late to make any difference. Although the possibility for warmer relations was formally present, the conception of an expansion of ties was now foreign to the kind of thinking that predominated in Soviet public discourse. Coverage of the long-awaited moment when Maksim Litvinov went to Washington to settle final outstanding issues with Roosevelt was anticlimactic. The issue of economic or cultural ties was hardly mentioned in *Pravda*, where recognition was presented as a victory for Soviet foreign policy and a positive step in preserving world peace (P11/10–19/33). "The Growth of the Prestige of the USSR in Asia and Europe" was a revealing caption used to head a selection of foreign press reports about the recognition (P11/28/33). The author of the lead editorial on recognition in *Pravda* passed over the advantages of recognition without even considering trade or culture (P11/19/33). Peace had become the government's main concern.

The ambiguous and often positive image of America that had held sway through much of the 1920s was also gone. As long as the possibility of cooperation with capitalist nations remained, a double image of America persisted in the press, and unfavorable characterizations were balanced by favorable ones. The dichotomy lasted only until the end of the 1920s, however. Recognition came too late to weigh in the balance of perceptions. With collectivization, the First Five-Year Plan, and the seemingly endless internal persecutions, the Soviet Union turned inward, and Western opinion did not matter. At the same time, Europe itself slipped into the maelstrom. The idea of Soviet-American cooperation that was raised so often in the Soviet press during the 1920s became one among many paths not taken.

What was most important in the "Americanism" Soviet journalists advocated during the NEP was not the American economic model but the use of American techniques, energy, and human qualities to make Russia a "new proletarian America," in Bukharin's famous phrase (RM3/22/23). This "Americanism" became increasingly "un-American" as the NEP faded and the society Soviet publicists promoted diverged ever more sharply from that of the United States. By the late 1920s, Soviet "Americanism" was subsumed in the Cultural Revolution. The notion of special people who worked like Americans, but for Soviet objectives, became part of the larger effort to reform people, to create a new kind of person. The dream of a new person had permeated the intellectual discourse in Russia from the mid-nineteenth century, but America did not figure importantly in it until the popular culture of the early twentieth.[56] What Soviet publicists did was to borrow the image of the energetic Americans from popular culture and use it to promote Soviet ideals.

Yet the American metaphor was used only by the professional journalists; it was not picked up by the local correspondents and occasional letter writers whose contributions filled out the active sphere. In this respect, enthusiasm for the active Americans had a limited currency. It remained a feature of a metropolitan or authoritarian imagination, something that the activists were unwilling or unable to adopt. The apparent contradiction in the Soviet images of America was not a contradiction at all.

The Bolsheviks promoted American techniques and qualities, while they condemned America itself. This was not just enthusiasm for foreign things.[57] They wanted to use America to build their own future, but they rejected the American future—for themselves and the world. The double use of America as a metaphor for activists and and as the exemplar of the capitalist system illuminates a success and a failure. Bolshevik journalists were so successful in creating a shared purpose among their supporters that they could suggest borrowing American techniques, praise Americans as people to emulate, and use the American metaphor for successful Soviet enterprises without undermining faith in a Communist future. America had a secondary place in the explication of their larger goal, but not a negligible one. They used America with confidence in this sphere of discourse.

The largely negative portrayal of America in the columns for the common readers reveals a corresponding weakness. The journalists condemned America for an impressive assortment of shortcomings, but they were unable to put aside their argument with their readers' belief that life was better in America, freer, and with greater prospects for self-betterment. More damaging was their inability during the 1920s to create a popular Communist success story equivalent to those that figured so importantly in the popular culture of prerevolutionary Russia and of other market economies. Although Soviet journalists promoted social mobility among people of common origins, they did so largely in the columns for the activists.[58] They never succeeded in creating a substitute for the mythology of success that so effectively defused discontent and encouraged aspiration and enterprise in the market economies. Nor did they create an effective equivalent to the prerevolutionary popular media as a mechanism to translate their ideas into popular form. The continuing need to borrow from the rival constructs of an apparently hostile popular imagination testifies to this weakness. So did the prominence of America in the largely unsuccessful efforts to create a Soviet popular literature during the 1920s.[59]

The idea of American qualities circulated long after the 1920s. The Russian American sociologist P. A. Sorokin noted during World War II that "whenever there appears among Russians, an unusually energetic, efficient, inventive, and optimistic type of person he is often nicknamed 'our Russian American.'"[60] Well-executed tasks, he added, were "done in the American way," and fair play was considered a manifestation of "the American spirit." George F. Kennan remarked on a similar sympathy. He identified it as the "friendly and sometimes even admiring interest in the United States—a mixture of curiosity, eagerness for peaceful rivalry, and sometimes even real liking—that runs through the Soviet population."[61] Such stereotypes retain something of their original meanings.

What do we learn from this contorted discourse in which the denunciation of America was often coupled with a belief in its popular idealization, and the promotion of American qualities was linked with so much that was alien to Americans? The contradictory use of America was part of a larger process of cultural fragmentation, by which the dream of the new society and a new type of person was articulated for a limited and sympathetic audience. The discourse for the new local elites in which America figured as a metaphor conveyed confidence. Soviet journalists also articulated a Soviet alternative to the kind of individual success associated with the United States, but these success stories were addressed to those who belonged or wished to belong to the *aktiv*.

The journalists' use of America when they wrote for common readers revealed an uncertainty about shared goals that was perhaps the most tragic cultural legacy of the NEP. The Russian Revolution was a long revolution in the lives of revolutionary intellectuals, and a short one in the experience of ordinary people. As the portrayal of America and Americanism illustrates, the journalists often faltered in their effort to translate revolutionary dreams into a popular idiom, and when they did they appealed to opinions and attitudes they wished to supplant. The failure to find a common language with common readers made force seem a more plausible instrument of policy than persuasion.

## NOTES

1. This essay is part of a larger study of the Soviet press. Research support has come from the National Council for Soviet and East European Research (contract 802-11), the John Simon Guggenheim Memorial Foundation, and the International Research and Exchanges Board. The author would like to thank Lary May, Richard Stites, Sheila Fitzpatrick, and Hans Rogger for their comments.

2. Jürgen Habermas, *The Structural Transformation of the Public Sphere: An Inquiry into a Category of Bourgeois Society* (Boston, 1989).

3. See John Keane, ed., *Civil Society and the State* (London, 1988). The notion of the rebirth of civil society has also figured in studies of the deterioration of authoritarian regimes. See Guillermo O'Donnell and Philippe C. Schmitter, *Transitions from Authoritarian Regimes: Tentative Conclusions about Uncertain Democracies* (Baltimore, 1986).

4. Michael Schudson, *Discovering the News: A Social History of American Newspapers* (New York, 1978), pp. 152–53, describes the place of professionalism and objectivity in American journalism; see also Robert W. Desmond, *Windows on the World: The Information Process in a Changing Society, 1900–1920* (Iowa City, 1980).

5. Habermas, *The Structural Transformation of the Public Sphere*, pp. 175–250, argues that the bourgeois public sphere ceases to exist in the modern period; but whether one agrees with this notion or not, critical commentary remained a part of public discourse in a way that was inconceivable in the Soviet Union, even in the 1920s.

6. I describe communication problems in Jeffrey Brooks, "The Breakdown in the Production and Distribution of Printed Material," in *Bolshevik Culture*, ed. Abbott Gleason et al. (Bloomington, Ind., 1985), pp. 151–74, and "Studies of the Reader in the 1920s," *Russian History*, 2–3 (1982), pp. 187–202. See also "Public and Private Values in the Soviet Press," *Slavic Review* (Spring 1989), pp. 16–35.

7. Brooks, "The Breakdown in the Production and Distribution of Printed Material," pp. 151–74.

8. The classic statement of theories of the roles of newspapers is Fred S. Siebert et al., *Four Theories of the Press* (Urbana, Ill., 1963). The authors distinguish the communist idea of the press from models based on authoritarianism, libertarianism, and social responsibility; Richard Taylor, "Goebbels and the Function of Propaganda," in *Nazi Propaganda*, ed. David Welch (Totowa, N.J., 1983), pp. 29–44.

9. Oron J. Hale, *The Captive Press in the Third Reich* (Princeton, 1964), esp. pp. 233–36; 265–73.

10. Brooks, "The Breakdown in the Production and Distribution of Printed Material."

11. Peter Kenez, *The Birth of the Propaganda State: Soviet Methods of Mass Mobilization* (Cambridge, England, 1985), pp. 47–48.

12. Newspapers are identified as follows: P for *Pravda*, B for *Bednota*, and so on; the first number given is the month, the second the day, and the third the year.

13. Brooks, "The Breakdown in the Production and Distribution of Printed Material," pp. 151–74; Brooks, "Studies of the Reader," pp. 187–202.

14. Angus Roxburgh, *Pravda: Inside the Soviet News Machine* (New York, 1987), p. 9; Ellen Propper Mickiewicz stresses this function among others in *Media and the Russian Public* (New York, 1981), p. 51; See also Peter Kenez, "Lenin and the Freedom of the Press," in Gleason et al., *Bolshevik Culture*, pp. 131–50; Kenez, *The Birth of the Propaganda State*, pp. 1–14; Richard Taylor, *The Politics of the Soviet Cinema, 1917–29* (Cambridge, England, 1979), pp. 26–29; and also Alex Inkeles,

*Public Opinion in Soviet Russia: A Study in Mass Persuasion* (Cambridge, Mass., 1950), pp. 143–74.

15. The spheres described in this essay represent a refinement of the ideas I developed in "Public and Private Values in the Soviet Press, 1921–28," pp. 16–35. For the distinction between general information *(obshchaia informatsiia)* and columns on Party Life, Production, etc., see *Pravda* 12/4/24.

16. Doris A. Graber, *Processing the News* (New York, 1988), discusses the importance of schemata in the organization of information from the media.

17. See Shearon A. Lowery and Melvin L. De Fleur, *Milestones in Mass Communication Research* (New York, 1983, 1988), pp. 327–52, for a description of this research.

18. There is a large literature on counter-readings of popular culture materials, that is, reception that differs from the intention of the producers. See, for example, Jochen Schulte-Sasse, "Toward a 'Culture' for the Masses: The Socio-psychological Function of Popular Literature in Germany and the U.S., 1880–1920," *New German Critique*, no. 29 (Spring/Summer 1983), pp. 85–105.

19. These columns are taken from *Pravda*. There are some variations among the newspapers.

20. The *aktiv* could include nonparty activists as well as active party members during the 1920s when it was still relatively small, as Sosnovskii observes in P7/5/25.

21. *Sovetskaia demokratiia. Sbornik*, ed. Iu. M. Steklov (Moscow, 1929), p. 203; see also V. A. Kozlov, *Kul'turnaia revoliutsiia i krest'ianstvo, 1921–27* (Moscow, 1983), pp. 160–76; G. V. Zhirkov, *Sovetskaia krest'ianskaia pechat'—odin iz tipov sotsialisticheskoi pressy* (Leningrad, 1984).

22. Only 863 party members worked as professional journalists in November 1921, and most of these were part-time (P3/30/22). In Moscow in September 1922, there were only 26 party members working as journalists in the trade union press, 22 in the military press, and 21 in the provincial press (P9/17/22). According to the same source, there were 32 party members working at *Pravda* and 18 working at *Izvestiia*. Vareikis complained as late as 1925 that the development of party cadres in the press was very slow (P8/23/25).

23. Graber, *Processing the News*, pp. 119–78.

24. On popular culture see Jeffrey Brooks, *When Russia Learned to Read: Literacy and Popular Literature, 1861–1917* (Princeton, 1985, 1988), pp. 141–46, 207–209; on intellectual history, see the articles by Hans Rogger, "*Amerikanizm* and the Economic Development of Russia," *Comparative Studies in Society and History*, vol. 23, no. 3 (July, 1981), pp. 382–420; "America in the Russian Mind—or Russian Discoveries of America," *Pacific Historical Review*, vol. 47 (Feb. 1978), pp. 27–51; "America Enters the Twentieth Century: The View from Russia," in *Felder und Vorfelder russischer Geschichte. Studien zu Ehren von Peter Scheibert*, ed. Inge Auerbach et al. (Freiburg, 1985), pp. 387–88; "How the Soviets See Us," in *Shared Destiny*, ed. Mark Garrison and Abbott Gleason (Boston, 1985), pp. 107–46.

25. This is based on a sampling of articles about America published in *Pravda* in the years 1921–28, 1931, 1933, 1935. The sample included every fifth article over twenty inches on a Ducane Manual Direct Projection film reader with the zoom lens expanded to the maximum close-up (roughly 132 lines), and every tenth article of twenty inches or less. All articles about America in *Krest'ianskaia gazeta* 1923–28 were also counted.

26. This is on the basis of my reading of *Pravda, Trud, Rabochaia gazeta, Krest'ianskaia gazeta, Rabochaia Moskva,* and other newspapers.

27. Rogger, "*Amerikanizm*," pp. 391–415; Hans Rogger, "Russia and the Civil War," in *Heard round the World*, ed. Harold Hyman (New York, 1969), pp. 179–256.

28. Rogger, "America in the Russian Mind," pp. 30–31, 40–42.

29. On the promise of America, *Russkoe slovo* (8/29/12, 2/25/11) and *Gazeta kopeika* (2/23/10). The nationalistic and popular journalists at *Russkoe slovo*, Vlas Doroshe-vich and V. S. Nemirovich-Danchenko, were most critical of America. See *Russkoe slovo* (1/24/08 and 4/13/06).

30. Hans Rogger linked Soviet and prerevolutionary ideas under the rubric of *"Amerikanizm"* in three important articles, *"Amerikanizm"; "America in the Russian Mind,"* pp. 27–51; and "America Enters the Twentieth Century," pp. 160–77. He notes the Bolsheviks' different objectives but sees Soviet Americanism as an exten-sion of prerevolutionary traditions and as an alternative to Marxism. *"Amerikanizm,"* pp. 387–88.

31. I discuss this movement in "Popular Philistinism and the Course of Russian Modernism," in *Literature and History: Theoretical Problems and Russian Case Studies,* ed. Gary Saul Morson (Stanford, 1986), pp. 90–110; I discuss the popular success stories in *When Russia Learned to Read,* chapter 8.

32. Brooks, *When Russia Learned to Read,* pp. 141–46, 207–208, 366–67.

33. Ibid., p. 65.

34. Taylor, *The Politics of the Soviet Cinema,* pp. 64–65, 95.

35. Ibid., p. 183, n. 14.

36. Lary May, *Screening Out the Past: The Birth of Mass Culture and the Motion Picture Industry* (Chicago, 1980), p. 109; Sheila Fitzpatrick, *Education and Social Mobility in the Soviet Union, 1921–34* (Cambridge, Mass., 1979), pp. 12–14, on the importance of upwardly mobile workers in Soviet society in the 1920s.

37. May, *Screening out the Past,* p. 216.

38. Ian Christie, "Soviet Cinema: Making Sense of Sound," *Screen,* vol. 23, no. 2 (July–August 1982).

39. On the Soviet attraction for American technology, see Kendall E. Bailes, "The American Connection: Ideology and the Transfer of American Technology to the Soviet Union, 1917–41," *Comparative Studies in Society and History,* vol. 23, no. 3 (July 1981), pp. 421–48.

40. See, for example, early descriptions in *Pravda* 1/24/23, 1/31/23, and 2/2/32. See also the remarks of Gastev, the founder of the Central Institute of Labor (P8/9/23). The idea of the scientific organization of labor and the doings of its many proponents were popularized in regular newspaper columns in the central press in 1922 and the provincial press in 1923 (P1/5/24). See Richard Stites, *Revolutionary Dreams* (New York, 1989), pp. 145–64.

41. See also Kuibyshev's remarks (P3/9/24).

42. S. Shvedov, "Obraz Genri Forda v Sovetskoi publitsistike 1920–1930-x godov," in *Vzaimodeistvie kul'tur SSSR i SShA XVIII–XX vv.* (Moscow, 1987), pp. 133–42, provides some description, but his unsystematic essay is based on an odd collection of professional and technical journals rather than the press as a whole. See also Bailes, "The American Connection," pp. 435–42, and Stites, *Revolutionary Dreams.*

43. See the series by Shafir on "The Miracle of the American Economy" and that of Sosnovskii, "Well, How Are Things at Ford," both in *Rabochaia gazeta* (8/24/26; 8/28/26; 9/3/26; 10/2/26; 1/7/27; 1/16/27; 1/27/27; 2/5/27).

44. Charles S. Maier, "Between Taylorism and Technocracy," *Journal of Contem-porary History,* vol. 5, no. 2 (1970), p. 29.

45. Antonio Gramsci, *Selections from the Prison Notebooks,* edited and translated by Quintin Hoare and Geoffrey Nowell Smith (New York, 1971), pp. 302–303.

46. See, for example, "Ford at Shipka," an article about "Soviet Fords" (*Sovetskie fordy*) (RG1/1/28).

47. See, for example, RM3/29/23.

48. This was not a sample article, but it was so important that I decided to include it for purposes of clarification anyway. The article is by P. A. Bogdanov.

49. George F. Kennan, "After the Cold War," *New York Times Magazine*, February 5, 1989, p. 32.

50. Richard B. Day, *Leon Trotsky and the Politics of Economic Isolation* (Cambridge, England, 1973).

51. H. H. Fisher, *The Famine in Soviet Russia, 1919–23* (New York, 1927), pp. 553, 556–57; Benjamin M. Weissman, *Herbert Hoover and Famine Relief to Soviet Russia, 1921–23* (Stanford, 1974); Bert Patenaude, "Say It Ain't So Comrade: Hoover's ARA in NEP Russia," unpublished public lecture, Stanford University, November 19, 1987.

52. There were few early comments on the ARA effort in *Pravda, Krest'ianskaia gazeta, Bednota,* or *Rabochaia gazeta.* It is conceivable, however, since not all of these runs were complete, that an article or two may have escaped me.

53. The ARA initially directed its aid to children, but it later opened its cafeterias to all hungry people.

54. P5/11/22; P7/1/23. The only sympathetic coverage in *Pravda* was a formal exchange of statements between Kalinin and the ARA, published in September 1922 (P9/8/22; P9/16/22). *Pravda* also published the ARA's own statement pursuant to ending the famine aid (P3/11/23).

55. The mass newspaper for workers *(Rabochaia gazeta)* had little to say about the ARA, although reporters found space to describe the incidental aid by American workers (RG10/7/22).

56. See Régine Robin, *Le réalisme socialiste: une aesthétique impossible* (Paris, 1986), forthcoming in English from Stanford University Press, for a discussion of literary aspects of this concern with a renewal of Russia.

57. Richard Stites stresses this point with respect to the cult of Ford and Taylor in *Revolutionary Dreams,* p. 148; David Joravsky links Taylorism with scientific rationality in *Russian Psychology: A Critical History* (Oxford, 1989), p. 344.

58. Jeffrey Brooks, "Information and Power: The Soviet Paradigm for Revolutionary Cultural Change, 1921–28," Final Report to the National Council for Soviet and East European Research, March 1985.

59. The best-known example is Marietta Shaginian's serial *Mess Mend, or a Yankee in Petrograd* and the sequel, *Laurie Lane, Metalworker.* The original versions are reprinted in Marietta Shaginian, *Sobranie sochinenii,* vols. 3–4 (Moscow, 1935). In volume 1, p. 71, she explains that the serials were reprinted in Comintern publications. Carol Avins, *Border Crossings: The West and Russian Identity in Soviet Literature, 1917–34* (Berkeley, 1983), discusses the place of *Mess Mend* in literary presentations of the West. Other examples include A. I. Evstigneev's "The Struggle for the Warm Current," in *Bednota* in April and May of 1922, and Ia. Okunev's "The World of the Future—A Utopian Novel," in *Rabochaia gazeta* (11/2/22, nos. 202–24). See also Stites, *Revolutionary Dreams,* pp. 180–81.

60. Pitirim A. Sorokin, *Russia and the United States* (New York, 1944), pp. 170–71.

61. George F. Kennan, *The Nuclear Delusion* (New York, 1976), p. 45.

# XV

# POPULAR LITERATURE
# OF THE 1920s
## RUSSIAN PEASANTS AS READERS

### Régine Robin

Russian peasants did not become readers, either on the morrow of the revolution or during the NEP. Only in the thirties, in the aftermath of forced collectivization and the mass literacy campaign of the 1920s, did certain strata of the peasantry start to assimilate not only the current vocabulary but also the new constructivist ethos of the positive hero.

This essay, part of a research project on Soviet reading and readers in the late 1920s and 1930s, focuses on the influence of the reader and of popular taste on the development of the official aesthetic that became known as socialist realism. Methodologically, the essay draws on an important movement in literary theory concerned with the act of writing and its reception. Within the structure of this project I have defined four types of readers and reading.

The first type comprises the ideal, "longed-for," or "utopian" readers as defined by the authorities: typical, average readers, who did not exist, sociologically speaking, but who were given stature as the new workers and peasants, who had triumphed over illiteracy, "peasant superstitions," and "petit-bourgeois" practices, as well as alcoholism and everyday violence. These ideal readers were the new docile but active Soviet citizens. They were peasants who had abandoned the traditional reading matter of the semiliterate: hagiographies, tales of knights and of simpletons, almanacs sold at fairs, and songbooks for evening gatherings. They were workers who had turned their backs on serialized literature and dime-store novels *(kopeiki)*, where Tarzan, highwaymen, and the adventures of some prodigal son made up the usual fare. The old culture of oral tradition or urban dime-store novels was replaced by new rural newspapers, featuring agronomy, political discourse, and new positive heroes such as Gladkov's Gleb

Chumalov, the hero of the novel *Cement*. These ideal readers were coopted in the thirties by the "ideal reading" postulated by the critics, who channeled reading in a monological direction, which dulled its messages, reduced their complexity, and served as a reading guide for the semiliterate masses. In this connection the concept of "plebeianization of culture," suggested by Marc Ferro, is very useful.

The second type of reader, the "reading character," was involved in the literary work of the twenties and thirties. Literature distributed by reading clubs, libraries, and newspapers played a key role in the development of this new social imagination. I have previously studied the pressure that readers put on writers, especially in Moscow at the 1st Congress of Soviet Writers in 1934.[1] Here, I wish to examine the way in which narrators treated the readers or reading characters in their texts, the books they were assigned to read, the system of evaluation to which they were subjected, and the message disseminated through narration by their reading activity. While stressing the concepts of sociocriticism (cotext, effect of asides, textual referents), I will analyze what the work's narratee (the narrator's fictive, implicit, accessory reader) knows and values in common with the narrator in order to decode the work.

I believe that there is a tension between the role of the reader-reading in the work, the positive hero or antisubject who develops a univocal, monosemic message, and the role attributed to the narratee, who enlists, even within the univocal structure of *romans à thèse*, hybridity, heterogeneousness, and plurilingualism. I will try to measure the disparity between the political authorities' "ideal" reader and the reader "represented," imagined by the literary authorities.

Third, there is the sociological axis, "real" readers and their development. Not much has been written about this topic, except for Jeffrey Brooks's outstanding works and those by Nicolas Werth on popular reading in the countryside. I will rely in addition on a number of unpublished works and on my own research to define these "real" readers and their development. Sources, although scattered, exist. Several serious studies done in the twenties can be used as a starting point.[2] Similar material is available for the thirties.[3] These real readers must be studied according to their rural or urban origins and their social milieu. A special source are the women's clubs and their specific reactions to portrayals of female characters in novels.

It is possible to construct a sociology of Soviet readership during the twenties and thirties. Documentation, although unsystematic and scattered, does exist, but analysis has not been undertaken because the overall problematic of most researchers has prevented them from asking such questions about the thirties, a time when "Stalinism" supposedly accounted for everything, and when people were supposed to have read only what the government wanted them to read. My hypothesis is that within the structure of an ideological and literary orthodoxy and ferocious censorship, readers were more active than has been acknowledged. Indeed, peasant readers projected their ancestral mental habits, traditions, and individual and collective fantasies onto the book to such an extent that they inadequately deciphered the messages that the government intended these works to instill.

The entire sociology of reading points to the active, dynamic, complex character of reading. I will attempt to show that active reading within Soviet society of the 1920s, far from being a reading of the *typical,* was syncretic; onto the positive hero it projected Tarzan, Pugachev and his rebellions, Saint George overcoming the dragon, Ivan the simpleton, the *bogatyri* of the *chansons de geste,* and traditional *byliny.* Reading and its reception were uncontrollable in this sense and held many surprises.

Finally, the fourth axis, the reader-author, is the most fascinating to analyze. This category deals with the production of writing by this type of reader who, at a certain point, became a reader-reporter, *rabkor* or *sel'kor,* a worker or peasant correspondent, who participated in agitation theatre, the formulation of watchwords and slogans, and the organization of new holidays (principally May 1 and the anniversary of the October Revolution). This category involved the writing of articles and essays in a genre that developed in the twenties and thirties, the sketch or *ocherk.*

My aim is to reconstruct the history of these worker and peasant correspondents, to draw up a typology, and to analyze the popular cultural productions that grew out of them: wall posters, *agitki* (agitation plays), songs, *bouts rimés* rooted in ancient folklore and renewed in politics, articles sent to newspapers, reporting competitions, short novels, new folklore (taken from the oral tradition, epic songs and poems dealing with knights, but which in their traditional form were about Lenin, Stalin, kolkhozes, etc.), and workers' and peasants' autobiographies.

These four axes, through sociological approaches, textual analysis, and the qualitative and quantitative processes of the historian of mentalités, should uncover an unexplored continent: mentalités; cultural syncretism; "tinkering" between the old traditional forms and the new ideological norms; conflicting articulation between an old and a new ideological acculturation which was accepted only because reading could project onto it systems of location and identification that included the old values, while shifting their emphasis. Within the structure of these four axes I will consider a number of issues.

The end of the NEP witnessed a certain setback on the cultural front. The campaigns against illiteracy had not produced the intended results.

The 1926 census and the results of surveys on literacy showed that 55 percent of the rural population was still illiterate, and 40 percent of seven- to eleven-year-old children had not yet been provided with schooling. According to Ia. Shafir, of the 3,200 daily copies of *Pravda* distributed in Voronezh in May 1924, 1,150 were sent to rural soviets and party cells and 930 went to rural clubs. There were 216 subscribers, 90 percent of whom were distributors. In this province of 3 million inhabitants, only 617 copies were sold individually.[4] How do we explain this?

The Bolsheviks, for the most part, had their roots in urban culture and the Enlightenment. Despite their discourse on the necessary alliance be- tween workers and peasants, they had inveterate ideological and cultural prejudices against the peasantry. This relative blindness shaped their whole cultural policy and their inability to take into account, consciously at least, the immense heritage of the traditional, oral culture.

The Bolsheviks did not manage, within the structure of the campaign against illiteracy and the reorganization of cultural institutions, to make themselves understood by the peasants and the masses in general. In 1922, Ia. Shafir undertook a journey in the Voronezh region on behalf of the Central Committee's agitation-propaganda section. He described this trip in his book *Gazeta i derevnia*. Shafir observed that, generally speaking, newspapers had neither subscribers nor readers in the Russian country- side. They were used mainly to roll cigarettes. Furthermore, peasants did not know how to read the paper. They understood neither the vocabulary nor the syntax.

Shafir reported on a survey conducted in a Red Army battalion regard- ing an article published in *Pravda* on March 14, 1923, about the assassina- tion of the Soviet ambassador Vorovskii in Lausanne. The article was entitled "The Impertinence of Killers." Problems began with the title. No one understood its meaning, but each respondent thought about it and racked his brains, repeating "The Impertinence of Killers." At last, one of the recruits had a flash of inspiration: "It means: they really killed him, not just hurt him. . . ." Obviously, no one had heard of Vorovskii or the foreign minister, Chicherin. No one knew what an ambassador was. Some of them had a vague idea of what Switzerland was: "a country over yonder." A "diplomatic note" was "a big noise." No one understood the meaning of the sentence "The Swiss government refuses to give the Soviet government satisfaction on this point." "What satisfaction are they talking about?" asked one. "Who is happy?" asked another. "What point? A man is dead," said the third. The following sentence left everyone puzzled: "This attitude of the Swiss government only reveals its complicity in the murder case of C. Vorovskii." They did not understand the words *reveals* or *complicity*, the use of *only*, or the abbreviation *C.* for *Comrade* (in Russian *T.* for *tovarishch*).[5]

The same survey, conducted among sixty-four soldiers who read the newspaper regularly, confirmed that the vocabulary was not understood. Werth listed the number of readers who did not understand certain words:

| | |
|---|---|
| USSR | 8 |
| sovnarkom | 10 |
| territory | 10 |
| class enemy | 12 |
| anecdote | 16 |
| horizon | 19 |
| officially | 21 |
| diplomatic note | 22 |
| system | 23 |
| ultimatum | 24 |
| regularly | 26 |
| element | 28 |
| initiative | 31 |
| complicity | 33 |
| occupation | 36 |
| publicity | 40 |
| memorandum | 42 |
| intrigue | 46 |
| reparations | 48[6] |

The peasants understood neither subordinate clauses nor abbreviations. Unable to understand the meaning of what was written in the papers, some peasants requested translations, "so that everything may be explained in our language, on a special page." Others asked that more be written about country life.

A. M. Selishchev stated that political language remained inaccessible to the Russian peasantry. Furthermore, new terms used by peasants lost some of their abstract character and took on new meanings. Peasants assimilated only the semantic aspects directly related to the functions of country life. They not only altered pronunciations, they also "remotivated" words, referring in some cases to folk etymology.

| | |
|---|---|
| Kamunist, Kamenist | one who does not believe in God |
| Karlo Mars | it's like Lenin |
| Komsomolets, Kosomolets | grind crookedly |
| Kosorylyi | reminiscent of "twisted mouth, it's like Communists" |
| Proletaria | the poor |
| Rekvizirovat' | to remove the wheat |
| Sitsializm | 1. it's living in the new way |
| Sitsializma | 2. I don't know, but I use it |

The Soviet press's inaccessibility to the popular masses was unanimously
noted. Lenin mounted a campaign against newspapers' style and what was,
in his opinion, their too-frequent recourse to foreign words.[7]

V. Karpinskii, in the December 12, 1923, edition of *Pravda*, and L.
Sosnovskii, at the Worker Correspondents' Congress (*Pravda*, November
21, 1923), severely criticized the Soviet press's methods. Karpinskii said
that the press's language was nothing more than slang elaborated by a
privileged minority. It was full of barbarisms, lexical as well as syntactic,
that were incomprehensible to workers and peasants. Sosnovskii proposed
reconciling newspaper language with the peasants' language by shortening
sentences (simple people do not use subordinates) and reducing the vocabulary (the muzhik's vocabulary was composed of only 2,000 words). Shafir[8]
and V. Mints[9] shared the same point of view: It is necessary to try to
reconcile literary language with popular language, to use more verbs and
fewer nouns, to replace bookish turns of speech with everyday expressions.

But it was a viewpoint opposite to that of linguists such as Vinokur,
Iakubinskii, and Shcherba. While aware of the communication problems
presented by the press, they were absolutely opposed to reconstructing
literary discourse in the image of the middle reader. They believed it was
necessary to educate the masses, to raise their cultural level. Shil'rein[10] as
well as L. Uspenskii[11] defended an intermediate position. In brief, toward
the end of the twenties when the results of the cultural NEP appeared
unsatisfactory, cultural authorities were still wondering how they could
reconcile ordinary speech with poetic speech, on the one hand, and popular language with the new language of the government, on the other
hand.

The very notion of the emergence of a new mass reader did not facilitate
the integration of the peasantry into the new cultural power. It was a
paternalistic and patronizing notion that was constantly aimed at instilling
good reading, like a catechism, and protecting the masses from bad reading. As a prophylactic, the government promoted collective reading intended to facilitate social control and superimpose ideological and symbolic
values. Peter Kenez reports the following comment made by Nadezhda
Krupskaia in 1924 when, while in charge of the purification of libraries,
she came upon a list of books to be banned.

> In the circular there was no "defect," yet a defect was there all the same. To
> the circular was affixed a thoroughly unfortunate list of books, a list com-
> piled by the Commission for the Reexamination of Books, attached to the
> circular I had signed, without my knowledge. As soon as I saw this list I
> cancelled it. Why was this list unfortunate? In the first place because it was
> beside the mark. In it it was said that it was necessary to remove from the
> mass libraries Plato, Kant, Mach—in general, idealists. That idealist
> philosophers are harmful people is beyond question. But their presence in a

library for peasants or the worker masses is not harmful at all, it is senseless: a man of the masses will not read Kant. Hence the "list" did not alter matters in any way. Much worse was the fact that the list of books to be removed in the field of "religion" was extremely limited.[12]

This purely normative conception of mass readers did not take tastes or popular demand into account.

Jeffrey Brooks recently demonstrated the existence at the end of the old regime of a mass culture that also reached the countryside. First of all, there was the *lubochnaia literatura* with its religious and legendary heroic themes. In the second half of the nineteenth century there emerged a mass belletristic literature with secular themes and a large number of bandits. Rural literacy became more common, and non-*lubok* books filtered into the villages. Culturist intellectuals studied the reading public and its problems. Anski[13] relates that peasants engaged in three types of reading, books about religion, fairy tales, and secular themes, and that their reading values had been formed through their contact with religious books. These values included the sanctity of reading, expectation of truthfulness in printed matter, display of emotion when confronted with the text, and expectation of a moral from the text. At the beginning of the twentieth century adventure stories, from Tarzan to Nick Carter, were fashionable.

The Bolsheviks in power found themselves disabled in the face of this mass production. They reacted by suppressing it while trying to promote a new culture and a new literature, while facing the issue of whether or not to preserve the classical heritage. But they were on their guard against potential heresy in the heritage of popular, oral, and legendary mass culture.

In the area of the new mass culture, experimentation was primary. In the early twenties, it seemed obvious that an appeal could be made to the new audience if literature utilized such substandard plot-oriented genres as mystery, romance, or science fiction. The official encouragement of Nikolai Bukharin, an influential Soviet politician who believed that popular literature had a legitimate place within the new culture, led to the creation of sovietized versions of Western popular literature. *Krasnyi* Pinkerton or Red Detective enjoyed broad appeal. The works of Jack London were also popular, not to mention science fiction such as A. N. Tolstoy's *Aelita,* and Soviet versions of adventure and detective novels. Marietta Shaginian made her name with the latter. Her *Mess Mend ili Ianki v Petrograde* (1923–1924) and *Lori Len metallist* (1925) pleased the public with their adventures and their style, integrating cinematic techniques. Those works made use of a parodic, ironic play on the clichés and stereotypes of the former popular literature. The public, oblivious to the parody, liked this literature precisely because it reinforced mental habits and internalized clichés. This flood of literature was so great that Viktor Shklovskii proposed not only that the

Bolsheviks take an interest in cinema, journalism, and avant-garde literature—so far removed from the masses—but that they study mass literature
closely and not scorn it.

Therefore, there was, on the one hand, elitist experimentation and, on
the other hand, the empty space of a new mass culture. What appeared was
not aimed at the peasants. Books sent to the countryside did not suit
peasant readers. The peasant public did not like being called *muzhik*. It did
not appreciate the paternalism and condescension with which it was addressed. More important, the peasants detested *skaz* and all imitations of
peasant speech in writing, feeling that they were being made fun of. Even
the regime's efforts in the agronomic field were not always crowned with
success; the agricultural books were too general and did not take geographic and climatic particularities into account. Peter Kenez emphasizes:

> The basic problems besetting Soviet publishing remained unsolvable: At a
> time of a shortage of funds, how could they produce enough books? How
> could they get the books to the readers? How could they persuade the
> peasants to read what the Party leaders believed they should read? How
> could they produce books that were both ideologically useful and at the same
> time written in a language the peasants found attractive? Where could they
> find enough cadres who could write books for village readers? During the
> NEP period the Soviet regime succeeded in depriving the peasants of books
> it considered harmful. It did not yet have the strength to make the peasants
> read what it wanted them to read.[14]

Strangely enough, this relative failure paved the way for a new generation of readers and tastes. The following examples illuminate the yearning
for culture and the utopian enthusiasm of the twenties. A demobilized
poor peasant, thirty-eight years old, wrote to the editor of *Krest'ianskaia
gazeta* (1922):

> I thank you for your book and for the newspaper. Long live Marxism! Long
> live Leninism and the Communist proletariat all over the world! And long
> live our Union of Soviet Socialist Republics! And long live science that
> advances, not so that we'll kill ourselves, but so we can make electricity and
> one day grow bread without making such an effort. In any case, I un-
> derstand that one day science will produce artificial bread. Next, I confirm
> that I understood everything in the book *The Marvels of Thought and Reality*.
> The cover and illustrations are very good, very clear.[15]

The second example is a letter from a poor demobilized peasant in charge
of a rural club, in an editorial in *Krest'ianskaia gazeta* (1921):

> Send me a list of books published on the following subjects because I'm
> interested in everything: chemistry, science, technology, the planets, the sun,
> the earth, the planet Mars, world maps, books on aviation, the number of

planes we possess, the number of enemies the Union of Soviet Socialist Republics has, books on comets, stars, water, the earth and the sky.[16]

The enthusiasts, the new semiliterate cadres, the members of *aktivy*, the agit-prop, and the Komsomol in the countryside, were leaned on by the new cultural regime and constituted the target of the new cultural apparatus.

What were these avid new readers reading? Writers who toured factories, Red gathering places, and the reading izbas of kolkhozes and who were in contact with reading clubs always returned with the same demands. In 1927 the writer Serafimovich held a discussion with workers from the reading club of a Leningrad metallurgical factory. He was taken aside by workers complaining of finding only "bad language"—curses, colloquial language, and gibberish—in literature. However much Serafimovich tried to explain that the tongue uses everyday language, that life is often dirty and crude, and that one should not, therefore, always expect to see "good language," nothing would make them listen.[17] This reaction (similar to positions later taken by Gorky) was widespread. The search for good speech could even be turned against Gorky himself, against his novel *Mother,* considered, however, to be the precursor of socialist realism:

> Those who read the classics (usually the most "cultivated" peasants) are also looking for "good style," "beautiful descriptions," and "good speech" in literature. In this respect, the comment of a reader is revealing: Does M. Gorky not have any education? People should not be allowed to read that kind of book! Is that why books are written? To learn to swear, one does not need Gorky's help.[18]

In 1927 T. Kholodnyi gave an account of a "Communist Saturday" where readers stated their impressions and demands. The participants wanted books for relaxation. They rejected political lessons and begged for action, for contemporary everyday life. Kholodnyi explained: "Writers have gotten a proper dressing down. Even those who praised *Cement* reproached its author for his 'bad language,' his coarse language tinged with literature."[19] The mannered style and imitation of popular speech were criticized: *skaz* and ornamental prose were denounced. Workers also protested that they recognized themselves only in realistic and psychologizing forms. One of them declared: "What is good about old novels is that you see the whole of life. *You read them and see everything as if you were there:* a man is born . . . he is very small . . . he grows, the rascal. . . . And little by little, you see him become a man. . . . you see him live, and then die. That's what's important." Kholodnyi concluded: "The mind of the masses is expressed in that tirade."[20]

As the crusade against illiteracy moved into full swing, some extensive surveys and the Smolensk Archives give us a rough estimate of the tastes of actual readers, the true reception of literature (not that of the critics): library inventories, responses to surveys on reading, etc. Werth describes a survey of 360 young peasant readers, aged sixteen to twenty-four, in the Leningrad region. The nine works in greatest demand were:

| | |
|---|---|
| Neverov | *Tashkent, khlebnyi gorod* |
| Furmanov | *Chapaev* |
| | *Krasnyi desant* |
| Seifullina | *Virineia* |
| Dorokhov | *Ob Irtyshe* |
| Sinclair | *King Coal* |
| Serafimovich | *Zheleznyi potok* |
| Jack London | *The Sea Wolf* |
| Sikachev | *Kulak*[21] |

Other works in great demand were simple short stories used in basic reading classes such as "The Life of Avdotina," opposing alcoholism, and "Andrew Good-for-Nothing," combating the ill effects of ignorance. The Russian classics were represented by Chekhov, Tolstoy *(Anna Karenina),* and Pushkin *(The Captain's Daughter).* Foreign classics, from London and Hugo to Zola, made up 18 percent of the books represented.

Neither proletarian best-sellers *(Cement* by Gladkov) nor avant-gardists (Mayakovsky) were represented. Werth commented on this survey:

> Thus, among the most-read books, there are six adventure stories, which take place during the initial "heroic" years of the Soviet regime, two "foreign classics," dedicated to the worker's fight against money, one book about the "social reality" of the village, and only one book that belongs to the Russian classics. Generally speaking, adventure novels and spy stories that take place during the revolution and the Civil War constitute the nucleus of all rural libraries. All of these books (several hundred are listed) present some legendary Chekist or a brave soldier from the Red Army fighting victoriously against the White Guards and spies of a foreign power, and exalt a revolutionary romanticism to which the youngest readers (16 to 20 years), for whom the 1917–1920 era has already become a part of mythology, are particularly sensitive.[22]

Readers demanded not avant-gardist literature but writing that was readable and with which they could identify, material that provided an escape from daily life and at the same time idealized daily life. Popular audiences wanted linear plots, a spirit of adventure, revolutionary heroism and romanticism, lively dialogue, realistic scope, verisimilar background.

If mass readers wanted something new, it was thematic novelty: a Red Tolstoy, or even a Red Tarzan. Purely formal plays on language such as Khlebnikov's *Zaum* never hit it off with the masses; they preferred respectability and conformity in literature.

I have referred to "plebeianization." Marc Ferro has used the term *popular absolutism* to designate mass pressure that at times exceeded what the leaders were calling for.[23] In a similar vein, it did not require the April 22, 1932, decree imposing socialist realism for the masses to have succeeded in imposing their thirst for adventure and for heroes after their own image, their need to idealize an uncertain and rude present or to escape into the heroic past of Pugachev's and Stenka Razin's rebellions or popular tales revived through modern folklore.

Cultural plebeianization corresponded with orders from above, but, we may ask, plebeianization with respect to what and to whom? If the readers of the thirties are to be compared with the reading minority during the years immediately preceding the revolution, we can definitely point to a plebeianization, although the existence of a popular culture during the 1900s should not be forgotten. In the postrevolutionary period, the great campaign against illiteracy and the participation of workers and peasants in cultural development—although directed and supervised—resulted in autobiographies, factory histories, histories of particular localities during the Civil War, stories and tracts concerning everyday life, dekulakization, industrialization, and the campaign against alcoholism; individual or collective endeavors to write fiction, real-life sketches, portraits from factory correspondents, new bards springing up from the countryside and the cities and from national minorities in particular, and the revival of oral traditions. Despite the growing authoritarian character of the regime—and this is not the least of the contradictions with which the researcher is confronted—a whole new discourse was emerging. The fact that this new discourse may have been considered phony, delinquent, directed, and channeled in no way changes the phenomenon.

If this genuine cultural revolution is taken into account, the notion of "plebeianization" becomes a comparative one. The fact remains that this vast new discourse was another expression—this time from below—of the authoritarian word. It came into conflict with all those who gave priority, not to normalization of language but rather to changes in the way of life. Popular wisdom is not necessarily the path to innovation.

Peasant readers wanted a *readable* aesthetics. This led to conflicts between the elite and the rank and file at the level of language, representation, and message. In the late nineteenth and early twentieth centuries, numerous theorists, authors, and thinkers had already noted the Russian peasants' passion for verisimilitude. In iconography, we can trace the evolution from the traditional peasant *lubok* drawings to realism and relief. The *lubki* entered into the aesthetics of verisimilitude and mimesis. Although the avant-garde reused the traditional, naive *lubok*, popular taste settled on so-called authentic representation.

Narratologists describe a realist position that transcends the various schools and their different views. The realist project postulates a real and material external and knowable world (the extratext); it postulates that this reality "enters" the text by way of transparent writing that expresses it, and that the elements of the text are organized in such a way as to find themselves homologous to the various elements organized in the extratextual reality. Realist writing shows us a world identical to the real world and in the same spatio-temporal relationship.

Through this "mimetic" writing device, readers believe they are dealing with the real world, with something that relates itself through the transparency of the narration. This has been called the "referential illusion." In order for this illusion to be effective, the realistic text must be readable, devoid of harshness and opacity. Readability implies the setting up of a hypotactic device that guarantees the stability of the signs, the cohesion, the coherence, and the consistency of the textual universe which mimics or shows the extratextual universe. Such a device aims to ensure the transit of reading: necessity, adjacency, and metonymical relationships; stability of the actants, of the narrative functions, of the narrator's status; isotopic coherence; in other words, the presence of all the elements that guarantee logical and semantic coherence: anaphora, discrypticisms, redundancies, repetitions, recalls, enhancement of flashbacks, of prolepses, of commentaries.

To be effective, this referential illusion still needs a certain mode of narrative presence. Even if the point of view shifts, one will always notice a tendency toward omniscience, since the narrator per se must be as invisible as possible. Of course, one can always trace the narrator's voice in the text, in the form of detachable statements, maxims, locutions, or clichés which reinforce readability. Furthermore, the realistic text presupposes a transparency in writing, which as the vehicle and instrument of communication is the medium of representation, the means of expression. Second in rank, with respect to reality, it helps to designate it, to display and to judge it.

I have stressed this encounter between what became socialist realism and pressure from the first generation of readers, which included many peasants, because it seems to me that this phenomenon has not been given sufficient emphasis. What is more, it certainly seems that the relationship between realism and the popular masses from the nineteenth century onward, the industrial revolutions, the modernization and transformation of rural life, and the secularization of everyday life were coessential. P. J. Proudhon dreamed in this way of a people's aesthetics:

> I would give the Louvre, the Tuileries, Notre Dame—with the pillar thrown in—to have my own little house, built to my liking, where I would live alone, in the center of a small tenth-of-a-hectare piece of land where I would have water, shade, grass, and silence. Were I to erect a statue, it would be neither

Apollo nor Jupiter: I have nothing to do with those gentlemen, nor London's, nor Rome's, nor Constantinople's, nor Venice's sights—heaven forbid me from living there. I would put what I lack there: mountains, vineyards, prairies, goats, cows, sheep, harvesters, little shepherds.[24]

More recently, Pierre Bourdieu has demonstrated that given a photograph representing a woman's hands, a sample of people questioned in a survey on tastes was divided between those of bourgeois and intellectual origin, who emphasized the form, the material, the art ("What a pretty picture"), and those of popular origin, who saw the content—a representation, "pretty hands,"—and voiced a moral appraisal. Bourdieu adds:

One cannot *completely* understand the support that Zhdanov's theses, very close to Proudhon on more than one point, received without taking into account the similarities between his "aesthetics" and the popular or petit-bourgeois ethos of a fraction of the leaders of the Communist Party.[25]

I do not mean to suggest that socialist realism was purely and simply the insertion of a popular aesthetics into the official aesthetics. The matter is infinitely more complex. Socialist realism emerged from the encounter between three positions: political and didactic directives from above; a debate within the literary milieu, which from the beginning of the twenties had been quarreling over the search for a new realism; and the need, coming from the popular masses, to renew an aesthetics of the readable and clear message. Socialist realism grew out of a syncretism that aimed for the establishment of a consensus, by providing a middle ground where four social sources could coalesce. The state imposed the primacy of politics and ideology; the old intelligentsia attained recognition of its *savoir-écrire;* the former proletarian writers contributed their enthusiasm and their activating force; and the popular masses renewed an aesthetics of representation that permitted them entrance to this new high culture. All this is to suggest that the peasant reader played an active role in the genesis of socialist realism, contrary to previously accepted views.

I will conclude with a few words on the issue of peasant reading itself. Although we know or are beginning to understand what the peasants did or did not like, we do not know how they interpreted what they read, what went on in their imaginations. Reading is an active, plural, and heterogeneous process. Reception, even in an aesthetics that is meant to be clear and monological, can never be completely controlled. There are misinterpretations, corruptions of meanings that have surprises in store. What proof is there that the popular masses took the morals of the *romans à thèse* literally, that they did not project onto the positive heroes the decoding models of the adventure stories of which they were so fond? If this hypothesis has some validity, it should force us to take seriously reading in its double movement: that by which the social imagination is formed and at the same time that which resists closure and the narrowing of meaning.[26]

NOTES

1. Robin, *Le Réalisme socialiste: une esthétique impossible* (Paris, 1986).
2. During the twenties, for example, the works of Ia. Shafir, *Gazeta i derevnia* (Moscow, 1923); A. M. Selishchev, *Iazyk revoliutsionnoi epokhi* (Moscow, 1928); A. M. Bol'shakov, *Derevnia 1917–1927* (Moscow, 1927); N. Rosnitskii, *Litso derevni* (Moscow/Leningrad, 1926); M. I. Slukhovskii, *Kniga i derevnia* (Moscow/Leningrad, 1928); the 1924 Izba Libraries Competition in *Pravda;* and the memoirs of worker correspondents, such as, for example, I. Zhiga's work *Dumy rabochikh, zaboty dela (Zapiski rabkora)* (Moscow, 1929).
3. For example, *Trud*'s 1935 survey; press reports of reading clubs' activities; reports of writers' trips to factories and the countryside at the height of the dekulakization period or immediately afterward; readers' letters about novels or plays which, despite censorship and a certain "teleguidance" one must know how to measure and interpret, give an approximate idea of average tastes and of infatuations and refusals; the editions and reeditions of certain novels whose line was not necessarily the most official, but which attained great success nonetheless; the inventory of libraries and of the Smolensk Archives.
4. N. Werth, *La Vie quotidienne des paysans russes de la révolution à la collectivisation* (Paris, 1984), p. 237.
5. Quoted by Werth, "Alphabétisation et idéologie en Russie soviétique," *Vingtième siècle,* 10 (April–June 1986), p. 26.
6. Werth, *Vie quotidienne,* pp. 239–40.
7. *Lénine et les questions de langue* (Moscow, 1982).
8. Ia. Shafir, "O iazyke massovoi literatury," *Knigonosha,* 39 (1924).
9. V. Mints, "O nauchnoi postanovke izucheniia chitatelia," *Knigonosha,* 42 (1924).
10. Shil'rein, *Iazyk krasnoarmeitsa* (1928).
11. L. Uspenskii, "Russkii iazyk posle revoliutsii," *Slavia,* 10, no. 2 (1931).
12. P. Kenez, *The Birth of the Propaganda State* (Cambridge, England, 1985), p. 248.
13. J. Brooks, *When Russia Learned to Read* (Princeton, 1985); Anski, *The People and the Book* (1894; 1913).
14. Kenez, *Birth,* pp. 249–50.
15. Werth, "Alphabétisation," p. 27.
16. Ibid.
17. Quoted in L. Iddir-Spindler, "La Résolution de 1925 à l'épreuve de la pratique. Littérature soviétique et lutte contre l'opposition d'après la *Pravda* de 1927," *Les Cahiers du monde russe et soviétique,* 21, no. 3–4 (July–December 1980), pp. 361–99.
18. Quoted by Werth, *Vie quotidienne,* p. 232.
19. Iddir-Spindler, "Résolution," p. 380.
20. Ibid.
21. Werth, *Vie quotidienne,* pp. 229–30.
22. Ibid., p. 230.

23. M. Ferro, *Des Soviets au communisme bureaucratique* (Paris, 1980), p. 230.

24. P. J. Proudhon, *Du principe de l'Art et de sa destinée sociale, Oeuvres complètes*, t. II (Paris, 1939), p. 256.

25. P. Bourdieu, *La Distinction, critique sociale du jugement* (Paris, 1979), p. 52, n. 51.

26. I wish to thank Henry Elbaum for the help and information he gave me during the writing of this essay.

# XVI

## POPULAR SONG IN THE NEP ERA

### Robert A. Rothstein

The slogan "Carry Through the Struggle against Nepman Music" represented for a time one side in the competition for the Soviet mass musical audience in the first fifteen years after the October Revolution. While the Russian Association of Proletarian Musicians (RAPM), publisher of a 110-page tract with that title,[1] did manage to occupy the commanding heights in the Soviet musical world for a while, it was a political rather than a musical victory.

The "Nepman music" that the public preferred was primarily an urban product. There were songs published as sheet music, which probably remained largely in the cities among those who had pianos, musical education, and middle-class aspirations. There were also songs that were not published or were published only in popular songbooks (collections of texts) and reproduced as well in handwritten notebooks or albums.[2] These songs represented a kind of urban folklore that spread far beyond the big cities to workers and peasants all over the country. Examining some examples of both kinds of "Nepman music" can give us a sense of the moods and tastes of the 1920s—before a single, official musical culture took over.

At the time of the revolution, music publishing in Russia had had a history of nearly a century and a half. The first publication of Russian songs with music dates from 1776, when part 1 of Vasilii Trutovskii's *Sobranie russkikh prostykh pesen s notami* appeared in St. Petersburg. Like this collection, most of what followed over the next century contained arrangements and reworkings of folk songs and composers' imitations of such songs. Some specialized collections (e.g., soldier songs, songs for children) were also published in the second half of the nineteenth century, and the last three decades of that century brought the publication of sheet music for what in America is called "parlor songs," as well as albums containing "the favorite songs of the Moscow Gypsies" or songs from the repertoire of popular singers.

Such publications continued to appear up until the October Revolution. A decree of December 19, 1918, however, nationalized all musical publishing houses and print shops and all stocks of music. All of this was turned over to the musical section of the Commissariat for Education (Narkompros). MUZO, as it was known, lasted only until 1921 and seems to have published mostly revolutionary songs and a few collections of folk songs. It was succeeded by Gosudarstvennoe muzykal'noe izdatel'stvo, which in turn became Muzsektor Gosudarstvennogo izdatel'stva at the end of 1922.[3]

On December 12, 1921 the Council of People's Commissars issued a decree permitting the establishment of private publishing houses. The official Soviet bibliographical chronicle lists only a few pieces of privately published sheet music for 1922, but nearly two hundred for 1923.[4] Much of the music bore the legend "published by the author" *(izdanie avtora)*, i.e., by the composer. The music was published not only in Moscow and Petrograd but also in Kiev, Rostov-on-Don, Sukhumi, Nizhnii Novgorod, and perhaps other centers. Moscow composers had their own organization, the Association of Moscow Authors, which published sheet music, had its own store, and later (1927–30) sponsored Aleksandr Tsfasman's jazz band (Amadzhaz).[5] Available examples of privately published sheet music suggest that 1925–27 represented the height of the phenomenon. Although S. Frederick Starr refers to it (perhaps with tongue in cheek) as "samizdat," the music was printed at state printing houses and bore the imprimatur of the central censorship office (Glavlit) or of local censorship bodies. A contemporary critic complained that this production was being sold on a commission basis by state publishers and music stores.[6]

Early in 1930, however, AMA was liquidated and its director, Pereselentsev, was sentenced to four years at hard labor "for his shady deals" *(za svoi delishki)*.[7] I have found only one piece of privately published sheet music dated 1930, and none with any later date. In January 1930 a member of RAPM took on a high position *(rukovodiashchaia rabota)* in Muzsektor, and that publishing house abandoned the publication and sale of what was known at the time as "the light genre" *(legkii zhanr)*.[8] The elimination of AMA and the change in Muzsektor policy marked the end of NEP in the field of popular music. The year 1930 closed the door permanently on private music publishing, but greater tolerance in the area of repertoire would reappear periodically (e.g., in the later 1930s in the case of such performers as Izabella Iur'eva and Vadim Kozin).

Discussions about musical policy continued past 1930, but they were reflected in the press in a limited way because of the dominant position achieved by RAPM, a position it was to maintain until it, like all artistic and literary organizations, was dissolved by the Central Committee resolution of April 23, 1932, that also established centralized unions of writers, composers, etc. During the two years of its dominance, however, it affected not only publication but also performance, seeing to it, for example, that the Piatnitskii Choir, whose folk songs supposedly were inimical to socialism, did not perform on the radio.[9]

An ally of RAPM in controlling performance was Glavrepertkom (the Central Committee for the Control of Productions and Repertoire), an agency of Narkompros. It published various lists of what could and could not be performed, including a 1929 guide that contained, among other things, a list of around 400 acceptable songs from the "Gypsy repertoire" and a much longer list (some 1,500 "vocal works") of items that were banned from performance. A few songs published during the twenties were included in the approved list, but many more were on the banned list. We can also find a considerable amount of NEP-era sheet music offered for sale in a 1934 catalogue from Mezhkniga (with prices in American dollars).[10]

The songs that were published in the twenties, mostly as sheet music but also in some collections, fall into five (not entirely discrete) categories: revolutionary songs, "Gypsy" songs, dance tunes, "songs of the new way of life" *(pesni novogo byta)*, and "exotic" songs. (I leave out of consideration publications of traditional folk songs.) Among the revolutionary songs were the "classics," e.g., "Internationale," "Boldly, Comrades, in Step" *(Smelo, tovarishchi, v nogu)*, "Warszawianka," "We Are Blacksmiths" *(My kuznetsy)*, as well as post-October examples of *agitmuzyka*. Unlike the classic revolutionary songs, which were sung in both city and countryside (at least by the more politically conscious youth), almost all of the new revolutionary songs were met, according to Arnol'd Sokhor, with "total indifference" by the public. A few did achieve some popularity: Sokhor mentions "Red Youth" *(Krasnaia molodezh')*, words by Gerasim Feigin, who died at age twenty helping to put down the Kronstadt mutiny, music by one of the most prolific composers of the time, Dmitrii Vasil'ev-Buglai), "The Workers' Palace" *(Rabochii dvorets*, words by Aleksandr Pomorskii, music by Aleksei Turenkov), and "We, the Komsomol" *(My komsomol*, music [and words?] by Petr Alekseev). Two stanzas from "Red Youth" (in a very prosaic translation) give some idea of the genre:

| | |
|---|---|
| We will go without fear, | Мы пойдем без страха, |
| We will go without trembling, | Мы пойдем без дрожи, |
| We will go to meet | Мы пойдем навстречу |
| The dread foe. | Грозному врагу |
| | |
| We will break the locks, | Мы собьем запоры, |
| We will break the barriers, | Мы собьем преграды, |
| We have all been inspired | Все мы вдохновились |
| By the red struggle.[11] | Красною борьбой. |

The so-called "Gypsy genre" *(tsyganshchina)* is a large topic by itself, with a history going back to the late eighteenth century.[12] These songs were typically nonnarrative and usually dealt with the pain of love. They sometimes mentioned Gypsies or troikas, but tone was more important than the realia. The censors of Glavrepertkom made subtle distinctions, not only between banned and permitted songs but, in the latter category, between songs that were recommended, those that were allowed, and those that were allowed in moderation. Their *Repertuarnyi ukazatel'* of 1929 also listed separately songs that Glavrepertkom had not banned but that were often forbidden by local censors. In the preface N. A. Ravich listed some of the negative qualities of the banned songs: "decadence, unhealthy exoticism, propaganda for so-called 'free love,' [a tone of] drunken tavern debauchery [*p'ianyi kabatskii razgul*]," etc. The term *decadence (upadochnichestvo)* was a frequent epithet in those days. A theoretical statement of 1927 listed mysticism, eroticism, and fatalism as some of its characteristics and defined decadent literature (in a way that could also be applied to music) as follows: "Literature should be considered decadent if it is too feeble to organize the class will, if it reflects the disintegration of social forces and artistically fosters the growth of elements of disintegration by blunting the will to victory."[13]

From today's perspective, the practical implications of such criteria are far from clear. Consider the following texts. Among the songs that were banned in 1929 was Boris Fomin's "In Time We'll Forget Everything" (*S godami vse zabudem,* words by Mikhail Lakhtin, published by the composer in Moscow in 1927):

Why awaken sleeping declarations
Of unnecessary feelings, unnecessary words;
Idle rumor won't bring you
The importunate ravings of emotional suffering.

In time we'll forget everything,
We'll condemn what we love,
So go on by; I don't regret it.
Let happiness fade.
A star is still shining.
I'm not in the mood for sadness today.

Love has left, defeated by bad weather.
There's no doubt: parting is certain.
Why go looking for happiness?
Life's waves will knock us down again.

К чему будить уснувшие признанья
Ненужных чувств, ненужные слова;
Докучный бред душевного страданья
Не донесет к вам праздная молва.

С годами все забудем,
Что любим, то осудим,
Так проходите мимо, мне не жаль.
Пусть счастье увядает,
Звезда еще блистает,
Не по сердцу сегодня мне печаль.

Любовь ушла, разбитая ненастьем,
Сомненья нет, разлука решена,
К чему идти на поиски за счастьем?
Нас вновь собьет житейская волна.

Perhaps this song, with its fatalistic and pessimistic conclusion, does "blunt the will to victory," but not obviously more than the same composer's "Only Once" (*Tol'ko raz*, words by Pavel German, published by Fomin in Moscow in 1925), which was on the "permitted in small doses" list:

Night and day my heart lets caresses fall,
Night and day my head spins,
Night and day, like an agitated fairy tale
Your words ring in my ears.

> Only once in a life do encounters occur,
> Only once is the thread broken by fate,
> Only once on a cold, grey evening
> Do I want so much to love.

A ray of a forgotten sunset is fading away.
The flowers are shrouded in blue.
Where are you whom I once desired?
Where are you who awoke dreams in me?

День и ночь роняет сердце ласку,
День и ночь кружится голова,
День и ночь взволнованною сказкой
Мне звучат твои слова.

> Только раз бывают в жизни встречи,
> Только раз судьбою рвется нить,
> Только раз в холодный, серый вечер
> Мне так хочется любить.

Тает луч забытого заката,
Синевой окутаны цветы.
Где же ты, желанная когда-то,
Где, во мне будившая мечты?

One might claim that "Only Once" is slightly less pessimistic than "In Time We'll Forget Everything," but how about "Cut-glass Tumblers" (*Stakanchiki granenye*, words by Grigorii Gridov, a "very old melody" reworked by Boris Prozorovskii, published in Leningrad and Moscow by Russkoe izdatel'stvo, n.d.), which was included in the list of songs unnecessarily banned by local censors:

> The cut-glass tumblers fell off the table.
> *Romny mandè*, my handsome one, he has deserted me.
>
> I can't put back together the broken glasses on the floor
> And there's no-one I can tell about my longing and grief.
>
> My poor heart is not beating; I'm alone again.
> Farewell, bright joy. Farewell, my love!
>
> The bright sun doesn't warm my empty soul,
> My lover has given his warm caresses away to another.
>
> Parting, oh parting, and my life has ended
> Since the cut-glass tumblers fell off the table.[14]

> Стаканчики граненые упали да со стола.
> Ромны мандэ, красавец мой, побросил он меня.
>
> Мне на полу стаканчиков разбитых не собрать
> И некому тоски своей и горя рассказать.
>
> Не бьется сердце бедное, я одинока вновь,
> Прощай ты, радость светлая, прощай моя любовь!
>
> Не греет солнце яркое души моей пустой,
> Дружок мой ласку теплую отдал навек другой.
>
> Разлука, ты разлука, и жизнь моя прошла
> С тех пор, когда граненые упали со стола.

After 1930 such songs were not published again in the Soviet Union until the 1970s, when some of them made their way into collections of "old-fashioned romances" (*starinnye romansy*).[15] They were, however, performed by Soviet artists later in the thirties and continued to be part of the Russian émigré repertoire, published in sheet music and song collections by publishers all over the world: Zigzagi in Kharbin; Maski in Riga and Paris; Prosveshchenie and Zlatolira in Sofia; the Hebrew Publishing Company, Metro Music, and the Russian Music Company in New York, to name a few.

Dance tunes represented a large part of the sheet music output of the 1920s. One measure might be the number of titles listed in the Mezhkniga catalogue mentioned above. Waltzes, foxtrots, etc., amount to some 460 items, as compared to approximately 530 under the heading "Contemporary Gypsy Songs," i.e., the type just discussed. Although the foxtrot and *fokstrotchiki* were the target of particular polemical fire from RAPM[16] and are singled out for attention by Starr,[17] many more waltzes than foxtrots are listed in the Mezhkniga catalogue: 135 (including 24 items labeled "val's-boston," i.e., a kind of slow waltz) vs. 59. Among another 115 miscellaneous or unspecified dance tunes were 8 listed as "American dance," 4 listed as "eccentric dance," and 1 "American eccentric dance," all of which were probably tap-dance melodies.[18] The other dance genres represented in the 1934 catalogue were tango (20 titles), one-step (11), shimmy-foxtrot or foxtrot-shimmy (6), two-step (4), polka (4), two-step/one-step (1), shimmy (1), shimmy two-step (1), telephone-step (1), cakewalk (1), quadrille (1), and hopak (1). Separate mention should be made of a *menuèt foksè* [!] by Aleksandr Tsfasman. The list included works by foreign composers as well; among recognizable names were Irving Berlin, Imre Kálmán, Ferenc Lehár, W. C. Handy, and Vincent Youmans.[19]

The songs that were sometimes advertised as "songs of the new way of life" were attempts to write new revolutionary songs or songs with a more proletarian atmosphere or setting. The music, however, was often still in the style of *tsyganshchina* or *fokstrotshchina*. That was obviously the problem with a Komsomol song by two old practitioners of "the light genre," lyricist Pavel German and composer Iulii Khait. "The New Generation" *(Smena)* was attacked by Lev Lebedinskii of RAPM, who reproduced the text and music of the chorus as an illustration of "a music-hall song [*shansonetka*] with a 'revolutionary' text":

| We are coming to take the place of the old | Мы идем на смену старым |
| Weary fighters | Утомившимся бойцам |
| To ignite proletarian hearts | Мировым зажечь пожаром |
| With a world-wide fire.[20] | Пролетарские сердца. |

German also wrote texts with a proletarian setting, as did his colleague Boris Timofeev, whose song about love and betrayal at the spinning mill, "The Spinning Machine" (*Stanochek*, music by Boris Prozorovskii, published by Kievskoe muzykal'noe predpriiatie, n.d.), is a good example of the genre:

It happened at the factory,
At the spinning machine,
Where the every-day call of the factory whistle
Starts up a familiar song.

To the sound of the noisy wheels,
A girl's song is passionate.
It was there I chanced to fall in love
With a merry weaver.

>Oh machine, my machine,
>What are you singing about?
>People like my darling
>Are not to be found.[21]

Это было на заводе
У прядильного станка,
Где родную песнь заводит
Зов привычного гудка.
Под шумящие колеса
Песня девки горяча.
Там любить мне довелося
Развеселого ткача.

>Станочек, мой станочек,
>О чем поешь?
>Таких, как мой дружочек
>Ты не найдешь.

The song goes on to describe a movie date and concludes with the weaver abandoning the narrator for another woman. She, however, finds solace in her work in the factory collective.

RAPM publicists accused the authors of these songs of cynicism and worse; it is hard for us to judge to what extent the composers and lyricists were sincerely attempting to fit their art to the needs of new times and to what extent they were just attempting to survive. All we can note is that some continued as successful Soviet songwriters into the forties and beyond (e.g., Dmitrii and Daniil Pokrass, Matvei Blanter, Iulii Khait, Valentin Kruchinin, Pavel German), while others seem to have disappeared from the scene (e.g., Boris Prozorovskii, Konstantin Podrevskii, Oskar Osenin).

I have referred to the final category of printed music of the twenties as "exotic" since many of the songs that do not fit into any of the other categories were songs dealing with exotic places and people.[22] The Mezh-kniga catalogue, to be sure, arbitrarily lists many of them under the heading "contemporary Gypsy songs," and some of them may well have been dance tunes. A sampling of titles will give some idea of the genre: "Ricksha from Nagasaki," "Miss Butterfly," "It's Noisy at Night in Marseilles," "Redheaded Signora," "Fujiyama," "Creolita," "Calcutta," and two versions of "The Thief of Baghdad" (no doubt inspired by the Douglas Fairbanks film of the same name). The one text that I can cite is a case of domestic, ethnic exoticism: it is set in the Jewish *shtetl* of Ol'shany (near Kharkov). "Sarah" *(Sarra)*, subtitled "a Jewish *shtetl* melody," has words by Boris Timofeev and music, arranged by Boris Prozorovskii, taken from the Yiddish song "Daisies" *(Margeritkelekh,* composer unknown):

> In the town of Ol'shany lived Sarah,
> Radiant as the spring sun,
> Full of voluptuousness and secret ardor,
> A beauty, tra-la-la-la.
>
> Her father, the rabbi, was in the synagogue all day,
> *Di mame* was peevish and cross.
> Sarah's relatives were strict and stern,
> But to her it was all tra-la-la-la.[23]

> В местечке Ольшанах жила-была Сарра,
> Как вешнее солнце светла,
> Вся полная неги и тайного жара,
> Красавица, тра-ла-ла-ла.
>
> Отец ее рабби весь день в синагоге,
> Ди маме сварлива и зла.
> Родные у Сарры суровы и строги,
> Но ей все лишь тра-ла-ла-ла.

The song, set to a lilting waltz tune, goes on to tell how Sarah ran away with her gentile lover rather than marry the elderly, rich (Jewish) merchant who had become enamored of her. "Sarra" was not banned by Glavrepertkom in 1929 (unlike other songs by Timofeev and Prozorovskii), perhaps because of its progressive portrayal of interethnic relations and of religious tradition ("Oh, what did Sarah care now . . . about the gloom of ancient customs . . .").

Based on a sample of sixty-one items for which I have figures, it seems that most of the sheet music of the twenties was produced in small press runs, usually 2,000 copies or fewer (and most in runs of 1,000 or, for some reason, 1,050 copies). Of the sixty-one songs only seven were published in 3,000–3,150 copies, and only four in the range 5,000–5,500 (one of them being a collection of ten songs from the repertoire of Tamara Tsereteli, arranged by Boris Prozorovskii). Only five songs reached the 10,000-copy level (one of them, "We're Only Acquainted" [*My tol'ko znakomy*], by virtue of a Leningrad edition of 5,000 plus another 5,000 published in Nizhnii Novgorod). We have no real information about the customers for all this sheet music, but judging from accounts of what workers and peasants were singing in the late twenties and early thirties (some of which were mentioned above), almost none of the published music of the twenties was taken up by that potential audience.[24]

One songwriting team was successful in reaching them. Pavel German and Valentin Kruchinin's "Mine #3" *(Shakhta No. 3),* "Man'ka's Section of Town" *(Man'kin poselok),* and especially "Bricks" *(Kirpichiki),* three "songs of the new way of life," were widely sung. Two "contemporary Gypsy songs" also achieved similar popularity: the already quoted "Cut-glass Tumblers" (one of the songs in the Tsereteli collection) and "Little Bells" *(Bubentsy,* words by Aleksandr Kusikov, music by Aleksandr Bakaleinikov, published in 1925 by Muzsektor in Moscow in 10,000 copies—in old orthography, from old plates).[25] The first verse and the chorus of the song are as follows:

My heart seems to have awakened in a fright.
I now regret the past.
Let the horses with their flowing manes
And little bells whirl me away into the distance.

> I hear the ringing bells from afar.
> That's the familiar sound of a troika starting off
> And all around the sparkling snow
> Has spread out like a white shroud.

Сердце будто проснулось пугливо.
Пережитое стало мне жаль.
Пусть же кони с распущенной гривой
С бубенцами умчат меня вдаль.

> Слышу звон бубенцов издалёка.
> Это тройки знакомый разбег.
> А вокруг расстелился широко
> Белым саваном искристый снег.

If, as it seems, the songs being published by state publishing houses and by private publishers—with a few exceptions—were not being sung by workers and peasants, then what did constitute their repertoire? Part of it was rural in origin—traditional folk songs and at least some of the masses of *chastushki* (short, usually four-line rhymed songs) that were being sung (and written down by folklorists). The literature on *chastushki*—both collections and studies—is vast. One pertinent observation from 1924 by the eminent ethnographer Vladimir Tan-Bogoraz is worth citing. In his editorial comment to an article about contemporary *chastushki,* he pointed out how few of them deal with "current events" *(novye bytovye iavleniia),* namely, not more than 100 out of the 2,000 collected in 1923 by the authors of the article. (The other 95 percent were love lyrics.) He added that an earlier collection of 10,000 items (1919–20) contained no more than 1 percent relating to new phenomena.

> Moreover, there was not a single political *chastushka* favorable to the Soviet regime. At that time village youth sang about deserters with particular enthusiasm and looked at the course of Russian politics through deserters' eyes. Starting in 1921 . . . sympathy for the Soviet regime enters the *chastushka*.[26]

A large part of the worker/peasant repertoire could be called, in contradistinction to the songs discussed above, "unpublished urban songs." Once again it is possible to provide a partial taxonomy: "cruel romances" (*zhestokie romansy*), workers' songs influenced by the cruel romances, *blatnye pesni*, and others.[27]

The cruel romance is more mentioned than analyzed in the literature. Gerald Smith's definition is probably the best available: "The cruel romance is a ballad-type song, usually with a strong narrative element telling a melodramatic story of unrequited love or infidelity. Quite often revenge leads to a violent outcome. The style is one of open sentimentality, and the text frequently concludes with a direct appeal for sympathy from the audience" (p. 64). He further compares the genre with such English songs as "She Was Poor but She Was Honest." The main defect in Smith's definition is the lack of a clear distinction between the cruel romance and the ballad. The leading Soviet specialist on folk ballads, Dmitrii Balashov, defines the ballad as "an epic (narrative) song, dramatic in character." He goes on to discuss the influence (in the nineteenth century) of the (literary) romance on the ballad, pointing out that the boundary between the two is quite relative, with the only distinction sometimes being the third-person author's narration in the ballad as opposed to the first-person hero's narration in the romance (typical of lyric songs).[28] In fact, the cruel romance often combines the third-person narration of the ballad with the first-person narration and expression of emotion of the lyrical song. L. Iashchenko speaks of "exaggerated manifestation of emotion" (*nadryvnist'*) and "hypertrophy of feelings."[29]

These structural and emotional characteristics of the cruel romance can be seen, for example, in "Madwoman" (*Bezumnaia*), which begins with a series of anguished rhetorical questions:

| | |
|---|---|
| Why are you, madwoman, destroying | Зачем ты, безумная, губишь |
| The one who is enamored of you? | Того, кто увлекся тобой? |
| You clearly don't love me. | Наверно меня ты не любишь? |
| You don't love me? So be it. | Не любишь? Так Бог же с тобой! |

| Why did you entice me? | Зачем ты меня завлекала? |
|---|---|
| Why did you make me love you? | Зачем заставляла любить? |
| You probably didn't know then | Должно быть тогда ты не знала, |
| How serious it is to betray love.[30] | Как тяжко любви изменить! |

The first- and second-person focus of the opening three stanzas shifts into a largely third-person narration of the "heroine's" wedding to a rich bridegroom as bitter tears pour from her eyes. (The narrator also appears as observer.) The song ends with a reprise of the first two stanzas.

The original of "Madwoman" was written by the self-taught poet Matvei Ozhegov (1860–1931). Ozhegov mentions it as one of his songs that were being sung "incessantly" *(bez umolku)* in Moscow in the 1890s. A Soviet folklorist found it in the repertoire of "the female half of factory youth" in Orekhovo-Zuevo in the 1920s, and it was still being sung in the Voronezh region in the 1960s.[31]

The reason for the popularity of such songs has been documented in comments recorded by Soviet folklorists (in the sixties and seventies):

> What I like about them is that they're about love, about women's troubles and injuries, about betrayal, that they grab you by the heart.

> What I like about it is that it's about betrayal, but she found enough strength to stab him to death for betraying her.

> I stand there and bawl. [*Ia stoiu i revliu (revu).*][32]

As usual the folklorists are mostly interested in texts and tend to ignore the undoubted role of the melody in the spread of particular songs. Musicologists have provided some analysis of the urban song tradition in general, but their few comments on the cruel romance are no more enlightening than the following observation: "The melodies of such songs show a dominance of melodramatic 'overemotional' [*nadryvnykh*] melodic segments [*intonatsii*] and of trite 'hurdy-gurdy' [*sharmanochnykh*] and music-hall phrases."[33]

Thanks to the melodramatic character of both their music and text, the cruel romances provided an outlet for emotional release through the vicarious experience of intense feelings. Years later the popular Soviet composer Isaak Dunaevskii would attribute the continuing popularity of "Gypsy" singers to the otherwise unmet need for such release *(otdushina).*[34]

The melodrama was brought closer to home in songs that were probably created under the influence of the cruel romance, but in which the protagonists are clearly identified as workers. One such song, "Exhausted, Worn Out" *(Izmuchennyi, isterzannyi),* was based on the poem "The Fate of a Factory Hand" *(Dolia masterovogo),* published in 1901 by the peasant-poet Prokhor Gorokhov. The song begins:

Exhausted, worn out
By factory work,
Our brother, the factory hand,
Walks around like an apparition from beyond the grave.[35]

Измученный, истерзанный
Работой трудовой,
Идет, как тень загробная,
Наш брат мастеровой.

The highly emotional style of the cruel romance is present here in both the melody and the text, which portrays the worker, let go in the middle of the winter, returning to his consumptive wife and hungry children.

The influence of the cruel romance is even more striking in the case of "Oh, You Poor, Poor Sewing-Machine Operator" *(Akh ty bednaia, bednaia shveika)*, published in Moscow in 1912 in a songbook with the same title:

Oh, you poor, poor sewing-machine operator,
You started work at seventeen,
Your wages didn't come easy,
You had to bear much trouble and grief.[36]

Ах ты бедная, бедная швейка
Поступила с семнадцати лет,
Не легко доставалась копейка,
Много вынесла горя и бед.

After three more stanzas describing her hard life as a worker, the song relates how she found a better life at a brothel. Later, however, a victim of physical abuse and alcohol, she is discovered frozen on a Moscow street. The melody of "Shveika" was taken from a more traditional cruel romance of love unrequited, "Don't Reproach Me, Don't Rebuke Me" *(Ne korite menia, ne branite).*[37]

While workers and peasants may not have been drawn to the published "exotic" songs about Calcutta and Marseilles, there was one exotic component of Soviet reality that proved attractive. Like the stories of the Odessa underworld by Isaak Babel', the so-called *blatnye pesni* found a wide audience throughout the country, both contributing to and feeding on the romanticization of that milieu. The term *blatnye pesni* is usually translated or explained as referring to criminal or underworld songs, but there is reason to prefer Gerald Smith's more cautious formulation, "songs about life on the wrong side of the law," which he uses interchangeably with the two translations just mentioned (pp. 70ff.). The reason for the caution is that we know next to nothing about the origin of these songs. Indeed, some earlier critics argued that unlike *blatnaia muzyka* (underworld slang), the songs reflect "another spirit, another source of ideas," than the criminal milieu.[38] To see how complicated the question is, consider the history of the "national anthem" of the homeless children of the 1920s, the *besprizorniki,* which Glavrepertkom banned in 1929 but which then spread throughout the entire Soviet Union thanks to its use in the first Soviet sound film, *The Road to Life (Putevka v zhizn').* It goes back to an anonymous urban romance of the 1870s that began:

| | |
|---|---|
| She looked | Она посмотрела |
| Sadly into my face | Мне грустно в лицо |
| And silently put | И молча надела |
| A ring on my hand. | На руку кольцо. |

The ring was supposed to remain bright as long as she remained faithful to the narrator. But the ring turned dark, she left him, and he felt like an orphan. The song was widespread in rural Russia at the turn of the century in folklorized versions, one of which began:

| | |
|---|---|
| In the orchard by the valley | В саду при долине |
| A nightingale is singing | Поет соловей, |
| And I, far from home, | А я на чужбине |
| Have been forgotten by people.[39] | Забыт от людей. |

It was such a version that was taken up by the *besprizorniki* and reworked, with the ring motif disappearing in the process (the notion of literal orphanhood presumably being more relevant than that of being "orphaned" by an unfaithful love). The result was texts such as the one recorded by M. P. Afanas'ev in Zaporozh'e (Zaporizhzhia) in 1925 or 1926, which begins:

| | |
|---|---|
| In the orchard by the valley | Как в саду при долине |
| A nightingale was singing loudly, | Громко пел соловей, |
| And I, a boy, am far from home | А я, мальчик, на чужбине |
| And forgotten by people. | Позабыт от людей. |
| | |
| I've been forgotten, abandoned | Позабыт я, позаброшен |
| Since my young years. | С молодых юных лет. |
| I was an orphan | Я остался сиротою, |
| Without luck or good fortune. . . . | Счастья-доли мне нет... |
| | |
| So I'll die, I'll die, | Вот умру я, умру я, |
| They'll bury me; | Похоронят меня; |
| And no-one will weep | И никто же не заплачет |
| Over my grave.[40] | Над могилой моей... |

Note that "Forgotten, Abandoned" (*Pozabyt, pozabroshen,* one title for the song) has no particular underworld or criminal content, nor, as we have just seen, does it owe its origins to that milieu. Yet because of its association with the *besprizorniki,* who were usually viewed as juvenile delinquents, it was included among *blatnye pesni* by both Petrov in 1926 and Vaiskopf in 1981 (and others in between). We can still use the formulation "songs about life on the wrong side of the law," but we need to understand it somewhat broadly as not being limited to accounts of criminal behavior.

One other example can illustrate both the popularity of *blatnye pesni* and the problems of definition of the genre. Among the songs recorded by M. P. Haidai and N. Dmitruk in 1925 from inmates of a Kiev prison was one that began:

> A thief goes down to the station,
> Chum-chá-ra, chu-ra-rá,
> To check the train over,
> Cuckoo!
>
> He checked the train over,
> Stole a suitcase.[41]

> Урка (вор) топает (идет) на бан (вокзал),
> Чум-чá-ра; чу-ра-рá,
> Контролировать майдан (поезд),
> Ку-ку!
>
> Сконтролировал майдан,
> Окалечил (украл) чемодан.

According to V. Bilets'ka, the author of an article on the subject, a song with a "chum-chá-ra" refrain was being sung all over Kharkov in the fall of 1923 in numerous variants.[42] The most constant component of the various texts dealt with a horse thief who is caught and then appeals in turn to his mother, his father, and his wife to get him out of jail. Eventually the only constant element turned out to be the melody (more or less) and the structure of couplets with interspersed refrains. The first political texts set to it dealt with Lord Curzon's ultimatum of April 1923:

| | |
|---|---|
| Curzon sent us a note, | Керзон ноту нам прислал |
| Chum-cha-ra, chu-ra-ra, | Чум-ча-ра, чу-ра-ра, |
| And Chicherin answered: | А Чичерин отвечал: |
| Cuckoo! | Ку-ку! |

Later a kind of political catechism was set to this pattern and melody:

What does the GPU [secret police] talk about?
Chum-cha-ra, chu-ra-ra,
Keep silent.
Cuckoo!

What does the bourgeois talk to us about?
The hell with the revolution.

What does the SR [Social Revolutionary] talk to us about?
Not recognizing the USSR.

What does the Menshevik talk about?
I'm not used to dictatorship [of the proletariat].

What does Miliukov talk about?
Not recognizing the Bolsheviks.

What does the rabbi talk to us about?
We won't give up the synagogue.

О чем толкует Г.П.У.?
   Чум-ча-ра, чу-ра-ра,
Соблюдайте тишину.
    Ку-ку!

О чем толкует нам буржуй?
На революцию наплюй.

О чем толкует нам эс-эр?
Не признавать С.С.С.Р.

О чем толкует меньшевик?
Я к диктатуре не привык.

О чем толкует Милюков?
Не признавать большевиков.

О чем толкует нам раввин?
Синагоги не дадим.

Such political verses spread to Moscow and Leningrad in 1923–24. K. Postavnichev's *Massovoe penie* (published by Vserossiiskii Proletkul't in Moscow in 1925) included among its recommended songs a version of "Chum-chara" (p. 91) that included part of the above catechism set to a melody almost identical with that published by Haidai. The second part of the refrain was "Ish' ty! Aha!" rather than "Ku-ku!" and there were a few couplets not quoted by Bilets'ka, e.g.,

What has the profiteer started talking about?
We can't continue like this.

What does Smena Vekh [an émigré group] talk about?
There's no harm in a revolution.

What does a Communist talk about?
Chum-cha-ra, chu-ra-ra.
Our road to victory is rocky.
Well, then, let's go!

О чем там нэпман стал пищать?
Нельзя так больше продолжать.

О чем толкует Смена Вех?
И революция -- не грех.

О чем толкует коммунист?
    Чумчара, чурара,
Наш путь к победе каменист.
    Ну, что ж, идем!

Thus traditional folklore motifs about stealing horses and ransoming prisoners were reworked in the style and language of *blatnye pesni* (examples in Bilets'ka's article) and then the original motifs disappeared, but the structure remained to serve as the basis of both *blatnye pesni* and political couplets.

The final component of the "unpublished urban songs" consists of a number of songs that do not fit into any of the three categories already discussed. They include satirical songs *(kupletnye pesni)*, reworkings or updatings of older songs, and some songs that might well have fit into one of the categories of published songs but were deemed not worthy of publication (usually because of RAPM objections to their musical style). The satirical songs were often written to order for particular performers, as in the case of "Bublichki" ("Bagels"), a song about the tragic lot of a street peddler.[43] The émigré writer Donat Mechik, who knew Iakov Iadov, the author of "Bublichki," provides an interesting sidelight to the history of the song. He claims that the lines that are always sung "I v noch' nenastnuiu, menia neschastnuiu / Torgovku chastnuiu ty pozhalei!" ("And on a rainy night take pity on poor me, a private market woman") were originally "I v noch' nenastnuiu, menia neschastnuiu / Torgovliu chastnuiu ty pozhalei!" ("And on a rainy night take pity on poor me, private trade"). This puts a rather specific edge on what Mechik calls "the most popular song of the NEP period."[44]

While "Bublichki" was totally a product of the NEP period, "A Soviet Strip of Land" *(Sovetskaia poloska)* is an example of an older song (probably from the turn of the century) that went through various reworkings. In the 1934 Mezhkniga catalogue it can be found in the category "old Gypsy songs" listed as "Polosyn'ka—A Russian folk song" in two arrangements (by Ia. Prigozhii and A. Cherniavskii, both specialists in the Gypsy genre). In a 1966 collection of folk songs it is printed in the category "songs of city life" and begins:

| | |
|---|---|
| Once I was harvesting my strip of land, | Раз полосыньку я жала, |
| Tying up the golden sheaves, | Золоты снопы вязала,-- |
| A young woman, oh, a young woman. | Молодая, эх, молодая. |

and tells how, while Masha's husband and mother-in-law are waiting for her to finish the reaping, a young man shows up and the grain never does get reaped.[45] In a version reported as being sung in the Wilno region between the wars, the visitor is a soldier.[46] In the twenties the workers' theater group Siniaia Bluza popularized an updated version. K. Postavnichev printed a revised and expanded variant of the Siniaia Bluza text among the songs that he claimed had already entered "mass circulation" *(obkhod massovogo peniia).*[47] Postavnichev's text is worth quoting here in its entirety:

I used to harvest my strip of land,
Tie up the golden sheaves,
 A young woman, oh, a young woman.

And I never dared to say
That our women's situation
 Is a bad lot.

Soon everything changed:
A revolution occurred
 In our land.

We drove out the landowners
And took freedom for ourselves,
 Equality.

Now things are different
And work is in full swing,
 It's going great.

It's all right, now we don't grumble.
Women's work has become common work,
 Everything has opened up.

Sometimes I used to sing
"I was harvesting my strip of land"
   And I would sob.

The old ways are finished,
Now I elect delegates
   To the soviets.

My drunken husband used to come home,
Come up to me and get going,
   He'd grab me by the ear.

Now we're free,
If I take him to a people's court,
   He'll pay a fine.

Misfortunes have disappeared:
Now under Soviet rule
   There's equality.

We share work and rest,
So, brothers, let's break out in song
   And make a toast!


Я полоску раньше жала,
Золоту снопу вязала,
   Молодая, эх, молодая.


И всегда сказать не смела,
Что, мол, наше бабье дело --
   Доля злая.


Скоро все переменилось:
Революция случилась
   В нашем крае.


Мы помещиков прогнали
И себе свободу взяли,
   Равноправье.


Вот теперь другое дело,
И работа -- закипела,
   Заспорилась.


Ничего, теперь не ропщем,
Бабье дело стало общим,
   Все раскрылось.

Раньше я пою бывало
«Как полосыньку я жала»
      И рыдаю.

Песни старые пропеты,
Я сама теперь в Советы
      Выбираю.

Прежде пьяный муж вернется,
Подойдет да развернется,
      В ухо хватит.

Нынче мы -- народ свободный,
Как подам я в суд народный,
      Штраф заплатит.

Улетучились напасти:
Ныне при Советской власти --
      Равноправье.

Труд и отдых делим вместе;
Ну-ка, братцы, грянем песню
      Да за здравье!


The topic of women's rights was very much in the air in 1925, when Postavnichev published this text (alongside "A Working Women's Internationale," to the tune of the classic "Internationale"). The 1925–26 debate over family law culminated in the adoption of a new family code. (See Wendy Z. Goldman's essay, above.)

Postavnichev published his "Soviet Strip of Land" *(Sovetskaia poloska)* only after it had become popular. Our final example from the worker and peasant repertoire of the 1920s was not published until 1957. "Give Us a Ride on the Tractor, Pete" *(Prokati nas, Petrusha, na traktore!)* begins:

> Whether you're going along the bumpy road or the highway,
> We're going the same way!
> Give us a ride on the tractor, Pete,
> Take us to the edge of the village.[48]


По дорожке неровной, по тракту ли,
Все равно нам с тобой по пути!
Прокати нас, Петруша, на тракторе,
До околицы нас прокати!

The musicologist Tat'iana Popova calls "Give Us a Ride" the most popular Komsomol and Pioneer song of the late twenties. She claims that it was neither published nor broadcast at the time because of the dominance of the "erroneous opinion that the melodic form of the urban song tradition was inappropriate for contemporary Soviet life."[49]

Let us summarize. In the area of popular music, the NEP period continued at least until early 1930, when private (or independent) music publishing ceased. During the 1920s there was a dualism in popular musical culture. On the one hand, songwriters continued to produce (and private publishers—and, to a much lesser extent, state publishers—to publish) songs that were in the tradition of urban (especially "Gypsy") music of the late nineteenth and early twentieth centuries. There were attempts to update some of this music thematically, and as had been the case with nineteenth-century urban music, foreign influences (e.g., the foxtrot) made themselves felt. These songs were probably most popular among those Soviet citizens who had middle-class backgrounds or aspirations but—with rare exceptions (e.g., "Kirpichiki")—seem never to have become a mass phenomenon in the cities or in the countryside. This "Gypsy-tango-foxtrot" strain of music did, however, influence later Soviet popular music in the thirties and beyond.

The other stream, the "unpublished urban music," was a continuation and development of urban musical folklore. It is these songs that show up in accounts of the repertoire of workers and peasants. By definition one expects urban folklore to have wide circulation in the cities, but it was not limited to that milieu. Just as in the nineteenth century villagers were anxious to learn songs brought back from the city by seasonal workers and soldiers, so too in the twentieth century urban culture had its prestige in the countryside. In both centuries it was the lower-class elements of that culture that were most accessible to peasants and ex-peasants. Thus cruel romances and *blatnye pesni* continued to flourish in the 1920s in the cities and villages.

After 1930 these two cultures gave way to a single popular musical culture created through the effects of sound films (e.g., *Veselye rebiata*, 1934) and the official propagation of so-called mass songs. This culture was somewhat eclectic, with room, for example, for the march from *Veselye rebiata* and the tango "My Heart" *(Serdtse)* from the same film, both by composer Isaak Dunaevskii. Frederick Starr speaks of the "monoculture" of jazz—"or what was thought to be jazz"—as the dominant force in Soviet popular music in the period 1932–36.[50] Starr is correct as far as style of performance is concerned, but it was some of the mass songs of the 1930s that had a longer-lasting effect, as reflected, for example, in the melodies to which soldiers wrote new texts during World War II.[51]

At the same time, the "urban folklore" culture continued its unofficial, underground (not in any conspiratorial sense) existence, so that folklore expeditions of the sixties and seventies could still report the survival of cruel romances and the like in distant villages, and one can find them in the repertoire of Soviet émigrés of the younger generation who come from Moscow, Leningrad, or Odessa. Some of the published urban music of the twenties and its antecedents from the three decades or so before the revolution have been and are being revived as an object of nostalgia through the production of records and song collections with music. One suspects that this process is not entirely archaeological, that some of the tradition must have survived, however submerged, among native speakers.[52]

## NOTES

1. *Dovesti do kontsa bor'bu s nèpmanskoi muzykoi* (Moscow, 1931).
2. A 1931 account describes such notebooks belonging to young workers in the Donbass. The notebooks came under attack from the local Komsomol. They were seized "in a terrorist manner" *(terroristicheski)*, and part of the haul was ceremonially burned (L. Baikova, "'Lirika' v Donbasse," *Na literaturnom postu*, 1931, no. 29, pp. 37–42).
3. G. K. Ivanov, *Notoizdatel'skoe delo v Rossii: Istoricheskaia spravka* (Moscow, 1970), pp. 32–33.
4. On the Sovnarkom decree see A. I. Nazarov, *Ocherki istorii sovetskogo knigoizdatel'stva* (Moscow, 1953), p. 114. The first issue of *Knizhnaia letopis'* for 1924 announced that thenceforth sheet music would be listed only in every second or third issue. No subsequent listings of sheet music were published, however, until a separate publication, *Letopis' muzykal'noi literatury*, began to appear in 1931.
5. Aleksei Batashev, *Sovetskii dzhaz: istoricheskii ocherk* (Moscow, 1972), pp. 25–26. See also S. Frederick Starr, *Red and Hot: The Fate of Jazz in the Soviet Union, 1917–1980* (New York, 1985), pp. 65–66.
6. Starr's comment is on p. 329 (n. 19). The Soviet critic was Innokentii Bolotov, "Prodavtsy poshlosti," *Novyi zritel'*, 1929, no. 40, p. 10. There are even examples of liturgical music being printed at state printing houses (*Knizhnaia letopis'*, 1922, nos. 1808, 1809, 2607).
7. S. Korev, "Glaviskusstvo i rukovodstvo muzykal'noi zhizni," *Proletarskii muzykant*, 1930, no. 3, p. 27.
8. Letter to the editors of *Proletarskii muzykant*, reprinted in *Dovesti*, p. 97.
9. V. M. Potiavin, "Izuchenie russkoi narodnoi pesni (1917 g.–30-e gody)," *Ocherki istorii russkoi ètnografii, folkloristiki i antropologii*, Vol. 4 (Moscow, 1968), p. 186. In those days traditional folklore was also under attack from another direction. V. Blium, an influential music critic and leader of the Association for Modern Music, organized a "trial" of the Piatnitskii Choir by radio listeners, whose judgments were published in several issues of *Radioslushatel'* (Petr Kaz'min, *S pesnei* [Moscow, 1970], pp. 48–58). Blium, himself usually a target of RAPM attacks, agreed this time that the choir encouraged a cult of the old, prerevolutionary village.

10. The censor's list: *Repertuarnyi ukazatel' GRK*, ed. N. A. Ravich (Moscow, 1929). The sales catalogue: *Tsyganskie pesni (novye i starye) i tantsoval'naia muzyka*, Katalog No. 15 (Moscow, 1934).

11. Feigin's poem was set to music by Buglai in 1922; the text and music can be found in the first volume of *Slavim pobedu Oktiabria!* (Moscow, 1967), pp. 78–81. Sokhor's comments are on p. 110 of his *Russkaia sovetskaia pesnia* (Leningrad, 1959). On the urban and rural song repertoire of the mid-twenties see, e.g., P. Sobolev, "O pesennom repertuare sovremennoi fabriki," *Uchenye zapiski Instituta iazyka i literatury Rossiiskoi assotsiatsii nauchno-issledovatel'skikh institutov obshchestvennykh nauk* (Moscow), 1928, no. 2, pp. 42–69, and V. Chuzhimov, "Materialy po fol'kloru TsChO [Tsentral'no-Chernozemnoi Oblasti] (Fol'klor predkolkhoznoi derevni)," *Sovetskaia etnografiia*, 1934, no. 1–2, pp. 193–200.

12. Some brief remarks can be found in Robert A. Rothstein, "The Quiet Rehabilitation of the Brick Factory: Early Soviet Popular Music and Its Critics," *Slavic Review*, 1980, Vol. 39, pp. 373–88, especially 376–77. The subject will receive greater attention in my forthcoming *Songs of the City: Studies in Russian Popular Musical Culture*. See also T. Shcherbakova, *Tsyganskoe muzykal'noe ispolnitel'stvo i tvorchestvo v Rossii* (Moscow, 1984).

13. *Repertuarnyi ukazatel'*, 8–9. I. Grossman-Roshchin, "Tezisy ob upadochnichestve v khudozhestvennoi literature," *Na literaturnom postu*, 1927, no. 1, pp. 3–8.

14. The words *romny mandè* in the second line are in Romany, the language of the Russian Gypsies, but they mean 'my wife' or 'my Gypsy woman' and not 'my handsome one.' (See *Tsygansko-russkii slovar'*, compiled by M. V. Sergievskii and A. P. Barannikov [Moscow, 1938; reprint, New York, 1981].)

There is something mysterious about the Russkoe izdatel'stvo that published "Cut-glass Tumblers." Of the five pieces of sheet music from that publisher that are in my collection, two list the place of publication as St. Petersburg and Moscow and three as Leningrad and Moscow. None are dated, but we know that Petrograd became Leningrad in 1924. The three Leningrad/Moscow publications, however, do not bear any Glavlit or other censor's number, nor do they indicate how many copies were printed and where. All three items were normal on all sheet music (and other publications) of the time. Perhaps these were examples of the kind of illegal publication of which Pereselentsev, the head of AMA, was accused. ("Not satisfied that the 'gracious' censors permit *almost* everything, disagreeing with their 'friendly' prohibition of certain of the most shameless and 'savory' works, Mr. Pereselentsev *prints and sells them illegally*" [emphasis in the original]—"Na fronte bor'by s nepmanskoi muzykoi," editorial from *Proletarskii muzykant*, 1930, no. 3, reprinted in *Dovesti*, p. 33.)

15. See Rothstein, "The Quiet Rehabilitation," pp. 383–84 (n. 51).

16. "This is the song and the dance of the petite bourgeoisie in the period of the catastrophe of capitalism. They reflect the consciousness of a person who has been turned into a slave of capital, of the machine, who has been totally digested by capitalist society and has lost any capacity, not only for protest but even for thought." L. Lebedinskii, "Nash massovyi muzykal'nyi byt," *Proletarskii muzykant*, 1930, no. 9–10, p. 24.

17. See, e.g., his reproduction of sheet music for Fomin's "Taiti-Trot," based on Vincent Youmans's "Tea for Two." (The caption refers to "Begin the Beguine," but the correct identification is on p. 59.)

18. For an account built on the device of "making it strange" (*ostranenie*) see L. Lebedinskii, " 'Amerikanskii tanets,' " in N. Briusova and L. Lebedinskii, *Protiv*

*nèpmanskoi muzyki (tsyganshchiny, fokstrota i t. d.)* (Moscow, 1930), pp. 20–26, reprinted from *Za proletarskuiu muzyku*, 1930, no. 2.

19. One methodological caveat: The Mezhkniga catalogue is not a bibliography but a list of remainders. Since, however, it does include some of the most popular songs of the twenties, it would seem to be somewhat representative of the sheet music production of the period and not to be limited to music that no one in the USSR wanted to buy. Unfortunately *Letopis' muzykal'noi literatury* (the later *Notnaia letopis'*) did not begin publication until 1931.

20. "O shansonetke, 'voennoi muzyke' i Aviamarshe," *Na literaturnom postu*, 1931, no. 12, p. 41; see also his "Nash massovyi muzykal'nyi byt," *Proletarskii muzykant*, 1930, no. 9–10, p. 18.

21. The information about "Spinning Machine" comes from the cover of sheet music for another such song, "Little Star" *(Zvezdochka);* the text was transcribed from a recording by the émigré singer Petr Leshchenko, "Russian Songs and Tangos by Peter Lestchenko and Orchestra," vol. 2, Kismet K-31. The classic example of this type of song is, of course, "Kirpichiki," which was discussed in Rothstein, "The Quiet Rehabilitation."

22. A 1929 polemic sneers at "tavern ethnography" *(kabatskaia ètnografiia)*—M. Zagorskaia, "Dovol'no charl'sfoks-pliasov!" *Vecherniaia Moskva*, September 11, 1929 (#209), p. 3.

23. The original Yiddish text, written by Zalman Shneour in 1909, deals with a girl who goes to the woods to pick daisies and meets a handsome stranger. The text and music can be found, e.g., in Eleanor Gordon Mlotek's collection *Mir trogn a gezang!* (New York, 1972), pp. 40–41. My photocopy of "Sarra" shows no publication data other than the indication "izdanie avtora."

24. Needless to say, the question is not whether peasants and workers were buying sheet music for their piano benches but rather whether the published songs entered their repertoire.

25. Aleksandr (or Sandro) Kusikov was an imaginist poet, a friend of Esenin. Mayakovsky wrote about him:

> Mnogo est' vkusov,
> vkusits
> i vkusikov.
> Komu nravitsia Maiakovskii,
> a komu—
> Kusikov.

("There are lots of different tastes. / Some people like Mayakovsky and some, Kusikov."—A. M. Argo, *Svoimi glazami* [Moscow, 1965], p. 86.) "Little Bells" is mentioned, e.g., as being popular among workers at the Kaluga railroad yards, in M. Pereverzeva, "O gorodskikh pesniakh," *Prosveshchenie na transporte*, 1929, no. 7, p. 103.

26. Editor's note to N. M. Morev and N. Sh[printsin], "Sovremennaia chastushka," in *Staryi i novyi byt*, ed. V. G. Tan-Bogoraz (Leningrad, 1924), p. 117. Two interesting monographs are S. G. Lazutin, *Russkaia chastushka. Voprosy proiskhozhdeniia i formirovaniia zhanra* (Voronezh, 1960), and Brigitte Stephan, *Studien zur russischen Častuška und ihrer Entwicklung* (= *Slavistische Beiträge*, Vol. 38 [Munich, 1969]). For additional references see the several volumes of *Russkii fol'klor— Bibliografícheskii ukazatel'*, compiled by M. Ia. Mel'ts (Leningrad, 1966– ).

27. Some of these genres are discussed (and illustrated in translation) in Gerald Stanton Smith's *Songs to Seven Strings: Russian Guitar Poetry and Soviet "Mass Song"*

(Bloomington, 1984), pp. 64–87. See also Rothstein, "The Quiet Rehabilitation," pp. 377–79.

28. D. Balashov, "Russkaia narodnaia ballada," editor's introduction to *Narodnye ballady*, 2nd ed. (Moscow/Leningrad, 1963), pp. 7, 39.

29. "Ukraïns'ki narodni romansy," editor's introduction to the volume of the same title (Kiev, 1961), p. 32.

30. This text is based on versions published in *Zolotye pesni* (Riga, n.d.), pp. 421–22, and in Aleksei I. Chernov (Alexis J. Chernoff), *Narodnye russkie pesni i romansy*, Vol. I, 2nd. ed. (New York, 1959), pp. 79–80.

31. See M. I. Ozhegov, *Moia zhizn' i pesni dlia naroda* (Moscow, 1901), p. 22; Ia. I. Gudoshnikov, *Ocherki istorii russkoi literaturnoi pesni XVIII–XIX vv.* (Voronezh, 1972), p. 146; and his "Gorodskoi romans kak sotsial'noe i khudozhestvennoe iavlenie," in *Fol'klor narodov RSFSR*, vyp. 6 (Ufa, 1979), pp. 102–103. The information about Orekhovo-Zuevo is from P. Sobolev, "O pesennom repertuare," p. 52. Gudoshnikov *(Ocherki)* mentions the existence of three basic variants of the song: one containing the lyrical monologue of the first half plus the narrative part of the second, one limited to the first part, and one consisting only of the description of the wedding. He is referring to the situation in the 1960s, but in the twenties there are also references to a song, "The Bride Wore a White Gown" *(Nevesta byla v belom plat'e)*, i.e., presumably to a text that begins with the wedding description, the first line of which is "The bride wore a white gown."

32. E. V. Pomerantseva, "Ballada i zhestokii romans," *Problemy khudozhestvennoi formy* (= *Russkii fol'klor*, Vol. 14) (Leningrad, 1974), p. 203.

33. T. V. Popova, *Russkoe narodnoe muzykal'noe tvorchestvo*, vyp. 3 (Moscow, 1957), p. 153, under the heading "Psevdonarodnaia pesnia." Chapter 2 of Popova's book is devoted to "Gorodskaia narodnaia pesnia XVIII i XIX vekov." I hope to return to the question of the musical definition of the cruel romance.

34. I. Dunaevskii, "O narodnoi i psevdonarodnoi pesne," *Iskusstvo i zhizn'*, 1939, no. 5, p. 7.

35. The full text (in a folklorized variant of the Gorokhov original) together with music was included in an unusual three-volume collection published in 1936–37 by the Narkom Oborony SSSR (under the aegis of Politicheskoe upravlenie Raboche-Krest'ianskoi Krasnoi Armii): *Russkie narodnye pesni*, compiled by A. G. Novikov, Vol. 3 (Moscow/Leningrad, 1937), p. 10. The collection was unusual first of all for the fact that it contained a number of songs (such as "Exhausted, Worn Out" and several cruel romances) not otherwise published (especially with music) in the Soviet Union until relatively recently, if at all. Also unusual was the fact that it was printed very rapidly: the first two volumes, containing nearly five hundred pages of texts and music, were printed in some three months' time, according to one reviewer (Sergei Bugoslavskii in *Kniga i proletarskaia revoliutsiia*, 1937, no. 4, p. 90). The Gorokhov poem can be found in *Pesni i romansy russkikh poetov*, ed. V. E. Gusev (Moscow/Leningrad, 1965), pp. 864–65.

36. In the 1912 songbook the song is listed as "a new folk song." Pereverzeva mentions it as one of the songs being sung in the late twenties at the Kaluga railroad works ("O gorodskikh pesniakh," p. 101). In the late forties the same melody served as the basis for a song made popular by the weavers' chorus of Vichuga, "Motherland" *(Rodina [Zanialasia zaria raspisnaia])*. On this see Popova, *Russkoe narodnoe muzykal'noe tvorchestvo*, vyp. 2, 2nd ed. (Moscow, 1964), pp. 258, 296.

37. The text and melody of "Don't Reproach Me" can be found in *Russkie narodnye pesni: Melodii i teksty* (Moscow, 1985), p. 59.

38. Vladimir Bogdanov, review of V. F. Trakhtenberg, *Blatnaia muzyka*, in *Ètnograficheskoe obozrenie*, 1908, Vol. 76/77, no. 1/2, pp. 182–85. See also Viktor Petrov,

"Z fol'kloru pravoporushnikiv," *Etnohrafichnyi visnyk,* 1926, no. 2, p. 48, who disputes this view.

39. One such text was published by Èduard Zelenskii in his *Chto poet sovremennaia derevnia Pskovskogo uezda* (Pskov, 1912), p. 126, and another by Boris and Iurii Sokolov in their *Skazki i pesni Belozerskogo kraia* (Moscow, 1915), p. 499. The account of the history of the song is based on the comments of Zinaida Èval'd in E. V. Gippius and Z. V. Èval'd, *Pesni Pinezh'ia,* Vol. 2 (Moscow, 1937), pp. 431–32.

40. Published in Petrov, "Z fol'kloru pravoporushnikiv," p. 54. The text is clearly in Russian, although in Petrov's Ukrainian article it is printed in Ukrainian orthography. A similar version can be found in Iakov Vaiskopf, *Blatnaia lira: Sbornik tiuremnykh i lagernykh pesen* (Jerusalem, 1981), p. 51. A shorter version is included in an account of Russian songs sung in the interwar period in the then-Polish region of Wilno: Franciszek Sielicki, "Rosyjskie piosenki ludowe śpiewane na Wileńszczyźnie w okresie międzywojennym," in Ryszard Łużny, ed., *O poezji rosyjskiej* (= *Zeszyty Naukowe Uniwersytetu Jagiellońskiego* 668 = *Prace Historycznoliterackie,* z. 49) (Cracow, 1984), p. 36.

41. Each verse includes the refrains "Chum-cha-ra, chu-ra-ra" and "ku-ku" as in the first verse. The text was published in Petrov, "Z fol'kloru pravoporushnikiv," p. 60, and two versions of the melody in M. Haidai, "Melodii blatnykh pisen'," *Etnohrafichnyi visnyk,* 1926, no. 2, p. 165. The explanations of terms come from Petrov.

42. "Z studii nad suchasnymy pisniamy (Do istorii pokhodzhennia i rozvytku odniiei pisni r. 1923-ho)," *Etnohrafichnyi visnyk,* 1926, no. 2, pp. 38–43.

43. See Smith, *Songs to Seven Strings,* p. 65, for an English translation of one version, and Chernov, *Narodnye russkie pesni i romansy,* vol. 1, pp. 137–38, for a fuller text. Three verses together with the music were published by Gregory Stone in his collection *Gypsy Melodies* (New York, 1936), pp. 3–5, with a deathless English text by Carol Raven, who provided the following version of the chorus:

> Here come the Bublitchki,
> Bring in the Rublitchki,
> I bake 'em fresh and fresh-
> er every day.
> If you have friends for tea,
> Just give 'em Bublitchki
> They'll want the Bublitchki,
> To keep 'em gay.

Smith cites "Bublichki" as an example of the cruel romance, but neither the text (dealing with economic rather than romantic problems) nor the music (rather lively; half of the chorus is in a major key) fits the model of that genre.

44. Donat Mechik, *Vybitye iz kolei* (New York, 1984), pp. 31–32. On Iadov see also Konstantin Paustovskii, *Povest' o zhizni,* vol. 2 (Moscow, 1966), pp. 108–12. The émigré songwriter Oskar Strok wrote a response to "Bublichki" called "New *Bublichki,*" which began "I'm abroad, free as a bird" *(Ia za granitseiu, svobodnoi ptitseiu . . .).* The text was published in the undated Riga songbook *Zolotie pesni* (pp. 468–69) with no author/composer listed; Strok's name appears on a manuscript copy of the words and music in my possession.

45. *Russkie narodnye pesni,* ed. Az. Ivanov (Moscow/Leningrad, 1966), pp. 237–38. A similar text was printed in *Zolotye pesni,* pp. 237–38.

46. Sielicki, "Rosyjskie piosenki," p. 34.

47. K. Postavnichev, *Massovoe penie* (Moscow, 1925), pp. 57, 124–25. On Siniaia Bluza see Starr, *Red and Hot,* pp. 61–62, and the literature cited there. Pereverzeva, "O gorodskikh pesniakh," p. 103, mentions "A Soviet Strip of Land" as popular among Kaluga railroad workers.

48. *Slavim pobedu Oktiabria!,* vol. 1, p. 109.

49. Popova, *Russkoe narodnoe muzykal'noe tvorchestvo,* vyp. 2, pp. 257–60. The text of the song was based on a poem by Ivan Molchanov, written in response to a newspaper account about an attack on a young tractor driver, who was beaten unconscious, doused with kerosene, and set on fire. The incident took place in July 1929. In 1956 it was discovered that the tractor driver had survived the attack. (*Slavim,* Vol. 1, p. 154.)

50. Starr, *Red and Hot,* pp. 128–29.

51. See, e.g., P. F. Lebedev, *Pesni, rozhdennye v bor'be* (Volgograd, 1983).

52. This paper is based on research made possible by a fellowship from the Russian Research Center, Harvard University, and sabbatical leave support from the University of Massachusetts, and has been informed by the insights of Halina Rothstein.

# XVII

# BOLSHEVIK RITUAL BUILDING
# IN THE 1920s

## Richard Stites

Ritualism—the use of created forms of symbolic behavior for devotional and celebratory moments in life—found its way into many corners of the Russian Revolution. The emergence of a search for new ritual as part of a Bolshevik religion reveals much about the transition from the revolutionary utopianism of the Civil War period to the revolutionary experimentalism of the 1920s. Many Bolsheviks were seized by the vision of War Communism as a permanent order and an ideal structure. When this vision receded in the early 1920s, some revolutionaries turned to another form of utopia building—experimental life from the bottom up. The years of NEP were an ideal setting for social and cultural experimentation. On the one hand, the partial restoration of capitalism engendered fierce hostility among committed communists, particularly veterans, workers, and radical intellectuals. Some of these tried to fight, repudiate, or even forget the realities of NEP by creating experimental enclaves of equality, community, and innovative culture or by drastically reordering old institutions. On the other hand, the very atmosphere of peace and normality, of relative tolerance and pluralism, created a sympathetic environment for leisurely culture building on a trial-and-error basis.[1]

The ritual race for Russian souls was one of these experiments. Its roots can be found in the intellectual current within early Bolshevism known as god building, launched after the Revolution of 1905 by the writer Maxim Gorky and the future commissar of enlightenment Anatolii Lunacharskii. It was based on a desire to infuse socialism with a religious element. Although Lenin, the leader of the Bolshevik Party, fought it angrily, god building recurred in many guises in the first decade after the revolution of 1917: in the arts, in the debates over communist morality, in the cult of Lenin, in revolutionary festival. Lunacharskii bowed to Lenin's ban on god building as a movement but never abandoned its religious kernel. He envisioned socialism as immediate community and faith triumphant, its basic human attributes as love and solidarity, and its historical agent as the proletariat. This was expressed in his own writings and speeches, in the kind of art he favored, and in the content of the early festivals that he promoted—particularly the massive theatrical spectacles in Petrograd in 1919–20 that were enveloped in myth, martyrdom, sacrality, and holy joy. But the broad religiosity of the early outdoor festivals *(prazdniki)* diminished in the 1920s, giving way to a heavy politicization and instrumentalism.[2]

Bolshevik observers of culture in the early 1920s were alive to the ritual and theatrical elements unfolding in all kinds of arenas. There was often a kind of reductionalism in the rhapsodic appeals of some to turn all of life into theater and all of theater into church. But it became increasingly clear that revolutionary forms and symbols, modes of expression and gathering—the festivals of revolution—did not in and of themselves provide the basic elements of a new religion: community rites of celebration, dedication, or mourning that evoked emotional forces transcending political and civic needs. But what kind of rites were needed? How could they be constructed? Of what use would they be? On these matters considerable acrimony was called forth.

Part of the problem resided in the nature of the ritual that would be replaced. The peasant way of life *(byt)* was determined by a system of values, customs, and folkways, varying from one community to another according to local history and the organization of economic life. Inseparable from *byt* was *obriad* (literally rite or ritual), a system of symbols and symbolic behavior rooted in tradition, displayed or performed in connection with the seasonal and life cycles. The imagery and lexicon of traditional Russian ritual were drawn almost exclusively from the Orthodox church calendar, though often heavily infused with pre-Christian pagan elements. These rituals possessed theatrical and aesthetic values for people who had almost no contact with the art and theater of high culture. More important, they possessed practical and instrumental significance, in that peasants believed very concretely in their established function. Legitimacy and salvation were vested in the proper ceremony of naming children, entering wedlock, and laying souls to rest. For the community as a whole, periodic rituals provided a rich and colorful social life, punctuated by convivial feasts and often ending in the fleeting moment of release—freedom from backbreaking toil, drunkenness, brawling, and sexual misbehavior. Rituals embedded family history and life-cycle events in the memory of the entire village, thus affirming the importance of each person in it. Some of these practices—though diluted through adaptation—migrated to the urban milieu.[3]

Judging from the literature advocating and accompanying the new ritual, the advocates had two kinds of things in mind. On the political and practical side, they opposed the old ways in order to fight religion with their own "visible Church," introduce a tone of rationality into lower-class leisure, struggle against drinking and fighting, promote labor stability, teach loyalty to the regime, and in a general way impose an urban order upon a rural mass seen as backward. On the idealistic side, they proposed to emotionalize the revolution, promote a spiritual image of Bolshevism, and—it seems likely—provide some symbols of class consciousness for the working class at a time when such consciousness appeared to be ebbing.[4]

Recognition of the problem began during the Civil War but found a focus only after the debacle of the Young Communist (Komsomol) Christmas Carnival of 1922. Suggested by an enthusiastic promoter of atheism, the economist I. I. Skvortsov-Stepanov—who was also an ardent opponent of god building—this episode was one of the landmarks of the antireligious campaign of early Bolshevism. All over Soviet Russia, Young Communist agitators staged mocking parades parodying religious belief, the clergy, the saints, and even the gods of Christianity, Judaism, and Islam. The public reaction was so negative that the practice was discontinued and leaders began searching for a more subtle way to replace religion. One of these was ritualism. The main spokesmen for it were Mikhail Kalinin, "peasant" president of the republic; P. M. Kerzhentsev, a Proletkult theater specialist; Leon Trotsky; Emelian Iaroslavskii, founder of the Godless League; and the urbane and literary physician V. V. Veresaev. Kalinin quoted peasants who were asking him for surrogate rituals. Trotsky observed that workers were already creating their own ritual forms. Kerzhentsev viewed civic ritual as part of the theatricalization of life. Iaroslavskii stressed the need to move beyond the mocking carnival. Veresaev, the most thoughtful of them all, mapped out the relationship of ritual to the rich and healthy world of emotions. They all argued that since religion was being discouraged and taken away from the people, something had to be given back to them. To do so, they further argued, was not a capitulation to religion but an appropriate mode of peaceful competition with it—one that would give rise to a new communist spirit.[5]

After a good deal of conference talk and journalistic ventilation, the party in October 1923 issued a circular recommending communist public festivals and private rituals. Of the first, Iaroslavskii was the main interpreter. He promoted "revolutionary countercelebrations," sober and joyous—processions with revolutionary songs and music, lectures and reports, and reasonable games—all timed for the cycles of the seasons to compete with church holidays. These festivals, supplementing the already established holidays of the revolutionary calendar, were to eschew mockery and insult but were to offer fun as well as enlightenment, perhaps embellished by a voluntary act of labor in order to woo youth away from the prayers and drunkenness of the old holy days. After the misconceived Komsomol Christmas, a Komsomol Easter had been organized in 1923—not a one-day act of carnival but a kind of unholy week of antireligious consciousness-raising speeches replacing the mockery. Published guides on Communist Easters described reports, charades, songs, poems, tales, stories, legends, quotations from atheist "masters," and skits such as "The Political Trial of the Bible," "The Komsomol Petrushka," and a "Trial of God."

A foreign visitor who witnessed the Leningrad counter-Easter of 1924 tells of Pioneers singing "materialist" songs, displaying slogans such as "The Smoke of the Factory Is Better Than the Smoke of Incense," and performing an atheist play to an audience of a thousand. Eventually a whole new counterfestival calendar emerged made up of "parallel" days, opposing Electric Day to Elijah Day, Forest Day to Trinity Sunday, Harvest Day to the Feast of the Intercession, and the Day of Industry to the Feast of Transfiguration. The problem was that if the performances were salted with antireligious skits, they descended back to carnival; if they were not, they were dull.[6]

The result was a shift in the realm of invented traditions from public display to the more intimate spheres of community and family. In the local community the focus for new ritual was the club, envisioned by some as a surrogate church or civic temple. An early apologist for the Palace of Workers, repudiating the old tsarist People's House *(Narodnyi Dom)* as an arena for "bread and games" to lull the masses, and scorning the bourgeois clubs as shelters for the card games and banquets of the affluent, described the workers' palace as "a cultural building for a new, healthy life of the proletariat."[7] The problem was to transform the workers' club of the revolutionary period (which had been, like those of 1789 and 1871 in France, psychological staging areas of revolutionary political action) into something solemn, joyous, and celebrative of the new order, without descending to banality.

A barrier to the fulfillment of this ideal was the dichotomy between the designers and the users of the club—a dichotomy that has often beset religious congregations in modern times. The exterior forms and the interior space of the clubs were in many ways congenial to the utopian speculations that accompanied the revolution. Architectural experimentation, fueled by self-consciously radical impulses, coincided with the turn toward indoor ritual and a search for the forms of community. The earliest clubs were opened in the premises of confiscated mansions or public edifices. But almost at once there appeared grandiose plans for huge central palaces of labor, followed by projects for local clubs in neighborhoods and enterprises. They varied little in interior content: library, dining room, large auditorium for solemn occasions, music room, theater, and recreational facilities. Variations of the name "workers' club" *(rabochii klub)* abounded: Workers' Palace, House of Lenin, Proletarian House, House of Workers, Palace of Culture (and of Rest), and so on. The earliest projects bordered on fantasy, with grandiose structures resembling medieval cathedrals, the Hôtel de Ville in Paris, railway stations, and chateaux. In the mid-1920s, especially with the work of the brilliant architect Konstantin Mel'nikov, clubs become more functional and more like the places where their users worked. These buildings provided—on paper—a broad range of collective activities, public services, and a grand setting, often with imaginative use of partitions for self-changing space.[8]

A sense of what went on inside may be gained from the report, based on "long observations" of a workers' club written by a ritual advisor and specialist in the 1920s. The closest thing to a quasi-religious ritual was the frequent meeting to honor special people or events. According to his observations, the decor was uniformly artless, routinized, and often inappropriate: red table cover, a bust or portrait of a leader, slogans on the walls, and a dais; and on particularly "festive" occasions, the bric-a-brac of a bygone age—crepe paper, paper lanterns, a fir tree. Music was provided by a brass ensemble which offered "flourishes" to punctuate the proceedings and endless renderings of the "Internationale."

Meetings were usually poorly timed, too long, and stilted—consisting of repetitive speeches, the awarding of prizes, the marches of the honored up to the dais. The formalism and the passivity of the spectators led the observer to assess the whole routine as "boring, dreary, and tiresome." His offhand remarks about the eternal awkwardness of ushers who carried banners up to the front reveal in a flash how the easy grace of the outdoor festival with its stately reverence and its familiar catalogue of movements and gestures became cramped inside the artificial premises of the new "workers' church." In the schools, communist ritual took the form of antireligious propaganda: a skit about Science Triumphant, a mock church service, a choral singing of "the antireligious Internationale," a verse about "The Priest and the Devil," and a collective declamation called "Storming the Trust of Heaven."[9]

At the level of family life-cycle ritual, the Bolsheviks made an effort to drape the three main junctures of human life—birth, marriage, and death—in revolutionary clothing. Octobering *(Oktiabrina)*, the dedication of newborns (called Starring [*Zvezdina*] in some places), was the most celebrated of these. It began haltingly and sporadically in the Civil War but began to spread in the early 1920s. Trotsky, hearing of a mock ceremony of "inspection" of a newborn child of workers by their factory comrades, saw it as a spontaneous expression of a new workers' ritual culture. No survey of Octoberings was ever published, but it seems to have taken hold in factory towns in the early 1920s. One of the first recorded in detail (November 22, 1923) took place in Kharkov, where a baby daughter was Octobered and presented with a gift—a portrait of the infant Lenin. The parents delivered a verbal promise to raise the child in the spirit of communism, the "Internationale" was sung, and choruses performed folk songs. The reporter claims a wide influence thereafter in the vicinity of Kharkov.[10]

At an Octobering in a Moscow club, a detachment of Pioneers with flag and drum chanted "We are the Young Guard of Workers and Peasants" as they escorted a mother to the dais. "The child belongs to me," she declaimed, "only physically. For spiritual upbringing I present it to society." The Pioneers then folded the baby in a red banner and vowed to enroll her in their unit. Since the Soviet law of 1917 permitted all citizens to change their names at age eighteen, some adults began to follow suit. A group of women workers, hoping to promote Octobering, had themselves renamed at a club ceremony as the "Vanguard of the New Life" amid some muffled guffaws from the menfolk. After a few months, they reclaimed their old names, except for one, Avdotiia, who had taken the name Revolution (*Revoliutsiia*) and was ever after known as Auntie Revo (Tetia Reva).[11]

The new names given to Octobered babies offer a code to the values officially revered in the early years. The French Revolution had invoked the shades of classical figures (Brutus, Hannibal, Gracchus); and European Social Democrats had tried to popularize socialist names (Lassallo, Marxina, and Primo Maggio in Italy; Bebelina in Germany). The few dozen Russian "revolutionary" names that I have uncovered from the period divide in the following way:

*Revolutionary Heroes and Heroines*

Spartak, Marks, Engelina, Libknekht, Liuksemburg, Roza, Razin, Mara, Robesper, Danton, Bebel'; Vladlen, Vladlenina, Ninel, Il'ich, Il'ina (all variants of Lenin); Bukharina, Stalina, Budena.

*Revolutionary Concepts*

Pravda, Revmir (revolution and peace), Konstitutsiia, Revdit (child of the revolution), Dotnara (daughter of the toiling people), Era, Karm (Red Army), Barrikada, Giotin (Guillotine), Bastil', Tribuna, Revoliutsiia, Krasnyi (Red), Kommuna, Parizhkommuna (Paris Commune), Proletarii, Buntar' (rebel), Fevral', Mai, Oktiabrina, Serpina (from sickle), Molot (hammer), Smychka (alliance of workers and peasants), Volia (will or freedom), Svoboda (freedom), Dinamit, Ateist, Avangarda, Iskra (spark), Marseleza (Marseillaise).

*Industrial, Scientific, and Technical Imagery*

Tekstil, Industriia, Traktorina, Dinamo, Donbass, Truda, Smena (shift), Radium, Genii (genius), Ideia, Elektrifikatsiia.

*Culture, Myth, Nature, Place Names*

Traviata, Aida, Les (forest), Luch (light), Poema, Okean, Orel (eagle), Solntse (sun), Zvezda (star), Razsvet (dawn), Atlantida, Brungilda, Minevra [*sic*], Monblan (Mont Blanc), Kazbek, Singapur.

There were the usual cases of error, resulting from misunderstanding of words. In 1919, peasants in a commune named their daughter "Markiza" (Marquise), thinking it irreligious and somehow vaguely foreign. Other names chosen included Commentary, Embryo, and Vinaigrette.[12]

It is hard to assess the semiotic significance of this because we do not know how many people were given which of these names. But in musing about what kind of people endowed and bore them (mostly workers), one feels an element of magic. Names in fact are magical in many so-called primitive and not-so-primitive cultures. This particular invented ritual was an expression of the wish to create a new reality by means of imagery, to populate the world with humans called Spark, Joy, Will, Electric, Rebel, and Barricade, and to fashion living monuments to the recent and distant heroic past (Vladlen, Spartacus). But it was also an almost mystical quest for another world by giving image to what is perhaps the most intimate possession of any human being. In their variety, color, and rich associative capacities, the revolutionary names of the 1920s represented a sensibility exactly opposite to that of those people who aspired to a collective identity for the masses. And it was also a national and generational revolt against the Greco-Russian Orthodox culture of the past with its ancient and limited repertoire of Aleksandrs, Andreis, Sofiias, Petrs, and Tatianas, though some tried to do this by choosing pre-Christian Slavic names, such as Mstislav or Sviatopolk, that had fallen into disuse in modern times.[13]

From the perspective of the ritual designers, Octobering possessed many distinct virtues. By allowing the couple to choose the baby's name, it rejected the custom of many villages for the male head of the household to make that choice. By providing the parents with a suggested list of "revolutionary" names, it reduced the number of people bearing names of saints (among whom had been very few workers, peasants, intellectuals, or radicals), and also eliminated another excuse for holiday observance: the traditional name day of the saint. By holding the naming in a club or factory or village reading room and allowing the local Bolshevik or manager to officiate with the aid of a Pioneer detachment, it excluded the clergy. By skipping the watery immersion in a damp church building and substituting a red banner for the white baby shawl, it promoted both good health and Bolshevik symbolism. And by treating the mother as an equal and prominent celebrant, it visibly repudiated the church's practice of banning women from the church until forty days after childbirth.[14]

Getting married at a Red Wedding—instead of at the dry civil registry office or in the church—had a dual significance. Its form showed a desire for the solemnity, decor, and ritual that were wholly absent at marriage registry offices. Its content treated the wife and the husband as legally, politically, and symbolically equal. During the French Revolution, the policeman Josephe Fouché had wanted Temples of Love built to stage all weddings. Such edifices did not bloom in the Russian Revolution, and the civil office remained a cramped, crowded bureau where couples got married in twenty minutes without so much as a rose or a ring. Some people obviously wanted more, as did the prophets of the new ritualism.[15]

Red Weddings appeared at about the same time as the Octobering ceremonies. Critics such as Veresaev thought them banal. He described one, of December 1924, in a club of leatherworkers: a red covered table, a portrait of Lenin, the vows of bride and groom to each other and to communism, reports and speeches, a wedding gift for the new couple—works by Lenin and Zinoviev—and the mandatory "Internationale." Village Red Weddings added the traditional custom of *chastushka* (the declamation of witty folk sayings) and *khorovod* (round dance and song). Among the peasants, attempts were made to insert industrial imagery into the feast by employing the new Ford tractor, adorned with red flags, as a wedding carriage. But the custom did not catch on in the countryside—peasants wanted something longer, more solemn and elaborate, followed by a day or two of carousing. In 1925, according to one estimate, 75 percent of peasant weddings were still held in church. Even in the industrial towns, there is no sign that the Red Wedding became a universal or even mass phenomenon.[16]

Here, too, the Red Wedding had some advantages over the Orthodox wedding. It was shorter, requiring far less expenditure of energy, and it advanced and signaled the doctrine of the equality of the sexes, an official position of the regime. This had appeal to some urban elements. But for the peasants, it apparently had little. Furthermore, the Red Wedding, even at its most elaborate, lacked the stunning beauty and magnificence of the Orthodox nuptial service—the song, the incense, the costumes, the rings signifying an unbroken life together. Furthermore, the church wedding was preceded by extremely stylized and theatrical preliminary rituals of courtship, matchmaking, serenading, wailing, improvised jokes, and carefully choreographed movements; and it was crowned by a joyous feast of dancing, eating, and drinking. The lamentation on the coming loss of freedom for the bride and the graphic display of the bloodstained sheet from the wedding couch as proof of virginity may have seemed to Bolsheviks debasing to women, but these customs were part of an ancient tradition and thus were revered by most peasants. In fact, the village wedding was the central event in the life of every person, and, for women especially, its signs and gestures were interlocked with the whole culture of folk tales, folk songs, epics, laments, sayings, and customs. Desacralizing the wedding was an assault on rural culture as a whole.[17]

The revolutionary funeral—it is significant that no neologism was applied to it and it was officially called "civic burial"—was the most problematic of the invented rituals and the most resistant to innovation. At the root of the problem was its origin as a martyr's funeral. Drawing on nineteenth-century precedents, the genre had emerged in 1905 with the funeral of Nikolai Bauman and found artistic stylization in the painting *Red Funeral* by Isaak Brodskii (1906). This style was adopted and amplified in the first great Bolshevik interment, that of Moisei Uritskii, held in September 1918. With its guard of honor, the lying in state in luxurious surroundings, the huge cortege with ornate red catafalque, the carriage escort and lone caparisoned horse, rows of bedecked armored cars, and overflying aircraft, it far surpassed the obsequies of former martyrs of the revolutionary movement. The city boss Grigorii Zinoviev displayed the full power of Petrograd's ceremonial magnificence and mobilized an entire city for the most elaborate funeral seen there since the interment of Aleksandr III in 1894—and even more dazzling in that the public was in full presence for the entire day, with dispersed units touching almost every neighborhood in the huge city. It became a model for hero funerals in the Civil War and prefigured most of the elements in the Lenin funeral of 1924, an event of stupendous importance. For the next two years, revolutionary burials became a regular feature in the street life of Russia.[18]

But not all people who die are revolutionary martyrs or heroes. The Orthodox church panikhida, a work of extraordinary textual richness and beauty, continued to attract masses of people, and not only in the countryside. Even at radical Kronstadt in the early days of the revolution, fallen sailors were given an Orthodox requiem on Anchor Square followed by a general singing of the "Workers' Marseillaise." As tension between church and state mounted, people began searching for alternative and politically acceptable ways to bury their dead. A peasant in 1919 asked Kalinin what kind of service the regime had in mind and if it was really necessary for him to bury his son—who was no revolutionary—to the strains of "You Fell Victim." New forms began to appear ad hoc, uneasy blends of old pious forms and modern political speeches. Veresaev described them in the mid-1920s as arid: a sterile chamber for the wake, mourners with nothing to do, and the customary eulogy for the departed—all of it leaving a void instead of an affirmation of life for the survivors. For poor workers, the rites were empty and cold. Veresaev proposed a wholly new ceremony with original music (instead of the eternal Chopin or the revolutionary funeral marches): sounds of sorrow to evoke genuine emotion followed by triumphant cadences to celebrate continuing life, a choreographed tableau of white-robed young women (recalling the maiden mourners of Orthodox funeral rites), and the mourners' participation in a great catharsis—in other words, an unabashed public display of emotion in the company of loved ones. But even Veresaev conceded that a "symphony of scarlet and black banners and a forest of marvelous palms" was suitable for a great national leader—such as Lenin.[19]

Some hoped to achieve the democratization of death by the use of crematoria. The first European crematorium had been built in Milan in 1876, and many major cities of Europe had them; but none had been allowed in Russia because of the power of the Orthodox church. As early as 1919 architects began designing ceremonial crematoria, bearing such names as "To the Heavens" and "Phoenix" and taking the shape of basilicas, towers, castles, and churches. But in some of these, the lying-in-state halls came in different sizes, indicating hierarchy even in death. This was simply a reflection of the heroic burial culture that was well underway and of the fact that when "important" funerals took place, factories were sometimes closed. Yet the crematorium seemed to promise a mode of neat standardization. Trotsky urged speedy cremations and simple ceremony with red flags, the funeral march, processions, eulogy, and a rifle salute. The architect Mel'nikov devised a "crematorium-columbarium" for ordinary people where the "family ritual would be revolutionized in a stroke, transcendent beliefs broken down, and the cause of sound health advanced." The first Soviet crematorium was opened in 1927 in the nonfunctioning Donskoi Monastery in Moscow which possessed cellars deep enough for the construction of incinerators and machinery. It contained a Farewell Hall of 150 seats. By the end of 1928 over 4,000 bodies had been cremated there, most of them by "administrative" process (that is, cadavers assigned to it by various institutions, presumably hospitals and morgues). Among the first "volunteers" who requested cremation in their testament were Skvortsov-Stepanov and Aleksandr Bogdanov, who was working to extend human life through blood transfusion.[20]

The fiery machines of the crematoria were the perfect emblem for the Bolshevik way of death: clean, rational, and economical. But this particular fire did not spark the emotions of the majority of Russians who continued to look to the life-giving earth for their place of final rest. The sculptor Sergei Konenkov dreamed of a new kind of cemetery for the future:[21]

> The very concept of a "cemetery" will change. They will be parks of good memories. In them, the grateful descendants will "recall" those who did not spare themselves in the name of the common good. Young life will seethe around magnificent works of sculpture and under the canopies of beauteous trees. These parks will become places of leisure and the pride of every Soviet city.

Except for the seething youth, such places have in fact sprouted up in Soviet Russia: the Mars Field in Leningrad, the Revolutionary Necropolis on Red Square, the various military-revolutionary sections of the Novodevichi in Moscow and the Aleksandr Nevskii Lavra and Volkov Cemetery in Leningrad, and the huge memorial grounds containing those fallen in World War II. They are places of immeasurable sadness as well as of national pride and love of homeland—but in this they hardly differ from the overgrown Orthodox churchyards that continue to cover the Russian land.

Revolutionary funerals became the norm for party leaders and other prominent figures in Soviet life. They were also observed by ordinary people, provided—as often happened by way of compromise—that a priest could intone the last rites before the civil ceremony or that a church service was allowed to follow it. Again, Bolsheviks could claim a rational advance over traditional funerals where women and family members questioned the deceased in lamentations about why he had abandoned them by dying, and where women regularly received less ritualistic attention in their burial services. But the civil burials also displayed inequality of a different sort— expressed in size of musical accompaniment (often a guitar for a humble person and bands of varying sizes for the elite), length and complexity of ceremony, and symbolic importance of the interment site.[22]

The communist ritual movement of the 1920s did not become a mass phenomenon as it would in the 1960s.[23] Only limited sectors of the urban population, mostly workers and intellectuals, took to it; and the government made no serious effort to sustain it. Peasant dislike or indifference, too, is easily understood: rural people of the older generation missed the little glasses of vodka and appetizers, the cry of "it's bitter," the priest, and the dancing at weddings; the plates of food for the dead; the mysteries, beauties, joys, and ebullience of country-style ritual. One reporter described a "new" wedding in a small town where the guests were expected to partake of cakes and tea and listen to political messages! But there was hostility to ritualism among communists as well. Some Young Communist League members seemed to distrust acts of piety and "beauty" no matter how Bolshevized. A 1930 encyclopedia entry on rituals asserted that "with the development of culture, rituals lose their significance." In the same year we hear of Young Militant Godless children playing "antireligious" military games in which a correct answer about God or atheism enabled the answering team to capture an enemy soldier or fortress, a clear reversion to the tough mode of war on God. Militant and military now converged. Soviet institutions abandoned the rituals of the 1920s thereafter and succumbed to dry bureaucratic forms. Club meetings of the 1930s adorned their trees with red stars and bayonets and listened to such soul-searing lectures as "The Class Essence of Christmas."[24]

Vitalii Zhemchuzhnyi, a filmmaker and writer for the avant-garde *Novyi Lef*, put his finger on the malaise in a critique of ritual building in 1927. "The spreading or propagation of some sort of novel, invented ritual," he wrote, "is an absurd utopia." Archaic ritual, he conceded, symbolized reactionary values. But artificial ritual was worse, since it preserved old elements but had no link to popular psychology. Only an "organic" system of ritual, built over time, could replace the ritual of tradition. He was right and wrong. Invented political and social rituals in nineteenth-century Europe had shown themselves fully capable of taking root if given time to grow. At a more visceral level lurked the deophobia of some communists. Emelian Iaroslavskii, in a striking anecdote, told of a comrade who, in order to avoid the odious prospect of a Red funeral which he considered immoral and barbarous, had endowed his body to a soap factory. This was the fear of a "communist *dvoverie*"—the simultaneous existence of two religions (both retrograde): Christianity and the ritualized communism of a new priesthood, holy day, God (Marx), scripture (his works), angels (the Red Army), and hell (for class enemies). Bolshevism, in this phobic vision, was becoming a religion in reverse. The distaste for it was Lenin's hatred of god building taken to its logical conclusion.[25]

The collapse of Soviet ritualism was of course part of the larger failure of the Bolsheviks to create a new religion around their ideals, myths, and values. For a while, the cult of Lenin seemed to offer a suitable substitute for traditional religions. But, as Nina Tumarkin has shown, the power of that cult began to fade in time and was in the late 1930s weakened by a cult of Stalin. The intensification of the war against God during the First Five-Year Plan also spelled the end of Bolshevik ritual building. Christmas trees were banned in 1929, and Santa Claus was unmasked as an ally of the priest and the kulak; churches were closed, and the antireligious carnival was once again unleashed. A parallel termination of the interesting discourse on communist morality which had occupied many writers in the late 1920s undercut all the other elements of god building in that period. In a larger sense Bolshevism—as the journalist Maurice Hindus observed at the time—while possessing some outward attributes of a religious faith, was actually a nonfaith because it was not forgiving, possessed no deity, exalted science and technology, and offered a "revolutionary" ethics instead of a universal and humane one. Berdiaev noted Bolshevism's lack of inward drama and depth, its weakness in religious psychology, and its pedantry. Years later—and from an entirely different perspective—Mao Zedong voiced his view very succinctly and honestly: "Marxism-Leninism has no beauty nor has it any mystical value. It is only extremely useful."[26]

The relevance of this rather minor exploration of cultural forms of the Russian Revolution ought to be obvious. First of all, if the quest for ritual is seen in combination with other experimental or innovative practices of the period, it should lay low the myth that the 1920s were a "nonutopian" time—a period of hard-headed common sense flanked by the two great utopian and experimental eras of War Communism and the Cultural Revolution of 1928–31. If anything, the NEP period was even more experimental because various groups had the freedom, leisure, and security to test out new human relationships. They were also highly motivated to do so precisely in order to keep the flame of revolutionary myth alive in the drafty and dank landscape of semicapitalism and "bourgeois remnants" of the 1920s. Ritual building was part of a counterculture that sought to affirm October in the face of hard economic realities, harsh physical conditions, and the compromise with the old world (as many perceived the NEP to be). The debate in the Young Communist League over morality and "how to be a good communist" was a perfect reflection of this. Ritualism was its reified counterpart—the visual, kinetic, and symbolic edifice that every value system needs in order to take root or survive. Enthusiasts of a new Bolshevik ritual clearly wanted to enrich and vary life under Soviet socialism and not reduce it or render it less meaningful by submitting it to political or economic machinery. Finally, it goes without saying that the limited success of community and family rituals in the towns was not matched by any success at all in the countryside—a statement that can be made for a whole range of innovative experimentation during the 1920s. This was further proof that urbanites and peasants continued to dwell in two different worlds.

## NOTES

1. This is one of the arguments of my book *Revolutionary Dreams: Utopian Vision and Experimental Life in the Russian Revolution* (New York, 1989).

2. For a brief and competent summary of Lunacharskii's religious sensibility, see Jutta Scherrer, "L'intelligentsia russe: sa quête de la 'vérité' réligieuse du socialisme," *Le temps de la réflexion*, II (1981), pp. 113–52. For a reading of the revolutionary festivals, see James Von Geldern, *Festivals of Revolution* (forthcoming), and Stites, "The Origins of Soviet Ritual Style: Symbol and Festival in the Russian Revolution," in Claes Arvidsson and Lars Erik Blomqvist, eds., *Symbols of Power: The Esthetics of Political Legitimation in the Soviet Union and Eastern Europe* (Stockholm, 1987), pp. 23–42.

3. V. Ia. Propp, *Russkie agrarnye prazdniki* (Leningrad, 1963); Y. M. Sokolov, *Russian Folklore*, trans. C. R. Smith (Detroit, 1971); Mary Matossian, "The Peasant

Way of Life," in W. Vucinich, ed., *The Peasant in Nineteenth-century Russia* (Stanford, 1968), pp. 1–40; and K. V. Chistov and T. A. Bernshtam, eds., *Russkii narodnyi svadebnyi obriad* (Leningrad, 1978).

4. See Diane Koenker's essay, above, for the diminution of class consciousness among workers in the 1920s.

5. M. K. [M. I. Kalinin], "Novyi byt," *Krasnyi pakhar*, 1 (1919), pp. 13–15; *Deietali Oktiabria o religii i tserkvi* (Moscow, 1968), pp. 6–7; V. [P. M.] Kerzhentsev, "Teatr kak vneshkol'noe obrazovanie," *Vneshkol'noe obrazovanie*, 2–3 (Feb.-Mar. 1919), pp. 23–28; L. D. Trotsky, *Problems of Everyday Life* (1923; New York, 1973); Iaroslavskii, *Protiv religii i tserkvi*, 3 vols. (Moscow, 1932–5), vol. III, pp. 220–24; V. V. Veresaev, *Ob obriadakh starykh i novykh* (Moscow, 1926), pp. 5–8; C. Binns, "The Changing Face of Soviet Power: Revolution and Accommodation in the Development of the Soviet Ceremonial System," *Man*, 14 (Dec. 1979), pp. 594–95.

6. Binns, p. 595; Iaroslavskii, *Religiia i R.K.P.* (Moscow, 1925), p. 47; Iaroslavskii, *Protiv religii*, vol. III, pp. 61–63; *Komsomol'skaia Paskha* (Moscow, 1924); Ia. Rezvushkin, *Sud na bogom* (Moscow, 1924); P. Sheffer, *Seven Years in Soviet Russia* (London, 1932), pp. 34–39; F. Kovalev, *Kalendar' religioznykh prazdnikov* (Kharkov, 1930).

7. V. E. Khazanova, ed., *Iz istorii Sovetskoi arkhitektury*, 2 vols. (Moscow, 1963–70), vol. I, pp. 134–35.

8. Ibid., vol. I, pp. 134–43, 150–55, and vol. II, p. 7 (illust.); Kathleen Berton, *Moscow: An Architectural History* (London, 1977), pp. 211–12; Vittorio de Feo, *URSS: architettura, 1917–1936* (Rome, 1963), p. 112; S. F. Starr, *Konstantin Melnikov: Solo Architect in a Mass Society* (Princeton, 1978), pp. 128–47.

9. M. Danilevskii, *Prazdniki obshchestvennogo byta* (Moscow, 1927), pp. 3–13; F. F. Korolev et al., *Ocherki po istorii Sovetskoi shkoly i pedagogiki, 1921–1931* (Moscow, 1961), p. 294.

10. Trotsky, *Problems*, pp. 45–47; Ivan Sukhopliuev, *Oktiabriny* (Kharkov, 1925); A. M. Selishchev, *Iazyk revoliutsionnoi epokhi* (Moscow, 1928), pp. 179–80; and Jenifer McDowell, "Soviet Civil Ceremonies," *Journal for the Scientific Study of Religion* (1974), pp. 267–68, for examples of obscure places where these rituals were performed.

11. Veresaev, *Ob obriadakh*, pp. 22–26; Danilevskii, *Prazdniki*, p. 4.

12. M. Kol'tsov, *Izbrannye proizvedeniia*, 3 vols. (Moscow, 1957), vol. I, p. 574; R. Fueloep-Miller, *The Mind and Face of Bolshevism* (New York, 1965), pp. 193–94; Sukhopliuev, *Oktiabriny*, pp. 20–30; M. K., "Novyi byt"; and personal information from bearers of revolutionary names. For comparisons, see H. de Man, *Psychology of Socialism* (London, 1928), pp. 156–64, and E. M. Thompson, *The Making of the English Working Class* (New York, 1963), p. 407. Science fiction utopias of the period abound in names of this sort.

13. For invented ritual, see Eric Hobsbawm and Terence Ranger, eds., *The Invention of Tradition* (Cambridge, England, 1983). Diane Koenker's small sample of six renamed babies (her essay, above) presents an interesting case for analysis: two Vladimirs, two Rosas, one Margarita, and one October. Vladimir is the ultimate Russian Orthodox saint's name, but it was also widely adopted at that moment, in many variants (see my list), because it was Lenin's first name. Rosa or Rose (*Roza* in Russian), though not common (except among Jews), was not unusual, yet it was a popular revolutionary name also because of its association with the Polish-German revolutionary martyr Rosa Luxemburg. Margarita, more popular in some non-Russian areas of the Soviet Union, may have been the only conventional name in this sample.

14. Natalie Moyle, "Death in Life: The Role of Women in Russian Ritual," unpublished ms.; Janna Gross, "Krasnyi Obriad," unpublished ms. I thank the authors for access to their work.

15. For the civil (ZAGS) wedding, see Stites, *The Women's Liberation Movement in Russia* (Princeton, 1978), pp. 363–64. Fouché, cited in Ernest Henderson, *Symbol and Satire in the French Revolution* (New York, 1912), p. 409.

16. Veresaev, *Ob obriadakh;* Vadim Bayan [V. I. Sidorov], *Kumachevye gulianki: khorovodnye igry* (Moscow, 1927), pp. 16–25; G. B. Zhirnova, "Nekotorye problemy i itogi izucheniia svadebnogo rituala v russkom gorode serediny XIX–nachala XX v.," in Chistov and Bernshtam, *Russkii narodnyi svadebnyi obriad,* pp. 32–47; M. Hindus, *Red Bread* (Bloomington, 1988), p. 197; Trotsky, *Problems,* p. 46; R. Pethybridge, *Social Prelude to Stalinism* (London, 1974), p. 55 (wedding figures). See also Helmut Altrichter's essay, above.

17. Moyle, "Death in Life"; Zhirnova, "Nekotorye problemy."

18. On the Bauman funeral, see Abraham Ascher, *The Russian Revolution of 1905: Russia in Disarray* (Stanford, 1989), vol. I, pp. 262–64; *Vestnik Oblastnogo Komissariata Vnutrennikh Del,* 2 (Sept. 1918), pp. 64–71 (Uritsky's funeral, illust.). See also *Plamia,* 67 (Oct. 19, 1919), pp. 1–2, for the funeral of General A. P. Nikolaev, who was hanged by the Whites. The motifs of his and Uritskii's funerals are similar to those of a funeral of the 1860s depicted in *Sergei Vasilevich Gerasimov* (Moscow, 1951), p. 11. On Lenin's funeral, see Nina Tumarkin, *Lenin Lives!* (Cambridge, Mass., 1983).

19. P. Avrich, *Kronstadt* (Princeton, 1970), p. 173; M. K. "Novyi byt"; Fueloep-Miller, *Mind,* p. 196; Veresaev, *Ob obriakakh,* p. 9.

20. Khazanova, *Iz istorii,* vol. I, pp. 214–15; Trotsky, *Problems,* p. 46; Starr, Melnikov, p. 35; Gvido Bartel, "Istoriia i statistika Moskovskogo Krematoriia," *Zdravookhranenie* (1929), pp. 106–108; Alexander Bogdanov, *Red Star: The First Bolshevik Utopia,* ed. L. Graham and R. Stites, trans. C. Rougle (Bloomington, 1984).

21. Quoted in Vasily Komar and Alexander Melamid, "In Search of Religion," *Artforum,* vol. 18, no. 9 (May 1980), no pagination.

22. Moyle, "Death in Life"; Gross, "Krasnyi Obriad"; and Daniel Kaiser, "Death and Dying in Early Modern Russia" (Kennan Institute Occasional Paper, 1986).

23. For the revival of communist ritualism after Stalin's death, see Christel Lane, *Rites of Rulers* (Cambridge, England, 1981). Arguments at the time of the revival (in the early 1960s) parallel those of the 1920s about the need for emotion and beauty in ritual events: I. Kryvelev, "Vazhnaia storona byta," *Kommunist,* 8 (May 1961), pp. 65–72; D. Sidorov, "Vazhnaia forma ateisticheskogo vospitaniia," *Partiinaia zhizn',* 6 (Mar. 1963), pp. 49–51; and O. Poleshko-Polesskii, "Khoroshie traditsii," ibid., pp. 52–54.

24. McDowell, "Soviet Civil," pp. 267–68 (qu. p. 267); *Tseli i zadachi Soiuza Bezbozhnikov* (Ulianovsk, 1928), pp. 41–42; N. Amosov, *Na detskom antireligioznom fronte* (Moscow, 1930), pp. 47–48; Merle Fainsod, *Smolensk under Soviet Rule* (New York, 1963), p. 440.

25. Vitalii Zhemchuzhnyi, "Protiv obriadov," *Novyi Lef* (Jan. 1927), pp. 43–47; Iaroslavskii, *Protiv religii,* vol. III, p. 223. For Europe, see Hobsbawm and Ranger, *Invention.*

26. Hindus, *Great Offensive* (New York, 1933), pp. 182–89; idem., *Humanity Uprooted* (New York, 1930), p. 41; Nicholas Berdyaev, *The Origin of Russian Communism* (London, 1937), pp. 158–78. Mao is quoted in W. Rosenberg and M. Young, *Transforming Russia and China* (Oxford, 1982), p. 182.

# XVIII

## CONCLUSION

### UNDERSTANDING NEP SOCIETY
### AND CULTURE IN THE LIGHT OF
### NEW RESEARCH

*William G. Rosenberg*

By now the readers of this volume will hardly need to be persuaded about the intrinsic importance of social and cultural history to our understanding of Soviet Russia in the 1920s. Without positing the notion of social or cultural autonomy, it is still obvious that the political issues that traditionally preoccupy historians of this period were remote from the day-to-day matters with which millions of ordinary Russians were concerned, especially in the countryside. And if, as Sheila Fitzpatrick suggests, the vehicle of cultural analysis has helped us finally to arrive at a social history that is not primarily about politics, we can now appreciate even further, nonetheless, the degree to which the political process itself in the 1920s and afterward was affected by Soviet Russia's social and cultural environment.

If we ask what we have learned from these essays about NEP as a period of transition, from what tsarist Russia had been to what Stalin's Russia was about to become, as it was phrased above, the answer has to be quite a lot. Most important, these essays make it clear that the new regime's very *agenda* in these years—to build a modern, industrial, socialist Soviet Union—was deeply at odds with the immediate concerns of many of its social constituents, particularly in the countryside. And if we begin to think again about the role of the party and the state in this process—issues which have not been directly before us in this volume—this alone helps us understand why, if not how, both acquired in the course of NEP a particular social base, the bureaucracy, which, as Moshe Lewin suggests, the party itself neither intended to acquire nor wanted.[1]

The party's "retreat" to bureaucracy clearly occurred, moreover, as the essays of Neil Weissman and Alan Ball indicate, partly because the traditional instruments of social control (police, militia) were extremely weak, and partly because the regime's control over its economy was soon deeply compromised, whatever the intentions of party leaders. Weissman shows quite clearly how the Bolsheviks attempted in the aftermath of 1917 to insulate the ordinary police and militia from baneful local influences, and how traditional habits of arbitrariness and caprice were foresworn in favor of respect for law, at least officially. Yet revolutionary Russia simply lacked an adequate complement of personnel for the tasks at hand, or the resources to support them. Villages soon developed their own "informal" means of policing, especially for petty crimes. The militia itself, poorly trained and paid and increasingly isolated, retreated rather quickly to the punitive and arbitrary methods that had characterized its tsarist antecedent.

The importance of this has not simply to do with rural culture. Among other things, the militia represented the official arm of the state under NEP, along with the tax collector, the grain procurement agent, the army recruiter, and the local soviet. The functions of the militia thus served as a point of interaction not only between town and countryside but also between state and society, and their problematic nature encouraged retreat on both sides—peasants more deeply into the insular life of the village, the state's agents more suspicious, wary, and defensive, even if defensiveness often took antagonistic forms.

The situation with private traders was similar, as Alan Ball's contribution suggests. Although there is still much work to be done on the social role of the private trader during NEP, as Ball recognizes, and while it is important to distinguish ordinary peasants from urban-based professionals who bought and sold goods for cash on a large scale, it is clear that the extent to which the purchase and distribution of scarce goods was beyond the state's control was necessarily a matter of great concern. Managing the allocation of commodities was an inherent part of socialist planning. Differential prices and the private traders' ability to earn huge, quick profits represented a siphoning of desperately needed capital, especially when professionals were adept at avoiding taxes. The very nature of trade in the early years of NEP, in fact, and the constant, if sometimes implicit, scorn with which party leaders regarded this most "bourgeois" of activities, invited concealment. In turn, this encouraged efforts at regulation, which could be done only bureaucratically, and poorly at best.

The social aspects of these interactions, moreover, were in some ways as problematic as the activity itself. Private traders often developed extensive personal networks in the early years of NEP, building in many cases on old contacts and relationships. The mentality of "connections" was itself inimical to socialist values, but an even stronger potential danger lay in the way in which antagonistic relations with the state turned personal networks into potential (and actual) systems of oppositional collusion. What was involved was rarely political in the programatic sense, although many Bolsheviks worried about the political outlooks of this burgeoning group. The issue, rather, was the degree to which the Soviet "state-in-the-making" was becoming increasingly less able to affect primary forms of social and economic interaction at odds with its implicit and overt system of values. For most of NEP, as Ball points out, the danger was again addressed by the means of bureaucratic regulation, which in some ways only intensified the problem. At the very least, these trading networks would eventually have to be made compatible with goals of state-directed industrial growth. If they were absorbed by the state itself, the social relations they reflected would also be largely absorbed, subverting socialist values from within. Here, clearly, was a primary source of *blat* and the "family circles," which so affected Soviet Russia under Stalin. If they were simply repressed, as began, in fact, to occur during NEP, the result was likely to be an extension of the commodity "deserts" Ball refers to, as the state increasingly found itself unable to procure adequate amounts of goods.

One can also appreciate in this regard the "dangers" posed by what William Burgess described to the seminar as the "corporate independence" of the rural correspondents—*sel'korrespondenty* or *sel'kory*—particularly those who openly expressed their opposition to the party based on an understanding of official corruption. At the highest levels of the party, Bukharin and others apparently reacted to this criticism with menacing threats, despite the fact that the *sel'kory* had been established in part to consolidate party links with the countryside and to provide the center with a steady stream of accurate information. Whether or not the *sel'kory* could properly be characterized as an oppositionist tendency, the paradox of the "Sel'kor Party," as Bukharin apparently called it in 1926, was that this critical tendency reflected both the hostility of many in the countryside to the Soviet state, and the needs of the state itself to purge its own bureaucratic apparatus of corruption, especially, it seems, in rural soviets. There was good reason, in other words, in terms of the party's own commitment to integrity within the state and party apparatus, for developing rural opposition. And the sociocultural foundations of this dilemma, just as in the case of the militia and the private traders, posed fundamental difficulties to those who recognized the relationship between an effective, viable state order and Soviet Russia's ability to achieve its fundamental goals.

In this regard, the singular reliability of the army, as Mark von Hagen shows us, and then through its extension by means of Red Army veterans to the NKVD, reflects a process related not so much to Bolshevik ideology as to the more general need of any industrializing order for reliable instruments of social control. One need only glance at the history of the National Guard in America or that of the national police and army in

France and Britain to appreciate this alliance in the West; and as Russianists all know, this was precisely what was lacking in the last years of the old regime, and a major source of its weakness. While I am leary of the linkage between a reliable military (or police) and the tasks of industrial state administration, links that Samuel Finer and others have emphasized,[2] it does seem clear that the problem of social control in the broadest sense is one that industrializing societies simply must solve in one form or another. In simple and stark terms, NEP posed this problem for the fledgling Soviet state in the 1920s; and its inability to find adequate solutions was at least partly rooted in the society and culture of NEP itself.

One way in which social control can be achieved, of course, is through the development of a broad popular consensus, since the degree of coercion obtaining in any state order is at least partly related to the pervasiveness of consensual values and commitments. Bolshevik leaders understood this very well. Although the emphasis of Peter Kenez's important book on the "propaganda state" centers on mass mobilization, the party's methods of political indoctrination were also clearly intended to internalize new social values and inculcate passive controls on social behavior. The "retreat" from terror under NEP, in fact, made the propagandists' task all the more urgent.[3]

Why it was so difficult to cultivate such a consensus in NEP society is apparent from the essays of Hiroaki Kuromiya, Wendy Goldman, Diane Koenker, and Helmut Altrichter, as well as other seminar contributions, especially that of John Hatch. Each deals with the ways in which prerevolutionary social relations and cultural traditions carried over into NEP, and with the manner in which social and economic circumstances in the 1920s contradicted in varying degrees the very system of values the party hoped to develop. The result in quite diverse milieus was a common tendency to insularity and resistance.

Kuromiya shows us, for example, that in some forms of social organization themselves, in this case the artel, a powerful, independent, and *functional* authority influenced the ways workers thought and acted; we learn from him by implication that the state's task with regard to the artel under NEP involved not only supplanting an autonomous with a subordinate authority but also maintaining the functional integrity of the work unit itself—something which he suggests Stalinists ultimately managed to do only by creating the shock brigades. The proposal of Aleksei Gastev, the period's best-known proponent of industrial "modernization" through the rationalization of work processes, that the artels had to be either "smashed or utilized cleverly" reflected an intractable dilemma. An all-out assault on this traditional system of production (and production relations) would clearly have intensified worker opposition to the proletarian state, itself an obviously troublesome contradiction; but any form of accommodation, even the most clever, perpetuated work values at odds with the state's pressing interests in industrial development.

John Hatch's contribution suggests the extent to which worker resistance in and outside the artels already centered under NEP on the Bolsheviks' reintroduction of highly differentiated wage scales and the piece rate system, regarded by some as among the worst aspects of capitalist industry. Highly differentiated wage scales reinforced a sense of privilege and hierarchy; piece rates not only tied wages to the speed of production but also liberated employers—now often the state itself—from most wage obligations when there were not enough goods to produce. The problems were similar with *khozraschet* and other systems of economic accountability, all of which led to cost cutting. NEP brought hardships for workers, plant failures, and the equivalent of bankruptcies even as the industrial economy was expanding, none of which encouraged the Bolsheviks' broadest base of social support to consider the state "theirs." As Diane Koenker shows in her exemplary essay, the very elements of proletarian solidarity and self-consciousness that had proved so important to the revolutionary process in 1917 were very much weakened under NEP, partly because victory itself made class consciousness less urgent, partly because of the intrinsic difficulty of "replacing the old with the new." And since one's sense of being a "worker" depended so much on an identifiable class enemy, proletarian consciousness could be cultivated under NEP only at the expense of the state and its agents, or through an implicit critique of NEP itself.

Wendy Goldman, meanwhile, shows us how strongly working women (also, ostensibly, an important social base of state support) were united in their criticism of (and hostility to) not only the new patterns of male-female relationships sanctioned by the new order but also the state itself for inadequately shouldering the burdens of family maintenance and support. As she tells us, new socialist values, particularly the progressive legislation on divorce, were sharply at odds with working women's social circumstances as well as basic economic facts. High female unemployment, low wages, and inadequate state resources undermined the Bolsheviks' vision of a free union between equals. Most working women remained dependent on men for their economic well-being, especially if they had families. Conservative sexual policies served to preserve the family as a viable economic unit, even at the cost of increased family insularity and the state's own ideological credibility.

All of this suggests in one way or another that the agenda of the state under NEP was fundamentally at odds in important respects with the agenda of society at large, and certainly with that of important bases of social support. Even for the most "respectable" members of the new social order, such as Goldman's working women, Koenker's printers, or those who made up Kuromiya's industrial artels, the imperatives of NEP were immediate, not future-oriented; personal and particular, not abstract or ideological; and focused overwhelmingly on local conditions and needs, not those of the state as a whole, however much these were of interest. And if there was, as Diane Koenker suggests, a need for new self-definition within Soviet society at large under NEP, this pattern of disjuncture could only make that particular task more difficult as well, further complicating the burdens of "modernizing" in this period of transition.

That NEP involved such burdens for the fledgling Soviet regime is hardly a new idea. I take it that this is what Moshe Lewin means when he writes of "the 'superstructure' rushing ahead" to a future of its own definition in the face of a basically rural, and hence local, social structure.[4] Nor, of course, did the problem spring up suddenly in Russia under NEP. One need only recall the near-universal alienation of virtually all social groups from the tsarist regime in its last years to appreciate the degree to which the task of integrating state and society in a functional way was inherited by Lenin and his comrades along with the need itself to further the processes of industrialization. Nonetheless, if we are to understand NEP broadly as a period of "transition," using that term in what I have suggested above is its proper historical sense, we must appreciate not only the very character of NEP society in and of itself but also the lack of correspondence between important elements of this character and the state's needs, as I have suggested, and, perhaps more important, the *effect* of this lack of correspondence, ultimately, on the way in which the Soviet state and its social institutions developed.

The same was true for NEP culture, in all of its senses. As Helmut Altrichter argues in his most interesting essay, and as V. P. Danilov, Teodor Shanin, and other students of the countryside have demonstrated in their work, such central elements of industrial culture as the measurement of value in terms of time or the importance of the division of labor were essentially alien to the Soviet village of the 1920s, as they had been before. And whether or not one sees the problem in terms of the degree to which "capitalism had penetrated the countryside" before 1917, as some of our Soviet colleagues are inclined to do, there seems little question that the Civil War wrecked any vestige of "progress" in those terms, and that as Moshe Lewin again reminds us, *aziatskaia bezkul'turnost'*, the expression of the time, had its justification.[5] The racist adjective itself, in fact, reflected not only a feeling about the cultural primitiveness of the village, suggested so well in Altrichter's descriptions of village feast days, but even more the cultural distance of the village from the industrial West.

This, I think, is what Régine Robin's fascinating account of peasants as readers is also describing, although in a way much more sympathetic to the village in terms of its resistance to (and even lack of comprehension of) the efforts of the party and state to penetrate its boundaries. Jeffrey Brooks's account of Russia's "American dream" paints a similar picture. The very ambiguity of popular attitudes in the city toward "technological" America was itself an important cultural residue of the past; and the notion that somehow hard work and "technological wizardry," as Brooks puts it nicely, were part of the American character, and that capitalist and exploitative America was simultaneously a metaphoric model for human effectiveness, reflected in one sense only the comparable tasks, urban and rural, of Russia's cultural transition to industrial "modernity," the task of creating, in effect, an industrial culture appropriate to the state's agenda for development.

I use the phrase "industrial culture" deliberately, for again it seems to me that the work here tends to concern not so much rural or urban society and culture (or culture in a rural or urban setting) as the sociocultural parameters shaping Soviet Russia's development under NEP, and the ways in which these parameters in turn both defined and redefined the tasks of the state itself in pursuing its own objectives. *Any* industrializing state, in other words, whether or not it considered itself "proletarian," as the Soviet state under NEP clearly did, simply *had* to confront in some fashion the insularity of the village, its cultural base, its lack of "comprehension" of industrial values, its militant resistance to outside authority, and the relationship between attachment to cultural traditions and resistance to change. The same was true in towns and cities, insofar as attitudes toward work, the quality of production, or even productivity itself reflected cultural impediments to technological progress.

It is in these terms, among others, that Katerina Clark's essay is so illuminating. The process of "sovietization" of Russian intellectual life that she reviews so well seems to have been both complementary to and *necessarily* complementary to the sovietization of Russian society, culture, and the state. One could hardly sustain for very long the processes of transition in circumstances where the dominant tendencies of intellectual life contradicted and opposed these efforts in comprehensive and fundamental ways. That arts and letters were not so much "proletarianized" as "routinized" as Soviet culture with a capital S simply parallels in logical fashion the process whereby the Soviet state-in-the-making, too, was not proletarianized but routinized, in all of its many limitations. Social relations, especially the relations between men and women, soon bore the marks of tradition and routine, as well, at least as strongly as new Bolshevik values. Routinization, moreover, implies social or cultural hegemony as well as the emergence of bureaucratic systems. It is consequently hardly surprising, at least from this perspective, that the question of *kto kogo* in intellectual life was answered during these years, considering that the overall direction and course of Soviet development itself—that is, from an essentially agrarian to an essentially industrial order—was also set during NEP, although not, of course, the means.

I suspect that another way of understanding the "sovietization of culture" is to see it as the "nationalization" of culture, not in the administrative sense of the term (although there was obviously plenty of that) but in the sense of the development of a "national" culture, loosely defined, complementing the official ideals, goals, values, and especially forms of the state. For Soviet intellectual life, in other words, NEP is both a period of exciting creativity and attractive diversity *and* a period of transition in which culture, like the state, becomes single-minded and intolerant rather than pluralistic, relentlessly determined rather than exploratory, and hopelessly dominated by official values and ideas, a consequence, as Clark shows us, of the shifting patterns of patronage.

In an important sense, however, this should not surprise us, for what NEP also reflects, in addition to everything else the seminar has touched upon, is the process of "nation building"—a jargon term I do not much like, but which I think one must use to designate the more subjective components of Soviet state development. I do not want to argue, like a sixth-grade textbook, that the "Soviet nation was forged in these years"; it may be that the concept "nation" was itself really inappropriate to the Soviet Union, in the past or especially now. But whether or not a nation existed or exists, the effort at building a nation certainly occurred during NEP, as it occurred elsewhere in the aftermath of the First World War, especially in Eastern Europe; and what our new understanding of NEP society and culture reveals to us again, I think, is the enormity of this task in postrevolutionary Russia, given the nature of social, economic, and cultural conditions, and especially the manner in which the revolution itself challenged and attempted to destroy the fundamental elements of political nationalism that helped cohere the old order.

Again I am referring to a complex process which is essentially anthropological and psychological in its essence, rather than simply political (although it also involves a deliberate strategy on the part of the party or state to inculcate a new "national feeling," and it is essential to the state's own *legitimacy*). And here, too, one of the important elements of NEP as a period of transition is the way the interactions between society and the state (or party) essentially defined the *limits* of this process in the 1920s and make Stalin's relatively greater success in this regard far more comprehensible. Consider, in particular, Richard Stites's analysis of community and family rituals. Among other things, what is interesting about the October-ings (and the marvelous assortment of names assigned to those duly "Octobered") is the way they simultaneously reflect conscious, programmed efforts on the party's part to transform the rituals of life in support of a new national consciousness, and the stumbling, limited nature of these efforts, each of which was to help create a unifying, legitimizing national identity. Many were subject to ridicule. Others, like the vaunted "Subbotniks," were regarded by many with cynicism, and even contempt. As Stites indicates, only limited sectors of the urban population took to the communist ritual movement, and many of these were already "converted."

What studying NEP from the perspective of society and culture tells us about this process, again, however, is how extraordinarily difficult it was, and how strong the resistance was to making this transition. This helps explain the curious history of urban songs that Robert Rothstein lays out for us. But it also helps explain why the more conventional efforts of Stalin and his supporters in this regard, evoking "heroic" traditions of Russia's past and conscientiously avoiding attacks on such traditional (and in many ways pernicious) values as "patriotism," ultimately proved so much more successful. Although this latter question is not on our agenda here, what is of relevance is the importance of understanding the cultural anthropology of NEP in these terms. If historians reexamine the particular forms that Soviet national identity eventually assumed—especially its non-Marxist political nationalism and its crude and passionate patriotism—they are now much more likely to find their origins not simply in Stalinist politics but in the society and culture of NEP.

I want to emphasize this as I turn briefly by way of conclusion to the last issue of NEP as a society in transition that I think deserves attention, its relationship to the formation of a Soviet "system," to use the phrase entitling a superb collection of essays by Moshe Lewin. The notion of a system is important to our understanding of NEP in at least three ways. First, and most generally, it prompts us to recognize that the interactions we have been examining between the various components of NEP society and culture are, in fact, interrelated themselves, and indeed constitute, in addition to everything else, a *system;* we need to remember, in other words, that while each of the essays here analyzes component parts of NEP, these parts together also form an organic whole. Second, and more particularly, it is important to recognize that the conflictual interactions themselves, between town and countryside, state and society, those "above" and "below," also produced during NEP the need for intensive state mediation, and were perhaps so strong as to beg mediation altogether. Some mechanism to reconcile clashing value systems and to inculcate further respect for and support of the new order simply had to be found. And third, I would suggest that it was precisely here, in terms of NEP as a "system," of the need for intensive mediation within that system, and ultimately of the failure of the new regime to do this successfully under NEP, that we must again bring back within our analytic purview the question of politics and the political process.

This last was a matter of some controversy among the participants at the seminar, and I do not wish to be misunderstood. I agree entirely with Sheila Fitzpatrick and others about the historical centrality of culture and society, the successful manner in which the study of cultural issues here illuminates our understanding about society itself, and the ways in which a new picture of NEP begins to emerge from our work precisely because of the added cultural dimension. As Fitzpatrick maintains, the "familiar political questions have been run into the ground."

For my part, however, I would emphasize the word *familiar;* and I would disagree in one important sense with her assertion that by the means of cultural and social analysis we have finally arrived at a social history that is not primarily about politics. That sense has to do with the ways in which relationships of power and control—politics—are themselves integral components of the important social and cultural elements we have been studying, even if—*especially* if—such relationships are not themselves familiar. In other words, even if one's objective is to explore NEP society and culture in and of themselves, one must ultimately pay attention to questions of power precisely because they affect virtually all social and cultural elements.

Let me put the matter in slightly different terms. As we have seen, central components of society and culture in NEP Russia were fundamentally related to traditional and prerevolutionary structures and values, rather than the "modern" elements postulated by Bolshevism as essential to the emergence of a revolutionary socialist order. This was true in family relations, patterns of industrial production, policing and state administration, rituals, and even the ways in which the burdens of unemployment were distributed, among others. These elements consequently had, in some way, to be reconciled with the demands of industrial modernity if the goals of the party (and state) were to be realized. "Reconciliation," in turn, meant politics and the exercise of power. Thus the power latent in social and cultural forms themselves—to resist the state, to function autonomously, to perpetuate male domination, for example—was necessarily a vital part of the political process as a whole. And in turn, the ways in which relationships of power emerged—between men and women, managers and workers, village elders and the militia—were also instrumental in determining the very nature of NEP's social and cultural components.

Here, moreover, is where the notion of "system" is especially important. To my understanding, it was precisely the ability to mediate the many conflicts elucidated by the essays above that was largely absent in Soviet Russia under NEP. In effect, tsarism and the revolutionary upheaval both left Russia without an effective and accepted political mechanism capable of facilitating a less traumatic (but by no means painless) postrevolutionary evolution. And if Soviet Russia's transition to a modern, industrialized, socialist order required the inculcation of more or less uniform values, recognized as legitimate and consequently reinforcing the legitimacy of the regime, not only was an effective mechanism for this largely absent under NEP, but so was any consensus as to what these values actually should be. In Jeffrey Brooks's felicitous phrase, the state simply could not *manage* the village. Nor could it manage the workplace or the family, insofar as "manage" implies an ability to ensure compatible values, behavior, and social relations. And what our explorations of society and culture here suggest, and what helps make them so important to our overall understanding of NEP, is the way in which NEP society and culture contained within its particular forms, in varying ways and degrees, the power to affect the nature of the developing system. Politics in this sense not only remains a desirable point of interest even for social historians but indeed is essential for our understanding of all forms of social interactions, and hence the very nature of society and culture. The problem of leaving politics out, in other words, is that it leads us to a distorted vision even of our cultural or social subjects, which act and are defined in no small measure in relation to power, political authorities, and their methods of control.

None of this, however, should detract in the least from the singular achievements of the seminar and this volume. Questions of social and cultural history have rightly been restored to a position of primacy in our understanding of NEP even as a period of transition, and by implication, to the whole course of Soviet development.

## NOTES

1. Moshe Lewin, *The Making of the Soviet System: Essays in the Social History of Interwar Russia* (New York, 1985).
2. Samuel E. Finer, "State- and Nation-Building in Europe: The Role of the Military," in Charles Tilly, ed., *The Formation of National States in Western Europe* (Princeton, 1975).
3. See Peter Kenez, *The Birth of the Propaganda State: Soviet Methods of Mass Mobilization, 1917–1929* (Cambridge, England, 1985).
4. Lewin, *Making*, chap. 11.
5. Lewin, *Making*, chap. 10.

# SELECTED BIBLIOGRAPHY

## Lori A. Citti

The monographs and articles included in this bibliography represent a selected list of secondary works on political, economic, and social issues of the NEP period. The list is by no means complete, especially as pertains to periodical literature.

### Soviet Monographs

Abramov, A. *O pravoi oppozitsii v partii.* Moscow, 1929.
Aleshchenko, N. M. *Moskovskii sovet v 1917–1941 gg.* Moscow, 1976.
Bakhtin, M. V. I. *Lenin o soiuze rabochego klassa i krest'ianstva v vosstanovitel'nyi period, 1921–1925 gg.* Gorky, 1960.
Berkhin, I. B. *Voennaia reforma v SSSR, 1924–25.* Moscow, 1958.
Bol'shakov, A. M. *Derevnia 1917–1927.* Moscow, 1927.
Bukharin, N. *Ekonomika perekhodnogo perioda.* Moscow, 1920.
Bukharin, N., and Preobrazhenskii, E. *Azbuka kommunizma.* Moscow, 1920.
Chugaev, D. A., ed. *Istoriia natsional'no-gosudarstvennogo stroitel'stva v SSSR.* 2 volumes. Moscow, 1968–1970.
Danilov, V. P. *Rural Russia under the New Regime.* Translated by Orlando Figes. Bloomington, 1988.
Dmitrenko, V. P. *Torgovaia politika sovetskogo gosudarstva posle perekhoda k nepu, 1921–1941.* Moscow, 1971.
Ehrenburg, I. *Memoirs, 1921–1941.* Cleveland and New York, 1964.
Ermakov, V. T. *Istoricheskii opyt kul'turnoi revoliutsii v SSSR.* Moscow, 1968.
*Fabrichno-zavodskaia promyshlennost' goroda Moskvy i Moskovskoi gubernii, 1917–1927.* Moscow, 1928.
Fediukin, S. A. *Bor'ba s burzhuaznoi ideologiei v usloviiakh perekhoda k nepu.* Moscow, 1977.
———. *Sovetskaia vlast' i burzhuaznye spetsialisty.* Moscow, 1965.
———. *Velikii Oktiabr' i intelligentsiia.* Moscow, 1972.
Genkina, E. B. *Gosudarstvennaia deiatel'nost' V. I. Lenina, 1921–23 gg.* Moscow, 1969.
———. *Perekhod sovetskogo gosudarstva k novoi ekonomicheskoi politike, 1921–22 gg.* Moscow, 1954.
———. *SSSR v period vosstanovleniia narodnogo khoziaistva, 1921–1924 gg.* Moscow, 1955.
Glezerman, G. *Likvidatsiia ekspluatatorskikh klassov i preodolenie klassovykh razlichei v SSSR.* Moscow, 1949.

Goncharov, A. F. *Sovetskoe gosudarstvo i pravo v period vosstanovleniia narodnogo khoziaistva SSSR, 1921–1925.* Moscow, 1960.

Iakubovskaia, S. I. *Stroitel'stvo soiuznogo sovetskogo sotsialisticheskogo gosudarstva, 1922–1925 gg.* Moscow, 1960.

Institute of History of the USSR, Academy of Sciences of the USSR. *Kul'turnoe stroitel'stvo v SSSR, 1917–1927: razrabotka edinoi gosudarstvennoi politiki v oblasti kul'tury.* Moscow, 1989.

————. *Novaia ekonomicheskaia politika. Voprosy teorii i istorii.* Moscow, 1974.

Kabo, E. O. *Ocherki rabochego byta.* Moscow, 1928.

Katagorin, I. I. *Istoricheskii opyt KPSS po osushchestvleniiu novoi ekonomicheskoi politiki, 1921–1925.* Moscow, 1971.

Kim, K. P. *Kul'turnaia revoliutsiia v SSSR, 1917–1965.* Moscow, 1967.

Lebakova, E. R. *Opyt KPSS po probishcheniiu mel'koi burzhuazii goroda k stroitel'stvu sotsializma.* Moscow, 1970.

Lenin, V. I. *O kooperatsii.* Moscow, 1965.

————. *O soiuze rabochego klassa i krest'ianstva.* Moscow, 1969.

Mamedov, M. R. *NEP i politicheskoe vospitanie rabochego klassa.* Baku, 1966.

Matsa, I. L. *Sovetskoe iskusstvo za 15 let: materialy i dokumentatsiia.* Moscow, 1933.

Morozov, L. F. *Organy TsKK-RKI v bor'be za sovershenstvovanie sovetskogo gosudartsvennogo apparata, 1923–1934 gg.* Moscow, 1964.

————. *Reshaiushchii etap bor'by c nepmanskoi burzhuaziei: iz likvidatsii kapitalisticheskikh elementov goroda.* Moscow, 1960.

*Moskovskie bol'sheviki v bor'be s pravym i 'levym' opportunizmom, 1921–1929 gg.* Moscow, 1969.

*Nauchnaia organizatsiia truda, proizvodstva i upravleniia: sbornik dokumentov i materialov, 1918–1930 gg.* Moscow, 1969.

*Partiia v bor'be za vosstanovlenie narodnogo khoziaistva, 1921–1925: dokumenty i materialy.* Moscow, 1961.

Poliakov, Iu. A. *Perekhod k nepu i sovetskoe krest'ianstvo.* Moscow, 1967.

Preobrazhenskii, E. A. *Ekonomicheskie krizisy pri NEPe.* Moscow, 1924.

Shlikter, A. G. *Agrarnyi vopros i prodovol'stvennaia politika v pervye gody sovetskoi vlasti.* Moscow, 1976.

Suvenirov, O. F. *Kommunisticheskaia partiia—organizator politicheskogo vospitaniia Krasnoi Armii i Flota, 1921–1928.* Moscow, 1976.

Tal', V. *Istoriia Krasnoi armii.* Moscow/Leningrad, 1929.

Tolmachev, V. N., ed. *Khuliganstvo i khuligany: sbornik.* Moscow, 1929.

Trifonov, I. Ia. *Klassy i klassovaia bor'ba v SSSR v nachale NEPa, 1921–1925.* Leningrad, 1969.

————. *Likvidatsiia ekspluatatorskikh klassov v SSSR.* Moscow, 1975.

————. *Ocherki istorii klassovoi bor'by v SSSR v gody NEPa, 1921–37.* Moscow, 1960.

Ulianovskaia, V. A. *Formirovanie nauchnoi intelligentsii v SSSR, 1917–1937 gg.* Moscow, 1966.

Zelenova, N. G. *Desiatyi s"ezd partii i ego resheniia: perekhod k novoi ekonomicheskoi politike; lektsiia.* Moscow, 1963.

Zis', A. Ia. *Stranitsy istorii sovetskoi khudozhestvennoi kul'tury, 1917–1932.* Moscow, 1989.

## Western Monographs

Abramsky, C., ed. *Essays in Honor of E. H. Carr.* Cambridge, England, 1974.

Atkinson, Dorothy. *The End of the Russian Land Commune, 1905–30.* Stanford, 1983.

Bailes, Kendall. *Technology and Society under Lenin and Stalin: Origins of the Soviet Technological Intelligentsia, 1917–1941.* Princeton, 1978.

Ball, Alan. *Russia's Last Capitalists: The Nepmen, 1921–29.* Berkeley, 1988.

Benet, Sula, ed. *The Village of Viriatino.* Garden City, 1970.

Berkman, Alexander. *The Bolshevik Myth: Diary, 1920–22.* London, 1925.

Bettelheim. Charles. *Class Struggles in the USSR: First Period, 1917–23.* Translated by Brian Pearce. New York, 1976.

————. *Class Struggles in the USSR: Second Period, 1923–30.* Translated by Brian Pearce. New York, 1978.

Bowlt, John E., ed. *Russian Art of the Avant-Garde: Theory and Criticism, 1902–1934.* New York, 1976.

Brinton, Maurice. *The Bolsheviks and Workers' Control.* London, 1970.

Brooks, Jeffrey. *When Russia Learned to Read.* Princeton, 1985.

Brzezinski, Zbigniew. *The Permanent Purge.* Cambridge, Mass., 1956.

Calvey, Charles E. "The Organizations That Coordinated the Kolkhozy from 1918–1933." Ph.D. diss., University of Illinois, 1984.

Carr, Edward H. *The Bolshevik Revolution, 1917–1923.* 3 volumes. New York, 1951–53.

————. *The Interregnum, 1923–24.* New York, 1954.

————. *Socialism in One Country, 1924–1926.* 3 volumes. New York, 1958–60.

Chase, William. *Workers, Society and the Soviet State: Labor and Life in Moscow, 1918–1929.* Urbana and Chicago, 1987.

Cohen, Stephen F. *Bukharin and the Bolshevik Revolution: A Political Bibliography, 1888–1938.* New York, 1973.

————. *Rethinking the Soviet Experience: Politics and History since 1917.* New York, 1985.

Cox, Terry. *Peasant, Class, and Capitalism: The Rural Research of L. N. Kritsman and His School.* New York, 1986.

Daniels, Robert. *The Conscience of the Revolution: Communist Opposition in Soviet Russia.* Cambridge, Mass., 1960.

————. *The Stalin Revolution: Foundations of Soviet Totalitarianism.* 2nd edition. Lexington, Mass., 1972.

Davies, R. W. *Soviet History in the Gorbachev Revolution.* Bloomington, 1989.

Day, Richard. *Leon Trotsky and the Politics of Economic Isolation.* Cambridge, 1973.

Deutscher, Isaac. *The Prophet Armed: Trotsky, 1879–1921.* New York, 1954.

————. *The Prophet Unarmed: Trotsky, 1921–1929.* New York, 1959.

————. *The Prophet Outcast: Trotsky, 1929–1940.* New York, 1963.

————. *Russia in Transition.* New York, 1960.

————. *Stalin: A Political Biography.* New York, 1967.

Dewar, Margaret. *Labor Policy in the USSR, 1917–1928.* London, 1956.

Drinan, Patrick. "Zinoviev and the Soviet NEP." Ph.D. diss., University of Virginia, 1972.

Dvinov, Boris. *Moskovskii sovet rabochikh deputatov, 1917–1922: vospominaniia.* New York, 1961.

Erlich, Alexander. *The Soviet Industrialization Debate, 1924–1928.* Cambridge, Mass., 1960.

Fainsod, Merle. *Smolensk under Soviet Rule.* Cambridge, Mass., 1958.

Ferdinand, C. I. P. "The Bukharin Group of Political Theoreticians: Their Ideas and Their Importance in the Soviet Union in the 1920s." D. Phil., Oxford University, 1984.

Fitzpatrick, Sheila. *The Commissariat of Enlightenment: Soviet Organization of Education and the Arts under Lunacharsky, Oct. 1917–1921.* London, 1970.

————. *Education and Social Mobility in the Soviet Union, 1921–1934.* New York, 1979.

————. *The Russian Revolution.* New York, 1982.

————. ed., *Cultural Revolution in Russia, 1928–1931.* Bloomington, 1978.

Gleason, Abbott, et al., eds. *Bolshevik Culture: Experiment and Order in the Russian Revolution.* Bloomington, 1985.

Graham, Loren R. *Science, Philosophy and Human Behavior in the Soviet Union.* New York, 1987.

————. *The Soviet Academy of Sciences and the Communist Party, 1927–1932.* Princeton, 1967.

Haimson, Leopold, ed. *The Mensheviks from the Revolution of 1917 to the Second World War.* Chicago, 1974.

Hatch, John. "Labor and Politics in NEP Russia: Workers, Trade Unions, and the Communist Party in Moscow, 1921–1926." Ph.D. diss., University of California, Irvine, 1986.

Holmes, Larry E. *The Kremlin and the Schoolhouse: Reforming Education in Soviet Russia, 1917–1931.* Bloomington, 1991.

Hough, Jerry, and Fainsod, Merle. *How the Soviet Union Is Governed.* Cambridge, Mass., 1979.

Huskey, Eugene. *Russian Lawyers and the Soviet State: The Origins and Development of the Soviet Bar, 1917–1939.* Princeton, 1986.

Jasny, Naum. *The Socialized Agriculture of the USSR.* Stanford, 1949.

————. *Soviet Economists of the Twenties: Names to Be Remembered.* Cambridge, England, 1972.

Joravsky, David. *Soviet Marxism and Natural Science, 1917–1932.* London, 1961.

Kenez, Peter. *The Birth of the Propaganda State: Soviet Methods of Mass Mobilization, 1917–1929.* Cambridge, England, 1985.

Lambert, Nicholas. *The Technological Intelligentsia and the Soviet State.* New York, 1979.

Langsam, David. "Pressure Group Politics in NEP Russia: The Case of the Trade Unions." Ph.D. diss., Princeton University, 1974.

Laqueur, Walter. *The Fate of the Revolution: Interpretations of Soviet History.* New York, 1967.

Lewin, Moshe. *The Gorbachev Phenomenon: A Historical Interpretation.* Berkeley, 1988.

————. *Lenin's Last Struggle.* New York, 1968.

————. *The Making of the Soviet System: Essays in the Social History of Interwar Russia.* Translated by Catherine Porter. New York, 1985.

————. *Political Undercurrents in Soviet Economic Debates.* Princeton, 1974.

————. *Russian Peasants and Soviet Power: A Study of Collectivization.* Translated by Irene Nove. Evanston, 1968.

McNeal, Robert. *The Bolshevik Tradition.* Englewood Cliffs, 1963.

Maguire, Robert. *Red Virgin Soil: Soviet Literature in the 1920s.* Princeton, 1968.

Male, D. J. *Russian Peasant Organization before Collectivization: A Study of Commune and Gathering, 1925–1930.* Cambridge, England, 1971.

Malle, Silvana. *The Economic Organization of War Communism, 1918–1921.* New York, 1985.

Mally, Lynn. *Culture of the Future: The Proletkult Movement in Revolutionary Russia.* Berkeley, 1990.

Medvedev, Roy. *Let History Judge: The Origins and Consequences of Stalinism.* New York, 1972.

Mirski, Michael. *The Mixed Economy: NEP and Its Lot.* Translated by Roger A. Clarke. Copenhagen, 1984.

Moore, Barrington. *Soviet Politics: The Dilemma of Power*. Revised edition. New York, 1965.

Narkiewicz, Olga. *The Making of the Soviet State Apparatus*. Manchester, 1970.

Nove, Alec. *An Economic History of the USSR*. London and Baltimore, 1969.

Pethybridge, Roger. *The Social Prelude to Stalinism*. London, 1974.

Pipes, Richard. *The Formation of the Soviet Union: Communism and Nationalism, 1917–1923*. Revised edition. New York, 1980.

Rees, E. A. *State Control in Soviet Russia: The Rise and Fall of the Workers' and Peasants' Inspectorate, 1920–1934*. New York, 1987.

Rigby, T. H. *Communist Party Membership in the USSR, 1917–1967*. Princeton, 1968.

———. *Lenin's Government, Sovnarkom, 1917–1922*. Cambridge, England, 1979.

Service, Robert. *The Bolshevik Party in Revolution, 1917–1923: A Study in Organizational Change*. New York, 1979.

Shanin, Teodor. *The Awkward Class: Political Sociology of Peasantry in a Developing Society, Russia, 1910–1925*. Oxford, 1972.

Solomon, Susan G., and Hutchinson, John F., eds. *Health and Society in Revolutionary Russia*. Bloomington, 1990.

Solzhenitsyn, Aleksandr. *The Gulag Archipelago*. New York, 1973.

Sorenson, Jay B. *The Life and Death of Soviet Trade Unionism, 1917–1928*. New York, 1969.

Stites, Richard. *Revolutionary Dreams: Utopian Vision and Experimental Life in the Russian Revolution*. New York, 1989.

———. *The Women's Liberation Movement in Russia: Feminism, Nihilism, and Bolshevism, 1860–1930*. Princeton, 1978.

Taniuchi, Y. *The Village Gathering in Russia in the Mid-1920s*. Birmingham, 1968.

Taylor, Richard, ed. *The Film Factory: Russian and Soviet Cinema in Documents, 1896–1939*. Cambridge, Mass., 1988.

Timasheff, Nicholas. *The Great Retreat: The Growth and Decline of Communism in Russia*. New York, 1946.

Toner, Glen. "The Politics of Energy and the NEP: A Framework and Analysis." Ph.D. diss., Carleton University, 1984.

Trotsky, L. *The Challenge of the Left Opposition, 1923–1925*. Edited by Naomi Allen. New York, 1975.

———. *The Revolution Betrayed: What Is the Soviet Union and Where Is It Going?* Translated by Max Eastman. 5th edition. New York, 1972.

———. *Stalinism and Bolshevism*. New York, 1972.

———. *Their Morals and Ours*. New York, 1937.

Tucker, Robert, ed. *The Soviet Political Mind*. Revised edition. New York, 1971.

———. *Stalin as Revolutionary*. New York, 1973.

———. *Stalinism: Essays in Historical Interpretation*. New York, 1977.

Tucker, Robert, and Cohen, Stephen F., eds. *The Great Purge Trials*. New York, 1965.

Tumarkin, Nina. *Lenin Lives! The Lenin Cult in Soviet Russia*. Cambridge, Mass., 1983.

Ulam, Adam. *The Russian Political System*. New York, 1974.

Vol'skii (Valentinov), Nikolai. *Novaia ekonomicheskaia politika i krizis partii posle smerti Lenina: gody raboty v VSNKh vo vremiia NEP: vospominaniia*. Stanford, 1971.

Von Hagen, Mark. *Soldiers in the Proletarian Dictatorship: The Red Army and the Soviet Socialist State, 1917–1930*. Ithaca, 1990.

Von Laue, T. H. *Why Lenin? Why Stalin? A Reappraisal of the Russian Revolution, 1900–1930*. Philadelphia, 1964.

Vucinich, Alexander. *Empire of Knowledge: The Academy of Sciences of the USSR, 1917–1970.* Berkeley, 1984.
Ward, Chris. *Russia's Cotton Workers and the New Economic Policy: Shop Floor Culture and State Policy, 1921–29.* New York, 1990.
Weiner, Douglas. *Models of Nature: Ecology, Conservation, and Cultural Revolution in Soviet Russia.* Bloomington, 1988.
Williams, Robert. *Artists in Revolution: Portraits of the Russian Avant-Garde, 1905–1925.* Bloomington, 1977.

## Periodical Literature

Abrams, Robert. "Political Recruitment and Local Government: The Local Soviets of the RSFSR, 1918–1921." *Soviet Studies,* 19, no. 4 (1967–68), pp. 573–600.
Avrich, Paul. "The Bolshevik Revolution and Workers' Control in Russian Industry." *Slavic Review,* 21, no. 1 (1963), p. 47.
Bailes, Kendall E. "The Politics of Technology: Stalin and Technocratic Thinking among Soviet Engineers." *American Historical Review,* 79, no. 2 (1974), pp. 445–69.
———. "Science, Philosophy and Politics in Soviet History: The Case of Vladimir Vernadskii." *Russian Review,* 40, no. 3 (1981), pp. 278–99.
Berkhin, I. B. "Nekotorye voprosy istoriografii novoi ekonomicheskoi politiki v SSSR." *Voprosy istorii,* 3 (1961), pp. 28–44.
———. "Novaia ekonomicheskaia politika i ee rol' v perekhodnyi period kapitalizma k sotsializmu. Iz opyta sotsialisticheskogo stroitel'stva v SSSR." *Kommunist,* no. 4 (1967), pp. 26–35.
Billik, V. I. "V. I. Lenina o sushchnosti i periodizatsii sovetskoi ekonomicheskoi politiki 1917–1920 gg. i o povorote k nepu." *Istoricheskie zapiski,* 80 (1967), pp. 126–69.
Blank, Stephen. "Soviet Institutional Development during NEP: A Prelude to Stalinism." *Russian History/Histoire Russe,* 9, no. 2–3 (1982), pp. 325–46.
Brooks, Jeffrey. "Studies of the Reader in the 1920s." *Russian History/Histoire Russe,* 9, no. 2–3 (1982), pp. 187–202.
Brovkin, Vladimir. "The Mensheviks and NEP Society in Russia." *Russian History/Histoire Russe,* 9, no. 2–3 (1982), pp. 347–77.
Brower, Daniel R. "The Smolensk Scandal and the End of NEP." *Slavic Review,* 45, no. 4 (1986), pp. 689–706.
Bukharin, N. "O novoi ekonomicheskoi politike i nashikh zadachakh." *Bol'shevik,* no. 8 (1925), pp. 3–14; no. 9 (1925), pp. 3–15.
Burbank, J. "Waiting for the People's Revolution: Martov and Chernov in Revolutionary Russia, 1917–1923." *Cahiers du Monde Russe et Soviétique,* 26, no. 3–4, pp. 375–94.
Cohen, Stephen F. "Bukharin, Lenin and the Theoretical Foundations of Bolshevism." *Soviet Studies,* 21, no. 4 (1969–70), pp. 436–57.
Dale, Paddy. "The Instability of the Infant Vanguard: Worker Party Members, 1928–1932." *Soviet Studies,* 35, no. 4 (1983), pp. 504–24.
Daniels, Robert. "The Secretariat and the Local Organizations in the Russian Communist Party, 1921–23." *Slavic Review,* 15, no. 1 (1957), p. 32–49.
Danilov, V. P. "Krest'ianskii otkhod na promyshli v 1920-kh godakh." *Istoricheskie zapiski,* 94 (1974), pp. 55–122.
Dmitrenko, S. L. "Certain Aspects of the New Economic Policy in Soviet Historical Scholarship of the 1960s." *Soviet Studies in History,* 2, no. 3 (1972–73), pp. 213–51; *Voprosy istorii,* no. 3 (1972).

————. "Sostav mestnykh partiinykh komitetov v 1924–27 gg." *Istoricheskie zapiski,* 79 (1967), pp. 77–108.

Dobb, Maurice. "The Discussions of the Twenties on Planning and Economic Growth." *Soviet Studies,* 17, no. 2 (1965–66), pp. 198–208.

Edvard, L. "Trudovye konflikty v pervoi polovine 1923 g." *Voprosy truda,* 4 (1925), pp. 90–98.

Ellison, Herbert. "The Decision to Collectivize Agriculture." *Slavic Review,* 19, no. 2 (1961), p. 189.

Fischer, Ruth. "Background of the New Economic Policy." *Russian Review,* 7 (1948), pp. 15–33.

Fitzpatrick, Sheila. "The 'Soft' Line on Culture and Its Enemies: Soviet Cultural Policy, 1922–27." *Slavic Review,* 33 (1974), pp. 267–87.

Genkina, E. B. "K voprosu o leninskom obosnovanii novoi ekonomicheskoi politiki." *Voprosy istorii KPSS,* no. 1 (1967), pp. 58–70.

————. "Vozniknovenie proizvodstvennykh soveshchanii v gody vosstanovitel'nogo perioda, 1921–1925." *Istoriia SSSR,* no. 3 (1958), pp. 63–89.

Gimpel'son, E. G. "On Workers' Control after the Passage of the Decree on Nationalizing Industry in the USSR." *Soviet Studies in History,* 23, no. 2 (1984), pp. 34–54; *Istoriia SSSR,* no. 4 (1981).

Gooderham, Peter. "The Komsomol and Worker Youth: The Inculcation of 'Communist Values' in Leningrad during NEP." *Soviet Studies,* 34, no. 4 (1982), pp. 506–28.

Graham, Loren. "Science and Values: The Eugenics Movement in Germany and Russia in the 1920s." *American Historical Review,* 82, no. 5 (1977), pp. 1133–64.

Haimson, Leopold. "The Problem of Social Identities in Early Twentieth Century Russia." *Slavic Review,* 47, no. 1 (1988), pp. 1–20.

Hatch, John. "The Politics of Mass Culture: Workers, Communists, and Proletcult in the Development of Workers' Clubs, 1921–1925." *Russian History,* 13, no. 2–3 (1986), pp. 119–48.

Igumnova, Z. P. "A Contribution to the History of the M. N. Pokrovskii Rabfak." *Soviet Studies in History,* 9 (1970–71), pp. 322–43; *Vestnik Moskovskogo universiteta,* no. 3 (1970), pp. 55–66.

Karpov, P. V. "V. I. Lenin ob ukreplenii soiuze rabochego klassa i krest'ianstva v period perekhoda sovetskogo gosudarstva k novoi ekonomicheskoi politike, 1921–1922 gg." *Trudy Leningradskogo bibliotechnogo instituta,* vol. 7. Leningrad, 1960.

Kenez, Peter. "The Cultural Revolution in Cinema." *Slavic Review,* 47, no. 3 (1988), pp. 414–33.

————. "Liquidating Illiteracy in Revolutionary Russia." *Russian History/Histoire Russe,* 9, no. 2–3 (1982), pp. 173–86.

Kimerling, Elise. "Civil Rights and Social Policy in Soviet Russia, 1918–1936." *Russian Review,* 41, no. 1 (1982), pp. 24–46.

Klimov, Iu. N. "Istoriografiia novoi ekonomicheskoi politiki." *Voprosy istorii KPSS,* no. 5 (1966), pp. 128–31.

————. "K voprosu o periodizatsii novoi ekonomicheskoi politiki." *Voprosy istorii KPSS,* no. 11 (1966), pp. 61–67.

Koenker, Diane, and Rosenberg, William. "Skilled Workers and the Strike Movement in Revolutionary Russia." *Journal of Social History,* 19, no. 4 (1986), pp. 605–29.

Korey, William. "Zinov'ev's Critique of Stalin's Theory of Socialism in One Country, December 1925–December 1926." *Slavic Review,* no. 4 (1950), p. 255.

Korzhikhina, T. P. "Obshchestvo starykh bol'shevikov, 1923–35 gg." *Voprosy istorii KPSS*, no. 11 (1989), pp. 50–66.

"Kruglyi stol: Sovetskii Soiuz v 20-e gody," *Voprosy istorii*, no. 9 (1988), pp. 3–58. Translation: "The Soviet Union in the 1920s: A Roundtable," *Soviet Studies in History*, 28, no. 2 (1989).

Kuromiya, Hiroaki. "The Crisis of Proletarian Identity in the Soviet Factory, 1928–1929." *Slavic Review*, 44, no. 2 (1985), pp. 280–97.

Kuz'min, V. I. "Novaia ekonomicheskaia politika i smychka sotsialisticheskoi promyshlennosti s melkotovarnym khoziaistvom." *Voprosy istorii KPSS*, no. 2 (1967), pp. 46–57.

———. "Osushchestvlenie leninskikh idei nepa v SSSR." *Voprosy istorii*, no. 4 (1970), pp. 69–86.

Lane, David. "The Impact of Revolution: The Case of Selection of Students for Higher Education in Soviet Russia, 1917–1928." *Sociology*, 7 (1973), pp. 241–52.

Lavrent'ev, V. N. "V. I. Lenin i stroitel'stvo sovkhozov v pervykh godakh sovetskoi vlasti, 1917–1925." *Nauchnye zapiski Moskovskogo finansovogo instituta*, no. 11 (1958).

Levin, Aleksey. "Expedient Catastrophe: A Reconsideration of the 1929 Crisis at the Soviet Academy of Sciences." *Slavic Review*, 47, no. 2 (1988), pp. 261–79.

Lewin, Moshe. "Who Was the Soviet Kulak?" *Soviet Studies*, 18, no. 2 (1966–67), pp. 189–212.

Lewis, Robert A. "Some Aspects of the Research and Development Effort of the Soviet Union, 1924–35." *Science Studies*, no. 2 (1972), pp. 153–79.

McNeal, Robert. "Lenin's Attack on Stalin: Review and Reappraisal." *Slavic Review*, no. 3 (1959), p. 295.

Male, D. J. "The Village Community in the USSR, 1925–1930." *Soviet Studies*, 14, no. 3 (1962–63), pp. 225–48.

Millar, James, and Nove, Alec. "A Debate on Collectivization: Was Stalin Really Necessary?" *Problems of Communism*, 25 (1976).

Miller, Martin. "Freudian Theory under Bolshevik Rule: The Theoretical Controversy during the 1920s." *Slavic Review*, 44, no. 4 (1985), pp. 625–46.

Miller, Robert. "Soviet Agricultural Policy in the Twenties: The Failure of Cooperation." *Soviet Studies*, 27, no. 2 (1975), pp. 220–44.

Morozov, L. F. "K voprosu o periodizatsii bor'by s nepmanskoi burzhuaziei." *Voprosy istorii*, no. 12 (1964), pp. 3–17.

Nove, Alec. "1926/7 and All That." *Soviet Studies*, 9, no. 2 (1957–58), pp. 117–30.

Pethybridge, Roger. "Concern for Bolshevik Ideological Predominance at the Start of NEP." *Russian Review*, 41, no. 4 (1982), pp. 445–53.

———. "Railways and Press Communications in Soviet Russia in the Early NEP Period." *Soviet Studies*, 38, no. 2 (1986), pp. 194–206.

———. "Social and Political Attitudes of the Peasantry in Kursk *Guberniya* at the Start of NEP." *Slavonic and East European Review*, 63, no. 3, pp. 372–87.

Poliakov, Iu. A. "Stimul, mera, temp: Nekotorye problemy novoi ekonomicheskoi politiki." *Voprosy istorii*, 7 (1964), pp. 21–32.

———. "20-e gody: nastroeniia partiinogo avangarda." *Voprosy istorii KPSS*, no. 10 (1989), pp. 25–38.

Rosenberg, William G. "Identities, Power, and Social Interactions in Revolutionary Russia." *Slavic Review*, 47, no. 2 (1988), pp. 21–28.

———. "Smolensk in the 1920s: Party-Worker Relations and the 'Vanguard' Problem." *Russian Review*, 36, no. 2 (1977), pp. 125–50.

Scherr, Barry. "Notes on Literary Life in Petrograd, 1918–1922: A Tale of Three Houses." *Slavic Review*, 36, no. 2 (1977), pp. 256–68.

Selunskaia, V. M. "V. I. Lenin o klassovoi bor'be v period perekhoda ot kapitalizma k sotsializmu." *Voprosy istorii KPSS*, no. 6 (1970), pp. 62–74.

Shanin, Teodor. "Socio-economic Mobility and the Rural History of Russia, 1905–1930." *Soviet Studies*, 23, no. 2 (1972), pp. 22–35.

Shelley, Louise. "Female Criminality in the 1920s: A Consequence of Inadvertent and Deliberate Change." *Russian History/Histoire Russe*, 9, no. 2–3 (1982), pp. 265–84.

Sochor, Zenovia. "Soviet Taylorism Revisited." *Soviet Studies*, 33, no. 2 (1981), pp. 246–64.

Sokolov, N. G. "The Use of Barter during the Transition to NEP." *Soviet Studies in History*, 23, no. 2 (1984), pp. 54–61.

Solomon, Peter H. "Criminalization and Decriminalization in Soviet Criminal Policy, 1917–1941." *Law and Society Review*, 16, no. 1 (1981–82), pp. 9–43.

Stevens, Jennie. "Children of the Revolution: Soviet Russia's Homeless Children *(bezprizorniki)* in the 1920s." *Russian History/Histoire Russe*, 9, no. 2–3 (1982), pp. 242–64.

Teptsov, N. V. "Voprosy agrarnoi politiki partii v 20–30-e gody: po materialam periodicheskoi pechati." *Voprosy istorii KPSS*, no. 11 (1989), pp. 138–43.

Vasil'ev, O. M. "V. I. Lenin o sushchnosti i znachenii novoi ekonomicheskoi politiki." *Sbornik nauchnykh rabot*, no. 1, Kharkov, 1960.

Vol'skii (Valentinov), Nikolai. "Non-party Specialists and the Coming of NEP." Translated by Randell Magee and Gregory Guroff. *Russian Review*, 30 (1971), pp. 154–63.

Weissman, Neil. "Prohibition and Alcohol Control in the USSR: The 1920s Campaign against Illegal Spirits." *Soviet Studies*, 38, no. 3 (1986), pp. 349–68.

Wolfe, Bertram. "Valentinov-Volskii on the NEP: An Insider's View." *Russian History*, 29 (1970), pp. 422–32.

## Selected Newspapers and Journals

Readers seeking a more comprehensive reference to Soviet periodicals may wish to consult the following:

Smits, Rudolf. *Half a Century of Soviet Serials, 1917–1968: A Bibliography and Union List of Serials Published in the USSR*. 2 volumes. Washington, D.C.: Library of Congress, 1968.

*Administrativnyi vestnik*
*Bednota*
*Ekonomicheskaia gazeta*
*Ekonomicheskaia zhizn'*
*Izvestiia*
*Kommunisticheskaia revoliutsiia*
*Komsomol'skaia pravda*
*Krasnaia letopis'*
*Krasnaia nov'*
*Krasnaia pechat'*

*Krasnoe studenchestvo*
*Krasnyi arkhiv*
*Krest'ianskaia gazeta*
*Leningradskaia pravda*
*Molodaia gvardiia*
*Novyi mir*
*Novyi zhurnal*
*Pod znamenem marksizma*
*Pravda*
*Proletarskaia revoliutsiia*
*Rabochaia gazeta*
*Rabochaia Moskva*
*Sotsialisticheskii vestnik*
*Stroitel'stvo Moskvy*
*Vestnik statistiki*
*Vlast' sovetov*
*Voprosy truda*
*Zhurnalist*

# CONTRIBUTORS

**Helmut Altrichter** is Professor of East European History at Friedrich-Alexander Universität Erlangen-Nürnberg and author of *Konstitutionalismus und Imperialismus: Der Reichstag und die deutsch-russischen Beziehungen 1890–1914; Staat und Revolution in Sowjetrussland 1917–1922/23;* and *Die Bauern von Tver: Vom Leben auf dem russischen Dorfe zwischen Revolution und Kollektivierung.*

**Alan Ball** is Associate Professor of History at Marquette University. He is the author of *Russia's Last Capitalists: The Nepmen, 1921–1929* and is completing a study of abandoned children in the Soviet Union.

**Jeffrey Brooks** is Professor of History at the Johns Hopkins University. He received the Vucinich Prize for *When Russia Learned to Read* and is currently completing a study of the Soviet press, 1921–45.

**Lori A. Citti** is a doctoral candidate in Soviet history at Indiana University.

**Katerina Clark** is Associate Professor of Comparative Literature and Slavic Languages and Literatures at Yale University and the author of *The Soviet Novel: History as Ritual* and (with Michael Holquist) *Mikhail Bakhtin.*

**Sheila Fitzpatrick** is Professor of History at the University of Chicago. Her publications include *Education and Social Mobility in the Soviet Union, 1921–1934; Cultural Revolution in Russia, 1928–1931;* and, most recently, *A Researcher's Guide to Sources on Soviet Social History in the 1930s,* coedited with Lynne Viola.

**Wendy Z. Goldman** is Assistant Professor of History at Carnegie Mellon University. She is currently completing a study of Soviet family policy and social change, 1917–1936.

**John B. Hatch** is Assistant Professor of History at the University of California, Los Angeles. His articles have appeared in *Slavic Review, Soviet Studies,* and *Russian History,* and he is currently completing a study of party-worker relations in NEP Moscow.

**Robert E. Johnson** is Associate Professor of History at Erindale College of the University of Toronto. He is the author of *Peasant and Proletarian: The Working Class of Moscow at the End of the Nineteenth Century.*

**Diane P. Koenker** is Professor of History at the University of Illinois at Urbana-Champaign. She is the author of *Moscow Workers and the 1917*

*Revolution,* coauthor of *Strikes and Revolution in Russia, 1917,* and coeditor of *Party, State and Society in the Russian Civil War.*

**Hiroaki Kuromiya** is Assistant Professor of History at Indiana University, Bloomington. He is the author of *Stalin's Industrial Revolution: Politics and Workers, 1928–1932* and is completing a study of the Donbas.

**Alexander Rabinowitch** is Professor of History at Indiana University, Bloomington. He is author of *Prelude to Revolution: The Petrograd Bolsheviks and the July 1917 Uprising* and *The Bolsheviks Come to Power: The Revolution of 1917 in Petrograd* and coeditor of *The Soviet Union since Stalin.*

**Régine Robin** is Professor of Sociology at the Université du Québec à Montréal. She is the author of *Le réalisme socialiste: une esthétique impossible,* which received Canada's Governor General Award for Non-Fiction. A translation is forthcoming from Stanford University Press.

**William G. Rosenberg** is Professor of History at the University of Michigan, author of *Liberals in the Russian Revolution: The Constitutional Democratic Party, 1917–1921,* and coauthor of *Transforming Russia and China* and *Strikes and Revolution in Russia, 1917.* He also edited *Bolshevik Visions: First Phase of the Cultural Revolution in Soviet Russia.*

**Robert A. Rothstein** is Professor of Slavic Languages and Literatures and of Judaic Studies at the University of Massachusetts, Amherst. He is the author of numerous articles in the areas of Slavic linguistics, paremiology, and Slavic and Yiddish music.

**Richard Stites** is Professor of History at Georgetown University and author of *The Women's Liberation Movement in Russia* and *Soviet Popular Culture* (forthcoming). His book *Revolutionary Dreams: Utopian Vision and Experimental Life in the Russian Revolution* received the Vucinich Prize of the AAASS in 1990.

**Mark von Hagen** is Associate Professor of History and Associate Director of the W. Averell Harriman Institute for Advanced Study of the Soviet Union, Columbia University. He is the author of *Soldiers in the Proletarian Dictatorship: The Red Army and the Soviet Socialist State, 1917–1930.*

**Douglas R. Weiner** is Assistant Professor of History at the University of Arizona. He is author of *Models of Nature: Ecology, Conservation and Cultural Revolution in Soviet Russia* and is currently completing a sequel volume which examines Soviet environmentalism from Stalin's death to the present.

**Neil Weissman** is Professor in the Department of History, Dickinson College. He is author of *Reform in Tsarist Russia: The State Bureaucracy and Local Government, 1900–1914* and is currently writing on police and deviance in early Soviet history.

# INDEX